Moral Discourses of the Economy in Eighteenth-Century Britain

Hye-Joon Yoon

Moral Discourses of the Economy in Eighteenth-Century Britain

palgrave
macmillan

Hye-Joon Yoon
Yonsei University
Seoul, Korea (Republic of)

ISBN 978-981-95-0957-7 ISBN 978-981-95-0958-4 (eBook)
https://doi.org/10.1007/978-981-95-0958-4

This Palgrave Macmillan imprint is published by the registered company Springer Nature Singapore Pte Ltd.
The registered company address is: 152 Beach Road, #21-01/04 Gateway East, Singapore 189721, Singapore

Preface

This book endeavors to present a comprehensive picture of the eighteenth-century British authors' engagement with their society which was becoming increasingly dominated by commercial concerns. It will do so by connecting the realms of economics, religion, law, and ethics, which have been assigned to different disciplinary specialties determined by current academic structure. Academic disciplines, being naturally interested in keeping its autonomy recognized, respected, and remunerated, have inevitably been focused on setting up self-enclosed canons of classic authors in each field and on writing an internal history of their mutual influence and difference. Such institutional autarky may be rewarding to those protected by each academic enclosure, but it fails to do full justice to the actual historical facts which established scholars purport to explicate and elucidate. Economics, like many other sciences, came into being in the eighteenth century, yet economic writings of the age have been somewhat neglected by the historians of the Enlightenment, who generally seem to accept the necessity of selecting and sanctifying a restricted list of political and philosophical works, as can be inferred from the names of the two series of scholarly editions published by Cambridge University Press, "Cambridge Texts in the History of Political Thought" and "Cambridge Texts in the History of Philosophy." David Hume's *Political Essays*, which contains a substantial amount of economic reasoning, takes part in the former series, while Adam Smith's *Theory of the Moral Sentiments*, very much alert to the practical circumstances of a commercial society, features in the latter series. Interestingly, Smith's *The Wealth of Nations* is not accommodated by any series of primary texts issued by this illustrious academic publisher.

Economic works of lesser fame which the long eighteenth century produced, regardless of their individual merits, have not been given proper respect, while modern economics has ceased to rely on verbal disquisition as it came to give exclusive credence to mathematical explication. Indeed, the noble scheme of intellectual historians to pay tribute to the genuinely inter-disciplinary communion of minds in the Age of Enlightenment tends to falter when one reaches the assorted legacy of economic writings, which in my view ought to include not only the third but all three titles by the two famous authors mentioned above. This book seeks to remedy this defect by extending the range of primary sources beyond Smith and the so-called pre-classical economists in two directions: first, to the less reverently remembered and even forgotten authors, and second, to those authors consigned to other specialist histories. The unobtrusive phrase leading the title of this book, "moral discourses," intentionally coming in the plural form, pledges to keep the door of the book's sources open to all who have said something relevant on the topic, "the economy," which I also hope will be understood in the broadest possible sense of the term.

The approach of this book to the gathered sources, simply put, is one that pays attention to what they say. Commentaries and analyses will be kept to the minimum, as ample space will be provided to the authors themselves. Even though the more articulate, and therefore the more celebrated, authors will take up more space than those that are not, a forum for open dialogue between all authors will be set up, regardless of their current status in the academic disciplines. Canonized luminaries will be placed side by side, whether they would have relished it or not, with obscure and anonymous authors. Authors opposed politically or religiously will also be invited to share the same page or paragraph, their mutual animus notwithstanding. Such inclusiveness and respect for works handed down to us certainly reflect my background in literary studies, where, until recently, primary texts were given full opportunity to speak for themselves without being prosecuted for their remarks in the court of political correctness. It also can find justification in the very inclusiveness or porousness of the free-market of print which came into being in eighteenth-century London. Thinking and writing about the economy in eighteenth-century Britain was by no means a hieratic art practiced by those qualified by institutional training. Academics, divines, doctors, parliamentarians, and businessmen all wrote on matters economic in a prose accessible to the general common reader. Some authors certainly have left their contemporaries far behind in the race for lasting renown, and at least one, Adam Smith, is revered as the founder of the mighty science of economics. But in his own time, Smith was just one among many authors who wrote for and was paid by the "booksellers," as publishers were called at the time. Not being a professional economist, Smith would not have minded finding himself placed in this book in the company of other non-specialists. Even Hume, an almost august name in our time, was one such lay author expressing his thoughts on matters economic in the form of short "essays." The plural noun "discourses" in the title of this book underscores this unpartitioned state of the eighteenth-century print market.

The organizing principle I follow in this book similarly is neither arcane nor abstruse. Each chapter pursues the vicissitudes of certain key words, although some chapters can be geared more toward exploring the semantics of the terms, while others, such as the last two, put more weight on the events the words refer to. The first chapter, being the introduction to the rest, traces the senses of the key words of the title, "moral," "discourse," and the "economy," first as they were understood and used in the period, and second, where relevant, in conjunction with later studies on the nexus between the moral, the religious, and the economic. To anticipate what will be elaborated there at length, the "moral" did not just mean what it came to signify in our time, but was linked to a far broader range of referents, at one extreme denoting customary or habitual practices of people with no normative connotations mixed with it, and at the other extreme those ethical or legal obligations founded on natural and revealed religion. By "moral discourses," therefore, I refer to this loose but comprehensive cluster of senses, even as some elements of that semantic family will gain greater or lesser spotlight in different contexts in the subsequent chapters. Terms used to name economic activities, likewise, were different from the modern usages. "Trade," "commerce," and "traffick" (often spelled in this archaic form) rather than "economy" were the words usually employed in various contexts dealing with economic issues. The "economic" in our title embraces these terms that triggered debates about moral questions, such as vice (Chap. 2), idleness (Chap. 3), and luxury (Chap. 4), as well as controversies over political morals, such as corruption (Chap. 5) and slavery (Chap. 6).

Standing between the main body of the book and the introductory chapter is the second chapter devoted to discussing Bernard Mandeville's two key terms, "vice" and "benefit." Private "vices" were lifted out of the moral limbo by Mandeville to be legitimized as positive forces bringing "benefit" to a desire-driven commercial society. The causal connection between moral vice and economic gains proposed by Mandeville was at once contentious and undeniable. Whether accepting his unsavory formula explicitly or not, the "moral" and the "economic" were embroiled in an almost century-long debate thanks to Mandeville, for which reason, his writings come before others.

The chapters that follow deal with the key terms which stood at the core of the eighteenth-century discussions related to the economy and which were believed to be highly important. For virtually all authors, regardless of their political or religious stances, "industry" was regarded as a sacrosanct virtue, frequently placed in sharp contrast to the universally proscribed vice of "idleness." Chapter 3 covers this dichotomy and traces its dominion all the way to the dark recesses of debtors' prisons. Chapter 4 traces both the vilification and the vindications of "luxury," on moral, religious, and economic grounds, after first delineating conceptions of "consumption," which was a term that encompassed physiology, morality, and commerce. The chapter's latter sections recount the attempts to neutralize the shady moral pretentions of "luxury" by polite comportment prescribed by "refinement" and by sensible gratification guided by "prudence."

Changing course slightly at this stage from the previous chapters whose major terms and issues concerned the morals of private individuals, Chaps. 5 and 6 deal with public or political morality. First to be considered in Chap. 5 are the "projects" or schemes for profiteering that pretend to benefit the public. For many authors, closely related to this species of moral and economic conspiracy, was the monopoly, which, though sanctioned by laws, inherently perverted the natural law of free trade, and, in the case of the "Nabobs," even the natural law of universal morality. Chapter 6 covers the moral crusade against the slave trade and slave labor. Purchase and ownership of African slaves were defended in the name of Britain's national interests and as a constitutional right of free-born British subjects. Battling this stronghold of political and economic justification called for an alignment of ethics, religion, politics, and economics. Being the longest of all, this chapter reconstructing the language, argument, and rhetoric of the Abolitionists and their opponents is the high point of this book that names itself "moral discourses of the economy in eighteenth-century Britain."

Whereas Chap. 6 is the longest, the last chapter is the shortest. Chapter 7 is an "epilogue" rather than a conclusion, where, instead of some key words taking the stage, two famous authors, Edmund Burke and Jeremy

Bentham, will be summoned as proponents of two contrastive philosophies. Burke castigated France under the "Jacobins" for disrupting the moral framework of society, economy, and politics. To Bentham, the intrusion of morals into economics, which this book charted all the way from Mandeville to the Abolitionists, was an outdated superstition that had to be thrown overboard. Placing the two side by side concludes nothing, of course. The flows and streams of Britain's intellectual history can never be contained by any contrastive pairing. But the unbridgeable rupture between the maximalist conception of morality held by Burke and the minimalist moral calculus of Bentham does serve both as a dead end of the discursive practices I describe in this book and as a signpost to later developments. Hence, there I terminate my investigation.

In this final as in all the previous chapters, I try to play the role of a moderator, or an impresario, who brings together the authors—once again, both celebrated and neglected, both named and nameless—as I give them as much space as feasible so that they can deliver their thoughts on the key issues in each chapter. Where a thicket of academic inquiries awaits them, for instance, in the parts covering the debates on "luxury," Burke's impeachment of Warren Hastings, or the slave trade, I attempted to recognize at least the most significant secondary sources. But I confess from the outset that I feel neither competent nor compelled to take the heavy responsibility of contextualizing each author and adjudicating quarrels between themselves or between them and posterity. The archenemy of historical research was identified by Herodotus as amnesia. Remembering the glorious and inglorious deeds of the past heroes and villains will be the chosen task for many historians, but for others, such as myself, the past can be salvaged from oblivion also by recollecting the words that embody the spirit of the age. Selective and partisan remembrance adhering to the ideologies in vogue have become something of a new normal in current humanities. The author of this book begs to be allowed to pursue a more old-fashioned path of reconstructing what those who lived and died in the past centuries thought, felt, and said about those issues that mattered to them most.

The outcome of my efforts surely must look shabby to many, but if there are any merits to be found here, the credit must go to others rather than to the person who wrote this book. While the labor that went into preparing for and writing this book is surely mine, I am indebted not only to those scholars whose works I consulted but to friends and colleagues who have directly or indirectly helped and encouraged me in this project for the past eight years or so. Paul Tonks, my colleague and friend at Yonsei, deserves to be mentioned first, for this book owes a great deal to his support and suggestions. Other names I am pleased to mention with gratitude include (in a chronological order of their contribution) my colleagues at the Korean Society for Eighteenth-Century English Literature, Ian McDaniel, Nicholas Brownlees, Charles Bradford Bow, Michael Ratnapalan, Hyon-Jin Kim, Hiroki Ueno, Michael Brown, and Sora Sato. I also thank the British Library and Yonsei University Library, whose collections and services were indispensable to my research, as well as the graduate students of Yonsei who patiently sat in my courses on the eighteenth-century thinkers for the past decade or so. My deepest gratitude goes to my wife, Young-Mi, without whose support I could never have gathered the strength, both moral and physical, to carry on this arduous task. Finally, I give thanks to Him whose Providence guided me to through this work.

Seoul, Korea (Republic of) Hye-Joon Yoon

Competing Interests The author declares the following as potential competing interests: This work was supported by the Ministry of Education of the Republic of Korea and the National Research Foundation of Korea (NRF-2021S1A6A4046091). A part of Chapter 2 was published as "Bernard Mandeville as a writer: A bibliographical and critical overview of his miscellaneous works," in The Journal of Eighteenth-Century English Literature 19 (2022), 99-129 (DOI: 10.46345/ecel.2022.19.2.000), published by the Korean Society for Eighteenth-Century English Literature.

Contents

CHAPTER 1

Introduction: Discourses, "Moral," and the Economic

1.1 Discourses

Let us begin with Samuel Foote's *The Nabob*, a popular comedy performed in three different seasons (1772, 1774, and 1781). If not one of the gems of English stage, it has the virtue of representing the dominant sentiments of educated or polite segments of English society of the period regarding some key topical issues considered to be at once moral and economic. The estate of Sir John Oldham, of a venerable ancient stock, is distressed by debts and the owner faces the imminent threat of foreclosure by Sir Matthew Mite, poor in pedigree but rich in cash amassed in India. Mite has an eye on Sir John's daughter Sophy. Mite the "Nabob" tells Sir John that if he gives away Sophy to become his wife, all debts will be forgiven. Lady Oldham is dead set against this demeaning proposal made by this upstart who came to their quiet country, "preceded by all the pomp of Asia." By "profusely scattering the spoils of ruined provinces," the Nabob corrupted the "virtue and alienated the affections of all the old friends to the family." But this hateful intruder commands a mighty arsenal of "contrivance and cunning," which is "an overmatch for a plain English gentleman," just as it was for "an innocent Indian" (Foote 1778, 4, 11). Even as he lusts after young Sophy, Mite is no romantic but a cool-headed investor in the stock market, employing two foreigners (presumably Jews), "Nathan" and "Moses Mendoz," as his stockjobbing agents. They do his bidding, asking him, "For de next settlement, would your honour be de

H.-J. Yoon, *Moral Discourses of the Economy in Eighteenth-Century Britain*, https://doi.org/10.1007/978-981-95-0958-4_1

bull or de bear?" Mite's assistant from his Bengal days "Touchit" is still in his service. He brags to his master's guest about the gallant art of getting their wealth in the East Indies: "[W]e cunningly encroach, and fortify by little and by little, till at length, we growing too strong for the natives, we turn them out of their lands, and take possession of their money and jewels" (Foote 1778, 41, 39). The only person capable of stopping this juggernaut is Sir John's brother Thomas, who is a successful merchant like Mite. It so happens that Thomas' son is in love with his cousin Sophy, which love is reciprocal. Lady Oldham had initially opposed their alliance, but with the imminent prospect of being evicted from her house and seeing her husband incarcerated in debtors' prison, she relents. Thomas pays off the money owed to Mite, and the young cousins are betrothed as the curtain closes. But before we reach that happy turn of events, Thomas reminds Mite, as one merchant to another, that money is not the only deity worshipped in England, that "there are superior spirits living, who would disdain an alliance with grandeur obtained at the expence of honour and virtue." Later on, Thomas the virtuous merchant preaches to the unscrupulous "Nabob" a lesson on sound political economy: "Your riches … by introducing a general spirit of dissipation, have extinguished labour and industry, the slow, but sure source of national wealth" (Foote 1778, 48, 66). In these and other interesting scenes, many of the key themes of this present book are touched upon. The play proposes that morally "superior" characters will not sacrifice their "honour and virtue" to the idol of mammon, that "labour and industry" are the "sure source" of a nation's prosperity, that stockjobbing and other such "projects" are dubious affairs, and that wealth acquired from the colonies should not be immune to moral scrutiny. It also admits that insolvency and luxury are pervasive problems affecting even the well-established landed families and that the new wealth, represented by the "Nabob," threatens to gain ascendency. All in all, the play illustrates the overlapping of moral and economic values, which both the playwright and his audience took for granted. No neat line was to be drawn between the domain of "riches" and "virtue," or better still, pecuniary wealth had to be subjected to moral accountability as well as monetary accounting.

This book aims at presenting a comprehensive picture of the extensive dialogue in the period between common-sense morality and economic forces Foote's *Nabob* exemplifies, by reconstructing the discourses of various eighteenth-century British authors who wrote on moral issues they felt were important to a society increasingly driven by commercial interests. If the "history of ideas," as J. G. A. Pocock states, may be "viewed as the history of the modes of explaining the world and its behaviour which have from time to time existed" (Pocock 1971, 204–205), the explanatory "modes" adopted by Foote and others writing in his century were characterized by a conflation of moral and economic arguments. To explain the eighteenth-century writers' "modes of explaining" their world, I follow the precedent they set of overstepping the boundaries separating the domains of economics, religion, law, and ethics, which are now assigned to different disciplinary specialties of academic institutions. The adjective "moral" in the title of this book denotes above all such inclusiveness, as does the noun "discourses." The "eighteenth-century" in the title accepts as the starting point the first phase of the "long" eighteenth century, namely the 1680s, when some of the early economic writers, such as Nicholas Barbon, published their thoughts. The end point of our chronology, however, subscribes to a "short" eighteenth century, as we end in the middle years of the 1790s,[1] primarily to terminate our journey with Edmund Burke, an author who devoted the last years of his life to wage war against the ideas and forces which he believed were tearing apart the moral fabric of the civilized world. Those who appear in this book, whether the relatively obscure Barbon or the supremely renowned Burke, do so as "authors" rather than thinkers or intellectuals. In fact, a large number of the voices heeded here are of those who are not celebrated as the representative "star" thinkers of the age, and some of whom remain completely anonymous. Of course, the more eloquent and articulate writers canonized by later scholarship (such as Burke) would receive more space than those who are not (such as Barbon). But the luminaries would be flanked by others of lesser fame.

Economics, like other branches of social sciences, did not exist as a professional realm of specialist knowledge in eighteenth-century Britain. Instead, matters related to the "economy" in the broadest possible sense, which is how I use the term in this book, were debated by writers coming from a broad range of backgrounds and creeds. Our first author is Bernard Mandeville, a Dutch-born London physician, while our last is Jeremy Bentham, a Londoner trained to become a barrister. Between the two, a significant portion of the space would be taken up by Anglican clerics of diverse ranks: bishops, deans, and parish priests. William Warburton's *The*

[1] These dates of the "long" or "short" eighteenth-centuries are those proposed by Langford (Langford 2002, 1).

Divine Legation of Moses Demonstrated, on the Principles of a Religious Deist, from the Omission of the Doctrine of a Future State of Reward and Punishment in the Jewish Dispensation, notwithstanding the impression the title conveys, features in this book, for the author has interesting things to say about the earthly reward and punishment attending one's economic behavior. William Blackstone's *Commentaries on the Laws of England* is given due attention in this book, as his majestic account of the English law keeps a steady eye on the economic realm. Those with a supposed first-hand knowledge of commerce such as Thomas Mortimer or Daniel Defoe, and political activists such as the indefatigable Thomas Clarkson, mix in the chapters of this book with nameless compilers of facts, for they all in their different ways illustrate the spirit of the age. The representative painter of the century William Hogarth also supplements our discussion with his pictorial narratives.

What lies behind our choice of the term "discourses," intentionally put in the plural, requires a more detailed account. First of all, the word refers to the relatively porous and gregarious synthesis of the authors with diverse provenances which we endeavor to construct in this book. It also underscores the approach adopted by this book of allowing these authors to speak for themselves rather than contextualizing or interpreting them constantly. The word "discourse," on the other hand, can claim solid historical lineage, for a number of these authors used the term in the titles of their works. Barbon and Dudley North both placed the word "discourse" in the titles of their treatises on commerce, as did another early economic writer, Josiah Child. Among the "moral" writings, one may cite Thomas Cole's *Discourses on Luxury, Infidelity, and Enthusiasm*, which exemplifies what "discourses" were expected to mean to contemporary readers: an unhampered exploration of topics both spiritual and political, moral and economic. It can even be suggested that "discourse" was understood in the period to signify something not that too different from Michel Foucault's "production of discourse," namely as a fluid social practice of "exclusion" and "prohibition" of arguments and ideas. Indeed, as Foucault himself points out, the "series of discourses" in the seventeenth and the eighteenth centuries about "money, production, commerce," authored by a motley crew of authors—merchants, clerics, politicians, and moralists—present a "strongly heterogeneous" picture that never attained the composure of a "discursive regularity" maintained by the academic science of economics (Foucault 1971, 10–11, 70). This book surely intends to fully acknowledge this "strongly heterogeneous" nature of the discourses of the period, but will do so without being influenced unduly by Foucault, a thinker who has no qualms about politicizing historical records as suits him. What this book does not aim at, even when the topics relate to the Britons' conduct in their far-off colonies, is to maneuver sources selectively to advance an implicit or avowed political agenda, since I have no ambition to be counted among the "leftist scholars" of which Siraj Ahmed, for instance, claims membership (Ahmed 2011, 127). Nor do I wish to put forth sonorous generalization about the trans-Atlantic slave trade such as those made by Ian Baucom, who confers on eighteenth-century Liverpool the honor of being one of the "capitals" of the "long twentieth century" (Baucom 2005, 31). If the name of Foucault still evokes a broadly "leftist" political disposition, I can then summon Quentin Skinner's reminder that to an impartial intellectual historian there "*is* no determinate idea to which various writers contributed, but only a variety of statements made with the words by a variety of different agents with a variety of intentions" (Skinner 1969, 38).

Skinner's anaphora of "variety" seems to urge some distancing from the established scholarly practices covering the eighteenth-century history of ideas, which generally concentrate on one major author or on a group of consecrated authors often with a view of constructing an internal narrative of influence, convergence, and divergence. Many studies of the "Scottish" Enlightenment, for instance, exemplify an adherence to a policy of closing the border of inquiry, as it were, along national or personal connections. A representative case would be Christoper Berry's *The Idea of Commercial Society in the Scottish Enlightenment*, where Josiah Tucker and Barbon, one Welsh and the other English, are given only a meager share of attention, the former in a footnote and the latter just once in the main text (Berry 2015, 85, 159). Daniel Defoe, an Englishman who wrote a great deal on commerce, receives no mention whatsoever. Those who have written on the contextual history of eighteenth-century British economic thought, encompassing both the English and the Scottish writers, have likewise tended to confine both the period and the main characters of their account to a handful of securely famous thinkers. Donald Winch's *Riches and Poverty: An Intellectual History of Political Economy in Britain 1750–1834* begins without fully explaining from the 1750s and is largely devoted to discussions of Adam Smith and Thomas Robert Malthus (Winch 1996). By putting in the title of this book the word "discourses" in the plural, I shall endeavor to balance this bias toward the venerated ancestors of economics by extending the range of primary sources beyond them to those writings and documents studied in political, philosophical, literary, and legal histories. We do so, of course, without claiming utter detachment from these and other important scholarly works, which we shall acknowledge in due course.

What is implied by "moral discourses" can further be clarified by contrasting the approach of this book to two well-known works that deal with the economic thinkers of the eighteenth century in a context embracing morals as well as economics. First is Emma Rothschild's *Economic Sentiments: Adam Smith, Condorcet, and the Enlightenment*, where she enlarges on Smith's suggestion that a certain "trucking disposition" may be inherent in human nature (Smith 1976a, 27 [I.ii.3]).[2] If Smith's premise is accepted, it follows that "traffic or commerce" is also a "traffic in opinions and sentiments" (Rothschild 2001, 8–9). Sentiments or disposition surely take up a respectable portion of what was understood to be signified by the term "moral" (as will be shown below), but that cannot possibly exhaust the entire domain of morals of the age. Therefore, I give to other components or departments of the moral realm, as recognized by the contemporaries of Smith, the respect they deserve. *Genres of the Credit Economy: Mediating Value in Eighteenth- and Nineteenth-Century Britain* by Mary Poovey, who has a literary background like myself, gives a fairly comprehensive and versatile role to the term "genres," which allows her to gather together fictional and non-fictional authors. My chosen category of "discourses" could be comparable in its intention to Poovey's "genres" as both bespeak a desire to jump across generic division. However, the primary sources quoted in this book is more restricted than Poovey's "genres," as I have no space to accommodate those she calls "economic writing" or "financial writings," such as reports of shipping and records of prices (Poovey 2008, 30–31), which cannot, in my view, have the same weight as essays and treatises composed to assign moral significance to economic actions. Nor does it seem warranted to read James Steuart's *An Inquiry into the Principles of Political Economy* as a fictional text not that dissimilar to Henry Fielding's *The History of Tom Jones, a Foundling* simply because both works resort frequently to digressions or because each "contains a narrator who directly addresses the reader and comments on the events and the nature of the narrative" (Poovey 2008, 131). Leaving everything else aside and just to take the words of the title for what they

[2] In accordance with the convention of Smith scholarship, when quoting Smith's works additional information about the source paragraph will be provided in square brackets.

mean, one reads that Steuart states what the topic of his "inquiry" is, however fictional his rhetorical devices may appear to be, whereas one would find it hard to grasp what economic principle or principles the "History of Tom Jones, a Foundling" offers to expound.

To some readers of this book, the two key terms in its title, "moral" and the "economy," could bring to mind E. P. Thompson's classic essay on the "moral economy" of the English food rioters in the eighteenth century. Ever alert to the pitfalls of grand theorizing, Thompson forbears from defining the "moral economy" as a clear-cut ideological position, not going further than to describe it as the "moral assumptions" held by the "poor," or the "notions" they "passionately held" about the "common weal" (Thompson 1971, 79). If usually quiescent, their belief in a "moral economy" becomes "in times of dearth" an inspirational force behind a certain "pattern of social protest" (Thompson 1971, 126). Thompson alleges that this "moral economy" of the working classes stood opposed to the "new political economy" represented by Smith's *The Wealth of Nations*, in that the latter "entailed a de-moralizing of theory of trade and consumption" (Thompson 1971, 89). While Thompson's meticulous account of the rioters' behavior and beliefs will most likely weather the changes in the academic climate, his views about Smith certainly will meet with loud protests in our time by those who respect the works of Rothschild and other scholars, such as Charles L. Griswold Jr. and Ryan Hanley (Griswold 1999, 261–264; Hanley 2009, 60–62), who demonstrated Smith's abiding interest in morals. Those who follow in the footsteps of Thompson tend to replicate Thompson's verdict about the "de-moralizing" intent of the "new political economy." Tim Rogan places Smith on the other side of the "moral economists' critique of capitalism" and its reduction of "human personality" to "terms suitable" for a "utilitarian calculus" (Rogan 2018, 12). Norbert Götz, even as he proposes to broaden the referential range of Thompson's "moral economy" to other cultures and periods, holds a simplistic view of Smith's stance as one that "elevated productivity" as the supreme criterion of the economy. Erecting an artificial barrier between the "moral" and the "economic" in order to claim that "morality was detached from the notion of economy in the middle of the eighteenth century" (Götz 2015, 148–149) has the potential to distort the context of what the eighteenth-century authors wrote and thought and as such would be a clear divergence from the rigorous contextual method of Thompson himself (Kirk 2025, 36). As far as this book is concerned, "moral economy" ought to be a comprehensive and inclusive notion that goes well beyond the confines of the political sentiments of food rioters. Many writers coming from the more comfortable classes—including but by no means confined to Smith—were very much concerned with the "moral" features of the economy. Smith and many others made "moral assumptions," more or less in the sense Thompson gives to the phrase, in their discussions of monetary economy.

The "moral" and the "economic" were inherently intertwined in the discussions sampled in this and subsequent chapters. The participants in the printed debates did not always aspire to accumulate a "moral capital" which Christopher Leslie Brown traces in his study of the Abolitionists (Brown 2006, 457). Different authors from different backgrounds, except perhaps in the rather exceptional case of those attacking the slave trade (to whom we devote Chap. 6) did not write with a conscious awareness of a shared purpose. One thing that held them together was, rather than their subjective sense of mission, the objective fact of being published by and for the London book market. Thinking and writing about the economy in eighteenth-century Britain, to emphasize again, was by no means a hieratic art practiced by those certified by institutional authorities. The "production of discourses" unfolded against the backdrop of a vibrant free market of print centered in London. In quantitative terms, the output of works dealing with economic issues, as calculated by Joseph Massie in 1754, was quite large indeed. Those Massie included in his list were highly diverse and mixed, ranging from statutes to revenue records (Hoppit 2017, 163, 166). This book cannot welcome this diffuse family of print, as it will admit only those works written by individual authors, known or anonymous, and published by "booksellers," as publishers were called so at the time. The market was free nominally, but was carefully or jealously managed by these "booksellers," whose main objective, albeit modified by their personal principles or affiliations, was reaping economic profit from the "copies," as the manuscripts were called, which they purchased from different authors.[3] On the title pages of the printed matters, naming the authors was not as mandatory as identifying the name (and address) of the publishers. The very form of the title pages in fact proclaimed the predominance of the publisher's role as the "creator of creators," to borrow

[3]On the eighteenth-century London book market, see Hoppit (2000, 176–181); Sher (2006, chap. 3 to chap. 5); Raven (2007, chap. 5 to chap. 10); Suarez et al. (2009). On the virtual monopoly London "booksellers" sought to enforce through litigation, see St Clair (2004, 97–100, 105–111).

from Pierre Bourdieu's terminology (Bourdieu 1993, 77; see also Sher 2006, 7–8). Be that as it may, a publisher needed authors to furbish him with the material to be printed. Those who offered their hand-written manuscripts encompassed a broad range of occupational backgrounds. Whether they had any practical experience in commerce or not, many of these authors chose to grapple with economic questions in a prose style attuned to the taste of the general common reader.[4]

One common feature they shared was their preoccupation with what they would readily identify as "moral" questions raised by the robust market economy that took shape in the century. Words rather than numbers mattered in the discussions of human attributes and attitudes affecting economic actions. William Petty's *Political Arithmetick* (1690) had claimed that in debates about politics and economics "intellectual Arguments" mobilizing "comparative and superlative Words" should give place to "Arguments of Sense," articulated in "*Number, Weight*, or *Measure*," which his own "Political Arithmetick" (Petty 1690, preface) exemplified. Petty's belief that natural laws of the body politic can be known through mathematics (McCormick 2009, 116) did not meet with that many adherents among those writing on economic topics in the subsequent decades, even as mathematical competence was becoming widespread and as government departments collected numerical data regularly (Hoppit 1996, 519–525; Innes 2009, 128–129). Charles Davenant hailed the "Excellent Computations" made by Gregory King of England's population in *An Essay upon the Probable Methods of Making a People Gainers in the Balance of Trade* (Davenant 1699, 23). Davenant and King were in the minority, ingenious as they were in their calculations (Hoppit 2000, 191). As the next century unfolded, "intellectual Arguments" using words rather than numbers prevailed, as many shared Defoe's suspicion that "judging by or from Calculations leads Men, of otherwise great Penetration, oftentimes into fatal Mistakes" (Defoe 1728, 214). Such "intellectual Arguments" were "discourses" using words, and those "Arguments" often resounded with moral intonation created by "comparative and superlative Words."

[4] A noteworthy precedent of our work can be found in Raven (1992, chapters 5, 8, and 9), although, by comparison, I place greater emphasis on what the luminaries of the period had written than on canvassing the general opinion reconstructed from a range of sources far broader than mine.

1.2 "Moral" and the Economic

What "moral" meant in the period, however, calls for some elucidation, which we shall conduct by inviting some representative authors in the mid-decades of the century to aid us. In his monumental *Dictionary of the English Language* (first edition, 1755–56; revised fourth edition, 1773), Samuel Johnson gives three different but related definitions of "moral." "Relating to the practice of men towards each other, as it may be virtuous or criminal, good or bad," is the first, while "[r]easoning or instructing with regard to vice and virtue" comes second, followed by the third and last, "Popular; customary; such as is known or admitted in the general business of life." The sample sentences he selected for each definition provide clear hints as to what Johnson meant by these definitions. For the first, Johnson takes three sentences from Richard Hooker, the sixteenth-century Anglican theologian. "Keep at the least within the compass of *moral* actions, which have in them vice or virtue" is the first of these three. Moral actions are those that are bound by the minimal criterion of "vice or virtue," which carries a broader denotation than the one given by Johnson's definition itself that the "moral" has to do with distinguishing the "virtuous or criminal, good or bad" among the "practice of men." The third and last of Hooker's statements assert that in "*moral* actions divine law helpeth exceedingly the law of reason to guide life, but in supernatural it alone guideth." The adjective "moral" stands here opposed to the "supernatural," which makes it close to "natural" or customary, and thus steers close to Johnson's third definition. The second definition is illustrated by a single sample, taken from William Shakespeare's *King Lear*. It features the phrase "a *moral* fool," that is, a cowardly fool given to fruitless moralizing. The choice is interesting for the expression is attended with starkly negative connotations, even when one remembers that the line is spoken by Goneril, a character totally devoid of any moral scruple.[5] The line from Shakespeare sounds almost like a sardonic gloss on Johnson's definition. Is Johnson suggesting that "Reasoning or instructing with regard to vice and virtue" is something only a "*moral* fool" indulges in and, as such, a pointless, if not outright ludicrous, exercise? The third definition is garnished with four quotations each taken from

[5] The Duke of Albany, thus insulted by his wife Goneril, retorts, "See thyself, devil! / Proper deformity shows not in the fiend / So horrid as in woman" (Shakespeare 2020, 4.2.58–60).

different authors, first of which contrasts "*moral* certainty" to "Physical and mathematical certainty." This binary opposition more or less is retained in the second and third samples. The fourth sample, on the other hand, speaks of a "*moral* universality," which is a term in logic referring to a "predicate [that] agrees to the greatest part of the particulars which are contained under the universal subject" (Johnson 1773, s.v. "Moral"). In this sense, one can classify this sample sentence as demonstrating a "*moral* certainty" in that it stands opposed to a strict "mathematical certainty" which demands a complete agreement of all the particulars with the universal proposition to which they are subjoined. As can be inferred from Johnson's definitions and illustrations, the "moral" in general was considered to be a word closely related to those practical affairs of daily life which could be adjudicated in the court of "customary" common sense. As such, the jurisdiction of that which was "moral" was separated both from that of supernatural revelation and from that of precise mathematical reasoning. What we mean by a "moral" discourse of the economy, then, is this relatively informal, "customary," and empirical apprehension and assessment of the "practice of men towards each other" as it relates to the "economy," the latter understood in the broadest possible sense.

"Moral" used as noun Johnson considers to be less firmly planted in the English language than its adjectival usage. The word can mean "Morality" or "practice or doctrine of the duties of life," but he adds that "this is rather a French than English sense." A more typical usage of the word as noun in English signifies the "doctrine inculcated by a fiction; the accommodation of a fable to form the morals." Similarly, "morality" is identified by Johnson as a loan word from French, "*moralité*, Fr.," and defined firstly as a "doctrine of the duties of life" compiled by philosophers. The second sense is more general as it refers to the "form of an action which makes it the subject of reward, or punishment," yet the sample sentence, taken from a printed sermon, makes it clear at what domain the "reward, or punishment" resides. The "*morality* of action," the sample statement maintains, "is founded in the freedom of that principle, by virtue of which it is in the agent's power, having all things ready and requisite to the performance of an action, either to perform or not perform it" (Johnson 1773, s.v. "Morality"). Free choices of free agents, presumably rational, are the premise upon which the subtle mathematics of modern microeconomics is founded. The "morality" of economic action which the "moral" discourses of the economy dilate on can be understood more in this latter "microeconomic" sense than in the former "philosophical" sense. Even in those instances where the "duties of life" become an issue, as in the debates about "luxury" or "idleness," the overriding concern was that such "vices" may erode the "agent's power" to "perform" properly. However, an important distinction has to be made here. Measuring the "moral" (customary) choices of free economic agents with "mathematical certainty" is what modern economics aspires to accomplish, but for Johnson and his contemporaries, such abstract certainty stood diametrically opposed to "moral certainty." This essential demarcation of the "moral" away from the "mathematical" or the "physical" was broadly accepted in the period by many authors. To cite one late example, Edmund Burke's diagnosis of where the ringleaders and cheerleaders of the French Revolution (to which we shall return in the very last chapter of this book) went wrong directed attention to their mathematical view of political "reason." Should a "computing principle" ever be relevant for politics, it ought to be so only as one of "adding, subtracting, multiplying, and dividing, morally and not metaphysically or mathematically, true moral denominations" (Burke 1998, 112–113). Measuring and evaluating "true moral denominations"—not "metaphysically or mathematically" but "morally"—imply a fundamental distrust of mathematical calculation and a staunch reliance on human language, on discourse and rhetoric, the weapons wielded by Burke the renowned orator. A "moral" discourse of the economy could very well be described, in this regard, as a cluster or collation of non-mathematical reflections on the economy, non-mathematical even when "true moral denominations" were added and subtracted in debates about highly contentious issues such as the African slave trade.

Interestingly, Johnson's sample sentence chosen for the first definition of "moral" as noun (signifying "practice or doctrine of the duties of life") pairs "moral" with "œconomy." "Their moral and œconomy, / Most perfectly they made agree" is the couplet scooped from Matthew Prior's "An Epitaph" by our lexicographer (Johnson 1773, s.v. "Moral"). The lines describe the happy marital consonance of a dead couple, "saunt'ring Jack and idle Joan," well-matched both in their reciprocal duties as man and wife (their "moral") and in their household management ("œconomy") (Prior 1721, 253). While the word in this sample usage clearly has a sense many steps removed from the current English noun "economy," Johnson's definitions, six in total, all derive their senses from the first, based on its Greek root "*œconomia*," the "management of a family; the government of a household." Other definitions listed by Johnson are "Distribution of expence," "Frugality; discretion of expence," "Disposition of things,"

"The disposition or arrangement of any work," and "System of matter; distribution of every thing active or passive to its proper place." Two of these definitions bear some partial resemblance to the modern sense of the word, but they in fact refer only to the management of funds for private consumption, as the quoted sentences testify:

> Particular sums are not laid out to the greatest advantage in his *economy*; but are sometimes suffered to run waste, while he is only careful of the main. *Dryden*.
>
> I have no other notion of *economy* than that it is the parent of liberty and ease. *Swift to Bolingbroke*. (Johnson 1773, s.v. "Economy")

In the first sentence, "economy" signifies one's personal expenditure ("his *economy*"), just as in the second, the "notion of *economy*" pertains to individual habits of spending money. The words referring to economic activities in Johnson's *Dictionary*, and in the general usage of the age, were "trade," "commerce," and "traffick," often used interchangeably. Not surprisingly, Johnson uses these terms to define one another. The first sense of "traffick" is "Commerce; merchandising; large trade," whereas that of "trade" is "Traffick; commerce." (Johnson 1773, s.v. "Traffick," "Trade"). The term "economy" would more often than not find itself coupled with decidedly non-economic words, as when Shaftesbury (Anthony Ashley Cooper) keeps in view the "economy of the passions" belonging to the "constitution" of a "particular creature or species" (Shaftesbury 1999, 198). Similarly, Joseph Butler finds the "economy and constitution of human nature" to be a "composition of various parts, body, spirit, appetites, particular passions, and affections" (Butler 1726, 39, 65). Human nature for these moral philosophers is likened to a household "economy," as it were, made up of various constituent members. To confer on "economy" a task greater and more comprehensive than the mission the word had carried out since antiquity within the walls of private household, or to remove it from the analogous significations attached to it by moderns (such as Shaftesbury and Butler), one had to add to it the adjective "political." Before we move on to that innovation, we first would have to understand what the expression "political" signified.

The adjective "political" was matched with "moral" at least by two authors of the period, one forgotten and the other keenly relished by current academia. The first is a churchman, Richard Hurd, whose *Moral and Political Dialogues* (1759) captured the fancy of no one less than the king himself. Thanks to his book, Hurd built a lasting friendship with George III, through whose support, he became bishop of Lichfield and Coventry (Sykes 1934, 400). Such political bounty was no doubt an unforeseen by-product of Hurd's platonic dialogues between known historical figures, but the "political" themes covered include a debate, in "Dialogue II," about the merits of renouncing the "drudgery of business" for a quite retirement after accumulating moderate monetary wealth (Hurd 1759, 98). If the economic realm is only indirectly visited by Rev. Hurd, no such reservation is to be found in David Hume. An author as versatile and erudite as Johnson, though one who did not share Johnson's or Hurd's attachment to the Church of England, Hume reminds us of the flexible role "political" played in the lexicon of eighteenth-century discourse. In fact, to Hume's *Essays, Moral and Political*, though later changed into "Moral, Political, and Literary,"[6] the title of this book I am writing pays homage. Indeed, if any precedent of aligning moral arguments with economic discussions needs to be proffered, one could readily point to Hume's *Essays*. "Political" was very much the term that covered the economic sphere, since, as we have seen, the term "economic" or "economy" did not neatly shed its Greek root referring to household management. Essays dealing patently with economic issues in Hume's collection belong to the "political" section in that the economics of a political community is what Hume focuses on. Yet a caveat is needed here. A large portion of Hume's "political essays" have recently been elevated to the status of his "contributions to economics," but to assert that Hume built an economic theory based on a "belief that there are tractable uniformities to human agency that produce observable patterns in the social realm" (Schabas and Wennerlind 2020, 3–4, 51) may be going a bit too far than the author himself intended. Hume consciously chose to name the collection of his economic writings "essays" rather than a systematic "treatise."

The tentative posture of an essayist also tinctures Hume's conception of "moral" used as an adjective. The primary opponent of "moral" in Hume's writings, as in Johnson's definitions, is "natural" or "physical." This can be illustrated by *A Treatise of Human Nature* (1739), which preceded his *Essays*. In his earlier metaphysical work, "moral" and "natural," or "moral" and "physical," even when their essential "distinction" is rejected, are generally placed in contrastive pairings (Hume 2000, 5–6, 115). The "moral"

[6] "Essays, Moral and Political" was the title from 1741 to 1758 (Miller 1987, xii–xiv). See also Sher (2006, 45–63).

is the opponent of the "natural" or "physical." In the later collection of his political essays, this opposition gains an even greater weight. For instance, "national characters" differ due to either "moral" or "physical causes," writes Hume in "Of National Characters." What then is meant by these phrases? "By moral causes" are meant "all circumstances, which are fitted to work on the mind as motives or reasons, and which render a peculiar set of manners habitual to us." This widely inclusive definition easily exceeds the boundary of the "moral" as we would usually understand the term, for the sense encompasses collective and institutional, as well as personal and intrinsic, parameters. Those constituting the "moral" embrace political factors such as the "nature of the government" or the "revolutions of public affairs." Economic conditions of the "plenty or penury in which the people live" also occupy a prominent place among the "moral causes." By contrast, "physical causes" are granted a more restricted jurisdiction, as they refer to the "air and climate" attending the geographical location of a particular nation. Between the two species of "causes," the former has a far greater preponderance, since a "nation," Hume points out, is "nothing but a collection of individuals" and since the "manners of individuals are frequently determined" by "moral" causes. These "moral causes" are saturated by economics and politics. "As poverty and hard labour debase the minds of the common people and render them unfit for any science and ingenious profession," Hume argues, "so where any government becomes very oppressive to all its subjects, it must have a proportional effect on their temper and genius, and must banish all the liberal arts from among them" (Hume 1987, 198 ["Of National Characters"]). "Moral" rather than "physical" factors play a key role in international trade, as well. China is physically removed far away from Europe, but Europeans desire to trade with China. Europe's "skill and ingenuity," both eminent items of "moral causes," are not inferior to those of China, yet Europeans are "never able to trade thither without great disadvantage." Why is it so? Surely not simply because China is a populous country at the physical level. It owes more to the fact that the Europeans crave the goods the Chinese manufacture and that the Chinese produce them in a particularly "industrious" manner. This illustrates how the "moral attraction, arising from the interests and passions of men" can be "as potent and infallible" as the "physical attraction" arising from proximity or contiguity (Hume 1987, 313 ["Of the Balance of Trade"]).

In the quoted passages above, "moral causes" or "moral attraction" played key roles in political and economic actions largely thanks to their being free from normative moral schemes condemning vice and commending virtue. Hume clearly prefers the third among Johnson's definitions. The "moral" is that which is tied to the customary "interests and passions" of a nation, "such as is known or admitted in the general business of life." This stance chimes in with Hume's view of "morals" as expounded in *A Treatise of Human Nature*. "Morals" affect "actions and affections" not so much because they follow the direction of "reason" as because they "excite passions" and by doing so "produce or prevent actions." "Reason of itself," in fact, is "utterly impotent in this particular" (Hume 2000, 294). What happens, then, to the distinction between virtue and vice? First thing to bear in mind is that these terms are "not qualities in objects, but perceptions in the mind" merely. They refer to "our own sentiments of pleasure and uneasiness; and if these be favourable to virtue, and unfavourable to vice, no more can be requisite to the regulation of our conduct and behaviour" (Hume 2000, 301–302). The corollary, then, would be that at the level of a political community, which is "nothing but a collection of individuals," the individual sentiments will vary randomly from individual to individual. However, the "moral causes," by which term Hume refers to specific political and economic conditions, ensure that some common standard would be shared in each community. As "moral causes" affect a given community, they are also affected in turn by circumstances specific to that community. This implies that the "ideas of morality and decency alter from one age to another," just as the political and economic "causes" tend to alter from one age to another. Within a particular age and within a particular society, "speculative opinions" can be proposed by individual thinkers about "moral principles," but what matters is the actual "judgement of manners" and the "sentiments of approbation or blame, love or hatred" shared by the society as a whole. These are determined by "long custom" which can never be changed so easily or promptly (Hume 1987, 246–247 ["Of the Standard of Taste"]). Such being the case, ostensibly "moral" essays—not that there are many of them in Hume's *Essays, Moral and Political*—keep an eye on the "manners" and "custom" with all their economic ramifications, while Hume's superb pieces on economics pay heed to the "moral" dimension of human action. Under the former category proper one can place "Of the Dignity or Meanness of Human Nature," where Hume vindicates "self-love" as a passion entirely compatible with a solicitude for other individuals. Few men can be found in a society who, "having a family, children, and relations, do not spend more on the maintenance and education of these than on their own pleasures." Such decision may very well "proceed from their self-love, since the prosperity of their family and friends is one, or the chief of their pleasures, as well as their chief honour" (Hume 1987, 85 ["Of the Dignity or Meanness of Human Nature"]). Self-love in this instance can never be a vice, for it incites a virtuous expenditure of one's material resources on those whose happiness one cares for. "Of Commerce," representing the latter category, sets up a dual proposition as the grand premise, first, that everything in the world is "purchased by labour" and, second, that "our passions are the only causes of labour" (Hume 1987, 261 ["Of Commerce"]). As the realm of the "moral" is inhabited by "passions" in Hume's perspective, the "moral" and the economic build a seamless connection denoted by the term "labour," itself fueled by "our passions," while producing all that our "passions" and our needs demand.

Another representative author of the century who hoisted the term "moral" on the title of his book, of course, is Adam Smith. *The Theory of Moral Sentiments* met with a warm reception much to the bemused envy of his older friend Hume.[7] The term "moral" features saliently in the title of Smith's first publication, yet the phrase "moral sentiments," despite being the titular hero of Smith's *Theory of Moral Sentiments* makes only a limited number of appearances in the text. Hume had commissioned nonrational "sense" (also called "feeling or sentiment") to provide the criterion of distinguishing virtue from vice. "An action, or sentiment, or character is virtuous or vicious" solely "because its view causes a pleasure or uneasiness of a particular kind" (Hume 2000, 303). Smith's theory of "moral sentiments," even as it follows Hume's precedent of equating the moral with "feeling or sentiment," broaches a broader list of subjects including passions, conscience, fashion, custom, wealth, virtue, and ethical theories. The expansiveness and flexibility of Smith's approach allow him to dispense with a frequent repetition of the phrase, yet when it is summoned in its full shape, the context tends generally to be negative. Our "moral sentiments" are exposed to the "corruption" caused by the "disposition to admire, and almost to worship, the rich and the powerful, and to despise, or, at least, to neglect persons of poor and mean condition"

[7] Hume wrote to Smith in 12 April 1759: "I proceed to tell you the melancholy News, that your Book has been very unfortunate: For the Public seem disposed to applaud it extremely. It was lookd for by the foolish People with some Impatience; and the Mob of Literati are beginning already to be very loud in its Praises." The "Mob" in question refers to three bishops or three "Retainers to Superstition," as Hume's cynical epithet puts it (Smith 1987, 35).

(Smith 1976b, 61 [I.iii.3.1]). This disposition is politically "necessary both to establish and to maintain the distinction of ranks and the order of society," yet it weakens the "moral sentiments" to such an extent as to entice those who aspire to possess what they admire to "abandon the paths of virtue" (Smith 1976b, 64 [I.iii.3.8]). The public utility of adulating the rich and the powerful, then, is inherently at odds with the individuals' moral sentiments, which bid one at least not to "despise" the poor and the lowly. Yet an extreme disposition to abhor and condemn worldly fortune in view of the rewards and punishments in the life after death can also be the antagonists of "our moral sentiments." Smith will not deny that our "happiness in this life is thus, upon many occasions, dependent upon the humble hope and expectation of a life to come" or that such hope "can alone illumine the dreary prospect of its continually approaching mortality, and maintain its cheerfulness under all the heaviest calamities to which, from the disorders of this life, it may sometimes be exposed" (Smith 1976b, 132 [III.2.33]). Yet to assert the superiority of the "futile mortifications of a monastery" over those "ennobling hardships" of honorable exertions in the secular world stands in "direct opposition to all our moral sentiments" (Smith 1976b, 134 [III.2.35]). Political passions and prejudice can also erode moral sentiments, since the "violence and rage of contending parties" tend to stifle and corrupt them (Smith 1976b, 156 [III.3.43]). But elsewhere in the book, Smith admits that "moral sentiments" themselves cannot avoid being conditioned by "custom and fashion," whose influence upon "moral sentiments," although not as great as political faction or fanaticism, remains an ineluctable part of what we deem to be appropriate, right, and beautiful. If the "custom and fashion" in question "coincide with the natural principles of right and wrong," they would not affect the moral sentiments adversely, but when a person "had the misfortune to be brought up amidst violence, licentiousness, falsehood, and injustice," that person's moral sentiments cannot avoid being severely disabled (Smith 1976b, 200 [V.2.2]). In fact, the society and the nation into which one is born largely determine one's moral sentiments. We have to presume that the "style of manners which takes place in any nation" is that which is "most suitable to its situation." "Hardiness," for instance, is "the character most suitable to the circumstances of a savage," whereas "sensibility" suits those living in a "very civilized society." When faced with this disparity, therefore, one cannot "complain that the moral sentiments of men," in either case, "are very grossly perverted" (Smith 1976b, 209 [V.2.13]). What can be gathered from these remarks is that

Smith's "moral sentiments" can never stay free from the complex and at times contradictory relationships of economic and political organizations, themselves heavily dependent on geographical and historical conditions. The "moral" realm, in other words, can and ought to partner with the political, of which economic issues (wealth, poverty, asceticism, fashion, and civilization) take up a sizable portion.

Smith was not content to remain as the celebrated author of *The Theory of Moral Sentiments*, but embarked on the titanic labor of writing his masterpiece on political economy. In this latter project of his, Smith was preceded by James Steuart, the author of *An Inquiry into the Principles of Political Economy* (1767). Smith wrote to one of his correspondents in 1772 that he was "preparing for the Press" his own contribution to the subject, promising that in his new book, "every false principle" Steuart falls prey to "will meet with a clear and distinct confutation" and that without "once mentioning it" (Letter to William Pulteney, 3 Sept. 1772, Smith 1987, 163–164). In the event, it took five more years for the work to be ready for the press, and we would likewise take advantage of that interval to visit the pages of Steuart's book to see what he meant by "political economy" and whether a "moral" dimension was recognized by him at all. As Steuart understands it, "political œconomy," built on what "œconomy is in a family," is an analogic expression used to describe an economic administration of a "state" (Steuart 1767, 15). Smith refers to Steuart's "principle," but Steuart in fact speaks mostly of the "art" of managing a political community. The main challenge for this "art" is to "secure a certain fund of subsistence for all the inhabitants, to obviate every circumstance which may render it precarious; to provide every thing necessary for supplying the wants of the society, and to employ the inhabitants." These inhabitants Steuart assumes to be freemen who act according to their inclinations and who will not let themselves be compelled to act against their wishes. Giving work to them, therefore, should be "in such a manner as naturally to create reciprocal relations and dependencies between them, so as to make their several interests lead them to supply one another with their reciprocal wants." This being as much an "art" as a "science," the "statesman" of a free society is obliged "to adapt the different operations" of his policy to the "spirit, manners, habits, and customs of the people" (Steuart 1767, 2–3). In fact, any attempt to simplify the complicated and compound management of a nation's "political œconomy" Steuart rejects as an error typical of the French economic writers, who indulge in building their "*Systèmes*." These theoretical models are "no more than a chain of contingent consequences, drawn from a few fundamental maxims, adopted, perhaps, rashly," and as such, they are "mere conceits" tending to "mislead the understanding, and efface the path to truth" (Steuart 1767, ix). Steuart's "spirit, manners, habits, and customs" can be subsumed under the third definition of "moral" by Johnson, "Popular; customary." Steuart, however, assigns the customary and popular standards of action and judgment to a higher category, the "spirit" of a particular people. The "spirit of people" is that which is "formed upon a set of received opinions relative to three objects; morals, government, and manners." When these three are "generally adopted" and "confirmed by long and constant habit," they are "never called in question" and become the bedrock upon which laws, government, and "what is commonly called the customs of a country" are erected. Of these three "objects," "manners" is the most difficult to grasp for an outsider, since they "are supposed by every one in the country to be so well known, so generally followed and observed, that it seldom occurs to any body to inform a stranger concerning them" (Steuart 1767, 8). That what Steuart calls "manners" can overlap to a large extent with Smith's "moral sentiments" affected by fashion and social prejudices is not difficult to grasp. On the other hand, "morals" proper for Steuart tends to be more normative than Hume would allow. They are founded on the "tenets" of a people's religion and concern the notions about an individual agent's "duty" in relation to his position in society (Steuart 1767, xiii). Thus "morals" in this narrower sense would matter less than the "spirit, manners, habits, and customs," for which Steuart's "principles of political economy" reserve an important place of honor, as we shall see below in his discussion of particular subjects such as "industry" (in Chap. 3) or "luxury" (in Chap. 4).

Morals as a measure of distinguishing virtue from vice can choose to stay at the level of "passions" and "sentiments" constituting human nature. Yet when morals purport to include obligations and duties, they cannot afford to do without religion, as Steuart admits. This was pointed out quite lucidly by John Locke in *The Reasonableness of Christianity, as Delivered in the Scriptures* (1695). "Natural reason," to judge from the "attempts of Philosophers" before the advent of Christ, reached only so far as to build "several Systems" that were many degrees removed from the "perfection of a true and compleat" morality. A "surer and shorter way" of reaching that perfection, Locke asserts, was secured by Jesus Christ, as "one manifestly sent from God, and coming with visible

Authority from him." As "King and Law-maker," the Son of God prescribed to humanity their "Duties" and commanded their "Obedience" to them (Locke 1695, 266). A generation or so later, William Warburton, who had huge respects for Locke (Sorkin 2008, 55–58), made an argument similar to that of Locke. Morality for Warburton implies an "*Obligation* in the Agent." If it does not, it remains an empty theory which has no relevance to real life. An obligation in turns "implies an Obliger," who must be different, by definition, from the "Obliged." Who then is the "Obliger"? An atheist will answer that it is "*Right Reason.*" Reason, however, is only an "Attribute" of the obliged, functioning as his "Assistant" in judging whether his obligation comes from the right obliger (Warburton 1738, 46–47). An obligation, furthermore, implies a "*Law*, which enjoins and forbids," which law can only be an "Imposition of an intelligent Superior, who hath Power to exact conformity thereto." A "blind unintelligent Nature" can never be this law-giver, neither can the "*Law of Reason*" or the "*Law of Necessity.*" These last two are merely "popular and figurative Expressions," the first referring to the "Rule that the Law-giver lays down for judging of his Will," and the second to the capacity of "forcing" a law upon the obliged (Warburton 1738, 48). To evade the inevitable admission that this "intelligent Superior" can only be the almighty Creator who revealed Himself in the Scriptures, certain philosophers (such as Hume, as we have seen above) choose to revive the Epicurean scheme which understands virtue as that which gives one pleasure and vice as that which does not. This is to confuse the "Natural" with the "Moral." Calling the "natural Good" such as "Food and Covering" a virtue will do little to set up an "Obligation" to prefer "Good to Evil." The Stoics, on the other hand, held the view that humans are compelled to be moral by the "Necessity" of "universal Nature." But this "Nature," itself being "blind and unintelligible," can make "Men obliged as Clocks are by Weights, but never as free Agents," whose voluntary acceptance of the "unnecessitating Command of an intelligent Superior" only "can make Actions moral" (Warburton 1738, 49–50). The moderns have come up with a new alternative to morals based on God's "unnecessitating Command." They suggest that a "*Moral Sense*" or "*Moral Instinct*" all humans are endowed with warrants some degree of virtue and goodness. The problem for Warburton is that this moral sense is far too "delicately interwoven into the human Constitution" and consequently "so easily and so frequently effaced." The "original Passions and Appetites" must first be "rightly tempered and balanced" before the "*Moral Instinct*" can hope to make itself felt in "any strong or sensible Operation." When the "Moral Sense" is made a rule of conduct, it often fails to maintain its authority in practice, for "it can never be shewn that one Appetite is righter than another, though they be contrary and inconsistent." Whatever appetite, therefore, which, "at the Present, is most Importunate to be gratified" becomes the norm, "how adverse so ever to the Moral Sense" (Warburton 1738, 57). Can customs come to supplement the fragility of the moral sense swayed by appetites? Not quite so. On the contrary, they will "insensibly effect the Idea of the Moral Sense" by long practice, exposing it to the whims of the "more violent Passions of Fear, Lust, and Anger." Moreover, that delicate "*Moral Instinct*" finds it almost impossible on its own to resist the potent assault of the "universal Passion of Self-interest" which spurs people to act by "Hopes and Fears" and which potentially threatens the peace and harmony of civil society. "To balance these Appetites," Warburton concludes, "what must be laid in the Scale of Virtue" are the "Rewards and Punishments, which Religion proposes" (Warburton 1738, 58, 60).

Can a religious morality that goes beyond natural "moral sense" to inculcate moral obligations be relevant for the economy? Here a brief excursus seems called for, as this question summons Max Weber's study of the influence of religious norms on economic actions. Weber not only detected a causal link between Puritanism and what he called the "spirit" (*Geist*) of "modern capitalism" (Weber 1948, 321) but sought to classify patterns of mutual dependence and tension between the "ethic of ultimate ends" (such as the rewards in afterlife) promised by all religions (including but not restricted to Christianity) and the "needs of economic life" (Weber 1978, 576–577). Compared with Weber's grand scheme of piling up religious traditions and their economic implications, my approach is not only myopic or even parochial, as we focus on a particular century and on a limited geography. But his ambition, though enviable, stands upon a premise which I do not accept. Weber sees religious morality and the "economic life" as two autonomous dominions, each with its own coded rules. Religion and the economy, as I see it, may be said to form an intertwined complex, an "overdetermination," to adopt Louis Althusser's term without subscribing to his Marxist faith in the "determination in the last instance by the economic" (Althusser 1977, 106–107). This "overdetermination" does not necessarily have to be a clinical symptom, for instance, of a religious bigot turning "daemonic" in his frantic business pursuits and displaying "both the qualities and limitations of his creed, in all their remorseless logic," as R. H. Tawney satirized the transmogrified "temper" of seventeenth-century Puritanism in later ages (Tawney 1938, 229). For one thing, the Anglican Church of our period, as one can see in Warburton's argument on obligation above, sought to harmonize reason with faith and to establish faith on reasonable arguments. The leaders and theologians of the Church did all their best to keep post-Puritan "enthusiasm" at bay (Holmes and Szechi 1993, 113–114; Hoppit 2000, 203–204). In such an ambience, the nodal point of "overdetermination" where some degree or species of religious sentiment would most likely leave its trace could very well be a quotidian issue of sober daily transactions such as that of obligation.

When like Hume, no religious premise is invited to sustain morality, an "obligation of morality" arising from promises, although patently an "invention for the interest of society," becomes "one of the most mysterious and incomprehensible operations that can possibly be imagin'd." Why are we obliged to perform what we promise? Because there is some "force" involved, answers Hume. This "force" of obligation attached to promises Hume identifies as that which is produced by natural motives of "hope or fear" (Hume 2000, 336–337). Yet, needless to say, hope or fear inspired by religious beliefs would be far more potent than those which are not. Even if it were an "invention," the "interests of society" will be far better served when sustained by sanctions of religion than when they are not. James Beattie, ever vigilant in dissecting the weaknesses in Hume's moral philosophy, reminded the reader of the plain fact that the "generality of mankind" would have difficulty appreciating the subtleties of Humean metaphysics, when they act according to their "internal powers" of moral sense and "do by their conduct declare, that they feel their authority." Most people "believe a certain mode of conduct to be incumbent on them in certain circumstances, because a sentiment of duty arises in their mind." If pressed to state their reason for doing so, they would answer, "I can give no further reason for it; but I *feel* that such is my duty." If pressed still further, the only viable answer can be that "I know that I ought to do what my conscience enjoins, because God is the author of my constitution" (Beattie 1771, 72–73). William Paley would take one step farther than Beattie to confer on the "sentiment of duty" implanted on humans by the "author" of their "constitution" the mission to guide one's pursuit of happiness in the domain of material transactions. The grounds and necessity of moral obligations are best explained when we accept that "private happiness is our motive, and the will of God our rule." An economic action, such as signing a contract, seeks to maximize one's "private happiness." When entering into a written compact, one assumes that each signatory will harbor some sense of obligation and will keep promises specified by the document. One who fears God would certainly feel more strongly obliged to discharge his promised mission than one who does not (Paley 2002, 36).

Obligations, in fact, played an increasingly important role in an economy that relied heavily on credit. Promises and promissory notes were crucial to daily transactions at all levels (Daunton 2002, 166–167). For purely practical reasons, moral obligations were vital to the economy. This is what Josiah Tucker, a cleric and economist, was firmly convinced of. For him there was no essential division between morals and commerce, as they were both built on the common foundation of religion. Commerce attests to the wisdom of the Creator, for the "Order of Things" is constituted by that "all-wise, just, and benevolent Being" in such a manner as to make nations, as well as individuals, stay mutually dependent for their "Self-preservation." "Morals" and "Trade," or our "*Duty*" and "*Interests*," can never oppose each other (Tucker 1774, 12). A fair and honest exchange of goods and services between a "town, or District" and its neighboring town, or between two foreign nations, not only satisfies the Christian duty of fraternal communion but serves the inextricably intertwined interests of both. Our prosperity on earth is linked to that of our neighboring cities or countries, for "were their Numbers to be diminished, or their Circumstances altered from Affluence to Want, we ourselves, in the Rotation of Things, should soon feel the bad Effects of such a Change" (Tucker 1774, 54). That Providence willed our mutual dependence is "perfectly legible both in the natural, and in the moral World." The "*natural* World" as made by "our bountiful Creator" is diversified into "different Soils" and "different Climates," enabling and encouraging the "Inhabitants of different Countries" to "supply each other with their respective Fruits and Products." By "exciting a reciprocal Industry," the nations of the world "carry on an Intercourse mutually beneficial, and universally benevolent." Furthermore, even when there exists "no remarkable Difference of Soil, or of Climates" between different countries, there exists a "moral" diversity, a "great Difference of Talents" displaying a "wonderful Variety of Strata in the human Mind" (Tucker 1774, 67). Predicated as it is on the consonance between the natural and the moral orders, Tucker's perspective can admit no conflict between the "*moral*" and the "*political*" or the moral and the economic (covered by the umbrella term "political"). "Providence has so ordained," Tucker asserts, "that every Nation may increase in Frugality and Industry, and consequently in Riches." What binds both the economic and the moral realm is the golden rule of reciprocity set by Jesus Christ Himself, "Whatsoever ye would that Men should do unto you, do ye even so unto them" (Matthew 7:12, Authorized [King James] Version). Apply this rule to politics proper, and "Liberty" would be preserved "without Licentiousness," and "Subordination" maintained without "Tyranny or Oppression." When applied to commerce, a "general Encouragement would be given to the Diligent and Industrious of all Professions." This will be attended by a "general Emulation" to exercise their "Genius and improve their Abilities." All the while, "every Man would find his own Account in doing to his Neighbour, as he wishes to be done to himself" (Tucker 1774, "Sermon 1," 12–13).

The last quotation above from Tucker on the benefits of morally acceptable conducts is taken from his sermon, where obviously revealed religion plays a palpable role. In the two "Sermons" appended to his *Four Tracts*, one can say Tucker develops a specifically "Christian" political economy that is more ethically oriented than his providential view of macroeconomic growth noticed by commentators (see, for instance, Urquhart 1995, 9). With the combined force of revealed and natural religions, Tucker endeavors to fend off all perversions of commercial morals. Would it not be more profitable if one dispensed with morals and religion? Would not "vice" be more beneficial for commerce? Against this impious argument (which will be the topic of Chap. 2) Tucker holds his grounds by asserting that a "System of Commerce, which is built upon Principles subversive of Religion and Virtue" will be "detrimental to the great Ends of Government" and thus "cannot be the just and proper Commercial System" but merely a "Deception" that cannot be "so lasting, or so extensive in its Consequences, as it might have been." Perhaps some "Individuals may be Gainers by it," but "upon the whole, it will be found to be as much repugnant to the trading Interests of Mankind, to the right Employment of their Time, and to national Wealth, Plenty, and Prosperity, as it is repugnant to Religion, and Civil Government" (Tucker 1774, "Sermon 1," 16). Tucker's optimistic view of the market economy as one that fits the scheme of both the natural and revealed religions did not rule out the need to castigate those who sought to disrupt this natural order by monopoly and war-mongering (as we shall see in Chap. 5). The greatest sin in political economy for Tucker is resorting to war for the "Sake of Trade." Just as it makes little sense to "oblige every County, Town, Village, nay, and every Shop among ourselves, to be engaged in civil and intestine Wars for the same End," nations should forbear from predatory violence, and keep to the path of amicable exchange of "those Stores of Providence, which are laid up in the natural World, and graciously intended for the Use of Mankind" (Tucker 1774, 69–70). That a high-ranking clergyman with no actual background in commerce could write on trade and politics with such conviction may appear somewhat outlandish in the eyes of atheistic posterity. But his contemporaries felt otherwise. Tucker was a respectable writer befriended by Lord Kames, the champion of the Scottish Enlightenment, and through Kames, by Hume as well (Shelton 1981, 166–171). More to the point is that Tucker's writings in its own context may be a salient but by no means an isolated specimen of a moral discourse of the economy derived from Christian premises.

Tucker's belief that a peaceable free-market economy was a morally "just and proper Commercial System" was widely shared by his contemporaries. It was given an extended and eloquent expression by a book which Smith had worked on for many years. When Smith finally published *An Inquiry into the Nature and Causes of the Wealth of Nations* in 1776, it was to seal his fame as the founder of economics, owing to the relatively systematic approach to the topic when compared with the comparatively diffuse and digressive work written by Steuart. Unlike the later generation of economists, however, that a systematic treatise on economics was written by someone famed as a moral philosopher did not appear particularly extraordinary. *The Monthly Review*, which pioneered in 1749 a new form of periodical journalism solely dedicated to reviewing new publications, had greeted Smith's first book with heart-felt enthusiasm, hailing the author as "one of the most elegant and agreeable writers, upon morals, that we are acquainted with" (Anon. 1759, 18). The magazine reviewed *The Wealth of Nations* upon its appearance in April 1776 by noting how the "respectable Author" succeeded in taking an "extensive and connected view of the several subjects in which the wealth of nations is concerned; and from an happy union of fact and theory has deduced a system, which, we apprehend, is on the whole more satisfactory, and rests on better grounds, than any which had before been offered to the Public" (Anon. 1776, 300). What the reviewer did not feel obliged to note was that this same "respectable Author" was formerly renowned for his work on moral philosophy, just as no one was surprised to find clerics of the Established Church, such as Tucker, authoring disquisitions on commerce. Both masterpieces of Smith easily fall under Johnson's understanding of "moral" as a synonym of "customary," for they deal with the practical and habitual interactions between humans in society. Smith's first book was never indifferent, as we have seen above, to the seminal problems of a commercial society driven by wealth and stirred by potentially misleading appearances of utility. *The Wealth of Nations*, in turn, does not so much construct an economic theory as embed the individuals' economic actions in a multi-layered context of moral, historical, and political conditions. Both books participate in the "moral" debates on the economy, albeit from different perspectives. *An Inquiry into the Nature and Causes of the Wealth of Nations*, as the nuanced and hedged words of the full title advise us not to forget, is hardly "a stupendous palace erected on the granite of self-interest," as George J. Stigler described it (Stigler 1982, 136). The architectural grandeur of the work emanates not so much from a single-minded purpose to devise a self-contained theory as from the "mosaic of details" and "the luxuriant foliage of illustrative fact," which Joseph Schumpeter, the venerable historian of economics, found admirable but rather pointless (Schumpeter [1954] 1994, 186–187). To emphasize yet once again, publications on economic topics emerged and remained in the long eighteenth-century Britain as a porous and hybrid genre, generally factual but at times hypothetical in its temper, mostly descriptive but at times prescriptive in its tone. Lacking a clear generic label, works dealing with matters economic were placed under the rubric of "miscellanies" in the booksellers' catalogue, which category also accommodated works on moral philosophy, history, and *belles lettres*, as is shown by the catalogue of Strahan and Cadell, who published Smith's *The Wealth of Nations* (Anon. [1781?], 7–10).[8] Authors felt free to pronounce their judgments on economic questions, dilating on the merits of "industry" against "idleness," expressing their misgivings about their society's craving for "luxury," and denouncing the "jobbery" of the "projectors" (to be covered in Chaps. 3, 4, and 5, respectively). Against such backdrop, a frontal attack charged with evangelical fervor (discussed in Chap. 6) on what to many was a vital national interest, the African slave trade and the West-Indies slave plantations, could be waged in the name of outraged morality. John Wesley

[8] This is a point I have already made in my book on Smith where I sought to honor the subtle textuality of *The Wealth of Nations*, as a worthy member of the "miscellaneous" family of non-fictional prose. By activating a "trivium" of approaches (grammar, logic, and rhetoric), I attempted to explicate the manner in which the former Edinburgh lecturer of rhetoric fortified and modulated his economic theory by the practice and substance of his writing (Yoon 2018, 24–25).

features in this book not so much as the founder of Methodism, but as a moral critic of slave trade and the idolatry of wealth that condoned it. "It is far better to have no Wealth, than to gain wealth, at the expence of Virtue," thundered Wesley in his *Thoughts upon Slavery* (1774). "Better is honest poverty, than all the Riches brought by the tears, and sweat, and blood of our fellow-creatures" (Wesley 1774, 38–39). Wesley's surely may be an extreme view about trade, profit, and wealth, yet that such voice was heard at all testifies to the complexity and flexibility of the discourses about the economy, which in what follows we propose to revisit and reconstruct.

References

Ahmed, Siraj. 2011. *Stillbirth of capital: Enlightenment writing and colonial India.* Palo Alto: Stanford University Press.

Althusser, Louis. 1977. *For Marx.* Translated by Ben Brewster. London: NLB.

Anon. 1759. The theory of moral sentiments, by Adam Smith. *The Monthly Review* July: 1–18.

Anon. 1776. An enquiry into the nature and causes of the wealth of nations, by Adam Smith. *The Monthly Review* April: 299–308.

Anon. [1781?] *Books, printed for W. Strahan, and T. Cadell in the Strand.* [London?]

Baucom, Ian. 2005. *Specters of the Atlantic: Finance capital, slavery, and the philosophy of history.* Durham: Duke University Press.

Beattie, James. 1771. *An essay on the nature and immutability of truth, in opposition to sophistry and scepticism.* 2nd ed. Edinburgh: A. Kincaid and J. Bell.

Berry, Christoper. 2015. *The idea of commercial society in the Scottish Enlightenment.* Edinburgh: Edinburgh University Press.

Bourdieu, Pierre. 1993. *The field of cultural production.* Edited by Randal Johnson. Cambridge: Polity Press.

Brown, Christopher Leslie. 2006. *Moral capital: Foundations of British abolitionism.* Chapel Hill: University of North Carolina Press.

Burke, Edmund. 1998. Reflections on the revolution in France. In *The writing and speeches of Edmund Burke, vol. 8: The French Revolution 1790–1794*, ed. L. G. Mitchell and William B. Todd, 53–293. Oxford: Clarendon.

Butler, Joseph. 1726 [1983]. *Five sermons preached at the Rolls Chapel and a dissertation upon the nature of virtue.* Edited by Stephen L. Darwall. Indianapolis: Hackett Publishing.

Daunton, Martin. 2002. The wealth of the nation. In *The eighteenth-century: 1688–1815*, ed. Paul Langford, 141–180. Oxford: Oxford University Press.

Davenant, Charles. 1699. *An essay upon the probable methods of making a people gainers in the balance of trade.* London: James Knapton.

Defoe, Daniel. 1728 [2000]. A plan of the English commerce. In *Political and economic writings of Daniel Defoe, vol. 7: Trade*, ed. John McVeagh, 115–341. London: Pickering & Chatto.

Foote, Samuel. 1778. *The nabob; A comedy, in three acts. As it is performed at the Theatre-Royal in the Haymarket.* London: T. Cadell.

Foucault, Michel. 1971. *l'Ordre du discours.* Paris: Gallimard.

Götz, Norbert. 2015. "Moral economy": Its conceptual history and analytical prospects. *Journal of Global Ethics* 11:147–162. https://doi.org/10.1080/17449626.2015.1054556.

Griswold, Charles L., Jr. 1999. *Adam Smith and the virtues of enlightenment.* Cambridge: Cambridge University Press.

Hanley, Ryan Patrick. 2009. *Adam Smith and the character of virtue.* Cambridge: Cambridge University Press.

Holmes, Geoffrey, and Daniel Szechi. 1993. *The age of oligarchy: Pre-industrial Britain 1722–1783.* London: Routledge.

Hoppit, Julian. 1996. Political arithmetic in eighteenth-century England. *Economic History Review* 49:516–540.

Hoppit, Julian. 2000. *A land of liberty? England 1689–1727.* Oxford: Oxford University Press.

Hoppit, Julian. 2017. *Britain's political economies: Parliament and economic life, 1660–1800.* Cambridge: Cambridge University Press.

Hume, David. 1987. *Essays, moral, political, and literary.* Edited by Eugene F. Miller. Indianapolis: Liberty Fund.

Hume, David. 2000. *A treatise of human nature.* Edited by David Fate Norton and Mary J. Norton. Oxford: Oxford University Press.

Hurd, Richard. 1759. *Moral and political dialogues: Being the substance of several conversations between divers eminent persons of the past and present age.* London: A. Millar.

Innes, Joanna. 2009. *Inferior politics: Social problems and social policies in eighteenth-century Britain.* Oxford: Oxford University Press.

Johnson, Samuel. 1773. *A dictionary of the English language.* 4th ed. London: Consortium.

Kirk, Neville. 2025. E. P. Thompson's moral economy and legacy. *Economic and Industrial Democracy* 46:27–48. https://doi.org/10.1177/0143831X241304912.

Langford, Paul. 2002. Introduction: Time and space. In *The eighteenth-century: 1688–1815*, ed. Paul Langford, 1–32. Oxford: Oxford University Press.

Locke, John. 1695. *The reasonableness of Christianity, as delivered in the Scriptures.* London: Awnsham and John Churchil.

McCormick, Ted. 2009. *William Petty: And the ambitions of political arithmetic.* Oxford: Oxford University Press.

Miller, Eugene F. 1987. Foreword to *Essays, moral, political, and literary*, by David Hume, edited by Eugene F. Miller. Indianapolis: Liberty Fund.

Paley, William. 2002. *The principles of moral and political philosophy*. Indianapolis: Liberty Fund.

Petty, William. 1690. *Political arithmetick*. London: Clavel and Mortlock.

Pocock, J. G. A. 1971. *Politics, language and time: Essays on political thought and history*. New York: Atheneum.

Poovey, Mary. 2008. *Genres of the credit economy: Mediating value in eighteenth- and nineteenth-century Britain*. Chicago: The University of Chicago Press.

Prior, Matthew. 1721. *Poems on several occasions*. London: J. Tonson.

Raven, James. 1992. *Judging new wealth: Popular publishing and responses to commerce in England, 1750–1800*. Oxford: Clarendon.

Raven, James. 2007. *The business of books: Booksellers and the English book trade 1450–1850*. New Haven: Yale University Press.

Rogan, Tim. 2018. *The moral economists: R. H. Tawney, Karl Polanyi, E. P. Thompson, and the critique of capitalism*. Princeton: Princeton University Press.

Rothschild, Emma. 2001. *Economic sentiments: Adam Smith, Condorcet, and the Enlightenment*. Cambridge, MA: Harvard University Press.

Schabas, Margaret, and Carl Wennerlind. 2020. *A philosopher's economist: Hume and the rise of capitalism*. Chicago: The University of Chicago Press.

Schumpeter, Joseph A. [1954] 1994. *History of economic analysis*. Repr. edited by Elizabeth Boody Schumpeter. London: Routledge.

Shaftesbury (Anthony Ashley Cooper). 1999. *Characteristics of men, manners, opinions, times*. Edited by Lawrence E. Klein. Cambridge: Cambridge University Press.

Shakespeare, William. 2020. *The tragedy of King Lear*. Edited by Jay Halio. Cambridge: Cambridge University Press.

Shelton, George. 1981. *Dean Tucker and eighteenth-century economic and political thought*. London: Macmillan.

Sher, Richard B. 2006. *The Enlightenment and the book: Scottish authors and their publishers in eighteenth-century Britain, Ireland, and America*. Chicago: The University of Chicago Press.

Skinner, Quentin. 1969. Meaning and understanding in the history of ideas. *History and Theory* 8:3–53.

Smith, Adam. 1976a. *An inquiry into the nature and causes of the wealth of nations*. Edited by R. H. Campbell and A. S. Skinner. Oxford: Clarendon.

Smith, Adam. 1976b. *The theory of moral sentiments*. Edited by D. D. Raphael and A. L. Macfie. Oxford: Clarendon.

Smith, Adam. 1987. *The correspondence of Adam Smith*. Edited by Ernest Campbell Mossner and Ian Simpson Ross. Oxford: Clarendon.

Sorkin, David. 2008. *The religious Enlightenment: Protestants, Jews, and Catholics from London to Vienna*. Princeton: Princeton University Press.

St Clair, William. 2004. *The reading nation in the Romantic period*. Cambridge: Cambridge University Press.

Steuart, James. 1767. *An inquiry into the principles of political economy*. Vol. 1. London: A. Millar and T. Cadell.

Stigler, George J. 1982. *The economist as preacher and other essays*. Chicago: The University of Chicago Press.

Suarez, Michael F. S.J., and Michael L. Turner, eds. 2009. *The Cambridge history of the book in Britain*. Vol. 5: *1695–1830*. Cambridge: Cambridge University Press.

Sykes, Norman, 1934 [1962]. *Church and state in England in the xviiith century*. Repr. Hamden: Archon Books.

Tawney, R. H. 1938. *Religion and the rise of capitalism: A historical study*. London: Penguin.

Thompson, E. P. 1971. The moral economy of the English crowd in the eighteenth century. *Past & Present* 50:76–136.

Tucker, Josiah. 1774. *Four tracts, together with two sermons, on political and commercial subjects*. Glocester.

Urquhart, Robert. 1995. David Hume and Josiah Tucker: Pagan and Christian political economy. *History of Economic Ideas* 3:1–33.

Warburton, William. 1738. *The divine legation of Moses demonstrated, on the principles of a religious Deist*. Vol. 1. London: Fletcher Gyles.

Weber, Max. 1948. *From Max Weber: Essays in sociology*. Translated and edited by H. H. Gerth and C. Wright Mills. London: Routledge & Kegan Paul.

Weber, Max. 1978. *Economy and society: An outline of interpretive sociology*. Translated by Ephraim Fischoff et al. Edited by Guenther Roth and Claus Wittich. Berkeley: University of California Press.

Wesley, John. 1774. *Thoughts upon slavery*. London.

Winch, Donald. 1996. *Riches and poverty: An intellectual history of political economy in Britain 1750–1834*. Cambridge: Cambridge University Press.

Yoon, Hye-Joon. 2018. *The rhetoric of tenses in Adam Smith's "The wealth of nations"*. Leiden: Brill.

CHAPTER 2

Private Vices, Pubic Benefits

2.1 Vices and Benefits

"Private Vices, Public Benefits." This formula welded to the title of Bernard Mandeville's *The Fable of the Bees* triggered an outraged response from many quarters for many decades, as it seemed to imply that economic benefits enjoyed by a commercial society which Britain had become in the eighteenth century were predicated on moral turpitude. In a somewhat oblique fashion, the author of this contentious work deserves to be placed among the "initiators of discursive practices," in Foucault's expression, who "established the endless possibility of discourse" by the works they wrote, although surely not of the same rank as Sigmund Freud and Karl Marx to whom Foucault reserves this honor (Foucault 1977, 132). To be more precise, Mandeville's is a rare case of a "negative" initiator of a discursive practice which we venture to call a "moral discourse of the economy," in that he triggered a cascade of critical reactions as well as modified applications of his thesis all throughout the century even as late as 1794 (Sekora 1977, 113–114). Quite unusually for a practically free market of print already well-established in London in the 1720s, when the second edition of the *Fable* came out in 1723, it was greeted with an attempt to suppress it with the force of the law. The Grand Jury of Middlesex accused the work as a "public nuisance" (Kaye 1924, xxxiv; Cook 1974, 117). A Grand Jury, unlike a trial jury, had the right to

H.-J. Yoon, *Moral Discourses of the Economy in Eighteenth-Century Britain*, https://doi.org/10.1007/978-981-95-0958-4_2

present indictments, generally in a written form, and thus initiate a criminal proceeding against the accused in the name of the monarch. Charges of public nuisances in London typically concerned creating health hazards such as piling rubbish on alleys, leaving the refuse of butchery in the gutters, and urinating in public buildings. Bawdy houses could also be subjected to public nuisance indictments (Baker 2007, 505, 433–434). For a printed matter to be labeled a "public nuisance," therefore, was an enormous infamy for the author and the publisher. The author was acquitted of the charges but his fame or notoriety was decisively put on a firm footing. What later writers of unimpeachable reputation such as David Hume or Adam Smith had to say by way of criticizing Mandeville has become a familiar chapter in the intellectual history of the period. Before adding our own small contribution to this venerable pile of scholarship, to which we will turn in due course, we shall first seek to make a better acquaintance with the author himself and to bring to light the distinctive moral or even theological framework within which he wrote and thought. While it cannot be refuted that Mandeville's ostensible purpose was to disrupt the moralistic pretensions of a commercializing society complaining about the immorality of its members, even as it welcomed the material advantages ensuing from that alleged ethical chaos, and to propose a less disingenuous means of legitimizing human desire, he yet spoke the language of morality, as the word "Vices" in the subtitle vocally testifies. We suggest, furthermore, that Mandeville was firmly convinced that the moral corruption inherent in human nature can never be cured. But first one has to start with the very name of the author himself.

"Mandeville" is the author of a family of works that joined the bustle and din of early eighteenth-century British print market. The author penned clearly more than *The Fable of the Bees*, though the work came to represent him exclusively. Discussions of Mandeville, past and present, generally tend to focus on *The Fable of the Bees*, but we need to remember that this representative work joins the company of other works known to have been written by him. Although some notable contributions to Mandeville studies in recent years, such as those by Markku Peltonen (2003, 265) and Robin Douglass (2020: 278–279), partially seek to correct this bias, the full corpus of Mandeville's writings are not always present even in these studies. The work itself is not always treated as a major landmark of the Enlightenment. *The Fable of the Bees* (henceforth abbreviated as *Fable*) has not enjoyed the honor of joining the acknowledged classics of intellectual history collected in the "Cambridge Texts in the

History of Political Thought" or the "Cambridge Texts in the History of Philosophy" series. F. B. Kaye's two-volume scholarly edition published in 1924 still remains the only complete standard version of the text. Phillip Harth's Penguin Classics edition of the *Fable* cares not to include Part II of the *Fable* presented in the form of philosophical dialogues. The editor mentions its existence only briefly in his introduction (Harth 1970, 12). Harth, on the other hand, applauds the *Fable* for being "an outstanding ornament of the greatest age of English satire," with which many may nod in agreement (Harth 1970, 12, 43). Is Mandeville a mere satirist, or does he deserve recognition as a serious thinker with a distinctive philosophical position? The answer by no means seems clear. Mandeville's worth, by those who take him seriously, is often measured by the relevance he had for other thinkers. Studies of Mandeville generally tend to allot a generous space to other thinkers in the larger European intellectual history preceding and following him. What matters is his influence on other established figures such as Francis Hutcheson or Smith. "Mandeville was an obsession with Hutcheson," remarks Kaye, in that Hutcheson "could hardly write a book without devoting much of it to attacking the *Fable*" (Kaye 1924, cxli). Donald Winch is interested in noting that Mandeville's "explanatory device of contrasting the private intentions or professed aims of individuals with their unintended social or public consequences" is adopted by the author of *The Wealth of Nations* (Winch 1985, 264–265). Other scholars are interested in who influenced Mandeville. E. J. Hundert, for instance, identifies Mandeville as a faithful follower of the seventeenth-century French moralists, such as Pierre Bayle, Pierre Nicole, and, to a less extent, Blaise Pascal. Equally important for Hundert is the fact that Mandeville's "thorough-going naturalistic anthropology" joins the movement to revive the Epicurean philosophy initiated by Pierre Gassendi (Hundert 1994, 31–35, 37, 45–47). While Mandeville's relationship to other thinkers tends to be almost a mandatory subject to all who write on him, his relationship to himself, or, in other words, the coherence of his thoughts as expressed both in the *Fable* and in other works composed by him, is not always elucidated with the same assiduity. All the while, the author himself remains something of an enigma. No reliable portrait exists to show us his countenance. Nor are we left with any extensive correspondence with other famous figures of the age. As Hundert aptly put it, in a sense, Mandeville "was less a person who wrote an infamous book, than an ideologically charged symbol constituted by the eighteenth century's intense and prolonged dispute about how to understand and evaluate the liberation of acquisitive instincts engendered in modern polities by the infusion of commercial relations into the centers of public life" (Hundert 1994, 2). One may add that this "symbol" left a distinctive trajectory marked by a series of apparently unconnected publications, including but not confined to the *Fable*.[1]

The *Fable* announces its thesis in the second part of the title, "private vices, publick benefits" with a fanfare loud enough to foreclose any careful scrutiny of the text. A mere glance at the title promptly convinces one of what the work aims at. Or one could just stop at the "Fable" itself. The narrative poem first published without prose remarks under the title of *The Grumbling Hive: or, Knaves Turn'd Honest* in 1705 can easily be taken as sufficient evidence of the author's licentious hedonism. Neil McKendrick, in offering the history of the "birth" of a "consumer society," for instance, praises Mandeville for having preached at the beginning of the eighteenth century that "man was a consuming animal with boundless appetites." This assessment is supported by a handful of lines taken from the poem only (McKendrick 1982, 16–18, 25). The plot of the "Grumbling Hive" seems plain and straightforward. While the bees were naughtily indulging their vices of "Lust" and "Vanity" in their rampant pursuit of "great Gains" through "Cheat" and "Deceit," a society propelled by "Luxury," "Pride," and "Envy" flourished (Mandeville 1924, 1: 18–20, 25). "Thus every Part was full of Vice, / Yet the whole Mass a Paradise." Things were prospering at such a splendid rate, when certain bees began to grumble about the pervasive fraud, crying out, "*Damn the Cheats.*" They even dared to complain to the gods, "*Had we but Honesty!*" Appalled by their "Impudence," Jove punished them by granting their wish (Mandeville 1924, 1: 24, 26–27). The beehive became honest, but soon the bees found themselves bereft of all the material benefits they had enjoyed thanks to their vices. The economy collapsed and the population dwindled. The remaining pitiful number of bees fled to a "hollow Tree." "The Moral" added to the verse narrative underscores its message with utmost clarity: "Fraud, Luxury and Pride must live, / While we the Benefits receive" (Mandeville 1924, 1: 35–36). If this is all there is to Mandeville's thoughts, there seems to be little left for the reader but to either reject his message upon moral grounds or accept it only on economic grounds. But

[1] The attribution of authorship to Mandeville and details about the editions of his works are based on the British Library catalogue, as well as on the English Short Title Catalogue (ESTC).

this deceptively simplistic blueprint of human behavior presented by *The Grumbling Hive* cloaks a more ambivalent and complex attitude toward McKendrick's modern "consumer society," particularly when we take into account Mandeville's other writings besides the *Fable*.

Why did Mandeville bother to write the *Fable* and other works? What we know about Mandeville's life rules out the possibility that his motive for trying his hand at writing was pecuniary gain, as it would have been for many other authors of the age. A Dutchman educated in medicine at Leiden University, an institution renowned internationally for its pioneering scientific research, Mandeville seems to have enjoyed a fairly lucrative practice as a London physician after moving from the Netherlands to England. He specialized in various psychological complaints typically afflicting the affluent citizens of the town, about which he published a steady-selling *Treatise of the Hypochondriack and Hysterick Passions* in 1711 (Kaye 1924, xxiii–xxvi; Cook 1974, 11–19). After settling in London sometime in the 1690s, he seemed to have swiftly and thoroughly mastered the language of the country he chose to live in. He married an English woman named Ruth Elizabeth Laurence in 1699 (Kaye 1924, xx). Four years later in 1703, he published his first works written in English, *Some Fables After the Easie and Familiar Manner of Monsieur de la Fontaine* and *The Pamphleteers: A Satyr*. Since the latter work is mentioned in the catalogue of titles advertised in the former, *The Pamphleteers* should be recognized as Mandeville's first published work in English. Quite fittingly, Mandeville praises in *The Pamphleteers* his fellow Dutchman William of Orange, extolling him as the special "Care of Providence." William "[s]ecur'd" Britain from the "Popish and Tyrannick Sway," thanks to which "we enjoy / Our dear Religion, Laws, and Liberty." With a new monarch Queen Anne on the British throne, the writer closes his poem by exhorting the nation's clergy to uphold the precedent set by Queen Anne's predecessor: "May they from Lust and Avarice be free; / Their Zeal and Doctrine Pure, and when they Teach, / As peaceful as the Gospel which they Preach" (Mandeville 1703a, 3, 9, 12).

Such public-spirited admonition about the dangers of "Lust and Avarice" seems at odds with what *The Grumbling Hive* preaches. But another voice is heard between the lines of *Some Fables*, whose literary genre clearly heads in the direction of the animal fable of *The Grumbling Hive* and whose tone at times is tuned to acerbic satire. For instance, Mandeville's version of "The Wasps and Bees" features "Justice Hornet" adjudicating a dispute between wasps and bees over "Some Honey Combs without a Tree" (Mandeville 1703b, 51). After six months the suit still drags on, but the bees have "heard of nothing but Vacations, / And Writs of barbarous Appellation." In the meantime, "The Honey every day grows worse, / And greedy Lawyers drain our Purse." The "Moral" of the tale targets the "greedy Lawyers":

> They lead us such a way about,
> Raise new disputes, make such a rout.
> Between the Plaintiff and Defendant;
> That, by the time they make an end on't,
> The Suit looks like an Oyster, where
> The Fish falls to the Lawyers share;
> And, if the Cause be manag'd well,
> Each of the Clients gets a Shell. (Mandeville 1703b, 55)

In *The Grumbling Hive*, the "Lawyers" of the beehive "kept off Hearings willfully / To finger the refreshing Fee" (Mandeville 1924, 1: 20). Thanks to their greed, the beehive as a whole prospered, for the fee refreshes other bees in its circulation. The moral stance about avarice appears to have shifted between the two "fables," but the terms of the argument, as well as the fictional mode, remain unchanged. *Some Fables*, then, rather than *The Pamphleteers*, although born in the same year, may be regarded as the first step Mandeville took in the path of becoming an "ideological symbol" of amoral selfishness.

Some Fables apparently met enough encouragement in the London print market to persuade its publisher, "Richard Wellington at the Dolphin and Crown at the West-End of St. Paul's Church-Yard," as the title page identified him, to issue an enlarged edition the next year in 1704, under a slightly different title, *Aesop Dress'd, or a Collection of Fables Writ in Familiar Verse*, moreover, with the author's name given below the title as "B. Mandeville, M.D." Justification of the revised title rested on ten new fables added to *Some Fables* of 1703, five preceding the fables of *Some Fables* and five following it. Among the former group one finds "The Hands, and Feet, and Belly," the "Moral" of which tale reminds the reader how "Plenty, Liberty, and Ease" are essential to the health of the "Body Politick." "The Dog and the Ass," belonging to the latter group of new fables, demonstrates how "None can live happily together, / Without assisting one another" (Mandeville 1704, 13, 92). Two years later, "B. Mandeville, M.D." apparently felt confident enough about his skill at composing English couplets to publish, anonymously, an animal fable conveying a highly abrasive message, *The Grumbling Hive: or, Knaves Turn'd Honest*. The broadsheet pamphlet printed on four pages without page numbers and divided into two columns told the story, summarized above, of bees who waxed prosperous as long as they stayed honest to their knavish nature, but became impoverished once they sought to aspire to honesty. Neither the name of the publisher nor the writer was given. "Printed in the Year, 1705" remains the only bibliographical information given at the bottom of the last page (Mandeville 1705). The poet who composed *The Grumbling Hive*, even as he turned to writing regular prose treatises, as we shall see below, never quite abandoned his penchant for composing satirical couplets. In 1712, his verses were collected under the title of *Wishes to a Godson, with Other Miscellany Poems*. The author's identity was half revealed by his initials on the title page, "By B. M." The pieces included in the duodecimo volume embraces vulgar sensuality with gusto. "May you never when y'are Drunk / Stumble on a rotten Punk" is one of the sincere "Wishes to a Godson." "On Celia's Bosom" informs the reader of what happens when one touches "th'inviting Skin" of Celia's breast: "I felt her Blood start up and fly, / And in her Veins boil Mountains high." "Outward Coldness is deceit" concludes the poem about this experiment (Mandeville 1712, 9, 17). What both *The Grumbling Hive* and *Wishes to a Godson* perform is an undressing of the external garment of respectability to prove that humans are in essence nothing but sensual creatures, whatever their pretensions may be.

One may feel tempted to jump straight from the taste for dismantling moral certainties evinced by Mandeville's satirical verses to the *Fables*, which after all developed into a series of prose "Remarks" on the satirical poem *The Grumbling Hive*. But Mandeville's solicitude for "public benefit," hinted by the last phrase of the title of the *Fable* ("Private Vices Public Benefit"), detains us at the level of philology, if not philosophy. Mandeville's very first publication in English was a political poem *The Pamphleteers*, lauding the champion of the Protestant cause William of Orange and entreating his successor to safeguard the true Protestant faith. In 1714, he engulfed his verse satire *The Grumbling Hive* with lengthy prose commentaries elaborating on the thesis stated in the title that "Private Vices" necessarily lead to "Public Benefits." Whatever may have been the author's true intention, the detailed "Contents" of the 1714 edition, coming right after the "Preface," underscored the author's interest in public welfare. "The Clergy of different Perswasions are beneficial to one another" asserts one entry in the table of contents, while another contends that "Luxury [is] not Destructive to the Wealth of a Nation" (Mandeville 1714a). Mediating between private desires and their impact on civil society was also the ostensive purport of another prose work born in the same year. Adopting a fictional format, it addressed the question of what women really gain from marriage. The full title of the work is worth quoting:

> The Mysteries of Virginity: or, A full Discovery of the Difference Between Young Maids and Old Ones. Set forth in several Diverting Dialogues of the Female Sex, on Love and Gallantry, Marriage and single Life, Dress and Behaviour, Batchellors and Husbands, Beauty and Courtship, Plays and Musick. With many other curious Subjects relating to Young Women not enter'd into the State of Matrimony.

Most of the dialogues depict the old-maid aunt doing her best to dissuade her young niece from forfeiting her virginity to men. The aunt feels sure that "every Woman that is Married" is no better than a "Slave to her Husband" (Mandeville 1714b, 127). But dialogues six and seven digress from the main path to pontificate on French military ambitions in Europe. *The Mysteries of Virginity* rested somewhat dormant until 1731, when it was reissued under a different title, *The Virgin Unmasked, or, Female Dialogues Betwixt an Elderly Maiden Lady and Her Niece, on Several Diverting Discourses on Love, Marriage, Memoirs, and Morals, &c. of the Times* (Mandeville 1731). Unlike in 1714, the author's identity in this edition was fully revealed on the title page as "Bernard Mandeville, Author of the *Fable of the Bees*." By contrast, it took less time for the *Fable* to be honored with a second edition. In 1723, the "Second Edition, Enlarged with many Additions" was printed along with two new essays, "An Essay on Charity and Charity-Schools" and "A Search into the Nature of Society." It was this edition, particularly the unsavory argument advanced in "An Essay on Charity and Charity-Schools," namely, that charity-schools can never achieve their purpose but only breed among the poor youth a "Habit of Sloth and Idleness and strong Aversion to Labour and Assiduity" (Mandeville 1924, 1: 274), which led him to become a pariah in the eyes of the establishment. The 1725 edition of the *Fable* included the author's "Vindication of the Book from the Aspersions contain'd in a Presentment of the Grand-Jury of Middlesex." The "Vindication" claims that the maligned work is in fact a "Book of severe and exalted Morality, that contains a strict Test of Virtue, an infallible Touchstone to distinguish the real from the counterfeited." Furthermore, far from being irreligious, his book pays tribute to the "unsearchable Providence" which "daily orders the Comforts of the Laborious, and even the Deliverances of the Oppressed, secretly to come forth not only from the Vices of the Luxurious, but likewise [from] the Crimes of the Flagitious and most Abandoned" (Mandeville 1725b, 466–467 [Mandeville 1924, 1: 404–405]). The author can be given some credit when he professes his serious concern for public welfare. The *Fable*, despite its fame or notoriety, forms a phalanx with his other treatises on social issues published in the 1720s. *A Modest Defence of Publick Stews: or, an Essay upon Whoring, as It Is Now Practis'd in These Kingdoms*, published in 1724 anonymously, offered a further variation on the theme of "Remark (H.)" of the *Fable* that "to preserve the Honour of our Wives and Daughters" against the incurable sexual drive of lusty males, "Markets of Love" should be allowed to serve their customers openly (Mandeville 1924, 1: 96–97). The defender of "Public Stews" in a similar vein reminds the reader of the futility of fighting the "Great Leviathan of Leachery [sic]" (Mandeville 1724, ii), for it is tantamount to denying the undeniable nature of human constitution. "[A]s long as it is that Nature of Man ... to have a Salt *Itch* in the Breeches, the *Brimstone* under the Petticoat will be a necessary Remedy to *lay* it," the author maintains (Mandeville 1724, preface). From this premise follows the conclusion that "publick Whoring is neither so criminal in itself, nor so detrimental to the *Society*, as private Whoring," if it is regulated by local governments and looked after by "two able Physicians, and four Surgeons at least" (Mandeville 1724, 2, 13). A work with a more somber tenor is *An Inquiry into the Causes of the Frequent Executions at Tyburn and a Proposal for Some Regulations Concerning Felons and Prisons*, published in 1725. The writer's diagnosis of the problem brims over with sound counsel. Crime against property should be capitally punished, but then, "it must be acknowledg'd, that where Men are without Shame and Education, and consequently not affected with the Ties either of Honour or Religion, Poverty itself is a strong Temptation to Thieving, when Opportunities offer." Public execution does little to achieve its purpose of striking "Terror," since the "small Concern, and seeming Indolence of the Condemn'd, harden the Profligates that behold them" (Mandeville 1725a, 36–37). Mandeville's prescription for severing the knot of this vicious circle is to transport the felons abroad—not to the milder climates of North America—and barter them with the Europeans kidnapped by the Muslim pirates on the "Coast of Barbary" and placed "under a miserable

Servitude." By doing so, one would "rid without Slaughter, or Probability of Return, the Country of the Vermin of Society, that, perpetually nibbling at our Property, destroy the Comforts of secure and undisturb'd Possession" (Mandeville 1725a, 48, 52). These and other remarks by Mandeville can be perhaps discounted as less than wholeheartedly genuine, but they certainly bid us see him as a versatile author with an interesting profile and not just "an ideologically charged symbol."

2.2 Vices and Virtue

Whatever Mandeville may have intended or believed, the work that predominantly represented him in the British publishing scene was *The Fable of the Bees* and the creed he stood for was one that was summed up by the title of his publication: the advocacy of "private vice" for the sake of "public benefits." The legal attempt to suppress the *Fable* by the Grand Jury of Middlesex in 1723 was followed by pamphlets committed to refuting the pernicious argument advanced by Mandeville. John Dennis, the author of *Vice and Luxury Publick Mischiefs: or, Remarks on a Book Intituled, The Fable of the Bees; or, Private Vices Public Benefits* (1724), was appalled by "so monstrous an Assertion," which is the "very Reverse of Truth," that "Vice and Luxury" can secure "publick Benefits." On the contrary, they are "publick Mischiefs" and "Political Infections and Civil Plagues" which "destroy the Liberties of a Free People." That "luxury" was singled out as the chief of vices typified the sentiments of many other moral and economic writers during the first half of the century, as we shall discuss in greater detail in Chap. 4, but for Dennis, the theological implications were even more astounding. That "Kingdoms and States have no way to flourish but by breaking the Commandments of God; by despising his Statutes and abhorring his Judgments" is a "manifest Contradiction to the Revelation both of the *Old* and *New Testament*," especially the latter. Christianity introduced a "more strict and severe Morality than was ever observed in the World before," but Mandeville alleges that Christ is an "Enemy to Civil Communities" by asserting that "Vices of the particular Members of them, are of so great Advantage to them" (Dennis 1724, 5, 11). So irreverent and impious an opponent can hardly be expected to respect the authority of revealed religion. Dennis, therefore, narrows his attack on Mandeville's representative vice of luxury, arguing how luxury "weakens Mens Bodies, stupefies their Minds, consumes their Substance, and wastes their Time, and keeps even those in a State of Indolence and

Inactivity, who are by Nature Diligent and Industrious." The political consequences are equally obvious. An "excessive National Luxury is sure to end at last in Slavery, which is always follow'd by the Diminution, if not the Ruin of Trade; for Men will not take Pains to accumulate Wealth, of the Possession of which, they are not secure" (Dennis 1724, 74–75). William Law's *Remarks upon a Late Book, Entituled, The Fable of the Bees, or Private Vices, Publick Benefits* (1726) took issue with the premise as well as the conclusion of Mandeville. He censured the author of the *Fable* for demolishing both "Man and Morality" by, first, considering "Man, *merely* as an *Animal*, having like other Animals, nothing to do but to follow his Appetites," and then ascertaining that this happy "*Animal*" was "cheated and flatter'd out of his natural State, by the Craft of Moralists." Moreover, by this dual operation, all virtues are exposed to be nothing more than the "*political offspring which Flattery begot upon Pride*," and thus "Man and Morality are here both destroy'd together," the former "declar'd to be only an *Animal*," and the latter an "Imposture" (Law 1726, 2–3). Where then does the intellectual "Faculty" reside in this animal driven by the immoral passions defended and even glorified by the author of the *Fable*? Mandeville himself demonstrates his thesis, since the author's deranged intellect is the handmaiden of his unseemly vices. Law ascribes the very act of writing and publishing such abhorrent work to the author's own exceeding "*Pride*" mixed with "Fear, Shame, Anger or Lust, or else to a beautiful Union and Concurrence of them all" (Law 1726, 4–5).

Defending the dignity of human morality or the economic health of the commonwealth from the onslaught made by the author of the *Fable*, which celebrated vice as both natural and beneficial, was a mission to be continued in the next decade. *Of Luxury, More Particularly with Respect to Apparel, Being the Substance of Two Discourses, on 1Tim.ii.9.* (London, 1736), unsigned but written by a clergyman, as was the case with William Law, sought to reconcile moral virtue and economic benefits which the *Fable* turned into mutual foes. Can "luxury," once again singled out as the chief among Mandeville's vices, ever be beneficial to commerce? "That in the making *rich brocaded Silks*, &c. many *Hands* are employed, and many *Families* handsomely maintained; so that this sort of *Luxury* promotes *Trade*, and consequently contributes to enrich the Nation; or, in a modern Phrase, *that private Vices are public Benefits*"—this argument is easily proven false, according to this author, by the "History of any Nation." On the contrary, history testifies that "*not Idleness, Luxury*, and *Lewdness*, which are the never-failing Attendants on this kind of Excess; but *Industry*,

Sobriety, and *Frugality*, do tend to *enrich*; and that *Religion, Justice*, and *Charity* (to all which this Vanity is an Enemy) are the *true Support* of a Nation." The contrast between "*Idleness*" and "*Industry*," which will be the topic of our next chapter, comes to fortify the author's censure of "*Luxury*." Yet it cannot be denied that "*Luxury*" does activate "*Industry*" at least in the production of "*rich brocaded Silks*, &c." Our author, therefore, would recommend placing moral restraints on economic production: "*Better* is it that these should be employed some other way: *better*, that some *few suffer, and that the whole Nation perish not*." Not all trades deserve equal encouragement, for unless one makes some distinction, one cannot answer the argument emanating from the thesis that "*private Vices are public Benefits*" which the "*Wanton* and *Intemperate* plead." These depraved creatures argue that unless one were "*Lewd*," the "*Bawd* must want *Bread*," and that unless one made a "*Sot* and a *Beast* of himself," the "*Vintners* would not be able *to pay their Rents*" (Anon. 1736, 49). Since these are extreme examples and since not all consumption depend on vice, the thesis loses its validity as a general proposition.

The first volume of William Warburton's *The Divine Legation of Moses Demonstrated*, also published in the same decade, contains a good deal of reflections on natural morality and on various non-theological issues. Warburton cannot let Mandeville remain either unrecognized or unrefuted. Indeed, the author of the *Fable* is given the distinction of being singled out as a writer who has succeeded in securing an "eternal Opprobrium" to "our Age and Country" by openly proclaiming "in a Book so intituled, that PRIVATE VICES were PUBLIC BENEFITS." This was an "unheard of Impiety, wickedly advanced, and impudently persisted in, against the universal Voice of Mankind." Warburton first follows in the footsteps of Dennis and Law in identifying the insidious intention of this impious author, which is to represent "*moral Virtue*" in general as the "Invention of Knaves," and "*Christian Virtue*," in particular, as the "Imposition of Fools." While this amounts to nothing less than an "Insult on common Sense," Mandeville cloaks it, as we have seen in the first section of this chapter, with a claim to serious moral pretentions, that his "Book is a System of most exalted Morals and Religion." This is an affront to "common Honesty." Far from building a "System" of morals and religion, Mandeville displays a fundamental weakness in his thinking, for his very definition of vice is unstable and ambiguous. What does he mean precisely by "vice"? Can it be an absolute category? The answer is in the negative for Warburton. One can classify some passion as vice "*only in a certain Measure, and to a certain Degree.*" The alleged utility of vice, similarly, arises not so much from its "essential Qualities" as from "some accidental Circumstance attending it." These latter may very well be "supplied by something that is not Vice, attended with the same Circumstance." What is meant by "public benefits," for instance, refers to the "Consumption of the Products of Nature and Art," which is the "Circumstance that makes States flourishing." If such "Circumstances" can consist of "Actions not naturally vicious," then a state can become "rich and powerful without the Assistance of Vice." Not all consumption but some species of consumption would be vicious, in other words. Mandeville labels consumption itself as "luxury" in a most ambiguous fashion, never content to confine the term to its proper sense as "*the Abuse of the Gifts of Providence.*" By doing so, he keeps "something like an Argument on foot, even when he has left all the rest of his Vices to shift for themselves" (Warburton 1738, 79–81). Warburton's discussion of luxury will be put aside to join that of other writers in Chap. 4, but we can note here that the clear distinction he wishes to make between consumption as a legitimate economic action and morally reprehensible "Abuse" shares the stance held by *Of Luxury, More Particularly with Respect to Apparel* published two years earlier.

Mandeville's thesis retained its fame or notoriety even in the later decades of the century. Hume and Warburton would not see eye to eye on religious issues, no doubt, but they stood on common ground in regard to the moral legitimacy of consumption, although the expressions used differ between them. Luxury or gratification deserves to be called vicious not for being sensual but for being exorbitant, namely when it "engrosses all a man's expence, and leaves no ability for such acts of duty and generosity as are required by his situation and fortune." It is what Warburton called the "*Abuse of the Gifts of Providence,*" and just as Warburton emphasized, it is not the only form that consumption or gratification invariably adopts. When you gratify your tastes for luxury while not neglecting your duties to your family, friends, and society, you give work to the "necessitous, and bestow satisfaction on hundreds." The "public benefit," therefore, arises not from "private vice" but from a mixture of virtue and vice, as it were. Moreover, not all vices have the same potential value for public economy. Compared with "*vicious* luxury," "indolence" can be far "more hurtful both to private persons and to the public." In fact, luxury even of a "vicious" kind can be preferable to utter sloth, which creates no public benefit whatsoever. In some cases, "two opposite vices" could have a chance of being "more advantageous than either of them alone." Some vices can either by itself or in combination yield some public benefit, but it does not follow from this that "vice in itself" is "advantageous." Hume, besides, cannot admit Mandeville's definition of "vice" as that which can be "beneficial" to society. If something caused the public to benefit from it, then it cannot possibly be called a vice (Hume 1987, 279–280 ["Of Refinement in the Arts"]). James Steuart never directly mentioned Mandeville in his work, but he also evinced his discomfort, akin to that of Hume, at the presence of "vice" in a discussion of economic issues. If there is any need to retain the terms "vice" and "virtue," in Steuart's view, they can at best convey only incidental meaning. "The vices of men," as far as he is concerned, "may no doubt prove the cause of their making a superfluous consumption, but the consumption they make can hardly ever be the cause of this vice." Or rather, an act of consumption in itself is no proof of any pre-existing vice. The "most virtuous man in France may have the most splendid table, the richest clothes, the most magnificent equipages, the greatest number of useless horses, the most pompous palace, and most extensive gardens," Steuart points out. Even the "most enormous luxury," even when considered a choice "directed to no other object than the consumption of the labour and ingenuity of man," can still be "compatible with virtue as well as with vice" (Steuart 1767, 142). Virtue and vice, in sum, are names of intrinsic human dispositions that are ill-suited to denote extrinsic actions of economic agents. By contrast, Mandeville, out of his peculiar moral and theological dispositions, relished the ambiguities and contradictions attending the thesis that "vice" was economically advantageous, precisely because it left little space for segregating rational or virtuous moderation of consumption from addiction or squander.

Hume's and Steuart's reluctance to admit "vice" into the causal nexus of economic actions was shared by other Scottish thinkers, such as Hutcheson, who taught Smith at the University of Glasgow and whom Smith praised in *The Theory of Moral Sentiments* as the thinker responsible, among all those who equated benevolence with virtue, for devising a system "beyond all comparison, the most acute, the most distinct, the most philosophical, and what is of the greatest consequence of all, the soberest and most judicious" (Smith 1976b, 301 [VII.ii.3.3]). As mentioned above, Kaye had alleged in his "Introduction" to the *Fable* that Mandeville was an "obsession with Hutcheson" and that "he could hardly write a book without devoting much of it to attacking the *Fable*" (Kaye 1924, cxli). Kaye's diagnosis of Hutcheson's "obsession" is not always borne out by the textual evidence of Hutcheson's works published during his lifetime. As Smith put it with a fair degree of justice, Hutcheson was more interested in constructing natural morality upon "benevolence" than on "attacking the *Fable*" itself. But that Mandeville indeed seemed to have posed a challenge to him formidable enough to trigger his intellectual labor can be reasonably inferred from his articles published in *The Dublin Weekly Journal* in the 1720s (McKee 1988, 128–132; Broussois 2015, 1097–1102) and which were collected in a posthumous edition published in Glasgow in 1750. Hutcheson would not deny the myriad "public benefits" of a commercial society which Britain was rapidly evolving into. The "conveniences and elegancies of life" produced by "mechanic arts" may not perhaps be "absolutely necessary," but they increase in their own way the "happiness of mankind." Likewise, "navigation and trade," at the core of commerce, "will support more men than domestic industry and barter," even though "it endangers many lives" of those who hazard the risks of navigation (Hutcheson 1750, 50, 52). What needs to be made clear, then, is what exactly is being referred to as "vice" by Mandeville which supposedly causes all these benefits. If "vice" is to be understood as the antithesis to "virtue," as those "affections or actions which tend to the public detriment," it cannot be compatible with the "improvement of arts, manufactures, or trade," all of which are public benefits. Mandeville credits in particular the vices of "intemperance, luxury, and pride" as the promoters of "industry," but these terms make sense only as relative and never as absolute denotations (Hutcheson 1750, 54–55). All three signify some degree of excess but that excess is "relative to a species or kind." If one can admit that it is possible that "in each constitution, station, or degree of wealth, a man of good sense may know how far he may go in eating and drinking, or any other expences, without impairing his health or fortune," he cannot possibly be said to be intemperate or given to luxury. What Mandeville intends to do is to confuse the meaning of these words, using the names of vices to designate virtues. The intended or inadvertent consequence will be that Mandeville's readers "will lose their aversion to moral evil in general, and imagine it well compensated by some of its advantages" (Hutcheson 1750, 57–59). When understood according to the "common meaning," those who deserve to be described as "luxurious, intemperate, or proud," even when they appear to spur commerce, are "not a whit the less odious, or free from inhumanity and barbarity, in the neglect of families, friends, the indigent, or their country," since they are absorbed solely by their "poor selfish pleasure." Whatever benefit that may arise from these creatures' indulgence in these pleasures is "no way owing to them, but to the industrious, who must supply all customers, and cannot examine whether their expences are proportioned to their fortunes or not" (Hutcheson 1750, 60). Moreover, in the long run, virtue induces more production than whatever vice may fortuitously occasion. The "temperate and frugal" would consume more wine than the intemperate drunker, since "all allow that they would probably live longer, and with better health and digestion." The frugal would have distributed parts of his fund to his family, friends, and those who borrow his money, who collectively would consume more than whatever can be credited to the "single luxury" of a prodigal (Hutcheson 1750, 61–63).

That Mandeville confounds the distinction between virtue and vice was the key point of Smith's criticism in his *Theory of Moral Sentiments.* Following in the footsteps of Hutcheson, Smith allots no less than nine paragraphs to refute the "wholly pernicious … system of Dr. Mandeville." Mandeville's argument is "pernicious" for it intends "to take away altogether the distinction between vice and virtue" (Smith 1976b, 308 [VII. ii.4.6]). Or better still, Mandeville puts virtue on such an inaccessibly high pedestal of a "complete self-denial" so that when measured by that extremely stern criterion, all human passions and actions fall down to the netherworld of vice:

> Wherever our reserve with regard to pleasure falls short of the most ascetic abstinence, he treats it as gross luxury and sensuality. Every thing, according to him, is luxury which exceeds what is absolutely necessary for the support of human nature, so that there is vice even in the use of a clean shirt, or of a convenient habitation. The indulgence of the inclination to sex, in the most lawful union, he considers as the same sensuality with the most hurtful gratification of that passion, and derides that temperance and that chastity which can be practised at so cheap a rate.

This is really an "ingenious sophistry of his reasoning," exploiting, as Warburton noticed, primarily the "ambiguity of language." Smith will rescue, like Warburton and Hume before him, virtue from this rigid extremism. Virtues of "temperance and chastity," for instance, far from dictating an "entire insensibility to the objects of the passions which they mean to govern," generally "aim at restraining the violence of those passions so far as not to hurt the individual, and neither disturb nor offend the society"

(Smith 1976b, 312 [VII.ii.4.11]). Smith also is in agreement with Warburton, though he makes no explicit mention of him, that vice for Mandeville cannot be an essential category but only a circumstantial attribute. Mandeville's "great fallacy" is to "represent every passion as wholly vicious, which is so in any degree and in any direction." By this "sophistry," Mandeville establishes his thesis that private vices lead to public benefits, for by Mandeville's definition, they may appear to do so. Indeed, "without the qualities upon which he thinks proper to bestow such opprobrious names," the "arts of refinement could never find encouragement, and must languish for want of employment" (Smith 1976b, 312–313 [VII.ii.4.12]). Smith, on his part, would choose the words that suit his purpose. For him what matters is the "arts of refinement" which cannot possibly be solely propelled by private vices such as "luxury." Mandeville's antagonist is in fact an anachronistic one, those "popular ascetic doctrines which had been current before his time, and which placed virtue in the entire extirpation and annihilation of all our passions." Having summoned this specter of puritanism, Mandeville could easily prove, first, that "this entire conquest never actually took place among men," and, second, that if that conquest of our natural passions were ever to succeed, it "would be pernicious to society, by putting an end to all industry and commerce, and in a manner to the whole business of human life" (Smith 1976b, 313 [VII.ii.4.12]). Upon this skewed premise, Mandeville urges that virtue is impossible, or that if it is possible, it is bound to be destructive, whereas vice is both possible and profitable. All this for Smith is clever but "destructive" (Smith 1976b, 313 [VII.ii.4.14]). What Mandeville assaults is the dignity of human nature and human passions, whose unavoidable shortcomings Smith acknowledges but will not condemn as incurable vices. Sound as Smith's refutation may be, however, Mandeville himself had some firm reason for adhering to the "ascetic doctrines" Smith rejects, as we shall see in what follows.

2.3 Human Nature and Passions

Mandeville wrote other works besides the much-maligned *Fable*, allegedly marred by "sophistry" and muddled with ambiguities in the eyes of his critics. As we have already seen, he composed pamphlets dealing with those subjects touching upon both private morals and public order, such as prostitution and burglary. Underlying and informing all these publications, as Smith detected, was his unflattering view of human nature as inherently corrupt and incorrigible. Apart from his *Fable*, the work that comes second in terms of popularity was *Free Thoughts on Religion, the Church, and National Happiness*, which was published in 1720 and went into three more editions during his lifetime (1723, 1729, and 1731). Mandeville here inveighs against not only the "Bigotry and Superstition of *Rome*" but the hypocrisies of all "Forms and Outward Devotion." He also exhorts Christians of all persuasions to "desist from Quarrelling, and taxing one another" in interminable disputes about inconclusive theological conundrums, such as predestination and free will (Mandeville 1720, 20, 24, 114). These statements of Mandeville do not make him a Voltaire right away. Religious controversy should be shunned not because rational philosophy shall wean the enlightened of such taste for irrational disputation but because true Christian faith requires genuine self-scrutiny. The first and the last duty of a good Christian is to live by the "Rules of Christianity," which is nothing else than to "conquer our Passions, and mortify our darling Lusts." This, however, is "what few of us earnestly set about." If that is the case, and if you cannot practice what you preach, you have no right to indulge in the "Hatreds and Animosities" toward other denominations, "especially such as are chiefly built on Prejudices" (Mandeville 1720, 8, 59). Years later in 1732, Mandeville wrote and published *An Enquiry into the Origin of Honour, and the Usefulness of Christianity in War*. Signing himself as "the Author of the *FABLE* of the *BEES*" on the title page, Mandeville dons in this treatise the solid protective armor of sound Protestantism. Christ's Gospel "teaches us many Things, which no Mortal could ever have known, unless they had been reveal'd to him; and several that must always remain incomprehensible to finite Capacities." The purity of the gospel, however, is corrupted by institutionalized religion, above all, by the Romish Church (Mandeville 1732, 30–31, 100). Religion was used as a pretext for endless wars among Christian powers and was mobilized to uphold the "most anti-christian Purposes of Tyrants and Usurpers." The final word, after a lengthy exposure of how Christianity has been manipulated as a political tool, is a confirmation of the author's faith in the "Doctrine of *Christ*, which can only be learn'd from the New Testament, where it will ever remain in its Purity and Lustre" (Mandeville 1732, 161, 208, 240). These two works containing the author's serious reflections on the tarnished history of Christendom should exempt Mandeville from being arraigned, in the language of the "Presentment" made by the Grand Jury of Middlesex, as one of the "*Zealots for Infidelity*" who make "Diabolical Attempts against Religion."

He was in his own way a zealot for genuine Christian faith, even as he laid bare the diabolical misdeeds of the religion. Nor did he simply recommend "Luxury, Avarice, Pride, and all kind of Vices, as being necessary to *Publick Welfare*," as the same document accused (Mandeville 1924, 1: 384–385) but proposed a more reasonable means of harmonizing incurable private vices with public welfare, if not in the *Fable* at least in his pamphlets on sex trade and thieves which we discussed in the first section of this chapter.

Mandeville's output as a writer, as we have seen so far, is respectable in both its breadth and depth. That money was no motivation for putting his energy and time into writing social treatises, as we have pointed out, should be obvious given his successful medical career. Something else must have compelled him to occasionally dip his pen to elaborate his thoughts. His writings testify to a robust mind working along a set of postulates that hinge upon his somber view of human corruption. Mandeville in the "Preface" to the *Fable* admits he has no illusions about the beneficial effect his work may have on the reader. "Mankind having for so many Ages remain'd still the same, notwithstanding the many instructive and elaborate Writings, by which their Amendment has been endeavour'd, I am not so vain as to hope for better Success from so inconsiderable a Trifle." If the "People, who continually find fault with others, by reading them, would be taught to look at home, and examining their own Consciences, be made asham'd of always railing at what they are more or less guilty of themselves," he would have achieved his modest end (Mandeville 1924, 1: 8–9). This chimes in well with his animadversion on hypocritical religiosity voiced in *Free Thoughts*, where it was accepted as a given fact that we humans cannot but heed the dictates of "our Passions" and "our darling Lusts." Mandeville can see no likelihood of humans becoming any better than what they naturally are. "Human Nature is always the same" (Mandeville 1924, 2: 153), even though "Genius, Wit, and Natural Parts" can be "sharpened by Application, and may be as much improv'd" (Mandeville 1924, 1: 275). What remains the same, more precisely, is the "love of Dominion and that usurping Temper all Mankind are born with" (Mandeville 1924, 1: 281). Indeed, the "Desire of Dominion is a never-failing Consequence of the Pride, that is common to all Men; and which the Brat of a Savage is as much born with, as the Son of an Emperour" (Mandeville 1924, 2: 204). Jack Malcolm regards Mandeville's "deterministic" perception of human nature as "mechanistic" (Malcolm 1987, 71). "Passions" and "Desire" in Mandeville's account, however, command subtle tools when they operate inside the human mind, which cannot simply be dismissed as "mechanistic." It would be fairer to Mandeville to place him among moral essentialists who subscribe to a "severe and exalted Morality," as he claimed in the "Vindication" of the *Fable*. The inherently vicious nature of humans, in his moral scheme, can hardly be altered by social conditions. Contrary to what Hume would argue a few decades later, variations of "physical" or "moral" causes—that is, climate, polity, or custom (Hume 1987, 198 ["Of National Characters"])—can make no significant change in human nature. Nor can humans hope to indulge in the "harmony of their hearts" which, for Smith, attends "that happy commerce" of "affections" felt "not only by the tender and the delicate, but by the vulgar of mankind" (Smith 1976b, 39 [I.ii.4.1]). On contrary, for Mandeville, from the least polite to the most refined, humans invariably show the same trait of the "usurping Temper" welling forth from their "Pride."

Yet this strict moralist, whose pessimism has been identified as bearing indelible marks of Calvinist (or Augustinian) influence by some commentators, has also been labeled a radical "utilitarian" by others (Adolph 1975, 161; Carrive 1980, 192; Malcolm 1987, 113–115; Hundert 1994, 34; Force 2003, 86). Jean Calvin declared in the *Institutes of the Christian Religion* that "man does not choose by reason and pursue with zeal what is truly good for himself according to the excellence of his immortal nature," but "like an animal … follows the inclination of his nature, without reason, without deliberation" (Calvin 1960, 286). Mandeville, though undoubtedly "steeped in the Calvinist tradition" of his native country the Netherlands, as Malcolm emphasizes (Malcolm 1987, 115), turns his argument away from Calvin's conclusion that salvation comes only from "God's free mercy" granted to those predestined for "eternal election" (Calvin 1960, 921). Instead, innate moral corruption of humans calls for an entirely earthly solution: "[N]ot the Good and Amiable, but the Bad and Hateful Qualities of Man, his Imperfections and the want of Excellencies which other Creatures are endued with," Mandeville believes, "are the first Causes that made Man sociable beyond other Animals the Moment after he lost Paradise" (Mandeville 1924, 1: 344). Fallen humanity, burdened with their "corrupt and defective Nature," had no choice but to submit themselves to the "vast Toil" required for their "Sustenance" (Mandeville 1924, 1: 286). Hence "the Necessities, the Vices and Imperfections of Man, together with the various Inclemencies of the Air and other Elements, contain in them the Seeds of all Arts, Industry and

Labour." But there is nothing glorious or heroic about human "Arts, Industry and Labour," for humans are whipped into diligence by their physical deficiency and moral depravity:

> Hunger, Thirst and Nakedness are the first Tyrants that force us to stir: afterwards, our Pride, Sloth, Sensuality and Fickleness are the great Patrons that promote all Arts and Sciences, Trades, Handicrafts and Callings; while the great Taskmasters, Necessity, Avarice, Envy, and Ambition, each in the Class that belongs to him, keep the Members of the Society to their labour, and make them all submit, most of them cheerfully, to the Drudgery of their Station; Kings and Princes not excepted. (Mandeville 1924, 1: 366)

Humans are vicious; therefore, they are prosperous. This paradoxical proposition jars against the elevated view of secular humanity which forms the core of mainstream Enlightenment thinking.

Mandeville's "Calvinist" stance on the human condition also makes it not entirely fair to classify him as an Epicurean hedonist, which is what Pierre Force and others have proposed (Goldsmith 1985, 159; Hundert 1994, 45; Force 2003, 79–80). The pleasure sought by the vast majority of mankind can hardly be distinguished from the pain of submitting to the "first Tyrants" of nature and the "great Taskmasters" of despotic human passions. Moreover, the pleasure of philosophical contemplation, to which a genuine Epicurean should aspire, can hardly subdue innate fear and anxiety. As he sees it, "there is no Difference between the original Nature of a Savage, and that of a civiliz'd Man." They are both "born with Fear; and neither of them, if they have their Senses about them, can live many Years, but an Invisible Power, will, at one Time or other, become the Object of that Fear; and this will happen to every Man, whether he be wild and alone, or in Society, and under the best Discipline." Civilization itself has its discontents, as we "know by Experience, that Empires, States, and Kingdoms, may excel in Arts and Sciences, Politeness, and all worldly Wisdom, and at the same time be Slaves to the grossest Idolatry, and submit to all the Inconveniencies of a false Religion" (Mandeville 1924, 2: 214–215). Humans are a bundle of contradictory passions, and civilized societies flourish not in spite of but by dint of these contradictions. "To me it is a great Pleasure," remarks Mandeville, "when I look on the Affairs of human Life, to behold into what various and often strangely opposite Forms the hope of Gain and thoughts of Lucre shape Men, according to the different Employments they are of, and Stations they are in"

(Mandeville 1924, 1: 349). One man's tragedy is a blessing to another. "The Fire of *London* was a great Calamity" for those who suffered from it. Yet it created splendid business opportunity for "Carpenters, Bricklayers, Smiths, and all, not only that are employed in Building but likewise those that made and dealt in the same Manufacturers and other Merchandizes that were Burnt." If these last were to "Vote against those who lost by the Fire; the Rejoicings would equal if not exceed the Complaints" (Mandeville 1924, 1: 359). The boisterous "Rejoicings" of those shaped by their "thoughts of Lucre" attest to the resilience of a society built on commerce. It also lays bare the spiritual dilemma of a commercial society, which Mandeville never minced words to embellish:

> We see daily Men rous'd from Sloth and Idleness, and spurr'd on to Emulation and useful Labour, by no better Principle than Envy; and it is generally taken for granted, that Covetousness and Pride are the chief Promoters of Trade and Industry: But can it on the other Hand be denied, that these Vices, against which the Gospel so justly cautions us, contain the Seeds of almost all the Iniquities and Disorders that are committed? (Mandeville 1720, 12)

The best one can do, if one cannot help relishing the benefits yielded by the "Vices, against which the Gospel so justly cautions us," would be to confess our "Errors and Follies," humbling one's pride, and "acknowledge" the wisdom of "Providence" (Mandeville 1724, preface) which granted us the bounty of material welfare despite our moral malady.

What runs through both Mandeville's representative work and his miscellaneous writings, to reiterate, is an unflattering anatomy of the pernicious passions at the heart of human society. Humans can never hope to rid themselves of their sundry vices, however much they may pretend to have done so. The hypocrisy of the self-rationalizing laymen, as well as the mystifying clerics, is what Mandeville feels it his duty to dismantle. Unlike some of his recent commentators (Peltonen 2003, 273–274; Douglass 2020, 293–294), whether polite sociability can support civil society was not a question that interested Mandeville. For him, what mattered were the elements in human passion sustaining and inciting commercial social networks. Economic expediency, however, cannot quite whitewash the inherent corruption of human nature. Mandeville, therefore, finds it incumbent to retain the terms of moral philosophy in describing the social mechanism of commerce. The cacophony breaking out in the *Fable* from the clash of a strict "Calvinist" premise of human depravity with the impersonal amorality of economics can be described in Mandeville's own words. Vigilant in his effort to "distinguish the real from the counterfeited" virtue, Mandeville marvels at the "unsearchable Providence" that welds material prosperity to moral pollution. This caustic view of human nature grated against the dominant sentiments of eighteenth-century British Protestantism, which opted to give greater credit to inborn human faculties than Mandeville or Calvin would allow. Among the representative voices of the age one may choose "Joseph Butler, L.L. D. Rector of Standhope, and Clerk of the Closet to Her Majesty," as introduced by the title page of his best-known work, *The Analogy of Religion, Natural and Revealed, to the Constitution and Course of Nature* (1736), which was universally extolled as Mandeville's *Fable* was universally censured.[2] The "Author of Nature," Butler assures us, has endowed human creatures with a generous amount of autonomy so that "all which we enjoy, and a great Part of what we suffer, *is put in our own Power*." That wise "Author" has enabled us to "provide ourselves with, and to make use of, that Sustenance, by which he has appointed our Lives shall be preserved." If we "have any one Kind or Degree of Enjoyment," we do so by "Means of our own Actions." By "Prudence and Care," then, "we may, for the most part, pass our Days in tolerable Ease and Quiet," while by "Rashness, ungoverned Passion, Willfulness, or even by Negligence," we "make Ourselves as miserable as ever we please" (Butler 1736, 47–48). Some indeed may contract "Habits of Vice and Folly of any kind, or have some particular Passions in Excess" and will "go out of their way, to gratify themselves in these Respects, at the Expence of their Wisdom and their Virtue." But those who preserve their "Prudence, or That reasonable Self-love" shun such folly (Butler 1736, 106). Even as they enjoy their worldly goods, they "manage their temporal Affairs with Prudence, and so pass their Days here on Earth in tolerable Ease and Satisfaction" (Butler 1736, 111). The path of "Prudence" is that of "Virtue," whereas that of "Vice" forfeits "Prudence." If someone decides to discard the terms "Virtue" and "Vice," Butler is willing to respect that choice, but he cannot deny that there is a "Faculty within us, which is the Judge of Actions, approves of prudent Actions, and disapproves imprudent ones" (Butler 1736, 461). Is "Virtue" really different in substance from our self-interest? That objection he

[2] Butler was made Bishop of Bristol in 1738, two years after the publication of this book. Butler was admired even by Hume the hard sceptic (Garrett 2012, 169–172, 185–186).

would concede, but with a caveat. If by a "*Sense of Interest* is meant a speculative Conviction or Belief," it can give us only "greater Uneasiness" rather than "Satisfaction." This would more or less correspond to Mandeville's "Virtue" placed on a pedestal beyond the reach of average humanity. But if by a "*Sense of Interest* is meant a practical Regard to what is upon the whole our Happiness," it not only is "coincident with the Principle of Virtue or moral Rectitude, but is a Part of the Idea itself" (Butler 1736, 134n). Virtue dwells in the realm of practical wisdom rather than that of abstract theory. Without mentioning Mandeville, Butler dealt him a severe blow by making "Virtue" rather than "Vice" beneficial in practice.

To oppose the "popular ascetic doctrines" of the past century, which, as Smith diagnosed, Mandeville was very much attached to, and "which placed virtue in the entire extirpation and annihilation of all our passions," the first thing to do was to release "virtue" from its forced antagonism to human "passions," as Butler's approach illustrates. The authority of an Anglican cleric handsomely remunerated by the Established Church for jealously safeguarding its "Forms and Outward Devotion" would not have awed Doctor Mandeville who claimed to know better about the "passions" constituting human nature. But there was no shortage of those who carried on the campaign of cleansing economic activities of the smear of "Vice." Thomas Cole, a junior cleric, writing about a generation later, begins his treatise by confirming Butler's proposition that the "Author of Nature" encourages and condones innocent pleasures. Humans were indeed created to seek and enjoy happiness in all they do. "Was there any thing criminal merely in the enjoyment of pleasure, our Creator would never have placed us under an inevitable necessity of incurring guilt this way," Cole muses. Seeking pleasure in itself is not sinning. Far from it, we find ourselves "absolutely constrained, as it were, to admit of a great variety of pleasures, in satisfying even the necessary demands of nature so that one can hardly conceive it possible for the most self-denying creature in the world, to defraud himself entirely of all those pleasurable recreations, which he is, at once, no less fully privileged, than completely fitted, to enjoy" (Cole 1761, 3–4). We shall have more to hear from this author in Chap. 4 as he takes part in the debate on luxury, but we need to trace his argument here to see how his premise leads to his refutation of the "author the Fable of the Bees" (Cole 1761, 15n). If humans were created by God that way, there can be nothing vicious about pursuing pleasures. The question as to whether certain private passions that are patently vicious can be beneficial to the public economy can easily be answered. On some occasions, private vices may be seen to promote the "circulation of wealth," but if the equation is to be established between the two, one has to prove that "there is no possibility of having the same thing effected by any other means," that "private virtues" can never be as "as serviceable to the publick in the very same way." Needless to say, they certainly can be as serviceable as vices. There is no reason "why a christian charity may not give as much, as any heathenish prodigality can throw away; why a liberal generosity may not as easily distribute its bounty through a circle of honest dependents, as the most profligate intemperance can scatter its rewards amongst the panders of iniquity." Moreover, when virtue rather than vice distributes wealth, it does so with "this very material difference; that the wealth of virtue will fall only into those hands, which need and deserve it most," whereas wealth derived from vice will become the "property of such as are the scandal and reproach, and must, in the end, prove the destruction of every nation, where they are supported and encouraged" (Cole 1761, 18–19).

Cole goes to the other extreme from Mandeville to argue that private virtue produces benefits for the public economy, which inherently cannot but stumble on the same objection that the average members of society are neither enslaved by exceptionally vicious passions nor capable of exercising extraordinary virtue. The terms "vice" and "virtue" could be empty names in themselves to the vast majority of self-interested individuals, modestly prudent and modestly hedonistic. Here we can return to Hume's thoughts about what "moral" signified, which we discussed in the previous chapter. "Vice and virtue," for Hume, "may be compar'd to sounds, colours, heat and cold," which are not "qualities in objects" but "perceptions in the mind." What is "more real, or concern us more" than these appellations are "our own sentiments of pleasure and uneasiness" (Hume 2000, 301–302). "An action, or sentiment, or character" is "virtuous or vicious" on account of its capacity to generate "pleasure or uneasiness of a particular kind." Vice or virtue, if so, cannot denote certain passions or actions that may be beneficial or detrimental to the public. They reside in the domain of subjective feeling. "To have the sense of virtue," Hume the metaphysician proclaimed, "is nothing but to *feel* a satisfaction of a particular kind from the contemplation of a character" (Hume 2000, 303). When writing on matters economic, however, Hume did not decline to use "vice" as a moral term in such a way as to give it greater substance than what he implied by the feelings of "pleasure or uneasiness" attending vice or pleasure. Avarice, for instance, features in some of Hume's essays, where they are used largely in the manner of Mandeville's positive re-evaluation. "Avarice" is a "spur of industry," and "industry," as we shall see in the next chapter, is a stalwart specimen of "virtue." Being a "passion" that is particularly "obstinate," "avarice" can assume the appearance of courage when it "works its way through so many real dangers and difficulties," disdaining to be "scared by an imaginary danger" (Hume 1987, 93 ["Of Civil Liberty"]). The dominion of "avarice" knows no boundary, for avarice, the "desire of gain," is a "universal passion, which operates at all times, in all places, and upon all persons" (Hume 1987, 113 ["Of the Rise and Progress of the Arts and Sciences"]). Other passions can be nobler, such as those devoted to public good, but they have the weakness of being "too disinterested and too difficult to support." A wise statesman, therefore, would know that it is "his best policy to comply with the common bent of mankind," and thus to "govern men by other passions, and animate them with a spirit of avarice and industry, art and luxury" (Hume 1987, 260, 262–263 ["Of Commerce"]). Avarice becomes a bedfellow of "industry," while "luxury," the chief vice for both Mandeville's *Fable* and its detractors, is coupled with "art." Surely this is tantamount to admitting that private vice ("avarice") yields public benefit? Hume would demure, no doubt, and say, once again, that whatever is conductive to public benefit cannot possibly be called "vice." In his early essay "Of Avarice" (1741), Hume had asserted that "we find no vice so irreclaimable as avarice" and that the "best excuse that can be made for avarice is, that it generally prevails in old men, or in men of cold tempers, where all the other affections are extinct" (Hume 1987, 571 ["Of Avarice"]). This essay was withdrawn from the editions of his collection after 1768, presumably because of the discord it creates with his later essays where "avarice" is no longer the favorite vice of classical and early-modern satirists. Avarice, for the mature Hume, is no longer a "vice," but whether it is labeled as such or not, the fundamental thrust of Mandeville's formula remains unchanged. Avarice, as one of the passions built into human nature, under whatever moral category they may be assigned, is the force that propels human society toward economic prosperity and political stability.

Smith's *Theory of Moral Sentiments*, not being ostensibly a work discussing economic life, may be expected to steer toward a more traditional conception of "avarice," which it indeed does, collating it often with "ambition." He asks, for instance, "[W]hat is the end of avarice and ambition, of the pursuit of wealth, of power, and preheminence?" To "supply the necessities of nature" cannot possibly be the answer, for the "wages of the meanest labourer can supply them." The real end is the "vanity, not the ease, or the pleasure" actually derived from wealth. The rich man "glories in his riches, because he feels that they naturally draw upon him the attention of the world, and that mankind are disposed to go along with him in all those agreeable emotions with which the advantages of his situation so readily inspire him" (Smith 1976b, 50–51 [I.iii.2.1]). This description fits "ambition" better than "avarice" or an inseparable concoction of the two. As far as they are dictated by a stronger passion or vice, that of "vanity," Smith's anatomy comes fairly close to what Mandeville says about the insidious capacity of "vanity" to stir people into diligence. "Vanity" and "Envy" are the "Ministers of Industry," and by satisfying "Lust and Vanity" of each other, his beehive thrives (Mandeville 1924, 1: 25, 18). Smith is less interested, however, about the economic benefits accruing from vanity puffed up by "avarice" and "ambition" than about their psychological effect on those possessed by them. "Avarice overrates the difference between poverty and riches," Smith observes. When stricken by "avarice," "ambition," or other such "extravagant passions," a person becomes "not only miserable in his actual situation, but is often disposed to disturb the peace of society, in order to arrive at that which he so foolishly admires." This is all sheer folly, for the "slightest observation" may remind him that "in all the ordinary situations of human life, a well-disposed mind may be equally calm, equally cheerful, and equally contented" without being thus disposed. While improving one's situation need not be discouraged, it never merits to be "pursued with that passionate ardour which drives us to violate the rules either of prudence or of justice" and in doing so to "corrupt the future tranquillity of our minds" (Smith 1976b, 149 [III.3.31]). The emphasis falls on the "rules" of conduct, which could keep one protected from the "passion for the objects themselves." "To be anxious, or to be laying a plot either to gain or to save a single shilling" would "degrade" even the "most vulgar tradesman" in the estimation of "his neighbours." "His situation may require the most severe oeconomy and the most exact assiduity," but his "parsimony to-day must not arise from a desire of the particular threepence which he will save by it, nor his attendance in his shop from a passion for the particular tenpence which he will acquire by it." This will make him a "miser" and not a "person of exact oeconomy and assiduity" who looks after his affairs in accordance with the "scheme of life which he has laid down to himself" (Smith 1976b, 173 [III.6.6]). A tradesman, indeed, should strive to "get what they call an extraordinary job, or some uncommon advantage" when such opportunity presents itself and when "he could acquire them without either meanness or injustice" (Smith 1976b, 173 [III.6.7]). The "meanness" or pettiness, then, is what Smith castigates, particularly when it is driven by a "passion" for the thing itself, the penny, shilling, and pound.

Smith offered a worthy counsel on how to preserve one's inner "tranquillity" in seeking to maximize one's material gain in *The Theory of Moral Sentiments*, where "exact oeconomy" was distinguished from miserliness, and "avarice and ambition" were placed under the injunction to observe the "rules either of prudence or of justice." *The Wealth of Nations*, written by the same author but from a broader perspective that cannot pay heed to individual moral distinctions, assumes that economic agents on average are not excessively imprudent or unjust in their motivations and actions. In fact, they are all almost by nature compelled to be prudent. Humans are capable of restraining their desire to spend money on "present enjoyment" thanks to the "principle which prompts" them to save, which is none other than the "desire of bettering our condition." This "desire" lies at the heart of human nature, as it "comes with us from the womb, and never leaves us till we go into the grave." In our journey from the womb to the grave, there is "scarce perhaps a single instant in which any man is so perfectly and completely satisfied with his situation, as to be without any wish of alteration or improvement, of any kind" (Smith 1976a, 341 [II.iii.28]). Thus, as all seek to better their situation, they are best left alone to pursue their interest "in the way that they judge most advantageous to themselves." To "prohibit" people from doing so amounts to nothing less than "a manifest violation of the most sacred rights of mankind" (Smith 1976a, 582 [IV.vii.b.44]). His conviction sounds most unassailable indeed:

> The natural effort of every individual to better his own condition, when suffered to exert itself with freedom and security, is so powerful a principle, that it is alone, and without any assistance, not only capable of carrying on the society to wealth and prosperity, but of surmounting a hundred impertinent obstructions with which the folly of human laws too often incumbers its operations; though the effect of these obstructions is always more or less either to encroach upon its freedom, or to diminish its security. (Smith 1976a, 540 [IV.v.b.43])

The foes to human happiness in *The Wealth of Nations* are no longer the "extravagant passions" for "objects themselves" but the unnatural government regulations, the "hundred impertinent obstructions" contrived by the "folly of human laws." Nor is Smith willing to denigrate the influence of "passions" on the contest among those exercising their natural "freedom" as investors. Left unhampered, the "private interests and passions of individuals naturally dispose them to turn their stock towards the employments which in ordinary cases are most advantageous to the society." Private agents are liable to make mistakes, but the "fall of profit" in some and the "rise of it" in others "dispose" them to "alter" their "faulty distribution." "Without any intervention of law," Smith emphatically maintains, "private interests and passions of men naturally lead them to divide and distribute the stock of every society, among all the different employments carried on in it, as nearly as possible in the proportion which is most agreeable to the interest of the whole society" (Smith 1976a, 630 [IV.vii.c.88]). Some "avarice and injustice" no doubt can be harmful, particularly if they provoke "princes and sovereign states" to pervert the economy, as proven by the dire consequences of their reducing the "real quantity of metal, which had been originally contained in their coins" (Smith 1976a, 43 [I.iv.10]). An "excess of avarice" can also be hurtful for private individuals, as is the case with a wholesale corn merchant who hoards his stock in view of imminent scarcity. But upon the whole, such "excess" is easily neutralized by considerations of interests. "Without intending the interest of the people," the merchant in question is "necessarily led, by a regard to his own interest, to treat them, even in years of scarcity, pretty much in the same manner as the prudent master of a vessel is sometimes obliged to treat his crew" (Smith 1976a, 525 [IV.v.b.3]). Smith's depiction of the individual's "freedom" sustaining the market economy does not vindicate Mandeville in his claim that private vices lead to public benefits, for surely there is nothing inherently vicious, to Smith, about the "private interests and passions" of individuals. In fact, it is the "most sacred rights of mankind" to "better" one's "condition" as best as one can. But the structural similarity cannot be denied. It is the "private interests and passions" of individuals that cause society to reach the "most advantageous" state. *The Wealth of Nations*, in these passages at least, inherits and fortifies the platform straddling the moral and the economic realms erected by Mandeville.[3]

To the extent that private passions play a pivotal role in moving the participants in economic drama toward particular directions, the domain of morals and that of economy overlap for Smith and Hume, except that they all accept human nature as it is, and do not offer to improve or reform it. Our last thinker in this chapter is Steuart, who deserves credit, if not as one who founded the discipline of political economy (as economics was first called), at least as one who baptized the field with that name in the title of his work, *An Inquiry into the Principles of Political Oeconomy*. Like Hume, Steuart deems it a wise policy to recognize the reality of human passions, and like Smith, he frowns at artificial interference by government in dealings based on the natural disposition of private individuals. "The best way to govern a society," Steuart thinks, is "for the statesman to form a system of administration, the most consistent possible with the interest of every individual, and never to flatter himself that his people will be brought to act in general, and in matters which purely regard the public, from any other principle than private interest" (Steuart 1767, 163). In fact, pretty much in line with Mandeville's fable, a commercial society should not be given too much to professing public disinterestedness. In a

[3] Here I modify my suggestion of moral neutrality or even aporia of *The Wealth of Nations* made in my previous book (Yoon 2018, 74–75, 79–81). Force insists on the essential difference between Smith and Mandeville as one between a "neo-Stoic conception" of society harmonizing with the "universe" and Mandeville's "Epicurean" view of commercial society founded on a paradox of self-love (Force 2003, 76–78). Hundert also sees Smith's Stoic position as the line that divides him from Mandeville, even as he applies Mandeville's "argument from unintended consequences" to his analysis of the "impersonal and anonymous relationships that characterized commercial society" (Hundert 1994, 222, 225). Istvan Hont and Michael Ignatieff consider Smith to be opposed to Mandeville in his belief that the "road to virtue and the road to fortune" could be "one and the same" at least in those for whom "market success" depended on a "reputation for probity and propriety" (Hont and Ignatieff 1983, 12). Winch, interestingly, finds a greater affinity between the two thinkers even at the level of style. Mandeville's "explanatory device of contrasting the private intentions or professed aims of individuals with their unintended social or public consequences" is employed by Smith in *The Wealth of Nations* "with a cynicism" that is "sometimes equal to that of Mandeville himself" (Winch 1985, 264–265). In Chap. 5 we shall see some demonstrations of Smith's "cynicism," but this is mostly reserved for the favorite target of his strictures, the monopolists. All these diverse interpretations, if we can emphasize again, concede to what we have called a "structural similarity" between the two writers in their pairing of the moral with the economic.

series of rhetorical questions, Steuart envisions a virtuous but disastrous society:

> Were a rich merchant to begin and sell his goods without profit, what would become of trade? Were another to defray the extraordinary expence of some workmen in a hard year, in order to enable them to carry on their industry, without raising their price, what would become of others, who had not the like advantages? Were a man of a large landed estate to distribute his corn rents at a low price in a year of scarcity, what would become of the poor farmers? Were people to feed all who would ask charity, what would become of industry? (Steuart 1767, 165)

Let private interests go their way, for otherwise "industry" will wither. More specifically, let competition be the rule of the game. When individual tradesmen come to the market to sell their ware to the "best advantage to himself," they enter into a "tacit competition." Each buyer, similarly, seeks to purchase the goods at a price most advantageous to himself. In this "double competition," that is, of among the sellers and among the purchasers, the "covetousness of the seller" wrestles with the "avarice of the buyer." Competition, activated by "avarice" or "covetousness," thus "works its effect on both sides" and "becomes double" (Steuart 1767, 196, 198). The economics of competition, in other words, takes good care of the moral vice of "covetousness." Of course, giving full rein to private interests does not rule out the need to direct human passions such as "avarice" to more productive outlets, particularly toward "industry," as Steuart emphasizes, and about which we shall have more to say in the next chapter. Denunciations of "luxury," whether they detain the consumers or not, can also be compatible with this acceptance of private interest as the driving force in the economy (as we shall see in Chap. 4), for one can argue that "luxury" erodes self-interest as an unnatural addiction that perverts natural passions. One way or another, that private passions and interests propel market economies should be accepted as an unimpeachable premise. Steuart, however, will make a distinction between the governed and those who govern them. "Public spirit," although "superfluous in the governed," should be "all-powerful in the statesman" (Steuart 1767, 164). When those who ought to have followed public spirit act in reality like private individuals, or abuse the public trust placed on them to pursue monopoly profits, they surely deserve to be denounced and literally impeached, as was the case with Warren Hastings the governor of Bengal (dealt with in Chap. 5). A turning point in the confluence of moral and economic debates was the Abolitionists' objection in the last decades of the century to the inordinate greed of those profiting from slave trade and slave labor (covered in Chap. 6). The "public spirit" demanding justice erupted from one part of the "governed" against the private interests of the other part of the "governed," as well as the supposed public interests of the government. But upon the whole, the sentiments and thoughts of the age are best represented by the following musings by Steuart's about the wisdom of the "Author" of nature:

> If it be said, that superfluity, intemperance, prodigality, and idleness, qualities diametrically opposite to the former [i.e. virtue], corrupt the human mind, and lead to violence and injustice; is it not very wisely calculated by the Author of all things, that a sober people, living under a good government, should by industry and moderation, necessarily acquire wealth, which is the best means of warding off the violence of those with whom they are bound in the great society of mankind? And is it not also most wisely ordained, that in proportion as a people contract vicious habits, which may lead to excess and injustice, the very consequence of their dissipation (poverty) should deprive them of the power of doing harm?

Always averse to extend his generalization too far, Steuart immediately adds to this passage a statement retracting this lofty meditation: "But such reflections seem rather to be too great a refinement on my subject, and exceed the bounds of political oeconomy" (Steuart 1767, 266–267). They may exceed the bounds of "political oeconomy" as Steuart defined it, but surely not the bounds of the vast array of moral discourses on matters economic, which we shall delineate further in subsequent chapters.

References

Adolph, Robert. 1975. Prose style in *the Fable of the bees*. In *Mandeville studies: New explorations in the art and thought of Dr. Bernard Mandeville (1670–1733)*, ed. Irwin Primer, 157–167. Hague: Martinus Nijhoff.

Anon. 1736. *Of luxury, more particularly with respect to apparel, Being the substance of two discourses, on 1 Tim. ii.9.* London: T. Green.

Baker, J. H. 2007. *An introduction to English legal history.* Oxford: Oxford University Press.

Broussois, Lisa. 2015. Francis Hutcheson on luxury and intemperance: The Mandeville threat. *History of European Ideas* 41:1093–1106. https://doi.org/10.1080/01916599.2015.1077150.

Butler, Joseph. 1736. *The analogy of religion, natural and revealed, to the constitution and course of nature*. London: J. and P. Knapton.

Calvin, Jean. 1960. *Institutes of the Christian religion*. Translated by Ford Lewis Battles, edited by John T. McNeill. Louisville: Westminster John Knox Press.

Carrive, Paulette. 1980. *Bernard Mandeville: Passions, vices, vertus*. Paris: Librairie Philosophique J. Vrin.

Cole, Thomas. 1761. *On luxury, infidelity, and enthusiasm*. London: J. Dodsley.

Cook, Richard I. 1974. *Bernard Mandeville*. Boston: Twayne Publishers.

Dennis, John. 1724. *Vice and luxury publick mischiefs: or, Remarks on a book intituled, The fable of the bees; or, Private vices public benefits*. London: W. Mears.

Douglass, Robin. 2020. Mandeville on the origins of virtue. *The British Journal for the History of Philosophy* 28:276–295. https://doi.org/10.1080/09608788.2019.1618790.

Force, Pierre. 2003. *Self-interest before Adam Smith: A genealogy of economic science*. Cambridge: Cambridge University Press.

Foucault, Michel. 1977. What is an author? In *Language, counter-memory, practice: Selected essays and interviews*, trans. Donald F. Bouchard and Sherry Simon, ed. Donald F. Bouchard, 113–138. Oxford: Basil Blackwell.

Garrett, Aaron. 2012. Reasoning about morals from Butler to Hume. In *Philosophy and religion in Enlightenment Britain: New case studies*, ed. Ruth Savage, 169–186. Oxford: Oxford University Press.

Goldsmith, M. M. 1985. *Private vices, public benefits: Bernard Mandeville's social and political thought*. Cambridge: Cambridge University Press.

Harth, Phillip. 1970. Introduction to *The fable of the bees*, by Bernard Mandeville, ed. Phillip Harth. London: Penguin.

Hont, Istvan, and Michael Ignatieff. 1983. Needs and justice in the *Wealth of nations*: An introductory essay. In *Wealth and virtue: The shaping of political economy in the Scottish Enlightenment*, ed. Istvan Hont and Michael Ignatieff, 1–44. Cambridge: Cambridge University Press.

Hume, David. 1987. *Essays, moral, political, and literary*. Edited by Eugene F. Miller. Indianapolis: Liberty Fund.

Hume, David. 2000. *A treatise of human nature*. Edited by David Fate Norton and Mary J. Norton. Oxford: Oxford University Press.

Hundert, E. J. 1994. *The Enlightenment's fable: Bernard Mandeville and the discovery of society*. Cambridge: Cambridge University Press.

Hutcheson, Francis. 1750. *Reflections upon laughter, and Remarks upon The fable of the bees*. Glasgow: Daniel Baxter.

Kaye, F. B. 1924. Introduction to *The fable of the bees, or, Private vices, publick benefits*, by Bernard Mandeville, ed. F. B. Kaye. Oxford: Clarendon.

Law, William. 1726. *Remarks upon a late book, entituled, The fable of the bees, or Private vices, publick benefits. In a letter to the author.* London: W. and J. Innys.

Malcolm, Jack. 1987. *The social and political thought of Bernard Mandeville.* New York: Garland Publishing.

Mandeville, Bernard. 1703a. *The pamphleteers: A satyr.* London.

Mandeville, Bernard. 1703b. *Some fables after the easie and familiar method of monsieur de la Fontaine.* London: Richard Wellington.

Mandeville, Bernard. 1704. *Aesop dress'd, or a collection of fables writ in familiar verse.* London: Richard Wellington.

Mandeville, Bernard. 1705. *The grumbling hive: or, Knaves turn'd honest.* London.

Mandeville, Bernard. 1712. *Wishes to a godson, with other miscellany poems.* London: J. Baker.

Mandeville, Bernard. 1714a. *The fable of the bees, or, Private vices, publick benefits.* London: J. Roberts.

Mandeville, Bernard. 1714b. *The mysteries of virginity: or, A full discovery of the difference between young maids and old ones.* London.

Mandeville, Bernard. 1720. *Free thoughts on religion, the church, and national happiness.* London.

Mandeville, Bernard. 1724. *A modest defence of publick stews: or, An essay upon whoring, as it is now practis'd in these kingdoms.* London.

Mandeville, Bernard. 1725a. *An enquiry into the causes of the frequent executions at Tyburn and a proposal for some regulations concerning felons and prisons.* London.

Mandeville, Bernard. 1725b. *The fable of the bees, or, Private vices, publick benefits. With an Essay on charity and charity-schools, and A search into the nature of society ... To which is added, A vindication of the book from the aspersions contain'd in a presentment of the grand-jury of Middlesex.* London.

Mandeville, Bernard. 1731. *The virgin unmasked, or, Female dialogues betwixt an elderly maiden lady and her niece, on several diverting discourses on love, marriage, memoirs, and morals, &c. of the times.* London.

Mandeville, Bernard. 1732. *An enquiry into the origin of honour, and the usefulness of Christianity in War.* London: J. Brotherton.

Mandeville, Bernard. 1924. *The fable of the bees, or, Private vices, publick benefits.* Edited by F. B. Kaye. Oxford: Clarendon.

McKee, Francis. 1988. Francis Hutcheson and Bernard Mandeville. *Eighteenth-Century Ireland / Iris an dá chultúr* 3:123–132.

McKendrick, Neil. 1982. Commercialization and the economy. In *The birth of a consumer society: The commercialization of eighteenth-century England*, ed. Neil McKendrick, John Brewer, and J. H. Plumb, 9–194. Bloomington: Indiana University Press.

Peltonen, Markku. 2003. *The duel in early modern England: Civility, politeness and honour.* Cambridge: Cambridge University Press.

Sekora, John. 1977. *Luxury: The concept in western thought, Eden to Smollett.* Baltimore: The Johns Hopkins University Press.

Smith, Adam. 1976a. *An inquiry into the nature and causes of the wealth of nations.* Edited by R. H. Campbell and A. S. Skinner. Oxford: Clarendon.

Smith, Adam. 1976b. *The theory of moral sentiments.* Edited by D. D. Raphael and A. L. Macfie. Oxford: Clarendon.

Steuart, James. 1767. *An inquiry into the principles of political economy.* Vol. 1. London: A. Millar and T. Cadell.

Warburton, William. 1738. *The divine legation of Moses demonstrated, on the principles of a religious Deist.* Vol. 1. London: Fletcher Gyles.

Winch, Donald. 1985. Adam Smith's "enduring particular result": A political and cosmopolitan perspective. In *Wealth and virtue: The shaping of political economy in the Scottish enlightenment*, ed. Istvan Hont and Michael Ignatieff, 253–269. Cambridge: Cambridge University Press.

Yoon, Hye-Joon. 2018. *The rhetoric of tenses in Adam Smith's "The wealth of nations"*. Leiden: Brill.

CHAPTER 3

Industry and Idleness

3.1 Industry

Of all the key concepts upon which various authors of the long eighteenth-century Britain built their moral discourse on economic issues, "industry" enjoys preeminence as an undisputedly positive signifier denoting all that is dynamic, durable, and dependable in the realm of individual and social actions. Donald Winch points out how the founder of economics Adam Smith always uses the term "industry" in "its eighteenth-century sense of a human quality or a general attribute of all economic activity" and never in the later sense of large-scale business organizations (Winch 1978, 142). One may add that in doing so Smith was joining a large family of others before him who upheld the supremacy of "industry" in both moral and economic vocabularies. Those who eulogized the virtues of "industry" hail from a broad range of intellectual position and stature. The Anglican divine Joseph Butler could shake hands with the agnostic sage David Hume over the unfailing rewards of "industry." The consensus easily transcended generational divide. Daniel Defoe writing in the 1720s and William Paley in the 1780s were both convinced that "industry" is that which never fails to bring forth prosperity. The juvenile stage of one's life is likened by Butler in *The Analogy of Religion, Natural and Revealed, to the Constitution and Course of Nature* (1736) to a state of "Probation," which "requires Diligence and Care" on the part of the youth as they practice "the voluntary Foregoing [of] many things which we desire, and

H.-J. Yoon, *Moral Discourses of the Economy in Eighteenth-Century Britain*, https://doi.org/10.1007/978-981-95-0958-4_3

setting ourselves to what we should have no Inclination to, but for the Necessity or Expedience of it." This experience acquired in the formative period of one's life inculcates "Labour and Industry, which the Station of so many absolutely requires." If "both were not accustomed to them in their Youth," people can hardly expect to be "capable of, and placed in, different Stations in the Society of Mankind" (Butler 1736, 129). This recommendation of the habits of "Diligence" as the indispensable foundation of "Labour and Industry" undersigned by Butler echoed in a somewhat latitudinarian mode the view held by the unnamed author of *A Discourse of the Necessity of Encouraging Mechanick Industry* (1690) that "industry" stood upon the solid foundation of revealed religion. "Industry" is the key to happiness bestowed on fallen humanity by God. The author believes that "whoever would under this *laps'd Oeconomy* and degenerated *Government* of the World, arrive to any tolerable degree of felicity in it, or to a participation of the Divine Favours and still bountiful Provisions of Soveraign Providence" must accept the fact that the "way to compass these naturally desired Accommodations, is, by *Labour* and *Industry*," that is, "by a diligent pursuit, and an industrious management in the World." As revealed religion tells us, the "*State* of *Original Purity* soon expir'd," but "pains and toil" were not just the "*Curse*" but the very cure prescribed by God to enable us to "taste of the Comforts and Emoluments of humane Life" (Anon. 1690, 2–3). In a similar vein, Samuel Bradford, bishop of Carlisle and Bernard Mandeville's contemporary, admonished in one of his sermons against the "eager desire of being hastily rich," and exhorted the audience to pursue the "way of Labour and Industry," for this it is none other than to tread the "paths of piety towards God, and justice and charity towards men" (Bradford 1720, 5). Temporality, as well as temper, matters in one's keeping to the path of pious industriousness, since "gradually gathering that measure of wealth which is best for us" is what one should aim at achieving. Whether rich or poor, our "*Labour* and diligence in our respective Callings" is the lot assigned by God to the humankind. Similar in argument, if not in ethos, to what Mandeville thought, Bradford asserts that due to "our degenerate Estate," our "*labour* is become more necessary" not only "to make us humble in a sense of our folly in disobeying our Maker," but to enable us, "by taking pains in some honest and useful employment," to "be preserv'd from evil courses, and become useful members of the great body of mankind." The "natural and appointed recompence of our *Labour* and diligence in our respective Callings" consists in the fact that "whilst we are in our several places promoting the benefit of the whole Body, we shall at the same time reap profit to our selves also, the *Labour* and industry of every other member redounding to our benefit, as much as ours does to theirs, and all together conspiring to the general good" (Bradford 1720, 12–13). The economic merit of "Industry" stands fortified with sanctions of theology and morality, and all this in a virtuous cycle of mutual advantage rather than the paradoxical traffic between private vice and public benefit heralded by Mandeville.

Even when shorn of the paraphernalia of religion, whether revealed or natural, the core message tended to remain essentially unaltered. Substituting "nature" for "God," and deleting all references to the Fall of our first parents from paradise, Hume, impersonating the voice of a typical "Stoic," remarks how for humans "[e]very thing is sold to skill and labour; and where nature furnishes the materials, they are still rude and unfinished, till industry, ever active and intelligent, refines them from their brute state, and fits them for human use and convenience." Hume's "nature," as much as the God Christians believe in, assigns "industry" as the human lot:

> If nature has been frugal in her gifts and endowments, there is the more need of art to supply her defects. If she has been generous and liberal, know that she still expects industry and application on our part, and revenges herself in proportion to our negligent ingratitude. The richest genius, like the most fertile soil, when uncultivated, shoots up into the rankest weeds; and instead of vines and olives for the pleasure and use of man, produces, to its slothful owner, the most abundant crop of poisons. (Hume 1987, 147–148 ["The Stoic"])

In Hume's broadened canvass of universal human condition, "industry" commands respect not just from those subjected to the "Necessity" of having to exercise "Mechanick Industry" but also from those bred for liberal professions, where even the "richest genius" can be of no avail without "industry and application." For all humans in their "different Stations in the Society of Mankind" (Butler 1736, 129) and in all "respective Vocations and Capacities" (Anon. 1690, 3), one thing needful is "industry." The unimpeachable status of "industry" as a supreme moral and economic virtue readily lent itself to be used for various justifications of private property and the pursuit to augment it. Lord Kames (Henry Home) stated his view with a blunt succinctness: "Without private property, there would be no industry; and without industry, men would remain savages for ever" (Kames 1774, 65). Preceding by some decades the leading voices of the Scottish Enlightenment, Hume and Kames, Defoe wrote in *A Plan of the English Commerce* (1728) that as "Industry of Mankind is set on Work" by commerce, "their Hopes and Views are rais'd, and their Ambition fir'd" (Defoe 1728, 142). In saying so, Defoe endorsed, whether consciously or not, Mandeville's dictum in his *Fable* that "Content" is the "Bane of Industry," as it makes people "admire their homely Store, / And neither seek nor covet more" (Mandeville 1924, 1: 34). Mandeville furthermore insisted on a stricter definition of "industry," so that it will not be confused with mere diligence. "Industry implies," for him, "a Thirst after Gain, and an Indefatigable Desire of meliorating our Condition" (Mandeville 1924, 1: 244). Defoe and Mandeville, writing anonymously, sought in the 1720s to convince their contemporaries to feel unashamed in pursuing their "Ambition" to appease their desire for "Gain." In a more circumspect tone, the author of *The Principles of Moral and Political Philosophy* (1785), William Paley, introduced on the title page as the "Archdeacon of Carlisle," affirmed the intimate relationship between property and industry, which inevitably made some richer than others. Paley found no reason to differ from Defoe, Mandeville, or Kames on the question of property. "Inequality of property," he concedes, is "an evil" morally considered, but it is one "which flows from those rules concerning the acquisition and disposal of property, by which men are incited to industry, and by which the object of their industry is rendered secure and valuable." The desire for private property puts to motion "industry," which in turn is rewarded by the unequal acquisition and possession of property protected by law. For Paley as much as for Kames, without private property there can be no "industry," and without "industry" activated by property there can be no civilization. "[E]ven the poorest and the worst provided, in countries where property and the consequences of property prevail," Paley observes, "are in a better situation, with respect to food, raiment, houses, and what are called the necessaries of life, than any are in places where most things remain in common" (Paley 2002, 65–66).

Here we need to pause briefly to address an obvious question about what is meant by the word "industry" in the different statements sampled above. The word in our current usage generally communicates a different meaning from one that was commonly understood by writers of the long eighteenth century. For us, the word refers either to business organizations (as in "heavy industry") or to sectors of business (as in "tourist industry"). By contrast, Samuel Johnson's *Dictionary of the English Language* (1755), first published at the mid-point of the century, gives an unequivocal and simple definition of "industry." The word signifies nothing else or more than "diligence; assiduity, habitual or actual laboriousness" (Johnson 1773, s.v. "Industry"). Mandeville proposed a clear distinction between "diligence" and "industry," but for the vast majority of English speakers apart from the Dutch immigrant Mandeville, "diligence" meant "industry" and vice versa. Besides, Mandeville's conception of "industry" as toiling to quench one's "Thirst after Gain," forward-looking as it may appear, dwells yet in the realm of individual's "habitual or actual laboriousness." Granting honor and respect to "industry," as an aspect or attribute of "laboriousness," by inference also honors "labour" as such, for "laboriousness" is in turn an attribute of "labour." As a moral virtue of "diligence," "industry" similarly presupposes an ongoing process of doing some important work. Quite fittingly, therefore, "labour" and "industry" often march together shoulder to shoulder in the quotations above to guide humanity to civilized living. To what extent "labour" contributes to "diligence" or "industry" and how far the achievements of "industry" can be credited to the account of the direct providers of "labour," however, tend to be less transparent than the nominal parity between "labour" and "industry."

John Locke can very well be considered to be a thinker best remembered by posterity, among other things, as one who championed the cause of "labour" and "industry." Like other writers we have already met, Locke also saw "labour and industry" as the driving force that moves social economy away from primitive savagery: "[W]hatever *Bread* is more worth than Acorns, *Wine* than Water, and *Cloth* or *Silk* than Leaves, Skins or Moss, that is wholly *owing to labour* and industry" (Locke 1988, 297). More important for him, however, was the legality of possessing and enjoying the worthy bread, wine, or cloth which "labour and industry" produced. His firm conviction was that natural "*Justice* gives every Man a Title to the product of his honest Industry" (Locke 1988, 170). Upon what grounds can one hold this view? It is founded on the proposition that "every Man has a *Property* in his own *Person*." Therefore, the "*Labour* of his Body, and the *Work* of his Hands … are properly his." My person (body) is mine; therefore, the product of my bodily labour is mine. This property, moreover, excludes the rights of all other individuals besides myself. "For this *Labour* being the unquestionable Property of the Labourer, no Man but he can have a right to what that is once joyned to, at least where there is enough, and as good left in common for others" (Locke 1988, 287–288). Compellingly solid as this argument may appear, it immediately gets embroiled in the question of agency, which is left unanswered:

> Thus the Grass my Horse has bit; the Turfs my Servant has cut; and the Ore I have digg'd in any place where I have a right to them in common with others; become my *Property*, without the assignation or consent of any body. The *labour* that was mine, removing them out of that common state they were in, hath *fixed* my *Property* in them. (Locke 1988, 289)

Through what means has "my Horse" come to be mine? Surely not exactly in the same manner as the "Ore I have digged" has "become my *Property*." A horse or any other animal needs to be bred and tamed "*per industriam hominis*," according to William Blackstone, before it can become a property, and even after that preparation, it remains a "qualified" property merely and never a "possession absolute" (Blackstone 1768a, 391), the last category being applicable only to "inanimate things" or "vegetable productions" (Blackstone 1768a, 389). Even more perplexing is the sudden introduction of "my Servant" who "has cut" the "Turfs" presumably according to my order, for it unfolds in a different domain from that simple picking of acorns and gathering of apples which Locke mentions earlier in the paragraph quoted above. If "every Man has a *Property* in his own *Person*," and if "my Servant" has every single right to belong to that category of "every Man," the "*Labour* of his Body, and the *Work* of his Hands," should be "properly his" rather than mine. If so, it would be "*Justice*" to give him, rather than me, the "Title" to the "product of his honest Industry," unless there is clear evidence of my "Industry" having joined that of "my Servant" when he sweated to cut turfs.

The moral and legal justification of appropriating the proceeds of hired "industry" would surface to the foreground later in the eighteenth century when those servants—slaves bought and brought from Africa—could under no pretensions be presented as voluntary agents fulfilling their part of the contract. But at least one voice among Locke's contemporaries sought to alert the readers to the importance of the "labourer" as well as of their "labour and industry." The Quaker reformer John Bellers proposed to set up a "Colledge of Industry of All Useful Trades and Husbandry" (as the title of his pamphlet described it) to provide work to the poor and to secure profit to investors. Such "Colledge" can extricate the poor from the vicious cycle of staying poor due to unemployment, of remaining "Miserable and Vagabonds" and that "for many Generations, from Father to Son." This can be rectified if one is enlightened about the plain truth about wealth creation, namely, that it is through labor that wealth is produced. Suppose one "had a hundred thousand Acres of Land, and as many Pounds in Money, and as many Cattle," he could get nothing out of it without laborers. When no workers are to be found, the rich landlord himself must do the work himself. "[W]ithout a Labourer, what would the Rich-Man be, but a Labourer?" Bellers asks. Therefore, the undeniable conclusion is drawn from this hypothetical case that "Labourers make Men rich." From this it further follows that the "more Labourers" there are, "there will be the more rich Men" (Bellers 1695, 2–3). In appealing to the self-interest of the "Rich-Man," Bellers would see to it that even as the rich benefit from the organized work in the "Colledge," the workers themselves "be made rich, by enjoying all things needful in Health or Sickness, Single or Married, Wife and Children" (Bellers 1695, 10–12). Bellers sounds original, but he also stands in the tradition of religious tracts and conduct books of the seventeenth century that inculcated habits of diligence and reverence for labor (Waddell 2012, 89–98). Those who did not share Bellers' version of Christian ethics or his solicitude for the welfare of the poor could still accept his contention that "industry," being more or less synonymous with "labour," ought to be recognized as the foundation of prosperity, both individual and social. "The greater number of people" means that "their greater industry" will be "serviceable in all cases; at home and abroad, in private, and in public," wrote Hume. A wise statesman would take care to keep "alive a spirit of industry in the nation," as it "encreases the stock of labour, in which consists all real power and riches" (Hume 1987, 283, 288 ["Of Money"]). In Hume's formula, "industry" is the dynamic power, which takes charge of maintaining and enlarging the "stock of labour." A nation functions or ought to do so like one vast "Colledge of Industry," where "industry" gives birth to "labour" and "labour" to "power and riches." This virtuous cycle, in Samuel Johnson's view, was more or less established in his own society. A supremely diligent man himself, Johnson wrote in *The Adventurer* no. 67 (June 26, 1753) that the "world is so adjusted that not only bread but riches may be obtained without great abilities, or arduous performances," since the "most unskilful hand and unenlightened mind have sufficient incitements to industry;" and since "he that is resolutely busy can scarcely be in want" (Johnson 1984, 262).[1] "Industry" means "diligence," according to Johnson's *Dictionary*; Johnson the essayist would add that it signifies a state of being "resolutely busy" in pursuit of livelihood and affluence.

For Johnson as well as for Bellers, "industry" presupposed a commercial framework or mechanism converting "diligence" of the "labourers" into "riches" at different levels, a better living even for the "most unskilful" poorer sorts and affluence for the "resolutely busy." The term which comprehensively denoted this process of wealth creation, both domestic and international, was "trade." "Trade is nothing else but an exchange of one mans labour for another" (Barbon 1685, 32), Nicholas Barbon asserted in *An Apology for the Builder* (1685), a pioneering but underrated work.[2] "Industry" being another name of "labour," it could be substituted for the latter in this formula defining the meaning of "trade." "Trade nourishes Industry, and Industry begets Trade," Defoe asserted (Defoe 1728, 160). In this species of syllogism, the premise necessitating the mutual interaction between "Trade" and "Industry" is the organic connection both categories have to innate human desires. "The main spur to Trade, or rather to Industry and Ingenuity," Dudley North declared in his *Discourses upon Trade* (1691), is the "exorbitant Appetites of Men, which they will take pains to gratifie, and so be disposed to work, when nothing else will incline them to it." Those captivated by the spirit of industry are not just the exceptionally diligent but all those who are stricken with insatiable appetites stemming from their several passions: "The Glutton works hard to purchase Delicacies, wherewith to gorge himself; the Gamester, for Money to venture at Play; the Miser, to hoard; and so others." As they are all compelled by their "Appetites" to become industrious, "other Men less exorbitant" also reap benefits from their labor. Even when the "exorbitant" person "doth not work, but profit by the Work of others," he yet contributes to the economy, for "those he sets on work have benefit by their being employed." A salutary contagion is thus spread throughout the entire fabric of society:

[1] This quotation illustrates how the terms "enlightened" and "unenlightened" were typically used in the period, as largely synonymous with "educated" or "cultivated." By contrast, the noun "Enlightenment" used as a historical and philosophical category was a translation of the German *Aufklärung* and imported by British intellectuals in the late nineteenth century. See Schmidt (2003: 421–443).

[2] Barbon is discussed extensively by Jonsson and Wennerlind (2023, 62–67), but their assessment of Barbon as a spokesman of the "Cornucopian zeitgeist" (76) is founded on their reading of *Discourse of Trade* only, as they care not to mention this earlier pamphlet.

> The meaner sort seeing their Fellows become rich, and great, are spurr'd up to imitate their Industry. A Tradesman sees his Neighbour keep a Coach, presently all his Endeavors is at work to do the like, and many times is beggered by it; however the extraordinary Application he made, to support his Vanity, was beneficial to the Publick, tho' not enough to answer his false Measures as to himself. (North 1691, 14–15)

Here one can obviously acknowledge North as a precursor of Mandeville in acknowledging the benefits private vices create for public economy, but more to the point is the way in which North's vision of emulation propelling even the "meaner sort" to "imitate" their superior's "Industry" complicates the traditional conception of "industry" as a term synonymous with the moral virtue of diligence. Inordinate, and therefore vicious, appetites compel those who are subjected to them to practice "Industry." Moreover, their immoderate desires ensure the perpetuity of diligence, since what they attain can never "answer" the "false Measures" of their immense cravings. In this new context, "industry" is loosened from its natural kinship with physical labor to appear increasingly as an artificial desire fermented by commerce. In a big town like London, remarks Barbon, "one is a Baker, the other a Brewer, a Shoo-maker, Taylor, &c." They exchange the products of their labor to "get not only a Livelihood" but to "grow rich." As they trade with one another, there "ariseth an emulation among them to out-live and out-vye one another in Arts." The rivalry "forceth them to be industrious, and by industry they grow rich" (Barbon 1685, 33). Bakers, brewers, and other tradesmen remain "industrious"—"resolutely busy," in Johnson's expression—due to their constant striving to "out-live and out-vye one another." Their "industry," coupled with their "emulation," will be interminable, since what it yields, as North diagnosed, will never be "enough to answer" the "false Measures" dictated by their immoderate "Appetites."

The tyranny of inordinate and unquenchable "appetites" could at times be looked upon as a hardship comparable to slavery, even as it promotes "trade" and guarantees "industry." Steuart, in discussing how humankind populates itself, finds the ancient and the modern eras at once different and similar in this regard. In the ancient times slavery contributed to the "peopling of the world," as slaves took on the burden of undertaking unpleasant but necessary tasks. In modern civilized societies, "trade and industry" play the same role assigned to the ancient slaves. In the darker ages men were "forced to labour because they were slaves to others," but in the enlightened age, "men are forced to labour now because they are slaves to their own wants" (Steuart 1767, 59). In general, however, this form of "slavery" was deemed by Steuart's contemporaries to be an indispensable component of the social mechanism activating and activated by "industry." Surely, no one would dare or care to question the moral authority of "diligence," into which "industry" could easily be translated back. Of course, when the "wants" exert their power to a dangerous degree on individuals and push them to deleterious excess, the word "luxury" could be summoned to admonish them, the debate about which we will examine in the next chapter. But the very word "trade" when attended by "industry" or "labour" would suffice to silence doubts about the moral implications of being led astray by "appetites" and "wants." Earlier in the century, Defoe enthroned "trade" as the initiator of all things useful and indispensable about earthly life: "Trade encourages Manufacture, prompts Invention, employs People, increases Labour, and pays Wages" (Defoe 1728, 135). In other words, "Trade nourishes Industry, and Industry begets Trade," to repeat Defoe's proposition quoted in the paragraph above. Later in the century, the unsigned author of *Luxury No Political Evil*, John Trusler, made a more nuanced plea on behalf of "wants" fostered by "trade":

> [T]he arts, whether useful or frivolous, create, without intermission, a variety of indulgences, many indeed of short duration, but which leave with us such a wish for their continuance, as to become afterwards a kind of want. Hence, a spirit of industry is kept up; hence, an abundance of every thing we wish; hence, a numerous population. This chain of effects brings wealth, brings strength, brings lasting felicity to an empire. (Trusler [1781?], 5)

What had at first been mere "indulgences" settle down to become a "want." At that stage, a steady "spirit of industry" is set afloat, which in turns allows "an empire" to enjoy a "lasting felicity." Between Defoe and Trusler stood Hume, who, now using the term "commerce" rather than "trade," established a direct causality between "commerce" and "industry":

> Commerce encreases industry, by conveying it readily from one member of the state to another, and allowing none of it to perish or become useless. It encreases frugality, by giving occupation to men, and employing them in the arts of gain, which soon engage their affection, and remove all relish for pleasure and expence. It is an infallible consequence of all industrious

professions, to beget frugality, and make the love of gain prevail over the love of pleasure.

Augmentation of "industry" in itself would be an unalloyed benefit derived from "commerce," but from the conjugal link formed between "commerce" and "industry" is born a passion or want, which is no mere "appetite" but the stalwart moral virtue of "frugality." This "frugality," however, is moved by a compulsive force, that of "want." It is a "frugality" sustained by the "love of gain" that resides in the soul of all who are engaged in diverse "industrious professions." What are these "professions"? Surely not the traditional liberal professions of law and medicine, for "lawyers and physicians beget no industry." The new heroes of modern society are the "merchants," who "beget industry by serving as canals to convey it through every corner of the state." These "merchants" exemplify "frugality" fueled by their "love of gain," since "by their frugality, they acquire great power over that industry, and collect a large property in the labour and commodities, which they are the chief instruments in producing" (Hume 1987, 301 ["Of Interests"]). "Industry begets trade," according to Defoe. For Hume, it is "trade" ("commerce") which begets "industry." As an offspring or servant of "merchants," "industry" submits itself to their "great power" and "arts" of maximizing "gain." At this juncture, the moral vestige of "industry" as diligence is quietly discarded. Even though "frugality," an expression noted by Christopher Berry (2015, 140–141), attends "industry" surrounding it with a halo of moral prestige, the typical mission of "industry" in Hume's understanding is primarily that of encouraging the "merchants" to amass a "large property."

The close liaison established between "commerce" and "industry" in Hume's essays is echoed by other authors, such as Steuart and Smith, who attempted a more systematic investigation of economic issues. Steuart is willing to allow some intangible "spirit of industry" to play its role in a nation's economic welfare, but the said spirit should matter only to the extent that it incarnates itself as the force that "prompt[s] the industrious to improve" their resources, that is, to become even more industrious. Or, at the other extreme, "industry" refers not so much to a "spirit" as to man-made devices of mechanical industriousness. Anticipating what later apologists of what came to be called the "Industrial Revolution," such as Andrew Ure in the next century, would say about the benefits of mechanization,[3] Steuart suggests that when a "machine" is "introduced into a manufacture," it never fails to "purge off hands which then become superfluous in that branch." This is no disaster for the purged "hands," for they can then "quickly be employed in another" branch. Therefore, machines serve as a "method of augmenting (virtually) the number of the industrious" (Steuart 1767, 118, 122–123). Smith, on his part, frequently summons the term "industry" to fortify his propositions, as has been pointed out by commentators (see, for instance, Jonsson and Wennerlind 2023, 92–93). The value of productive labor, a highly important category for Smith, should never be measured as mere quantities of time expended, for "there may be more labour … in an hour's application to a trade which it cost ten years labour to learn, than in a month's industry at an ordinary and obvious employment" (Smith 1976, 48 [I.v.4]). A crucial transformation of the word's significance is enacted in this formulation featuring "industry." The term no longer denotes a moral quality but has become an economic quantity calculated by discrete units, such as a "month's industry." Without the division of labor, which is the secret to increasing productivity for Smith, the famous but anonymous pin-maker in his opening chapters of Book 1 of *The Wealth of Nations* can "scarce, perhaps, with his utmost industry, make one pin in a day" (Smith 1976, 14 [I.i.3]). Our diligent pin-maker's "utmost industry" can or should be estimated only in terms of the quantity he produces, a pitiful "one pin in a day," rather than of his moral, spiritual, and emotional commitment to his vocation. Josiah Tucker, Dean of Gloucester, is often described by historians as a "leading spokesman for free trade" (Winch 1996, 139). His economic thoughts, however, were more comprehensive than that. Tucker's usage of the term "industry" very much signals the direction in which it will move in later decades and centuries, namely as a word signifying vigorous productivity. An increase in the total sum of "Gold and Silver" in itself cannot be a blessing for a nation, Tucker argues, but it is so only when it is "acquired by general Industry," for it will in turn "promote still greater Industry." On the other hand, an "Augmentation of Money" without a "preceding Increase of Industry" is "a national Curse—not a Blessing." The tropes of religion, "Blessing" and "Curse," adopted by Dean Tucker speaks not so

[3] Andrew Ure marveled at the workings of a "cotton mill" driven by power-loom, where the "perfection of automatic industry is to be seen." Of supreme importance for Ure is the quantity of output, the far greater "mass of productive industry a male adult is equivalent to, in power-driven manufactures, than in agriculture" (Ure 1835, 2, 5).

much of a moral or spiritual state of a commonwealth as of a material contrast, one between a "natural and healthy Growth" of a nation's economy and a "Tumour of Wealth." The key to health or diseases, to beatitude or damnation, is held by "industry" (Tucker 1774, 35–36). With Hume, Steuart, Tucker, and Smith, then, "industry" gradually parts company with "diligence," its old companion in moral semantics. "Industry" leaves "diligence" to pine in the unmeasurable, unproductive, uncommercial limbo of subjective dispositions, as it joins the gallant gentlemen engaged in the serious business of aiding and sustaining the accumulation of "Gold and Silver." Moreover, "industry," thus transformed into a countable entity, invites "Gold and Silver" to ratify its value, as when Smith moves on in Book 2 of *The Wealth of Nations* to "compute" the "quantity of industry" which "the circulating capital of any society can employ" (Smith 1976, 295 [II.ii.37]).

3.2 Idleness

Leaving "industry" to embark on its journey departing from moral qualities toward economic quantities, let us return to Hume's scheme according to which the "arts of gain" devised by "commerce" cultivate "frugality" on the part of the providers of "labour and commodities." "Industry" is begotten in the process, for the "love of gain" ordains the "industrious" agents to accept a life of diligence as their lot. What happens at the other end of the transaction, however, may not always be as praiseworthy. For it is more than likely that in that region where a "variety of indulgences," in Trusler's expression, are striving to transform themselves into "a kind of want," the "love of pleasure" could very well hold sway over human passions. The "love of pleasure" is often targeted and castigated as "luxury," but a more elusive or diffuse sort of opponent must also be subdued to clear the path for profitable "industry." The name of that adversary of "industry" is "idleness." The dichotomy of the two was engraved into graphic lessons by William Hogarth's pictorial narrative *Industry and Idleness* (1747), which depicted some twelve stages in the lives of two apprentices placed under the same master. The first plate contains all the seeds of later development. The "Industrious Apprentice" Francis Goodchild is busy working his shuttle, blithe and bright, while the idle apprentice Tom Idle fools away his time with eyes closed, frowning and dozing. The "Idle Apprentice" has no respect for religion, either, and soon would commit a series of crimes. Finally, caught red-handed as a murderer, he is put at the mercy of his former companion, who after a series of spectacular and well-deserved promotions—marrying his master's daughter, growing rich, being appointed Sheriff of London—is now an Alderman-magistrate. Distraught as the former "industrious" apprentice is, he can do little to save Tom Idle from being executed at Tyburn. The final plate celebrates Goodchild's election as the Lord Mayor of London (Hogarth 1747, plates 60 to 71). In the real world, of course, the contrast between "industry" and "idleness," as well as the respective trajectories of one and the other, could not be as spectacular as in Hogarth's popular prints. The ostensible morals of the visual narrative, as critics have pointed out, also contained ambiguities, with Hogarth's own autobiographical details built into it (Shesgreen 1976, 594–596; Cowley 2019/2020, 56). To the artist's contemporaries, however, the messages of the pictures appeared fairly transparent. Matching "Industry" with "Idleness" was considered by Hogarth to be a title that would meet with willing purchasers, as it indeed did (Barry 1997, 238). The opposition between the two was universally accepted as relevant not only by those who bought Hogarth's prints but by various authors discussing social and economic matters in pamphlets and books. The attraction of the dichotomy for those witnessing the changes Britain went through in the eighteenth century consisted in its conversion of economic disparity into moral distinction. The contrastive pairing of "industry" and "idleness" often provided a ready and indisputable answer as to why some ended up rich and others poor, all the way down to the early decades of the next century (Waterman 1991, 79).

One may begin with a work published in the same year as Hogarth's *Industry and Idleness* and which also targeted those concerned about the training and education of apprentices. The title given in full announces the book's content and intention:

> The London Tradesman. Being a Compendious View of All the Trades, Professions, Arts, both Liberal and Mechanic, now practised in the Cities of London and Westminster. Calculated for the Information of Parents, and Instruction of Youth in their Choice of Business.

The author, identified as "R. Campbell, *Esq.*" on the title page, in addition to fulfilling the promise made by the title, does not forget to provide moral counsel on how to succeed in any job or profession. The key to success or failure is held by one's conduct during apprenticeship. A good apprentice, who naturally wishes to "obtain his Master's good-Will," must be "diligent in his Business, and consider that it is a Crime against Moral Honesty to trifle away his Time, when he should be employed in his Master's Work." Diligence, another name of "industry," stands at the head of this practical maxim fortified with moral and spiritual authority:

> [H]e ought to be diligent, and apply closer in his Absence than in his Presence, and make Conscience of the Discharge of his Duty. By this Conduct he not only acquires his Trade sooner, and promotes his Master's Interest, but from it he may expect that Protection and Assistance of Divine Providence in his future Life; for this Reason also he must be faithful in every thing that is entrusted to his Care or Management. (Campbell 1747, 313)

Almost every stage of this promised sequence of blessings can be demonstrated by Hogarth's "Industrious" apprentice, who never failed to heed the calls of "Conscience" to enhance "his Master's Interest," for which good work the firm "Protection and Assistance of Divine Providence" accompanied him in his future career. To follow in the footsteps of such "diligent" and "faithful" apprentice, a "Lad grown to some Years must carefully avoid idle Company and Ale-Houses," since the "Time he spends there must be stolen from his Master, or encroach upon those Hours necessary for Rest." The company you keep now determines what you would become later. Above all, "Idle, profligate Fellows ought to be shunned," for their "Vices, by being frequent, become familiar to us, and by Degrees steal insensibly upon our Minds and convert us into one of themselves" (Campbell 1747, 314–316). One thing that Hogarth's Francis Goodchild, the upright apprentice, never does is to befriend Tom Idle either at their master's workplace or outside it. Having successfully kept the "Idle, profligate" Tom at bay, he could march on steadfastly toward his future glory.

Idleness, however, was a formidable opponent never so easily vanquished. *A Discourse of the Necessity of Encouraging Mechanick Industry*, cited above, detected idleness lurking at the very core of the English attitude toward trades and professions, particularly among those at the higher region of the social hierarchy. In Germany, even those families belonging to the "great Nobility" train their youth in some "*Manual Art*," so that when they are "reduced to Extremity," they may "earn" their "Bread rather than live upon the Charity and Benevolence of others" (Anon. 1690, 11). This being their practice, in "whole Provinces" of Germany, "there is not a Man that eats the Bread of *Idleness*, or of other Men's *Labour* and *Industry*." The English, however, would let "Idleness" be "fed," and "Luxury indulg'd, and Pride maintain'd, and Gentility supported" by looking down upon manual trade or "Mechanick Industry," giving their children a genteel education that would do little to improve their lot, rather than putting them to "some Trade or Employment" (Anon. 1690, 14, 22). This pamphlet was published in 1690, and by 1747, the year of Hogarth's *Industry and Idleness* and Campbell's *London Tradesman*, things presumably had changed. But apparently the same prejudice against useful but onerous "industry" misguided many parents and guardians to choose the wrong sort of profession for their youth. *The London Tradesman* found this to be not only wasteful but dangerous to the society:

> The Strength of the Commonwealth does not so much consist in the Number of its Subjects, as in the Number of People properly employed. Millions of Souls bred up in Idleness, or which is much the same Thing, Millions employed in Occupations for which Nature has not fitted them with proper Talents, instead of being an Advantage or Strength to the Society under which they live, are truly burthensome, generally become Beggars, and live upon the Labour and Industry of the more judiciously employed Part of the Inhabitants. (Campbell 1747, 14)

The "Occupations" indicted for fostering "Idleness" are mostly liberal professions in the law and the Church, where few can gain remuneration large enough to justify the expense that went into their education. "Had the Attorney been brought up a Country Farmer, or a grave plodding Shopkeeper, he might have made a Figure upon *Ludgate-Hill*, or *Cheap-Side*," Campbell laments (Campbell 1747, 9). The contrast between "Industry" and "Idleness" is thus extended further to a sectoral discrimination between those trades that can claim to be industrious and those that are not, particularly those in the cultural or entertainment sector whose "arts of gain," to put the case using Hume's expressions, aim to exploit people's "love of pleasure."

In the meantime, the roots of "Idleness" could also be traced further down to the very roots of the free-market economy sustaining British society. Thomas Sherlock, speaking as the Lord Bishop of London, was astounded by the manner in which the plague of "infidelity" nourished the vice of "Idleness" in his diocese. London being the center of the nation's publishing business, the "Press" there "for many Years past" has "swarm'd with Books, some to dispute, some to ridicule the great Truths of Religion, both natural and revealed," all in one way or another attempting to "tarnish the Gospel of Christ" and "all our Hopes in Christ" as "Delusions and Impositions." The "Earnestness with which these Books are sought after" is testimony to the fact that the book trade of London "beats all the World" in its ungodly fervor and has "become even the Mart for Infidelity" (Sherlock 1750, 7–8). "Infidelity" cultivated by the educated is "allied" with "Lewdness and Debauchery" of the uneducated lower classes, which composite vice "keeps them idle, poor and miserable, and renders them incapable of getting an honest Livelihood for themselves and Families" (Sherlock 1750, 9). Their very woes and worries, in turn, are tapped on by the sly "arts of gains" (Hume's expression) of the "Vintners, Coopers, Wine-Merchants, Distillers and Tobacconists," observes the author of *Luxury, Pride and Vanity, the Bane of the British Nation*. Owing to these "immediate Ministers to a Million of Vices and bad Habits," the "Œconomy and Industry of the mechanical Part of Mankind, hath of late Years been greatly impair'd" (Jones [1736?], 5). Smoking their pipes and sipping their liquors, the "mechanical" classes, Sherlock remarks, are given to haunting "Lewd Houses" and to perusing licentious publications:

> Have not all the Abominations of the Public Stews been opened to View by lewd Pictures exposed to Sale at Noon-day? Have not Histories or Romances of the vilest Prostitutes been published, intended merely to display the most execrable Scenes of Lewdness; Lewdness represented without Disguise, and nothing omitted that might inflame the corrupt Passions of the Youth of the Nation! (Sherlock 1750, 11)

Our good Lord Bishop declaims with a prophet's ire, but his solicitude extends to the practical as well as to the spiritual consequences of this dominion of "Infidelity and Immorality," to which Defoe the anonymous author of the "Histories or Romances of the vilest Prostitutes," *Moll Flanders* and *Roxana*, have made lasting contributions. In Hogarth's *Industry and Idleness*, the opening plate shows a page from "Moll Flanders" posted above Tom Idle's head (Hogarth 1747, plate 60). The Idle Apprentice at least is not all that slothful when it comes to reading this first-person narrative of a female thief with multiple male partners. The connection between immorality and idleness warned by Hogarth is what Sherlock is keenly aware of. The joint venture of "Infidelity and Immorality" exercises their ingenuity to inject a general "Spirit of Idleness and Indolence" (Sherlock 1750, 13) into the body politic as a whole:

> Is it to be wondered at, after so much Pains taken to corrupt the Religion and Morals of the People, that they should be indisposed to attend to any thing serious, or that they grow sick of Religion, which has no Comforts for them; that they fly from the Church and croud to the Playhouse: That they are tired of themselves, and their own Thoughts, and want to lose themselves in Company from Morning to Night? It is this unhappy, unsettled State of Mind, that has introduced a Kind of general Idleness among the People, and given Rise to almost infinite Places of Diversion in and about this Town; it were well if they were Places of Diversion only; but they are often Places for carrying on worse Business, and give Opportunities to the Profligate to seduce the Innocent, who often meet their Ruin, where they only came for Pleasure. (Sherlock 1750, 12)

This contagious "Spirit," however, as Sherlock admits, is remarkable for its industrious vigor. It is a "Business" sedulously endeavoring to capture people's interest in the "Playhouse" and other "almost infinite Places of Diversion." The state of miserable idleness of the populace is exacerbated and energized by a perverse sort of "industry," which potentially makes the disease incurable.

"Idleness" is a poisonous vice to guard against for all classes of society, but it becomes particularly alarming when the less affluent are seen to be addicted to it. The author of *Moll Flanders* Daniel Defoe, who could readily adopt fictional settings in his topical pamphlets, wrote under the pseudonym "Andrew Moreton, Esq." to complain about the audacity of the young girls answering his advertisement to hire maids at his house. They would unabashedly demand "five or six Pounds per Annum" as their wage, with the proviso that they decide what work they would do. Their common preference is the easier roles such as that of chambermaids. Precious few are willing to expend their physical energy at the kitchen or doing laundry. "In great Families indeed, where many Servants are requir'd," Mr. Moreton admits, "these Distinctions of Chamber-Maid, House-Maid, Cook-Maid, Laundry-Maid, Nursery-Maid, &c. are requisite, to the End that each may take her particular Business, and many Hands may make the Work light." But things cannot be the same "for a private Gentleman, of a small Fortune," who can ill afford "to keep so many Idle Jades, when one might do the Business." The audacity of the female servants is "intolerable" and needs to be recognized as a "matter of great Grievance" to those forced to hire them (Defoe 1725, 228). Andrew Moreton (or Daniel Defoe) may complain about the "Insolence, Pride, Exorbitant Wages" of the "Women-Servants" and "Footmen" (as the subtitle of his pamphlet specified), but doing without their assistance was becoming increasingly unthinkable for the middle classes living in towns. *Luxury, Pride and Vanity, the Bane of the British Nation* believed that "all sorts of People, Tradesmen as well as others" in London, Westminster, and "the Towns within ten Miles round," kept and fed "above an hundred Thousand more Maid-Servants and Footmen at this time … than used to be in the same compass of Ground about thirty Years ago." Each of these "Idle Jades" and equally idle lads dressed up as footmen earn at least 40 shillings a year, which is "more than the Wages of the like Number of Servants did amount to at the same Length of time past" (Jones [1736?], 10). A tributary to this vast pool of well-paid idlers kept by London "Tradesmen" and others below the highest rank of wealth flew from overseas. A pamphlet more or less contemporary with Defoe-Moreton, *A Trip Through London* (1728), was alarmed by the popularity of the English metropolis in Continental Europe. London, which "like the Ocean … receives the muddy and dirty Brooks, as well as the clear and rapid Rivers, swallows up all the Scum and Filth, not only of our own, but of other Countries." For many years, Italy and France have supplied London "with *Catcalls* and *Valet de Chambres*," but Germans have become equally visible "of late Years," as they "have endeavour'd to infringe upon them, by importing large Numbers of Slaves of their Growth into *London*, who from Lazyness and Lice, some have got themselves into lac'd Liveries, and good Places, and had begun to elbow out the *Welch*" (Jones 1728, 1–2). This characterization of Germans as particularly prone to be slothful may be vocally refuted by *A Discourse of the Necessity of Encouraging Mechanick Industry*, according to which pamphlet the Germans were the epitome of "Mechanick" or practical "Industry." What both would accept is the sectoral contrast between "industry" and "idleness," the latter here being identified with the domestic service market, in addition to the entertainment businesses discussed above.

The "Idle Jades" Defoe-Moreton castigates or the German "Slaves" entering the London servant market armed with "Lazyness and Lice" at least pose much less of a threat to the social order than those who are condemned to be idle for lack of any employment whatsoever in the nation as a whole and particularly among the distressed urban poor of London,

Westminster, and the Towns "within ten Miles around." Their presence was something the English law found impermissible. "Idleness" being a "high offence against the pubic œconomy," according to Blackstone's elucidation of the logic behind the law, the state saw it fit to punish it as such. All the "idle persons or vagabonds," defined by "antient statutes" as those "such as wake on the night, and sleep on the day, and haunt customable taverns, and ale-houses, and routs about; and no man wot from whence they come, ne[ither] whither they go," have not disappeared even in the prosperous and progressive eighteenth century, so that the "statute 17 Geo. II. c. 5." enacted in 1743 improved on the received tradition by classifying the idle offenders into three categories: "*idle* and *disorderly* persons, *rogues* and *vagabonds*, and *incorrigible rogues*." All were equally "offenders against the good order, and blemishes in the government," and therefore deserved to be punished, although with varying degrees of pain. The first group, the "idle and disorderly" were to be kept one month in prison or in a "house of correction," whereas "rogues and vagabonds" were first to be whipped and then be imprisoned for a maximum of six months. The pain reserved for the worst offenders, the "incorrigible rogues," was whipping followed by incarceration not exceeding two years (Blackstone 1770, 170).

Keeping the idle, whether roguish or not, in prison, of course, did little to inculcate habits of salutary "industry" in them, which, in all the varying conceptions of the term seen above, implied an element of voluntary choice motivated by "profit" or self-improvement. This was where the other, more humane department of English law also fell short. The Poor Laws, administered by the Established Church, ought to have discriminated those deserving Christian charity from those who patently did not. This distinction, however, was rarely made in practice. The pressure was acute particularly on London parishes, to which more and more "idle persons or vagabonds" flocked throughout the century (Daunton 1995, 454–455). Thomas Alcock, a clergyman himself, was deeply alarmed by this state of affairs. "If one Person by his own ill Conduct be brought into Distress, by Idleness, Sloath, Luxury, Drunkenness, Gluttony or Whoredome," Alcock urges, that person must not be treated in the same way as another who is "reduced by unavoidable Misfortunes, by Sickness, Old Age, Fire, Storm, loss in Trade, Shipwreck, a hard Farm, or sickly expensive Family." Even if the "Wants of these two Persons may be equal, surely their Claims to be relieved are far from being so." The inability to uphold this crucial distinction made the existing laws to have a "Tendency to hurt Industry, Care and Frugality," while tempting the "Sluggard" to "continue in Sloth." "The Fear of one Day coming to Want," Alcock asserts, "is a strong Motive with most People to be industrious, careful and sober," but "this Motive is much weakened, when a Man has the Prospect of Parish Pay to rely on in Case of future Wants or Misfortunes" (Alcock 1752, 9–11). Bellers' "Colledge of Industry," mentioned above, was a moral and economic scheme intended to make up for the shortcomings of English laws, civil and ecclesiastical, concerning the "idle" poor. It was Bellers' firm belief that "a full and regular Imployment of our Idle and Distress'd Poor ... in such Colleges" as he proposed, "upon our Lands, Buildings, Manufactures, and Fishery, will add much more Value to the Kingdom, than if we had a full Possession of all the Mines in the *Indies*" (Bellers 1714, 43). His "Colledge," in pursuing its charitable objective, was also destined to strengthen the nation's economy, for, as he asks, "how prudent is it to provide a good Education and Employ for the Poor, considering how many, for want of it, comes to be Miserable and Vagabonds, and continue so for many Generations, from Father to Son?" (Bellers 1695, 3). To this question of a relatively obscure Quaker thinker, Sir Josiah Child, with glittering record in trade and politics, would have given a ready consent. Child argued that the "Children of our Poor bred up in Beggary and Laziness, do by that means become not only of unhealthy Bodies, and more than ordinarily subject to many loathsome Diseases, whereof very many die in their tender Age," but "if any of them do arrive to years and strength, they are, by their Idle habits contracted in their Youth, rendered for every after indisposed to Labour, and serve only to stock the Kingdom with Thieves and Beggars." The only sensible approach is to make them industrious by giving them work. "He that gives to any in want does well; but he that gives to Employ and Educate the Poor, so as to render them useful to the Kingdom, in my judgment does better," Child contended (Child 1698, 81, 84). Charles Davenant made a similar case, on the strength of Gregory King's political arithmetic, according to which the "whole Body of the People" in England could be neatly separated into two groups, those "Increasing the Wealth of the Kingdom" and those "Decreasing the Wealth of the Kingdom." The former is computed to be 2,675,520 "Heads" and the latter 2,825,000 (Davenant 1699, 49–50). This discrepancy in numbers shows that the "Industry of not half the People maintains in some degree the other part." This needs to be rectified, Davenant proposes, by enacting laws against "voluntary Idleness" (Davenant 1699, 53, 35).

Similar to but yet different from Alcock, Child, or Davenant, for whom the poor remained a passive object of social policy, was Bellers in his strong belief in the supremacy of labor over all other components of his society's economic order. It is worthy returning to his views here, which we have already seen above. "Land, Cattel, Houses, Goods and Money are but the Carcas of Riches, they are dead without People," that is, without people who provide labor. "Men being the Life and Soul of them," abandoning the poor to stay idle as "vagabonds" or paupers has lethal consequences even for the rich and the comfortable. In his calculation, the "poorest Man in the Kingdom were worth a Million of Money," for, without the poor, the rich would have to do all the work themselves. There would have to be "as many of those rich Men Hewers of Wood, and Drawers of Water, Plowmen and Threshers, as we have of such Labourers now in the Kingdom, or else we should be under *Midas's Golden Curse*, Starve for want of Bread, tho' had our Hands fill'd with Gold" (Bellers 1714, 7–8). Once again, "industry" has to cure "idleness," all the more so since the "idleness" of the poor will jeopardize civilized living. Bellers is seconded by an unexpected and perhaps unwelcome ally on this point, Mandeville. One vice that the famous or infamous apologist of "Private Vices" cannot tolerate is that of sloth among the poor. "Labourers" should be made "cheap" by never giving them anything "worth saving," Mandeville advises. "If here and there one of the lowest Class by uncommon Industry, and pinching his Belly, lifts himself above the Condition he was brought up in, no body ought to hinder him." But it is the "Interest of all rich Nations," Mandeville instantly adds, "that the greatest part of the Poor should almost never be idle, and yet continually spend what they get" (Mandeville 1924, 1: 193–194). Charity, for the same reason, is anathema to society. "Charity," wrote Mandeville in "An Essay on Charity, and Charity-Schools," "seldom fails of promoting Sloth and Idleness, and is good for little in the Commonwealth but to breed Drones and destroy Industry" (Mandeville 1924, 1: 267). Keeping the poor from staying idle was considered vital to the happiness of a commercial society, whether one cared for the welfare of the poor (as did Bellers) or for the convenience of the rich who hire them (as did Mandeville). Institutions of philanthropy were established not just to rescue the poor from abject desolation but to wean them of their idle habits, as the very name of the "Society for the Reformation of Manners" formed in 1690s pledged (Daunton 1995, 469). While the "industry" of the poor carried a great deal of importance, "idleness" in turn could slip through the barriers of social class division to be used as a measuring, and at times chastising, rod on various other segments of society. Leaving aside the question of the "luxury" of the idle rich, which will be addressed in the next chapter, we can sample a fairly colorful range of diverse species of "idleness," both peaceful and violent, spreading across social, national, and ethnic borders.

We may begin with the Irish, whom the English loved to denigrate as notoriously slothful by nature. *A Discourse of the Necessity of Encouraging Mechanick Industry*, published in 1690 the year of the fateful Battle of the Boyne that put an end to all hopes of Irish independence from England, alleged that the Irish themselves admit that "before the English Conquest they lived in great Idleness and Sloth, having neither Arts nor any thing of labour amongst them; which put them upon a necessity of committing of what Rapin and Spoil they could, and continually to rob and prey upon one another." But thanks to the "English Laws and Government," they now "by vertue of their own Industry, make provision for their Children" (Anon. 1690, 7). William Robertson the Lowland intellectual found the same sort of moral weakness among the Scottish Highlanders. He applauds in *History of Scotland* (1759) the ultimately bootless attempt of James VI (before he became James I of England) to "civilize the Highlands and the Isles, a part of his dominions too much neglected by former monarchs." It was a civilizing mission very much in request, for the Highlanders, "retaining their natural fierceness, inured to rapine, infested their more industrious neighbours by their continual incursions." The king, however, found it "no easy matter to inspire the natives of those countries with the love of industry" (Robertson 1759, 233–234). The well-traveled Steuart was struck by the densely populated villages of Southern Spain sustained by a negligible level of "industry and labour." The secret lies in "charity." Spanish farmers, professing and practicing their popish Christianity, give one third of their yield to feed their poor peasants. As a result, "labour goes on mechanically, and without combination of circumstances, and the poor live in ease" (Steuart 1767, 90–91). Even the indolent and warm-hearted Spanish, however, when transplanted onto the Americas, could be incredibly industrious in putting the natives to hard work at the mines. The habit of the native Americans had for ages, as Robertson puts it in *History of America* (1777), been characterized by a "listless indolence in which they delighted to pass their days," not doing much to provide for themselves beyond the "little nourishment" barely sufficient to "invigorate" their "languid frame" (Robertson 1777, 177). They were ill-fitted for harsh labor, which quickly decimated them. To Child, what was as lamentable as the Spaniards' destruction of the Native Americans' lives was their misguided economic policy. The Spanish conquerors, instead of choosing the rational path of "Cultivating of the Earth" and "producing Commodities from the growth thereof," their "Intense and singular Industry" was applied solely to compel their "Slaves" to dig "Mines for Gold and Silver" (Child 1698, 202–203). In this unnatural instance, at least, "industry" rather than "idleness" turns out to be the bane blighting a nation's economy.

Anatomizing the foibles of the Spanish colonies in America in the sixteenth century, however, was not the primary objective of Child, for whom there were problems enough at home, all due to the unnaturally high interest rates, whose effect was to foster "idleness" for the benefit of the "*Griping Dronish Usurer.*" His proposal to restrict the rending rates, therefore, will injure "none but idle Persons that live at as little Expence as Labour." By the same token, to leave the rates as they are will be tantamount to permitting "Idleness to suck the Breasts of Industry" (Child 1698, 25, 21).[4] To put it in less graphic terms, the "Gain by Usury being so easie, certain, and extream great," not only the "Merchants and Tradesmen, but Land-men, Farmers, and Men of Possession" all "grow lazy in their Professions, and become Usurers" (Child 1698, 220). The duel between "industry" and "idleness" is by no means a simple contest. Child appreciates that the "corrupt Nature of Man" is far "more apt to decline to Vice, than incline to Vertue." From this premise, it follows that the vice of idleness entrenched in the "depraved nature of Man" can entice all humans, whenever possible, to indulge in "ease and pleasure." When compounded by "Covetousness," another strong passion lurking at the heart of human nature, nothing can stop those who can afford to do so from becoming "Country Gentleman or Usurer"—nothing, that is, except a strong government restraint that keeps the highest legal interest rate arrested at 4% (Child 1698, 53, 63–64). Not all shared this jaundiced view of the money lender. Thomas Mun, a London merchant with firm views on the merits of international trade (Wennerlind 2011, 231–232), claimed that money lent at interest enabled the "*younger* and *poorer* Merchants to

[4] Child's expression "to suck the Breasts of Industry" may remind one of Karl Marx's likening in *Capital* volume 1 of "capital" to a "vampire" that "lives only by sucking living labour" (Marx 1979, 342). Marx no doubt must have read Child, since Marx cites him in a footnote discussing money (Marx 1979, 184 n.9). Mark Neocleous fails to remember Child among the precursors of this gothic image of capital painted by Marx (Neocleous 2003).

rise in the World, and to enlarge their Dealings," for "if they want Means of their own, they may, and do, take it up at Interest: so that our Mony lies not dead, it is still traded." However "Dronish" the lender may be, the borrower more often than not is the beneficiary. "How many Merchants, and Shop-keepers have begun with little or nothing of their own, and yet are grown very rich by Trading with other Men's Mony?" asks Mun (1713, 57). But the syllogism implied in this justification assumes that the said "Merchants" and "Shop-keepers" must have been industrious in their business, for otherwise they could never have grown "rich" by "Trading with other Men's Mony." Besides, Mun also assumed that the interest rate was not too exorbitant as to prevent them from profiting from their loaned capital. This was exactly what Child advocated again and again. The Dutch, the great and formidable rival of the English during Child's time, knew how to keep themselves "Industrious" by never allowing for "any Use for Money … above the rate of Six in the Hundred." This cap on interest rate enabled the Dutch, "though they have no other Advantages of Industry and Frugality," to "out-Trade" the English, "if they make return of ten *per cent*, they almost double the Use allowed, and so make a very gainful Trade." The financial circumstances were quite different for the English. "But with us, where ten in the Hundred is so current, it is otherwise," Child points out. As a result, the Dutch merchants were much better off than the English: "[I]f we make not above ten, we are loosers, and consequently the same Trade being with them and us equally good for the Publick, is to the private Adventurers lossful with us, with them very gainful" (Child 1698, 218–219).

Tucker published his *Four Tracts … on Political and Commercial Subjects* in the 1770s when the interplay between "Covetousness" and pursuit of "ease and pleasure" had become far more pervasive than in the last years of the seventeenth century when Child expressed his envious admiration of the Dutch. Britain's overseas trade now definitely stood far ahead of those conducted by the Dutch or any other European rival (Thomas and McCloskey 1981, 88). Even so, Tucker reiterates Child's emphasis on the need to maintain good governance in order to keep the forces of the "*Griping Dronish Usurer*" from draining the vitality of the nation's economy. The path to a continuous prosperity can only be protected by "general Industry," that is by "exciting the Ingenuity and Activity of its People," which calls for bold and sagacious regulations. One should, for instance, by differentiated taxation, make "all Things hurtful to the Public Good" become "proportionably dear, and placed beyond the Reach of the Multitude," while at the same time encouraging "such Things as are necessary, or useful" to be produced sufficiently and provided at an affordable price. Through this and "every other conceivable Method," Tucker advises, "the Drones of Society" should be "converted into Bees, and the Bees be prevented from degenerating back into Drones" (Tucker 1774, 21). On the other hand, a mere increment in the volume of money unattended by any increase in "industry" can only push the country to slip into the deleterious "Way of National *Idleness*," a path in which "all Persons, whether Male or Female, would endeavour to put themselves in fortune's Way, and hope to catch as much as they could of this golden Shower" (Tucker 1774, 14–15). "Idleness" is not merely detrimental to Britain's political economy, but more damagingly, it poisons the spiritual health of her subjects, as Tucker admonishes his readers in one of the two "Sermons" appended to *Four Tracts*:

> [L]et every Man labour, working with his own Hands the Thing which is good, that he may have to give to him that needeth. Be not slothful in Business. In the Morning sow thy Seed, and in the Evening withhold not thine Hand. There are some which walk disorderly, working not at all, but are Busy bodies:—Now them that are such we command and exhort by our Lord Jesus, that with Quietness they work and eat their own Bread: For if any Man will not work, neither should he eat. (Tucker 1774, "Sermon 1," 18–19)

Be not "Busy bodies," for they are as bad as idlers "working not at all," but more importantly, be not "slothful in Business," for that is to spurn the express command of "our Lord Jesus" Himself. Tucker would most likely be scandalized to hear a self-proclaimed "Christian" economist of our time assert that "there is no Christian perspective on the economy for the same reason that there is no Christian perspective on organ transplants," and that one finds in the New Testament "an extraordinary disregard for almost everything in which economists are interested" (Heyne 2008, 113). This hasty conclusion evinces an "extraordinary disregard for" what the New Testament does say about matters economic, above all its advocacy of diligence or "industry." Tucker's contemporaries never brushed off religion in such a cavalier way when speaking of the economy. James Beattie, among others, offers a strong proof that the founder of Christianity held "industry" in high regard. "Our Saviour graciously forbids excessive anxiety with regard to the events of life, and the good things of this world," but "his religion ... is most unfriendly to indolence; and his apostles recommended industry, both by precept, and by example." In fact, our Lord practiced what he preached, for "there is reason to think that he himself had laboured with his own hands in his reputed father's profession: for otherwise his townsmen would not have called him the carpenter" (Beattie 1786, 111–112). Tucker relies less on the Scripture than Beattie, perhaps since he wishes to legitimize monetary commerce, about which not many favorable remarks can be found in the New Testament. In Tucker's homily, natural religion offers ample support. A wholesome "System of Commerce" in the eyes of God is one that gives a "general Encouragement" to the "Diligent and Industrious of all Professions." A culture of "general Emulation" built on such diligence of economic agents will "excite their Genius and improve their Abilities" (Tucker 1774, "Sermon 1," 12–13). For the same reason, a "System of Commerce" which fails to incite "industry" can never be a "Just and proper Commercial System" but a mere "Deception." Such a state of spurious commerce

> cannot circulate the Labour and Industry of Mankind as much as it ought to do; it is not so lasting, or so extensive in its Consequences, as it might have been; and tho' Individuals may be Gainers by it, yet, upon the whole, it will be found to be as much repugnant to the trading Interests of Mankind, to the right Employment of their Time, and to national Wealth, Plenty, and Prosperity, as it is repugnant to Religion, and Civil Government. (Tucker 1774, "Sermon 1," 16)

In admonishing against "idleness," both individual and structural, Tucker advances a doctrine of "industry" that can bridge the gap between morality, religion, and political economy.

The author of *The Wealth of Nations*, like Tucker, also had no sympathy for the "Drones" or slothful "Busy bodies," both high and low, ensconced at snug nooks and cranny of the society's framework. Artificial rules binding apprentices for "more than the usual number of years" are doubly detrimental to both parties, the master and apprentice. The master may fancy he profits from the unpaid work of his apprentices, but the "usual idleness of apprentices," who in general are more likely to behave like Tom Idle than Francis Goodchild in Hogarth's pictorial narrative, erodes their "industry" and the potential profit to be reaped from it (Smith 1976, 119 [I.x.b.8]). An apprentice, Smith generalizes, "is likely to be idle, and almost always is so, because he has no immediate interest to be otherwise" (Smith 1976, 139 [I.x.c.14]). Likewise, in the sphere of money market the contrastive interplay of "industry" and "idleness" displays their validity, but in contrast to Child, Smith focuses on the idleness of the borrower rather than the lender. Smith, unlike Tucker, puts great trust in the ability of the market to regulate itself in such a way as to prevent the dangerously idle from taking advantage of the market's freedom. "The man who borrows in order to spend will soon be ruined, and he who lends to him will generally have occasion to repent of his folly." While Smith concedes that this at times does happen, and that "gross usury" may motivate some to offer loans, he believes that "from the regard that all men have for their own interest," it "cannot happen so very frequently as we are sometimes apt to imagine." Smith evinces an unusual degree of confidence on this issue:

> Ask any rich man of common prudence, to which of the two sorts of people he has lent the greater part of his stock, to those who, he thinks, will employ it profitably, or to those who will spend it idly, and he will laugh at you for proposing the question. Even among borrowers, therefore, not the people in the world most famous for frugality, the number of the frugal and industrious surpasses considerably that of the prodigal and idle. (Smith 1976, 350 [II.iv.2])

One need not worry too much about the "Dronish Usurer," not only because businessmen know best what serves their interest, but because, more reassuringly, among the tribe of "borrowers" the "industrious" safely outnumber the "idle." Smith's belief that the market should be left to its own devices even when it comes to deciding the interest rate is not that different from one held by Blackstone, who makes a nuanced vindication of money lent on interest. Since "all other conveniences of life may either be bought or hired, but money can only be hired," Blackstone can find "no greater impropriety in taking a recompence or price for the hire of this, than of any other convenience." "To demand an exorbitant price is equally contrary to conscience, for the loan of a horse, or the loan of a sum of money," but a "reasonable equivalent for the temporary inconvenience the owner may feel by the want of it, and for the hazard of his losing it entirely, is not more immoral in one case than it is in the other" (Blackstone 1768a, 456). "A capital distinction," therefore, must be made between a "moderate and exorbitant profit." Quite appropriately, "to the former," people "usually give the name of interest," while "to the latter" they attach the "truly odious appellation of usury." The "former" reasonable interest is "necessary in every civil state," and all one has to do is to "exclude the latter, which ought never to be tolerated in any well-regulated society" (Blackstone 1768a, 457).

Behind the stone walls of ancient university colleges, however, far from the madding crowd of money lenders and borrowers, "idleness" enjoys a far greater security than would have been feasible elsewhere. Smith, himself a former student at Oxford (Ross 1995, 73–74),[5] waxes eloquent in his pitiless indictment. He first prepares the ground for his assault. "It is the interest of every man to live as much at his ease as he can," Smith sardonically asserts. If such is human nature, when "his emoluments are to be precisely the same, whether he does, or does not perform some very laborious duty, it is certainly his interest ... either to neglect it altogether, or, if he is subject to some authority which will not suffer him to do this, to perform it in as careless and slovenly a manner as that authority will permit" (Smith 1976, 760 [V.i.f.7]). This universal truth is nowhere better illustrated than in the illustrious university of Oxford:

> If the authority to which he is subject resides in the body corporate, the college, or university, of which he himself is a member, and in which the greater part of the other members are, like himself, persons who either are, or ought to be teachers; they are likely to make a common cause, to be all very indulgent to one another, and every man to consent that his neighbour may neglect his duty, provided he himself is allowed to neglect his own. In the university of Oxford, the greater part of the publick professors have, for these many years, given up altogether even the pretence of teaching. (Smith 1976, 761 [V.i.f.8])

On immature apprentices and on mature college dons, "idleness" exerts influence, as "idleness" can easily appeal to the "interest of every man." The only viable cure is to break the equality of "emoluments" and make them compete with each other. To the former group of idlers this prescription can be applied with some degree of success. To the latter, it most likely will not, in part because society seems to have agreed to leave

[5] Despite his strictures on Oxford, Smith seems to have made good use of his time at the English university. In fact, as his biographer points out, Smith owed "some gratitude to Oxford for the opportunity it gave him of reading solidly for six years, and for taking away anxieties about his accent and his Scotticisms, which plagued David Hume" (Ross 1995, 80).

alone a small portion of its idling academics to enjoy their slothful ease. There were clear exceptions, no doubt, such as Blackstone, the first Vinerian Professor of English Law at Oxford, but it does bespeak Smith's strong conviction that "idleness" in whatever guise should never be tolerated.

3.3 Insolvency and Incarceration

The dichotomy of "industry v. idleness," perennially dependent one upon another and permanently at war with each other, could also be dispatched to the margins of economic activity to manage and define its moral boundary. If "idleness" can be detected as dwelling in the university college common rooms, "industry" has its cousin in the less legitimate domain of insolvency. Here, too, the distinction between "industry" and "idleness" was frequently applied to distinguish the unfortunate bankruptcy of an industrious tradesman from the morally reprehensible insolvency of a profligate prodigal. Credit in the century was very often given on the basis of an assessment of the moral character of the debtor, with no other security than the expectation that the debt will be cleared when demanded (Hoppit 2000, 326, 332). Tradesmen and their clients with modest income would also experience frequent shortage of ready cash, so that they had no choice but to rely heavily on various forms of credit transactions (Finn 2003, 77–79). The hazards of business fluctuation, however, could easily overweigh the moral integrity of the debtor. For the wronged creditors, recovering their legitimate debt was never an easy process. The remedy was sought, often as a last resort, in the laws of England, which empowered the creditor to secure the body of the insolvent debtor. Seizing the debtors' goods rather than his or her person was certainly the more reasonable approach, but it ran into all sorts of ingenious impediments devised by insolvent debtors, such as concealing, dispersing, and disguising their goods and chattels (Finn 2003, 111–112). By contrast, seizing, or at least threatening to seize, the debtor's body was perceived to be an easier method of enforcing the payment of debts (Innes 2009, 231). When the debtor was indeed imprisoned, regardless of his or her moral responsibility and at times indefinitely, the debtor was being punished with a de facto sentence of enforced "idleness," if not outright starvation. Some could exploit the loopholes in the law by not paying back their debt and use what money they have to purchase comfort inside the debtors' prison. There were others, however, who ended up in jail because their businesses failed despite their best efforts to stay solvent by exerting their "industry." Insolvency, therefore, though patently a legal issue, was also considered to be an important subject of economic ethics which those outside the legal profession thought entitled to broach.

Not surprisingly, divines of different persuasions felt they had a duty to ponder on the moral implications of bankruptcy as an inevitable byproduct of a commercial society. Paley offered a sound common-sense view of the case:

> Whoever borrows money is bound in conscience to repay it. This, every man can see; but every man cannot see, or does not however reflect, that he is, in consequence, also bound to use the means necessary to enable himself to repay it. … An expectation which depends upon the continuance of his own life, will not satisfy an honest man, if a better provision be in his power; for it is a breach of faith to subject a creditor, when we can help it, to the risk of our life, be the event what it will; that not being the security to which credit was given. (Paley 2002, 94–95)

Paley counsels that if you have borrowed money from someone, use it cautiously, sacrifice your comfort, and never abuse your creditor's trust. John Wesley, on the other hand, expressed his sentiments with greater bluntness. In *A Serious Address to the People of England, with Regard to the State and the Nation* (1778), Wesley censured those alleging that the growing number of bankruptcies in England and particularly in London, which historians corroborate,[6] was a sign of her economic decay. "Do you not know," Wesley asks, "that the very Increase of Trade will of course increase Bankruptcies?" He offers a deceptively transparent reasoning. If "some Traders will gain," there will be others who "lose." Therefore, if there are more traders, there will be more bankrupts. Surely this cannot be all there is to it. Indeed, Wesley goes on to admit that many bankruptcies result from the "desperate irrational Boldness, never so common as now, which prompts such multitudes of men to enter upon Trade, with little or

[6] Bankruptcies increased from the 1770s in tandem with the growth in the financial services based on credit (Daunton 1995, 248, 252). Bankruptcies in London tended to be greater in frequency than in the provinces already in the 1730s (Hoppit 1987, 73). Hoppit also calculates the actual increase of London bankruptcies from the 1740s to the 1780s. It was 1 in 29.5 in the 1740s, increased to 1 in 43.7 in the 1750s, rose to 1 in 36.8 in the 1760s, further to 1 in 36.2 in the 1770s, and then stabilized into 1 in 42.8 in the 1780s (Hoppit 1987, 67).

no Capital." At the opposite end of the spectrum from the idle usurer, these tradesmen "attempting to trade without Money," relying solely on their "industry," constitute a large portion of the bankrupts (Wesley 1778, 26). Although Wesley would not say as much, the inference would be that these unfortunate tradesmen have no one else to blame but themselves. More interested in the spiritual failure of the "People of England," Wesley clearly simplifies the complicated circumstances and causes of business failure in a dynamic market economy. Nor does he extend his sympathy to those unfortunate bankrupts who languish in the debtors' prisons of London.

Half a century earlier, Thomas Sherlock, at the time Lord Bishop of Bangor, published *The Case of Insolvent Debtors, and the Charity Due to Them, Considered*, which was a "Sermon Preach'd before the Right Honourable the Lord-Mayor, the Aldermen, and Governors of the several Hospitals of the City of London, at the Parish-Church of St. Bridget, on Monday in Easter-Week, April 22, 1728," as the subtitle informs the reader. Sherlock would first draw the attention of the reader to the "Hard-heartedness and Cruelty which Men use towards their poor insolvent Debtors," which is generally connived at because "Men are apt to imagine that Conscience has nothing to do in it, and that they are secure from any Guilt, so long as they follow in a Legal Manner the Method prescribed by the Law." He will not criticize the law itself, but the lack of charity on the part of those creditors who use it as an "Instrument of Oppression and Revenge" ought to be blamed (Sherlock 1728, 7–8).[7] Creditors are justified to use whatever means against those who are "able, but not willing to pay," and to "delay poor Traders, or others, in the Payment of what is due to them, is always Injustice, and sometimes very barbarous Injustice" (Sherlock 1728, 11). Furthermore, those who live "idly and profusely, and are constantly diminishing what they have, and by so doing are rendering themselves less able every Day to pay their just Debts" hardly deserves charity. But when a debtor is "chargeable with no Fault, or Fraud, but is disabled by mere Poverty to satisfy his Debts," the rigors of the law should

[7] At least one creditor who sent his debtor to prison recorded his moral scruples in his diary. Thomas Turner, a Sussex shopkeeper, confessed in 1758 to his diary, "as soon as I had breakfasted I set out for Lewes in order to commit the management of the debt due from Master Darby to me into the hands of Mr Rideout." "Oh, what a confusion it is to arrest a person, for by this means he may be entirely torn to pieces," Turner could not but admit. "But then on the other hand," he checks himself immediately, "some of this debt hath been standing above 4 years" (quoted in Hoppit 1987, 41).

be applied sparingly, for the law was meant to "secure Men in their Properties" and not to "harass and torment a poor unfortunate Man." Imprisonment can be justified only when there is a "Prospect of recovering the Debt," through "Friends and Relations" who may pay it for the "Honour of the Family" (Sherlock 1728, 13–16). This possibility is more often than not entirely foreclosed for the vast majority of debtors:

> The unfortunate Persons ... for the most part, [are] such as have neither Money nor Friends to assist them; such as have fallen into Poverty by Misfortunes, by a Decay in their Business; or perhaps by the Largeness of a Family, which their utmost Diligence could not support. Were they at Liberty, they might probably be of Use to themselves, and their poor Families, and also to their Creditors, by following their honest Callings and Imployments. But now their Strength consumes in vain, they starve in Prison, and their Children out of it, or are thrown upon the Parish for a miserable Maintenance; and no Benefit or Advantage accrues, or can possibly accrue to the Person who confines them.

The imprisoned debtor unable to clear his debt is deprived of his "Liberty" to apply his "Diligence," as he is compelled to remain idle. Here, once again, the almost ubiquitous opposition between "industry" and "idleness" is invited to summarize the problem. As Sherlock sees it, incarcerating the debtor is to impose "idleness" on the insolvent as a punishment for his failed "industry" (Sherlock 1728, 17).

Sherlock pleads leniency toward the unfortunate debtors, but what was urgently called for was a more reasonable way of dealing with them. William Eden, an author trained in law, found the imprisonment for debt to be one of the weak spots of the English law in his *Principles of Penal Law* (1771). "From a numberless variety of accidental circumstances, which happen in the course of human transactions," Eden reasons, "it must fall to the lot of many, to become Insolvent." If so, the debtors, although "a species of Criminals, should in general be considered rather as unfortunate, than culpable" (Eden 1771, 45). Paley agrees with Eden on this point. Ideally, the creditor ought to use his "discretionary power" advisedly, not for mere "satisfaction or revenge" but to identify and punish "frauds relating to insolvency," Paley suggests. The presumption would be that "no discretion is likely to be so well informed, so vigilant, or so active, as that of the creditor" (Paley 2002, 95). Trusting the common sense of the creditor to make a sound and humane decision was hardly sufficient for the anonymous author of *The Case of Bankrupts and Insolvents Consider'd* (1734). A better guide for the creditor could be provided by the dichotomy of "industry" and "idleness." Like Sherlock, this anonymous author sees the incarceration of bankrupts to be an abuse of law, since "no Man ought … to be allowed to *indulge* his *private Revenge* against his Fellow-Subject." It also goes flatly against the "Rules of Christianity" which oblige us "to leave all Revenge to God, and to his Vicegerents on Earth, the Magistrates of the Society to which we belong" (Anon. 1734, 22). But some form of punishment would be justified for some categories of insolvents. It all depends on making a judicious distinction between their innocence and guilt. Our author classifies the unpaying debtors into four types. First are those "who have occasioned a Damage or Loss" to the creditor by their crimes. Second are those who have done so through some "culpable Action." Third are those who have injured the creditor by some "Negligence or Omission." Last in the list are those who came to be insolvent largely due to their "Misfortunes." This, for him, is the "*natural Division* of Insolvents," which "every just Municipal Law" ought to respect (Anon. 1734, 28). The first sort of offenders are characteristically those who, "after having contracted large Debts, *secrete* their Estate and Effects from their Creditors, and run beyond Seas, or into a Jail, with a Design never to make any Satisfaction to their Creditors, but to live beyond Seas, or to live idly within the Rules of a Prison, the remaining Part of their Lives, in order to *spend* in *Luxury* what they have got by *Robbery*" (Anon. 1734, 29). Also classified as belonging to the same group are "those who, without any Probable View or Expectation of better Circumstances, or of receiving speedily any large Sum of Money, or Estate, spend *idly* or *extravagantly* more than their Income can admit of, and by Pretences, which they know to be false and fraudulent, procure more than they can have any probable View of repaying." These inexcusable creatures should be regarded as no better than "common Cheats." Those in this category "deserve all to be hang'd" or punished severely (Anon. 1734, 30, 32). The second are those guilty of "Extravagance or Idleness," but not having had any criminal intention, they are merely "culpable." As such, they should be "subjected to some sort of *Punishment* or *Correction*, as a Terror to others." The third are those affected by "idleness" rather than "extravagance." They have been prodded "by the *Indolence* of their Nature," or was "led away by Company and Diversion," to accumulate large debts which they are unable to pay. Their idleness cannot go unpunished or at least must be "corrected," even though they "really deserve in some Measure to be pitied," as a "Terror to others," and to "rouse up the Attention and Application of those who are deviating, or who are by their Natures prone to fall into the same Road to Destruction." Lastly, the fourth group are those who have become insolvent purely "by *Misfortunes incident* to their Trade or Business; such as ill Success in their Projects of Trade, Losses by Sea, by Fire, or by bad Debt, &c. those who suffer by being *Security* or *Bail* for others, or by such like Misfortunes." By no means tarnished with criminality, culpability, or the moral defect of idleness, they are "*Real Objects* of Compassion; and it is most *barbarous* to leave it to the Power of a *splenetick*, or *revengeful Creditor*, to add to their Misfortunes, by throwing them into a Jail, where they must be in great Danger of Starving" (Anon. 1734, 33–35).

Parliament was not entirely unaware of the problems besetting the incarceration of debtors (Lemmings 2011, 142), but the laws of the realm made no distinction between the unfortunate, the profligate, and the culpable insolvents. Yet despite the accusations of critics such as Sherlock or Eden, the English law had its own reason—"artificial" and not "natural" reason, according to the famous dictum of Edward Coke's "Prohibitions del Roy (1607)" (Coke 2003, 481)—for treating the insolvent debtor with little humanity. A debt, as Blackstone explicates it, is one of the "private wrongs," and as such is a "privation of right" calling for an "adequate remedy" (Blackstone 1768b, 116). The non-payment is an "injury" for which the "proper remedy" is either "by action of debt, to compel the performance of the contract and recover the specifical sum due," or by an action of "*indebitatus assumpsit*" against the non-performance of the contract. The former action requires the sum in question to be stated exactly, whereas the latter is more flexible in that if any debt can be proven, the law will honor the claims of the plaintiff (Blackstone 1768b, 153–155). This latter action, "*indebitatus assumpsit*," empowers and obliges the sheriff to "produce" the defendant, which in practice means he can arrest the defendant, who is then either imprisoned "for safe custody" or put in "special bail" to the sheriff. The latter (bail) places the entire responsibility of securing the body of the defendant on the sheriff, which therefore is much less frequently adopted than the former (arrest) (Blackstone 1768b, 288, 290, 292). When the debt in question has been proven, the court issues a writ of "*capias ad satisfaciendum*," the intent of which is to "imprison the body of the debtor till satisfaction be made for the debt, costs, and damages" and which commands the sheriff to "take the body of the defendant and have him at Westminster, on a day therein named, to make the plaintiff satisfaction for his demand." If the defendant cannot satisfy the plaintiff as stated in the writ, he must be kept in custody by the sheriff until he does. If he is ever seen to be at large, it is considered an "escape" and the plaintiff may sue the sheriff to recover his debt (Blackstone 1768b, 414–415). As no sheriff would be willing to put himself under such predicament, he would make sure the debtor remains secure in prison, unless, of course, the creditor retracts his action. Such had been the practice of the English law for centuries, and the prisons of London, such as Fleet Prison and King's Bench, came to be part of the major institutions of London, listed by contemporary guide books to the metropolis. These prisons also evolved into becoming paralegal providers of accommodation and catering services to those who could pay (Innes 2009, 238–249; Finn 2003, 134–137). Furthermore, those who paid a certain "Sum" to the "Warden" were given the "Privilege of keeping Shops, and walking about to transact Business" in the "Liberties called the Rules of the Fleet" outside the walls of Fleet Prison (Anon. [1765?], 81).

However efficient the law may have been as a warning toward potential insolvents, and no matter how flexible the debtors' prisons at times were in their actual management, an indiscriminate incarceration of all insolvents could hardly answer the charge that it eroded the supreme principle of encouraging "industry" and discouraging "idleness." *The Case of Bankrupts and Insolvents Consider'd* leveled a poignant critical onslaught on this discrepancy in the way penal justice was meted out to insolvent debtors. The author held it to be evident that "every Man who has not his Hands employed in daily Labour, nor his Head employed in the Government of the Society, or in contriving Labour for others, is an *useless Person* to the Society, and must consequently be a *Burden* upon the Society." "Of these sort of *Drones* there will be abundance in every Society," but it is an "unpardonable Error in Politicks, to make any Laws, or to keep any Laws in Force, by which the Number of these *Drones* are necessarily *increased*," since those guilty of various offenses are left to stay idle in prison (Anon. 1734, 49). The absurdity, as well as the injustice, of the practice ought to be obvious to any reasonable observer:

> *That because a Man has been a Criminal, therefore he shall be maintain'd idly at the publick Expence.* This is what I think ought not, in any Case, to be practised; but, to make Imprisonment a Punishment for Insolvency, by which so many Hundreds are every Year rendered *idle*, and consequently

> *burdensome* to the Society, is a *monstrous Error* in Politicks: And the more so, because many industrious Tradesmen, and ingenious Mechanicks, get, by that Means, into such a Habit of *Idleness* and *Sotting*, that they can never after apply themselves to *Labour* or *Industry*. (Anon. 1734, 50–51)

The intransigence of the law bred a "Habit of *Idleness*" and dampened the spirit of "industry" among formerly "industrious" tradesmen and artisans. This could be rectified, this author believed, by adopting a fairly draconian but practicable measure: "*Workhouses* or *Bridewells* may be set up, and Criminals may there be confined and kept to hard Labour, for the Benefit of themselves, as well as of the Society" (Anon. 1734, 50). Some decades later, John Howard, based on his own visits to the prisons of the kingdom, published *The State of the Prisons in England and Wales* (first edition, 1772). Howard reported here how appalled he was to see felons mixing with debtors during daytime, leaving the debtor-prisoners to be "annoyed and corrupted by the wicked conversation of felons all day long." This had to stop. He proposed, first, to separate the two groups completely and, second, to set up a "large *work-shop* for such [debtors] as are willing to work." His scheme was based on his observations of some prison workshops already existing, where he found "basket-makers, shoemakers, &c. employed in their several trades," all "preserving their habit of industry" (Howard 1792, 24). His sound advice fell on deaf ears. Without addressing the fundamental contradictions of the law, or attempting to reform the prisons, Parliament occasionally passed laws to clear the prisons of all debtors, rather than finding means to segregate honest debtors from fraudsters and felons (Hoppit 1987, 34).

Bankruptcy, first made a crime by a 1543 statute, remained so in subsequent legislations of 1570 and 1604. The law began to relent a little toward the bankrupt in the 1706 statute, even though its title, "An Act to prevent frauds frequently committed by bankrupts," paid respects to the old attitude (Hoppit 1987, 19). In the mid-eighteenth century, a new statute (32 Geo.II.c.28, 1758) added a provisional clause permitting a defendant charged for an unpaid debt of less than £100 to be released from prison, with the creditor's consent, after making an "oath of his punctual compliance with the statute" and surrendering all his effects to his creditors, except for his "apparel, bedding, and tools of his trade" (Blackstone 1768b, 416). The statute thus intended to enable the defendant to extricate himself from the meshes of compulsory "idleness" and to use his "industry" again—outside the prison—to pay back his debt. The bankrupt, as Blackstone explicates, was "formerly considered merely in the light of a criminal or offender," but the modern law also wished to protect the "benefit of trade." The changes, never too drastic, were "founded on the principles of humanity as well as justice," as the new laws "confer some privileges, not only on the creditors, but also on the bankrupt or debtor himself" (Blackstone 1768a, 471–472). The amended legislation, averse to encourage profligacy, granted the "benefit of the laws of bankruptcy to none but actual *traders*" and not just to any trader but only to "industrious" traders (Blackstone 1768a, 473). A bankrupt's qualification to be deemed an "industrious trader" was specified by the statute. His subjective moral attitude was not the issue but only the nature of his business activity, for he had to be both a selling and buying trader. An inn-keeper, for instance, however diligent he may have been before he became bankrupt, fails to qualify as an "industrious trader" for he makes his living by letting the "use of his rooms and furniture" and his buying corn and selling victuals is only incidental to his trade. In addition, the amount of the tradesman's debt should not be inconsiderable. A minimum debt of £100 to one creditor, or £150 to two, or £200 to three and more must have been incurred (Blackstone 1768a, 475–476). Those who meet these criteria, upon the consent and the testimony of his creditors vouchsafing his "honest and ingenuous disposition" and confirming that his business failed due to "misfortunes, rather than to misconduct and extravagance," a certificate is signed by the creditors, by four out of five parts in number and value of his creditors, to grant him a minimum allowance and indemnity from imprisonment. By this means, "the bankrupt becomes a clear man again; and, by the assistance of his allowance and his own industry, may become a useful member of the commonwealth," Blackstone remarks, applauding the wisdom of the English law (Blackstone 1768a, 482–484). Whether the English bankruptcy law was genuinely inspired by "humanity" and "justice," as Blackstone claimed, could be a moot point. But what is far less doubtful is that the changes in the statutes ratified in the eighteenth century illustrate the pervasive presence of the dichotomy of "industry" and "idleness" in the minds of those seeking to impose some moral order on a volatile commercial society.

References

Alcock, Thomas. 1752. *Observations on the defects of the poor laws, and on the causes and consequences of the great increases and burden of the poor. With a proposal for redressing these grievances.* London: R. Baldwin.

Anon. 1690. *A discourse of the necessity of encouraging mechanick industry.* London, R. Chiswell.

Anon. 1734. *The case of bankrupts and insolvents consider'd.* London.

Anon. [1765?] *A companion to the plan of London, describing the government, churches ... City-companies ... general and penny-post offices, and other interesting particulars relative to the cities of London and Westminster, and borough of Southwark.* London: T. Kitchin and H. Parker.

Barbon, Nicholas. 1685. *An apology for the builder: or A discourse shewing the cause and effects of the increase of building.* London.

Barry, Wind. 1997. Hogarth's "Industry and idleness" reconsidered. *Print Quarterly* 14:235–251.

Beattie, James. 1786. *Evidences of the Christian religion; Briefly and plainly stated.* Vol. 2. London: A. Strahan, and T. Cadell.

Bellers, John. 1695. *Proposals for raising a colledge of industry of all useful trades and husbandry, with profit for the rich.* London.

Bellers, John. 1714. *An Essay towards the improvement of physick. ... with an essay for imploying the able poor; by which the riches of the kingdom may be greatly increased.* London.

Berry, Christoper. 2015. *The Idea of commercial society in the Scottish Enlightenment.* Edinburgh: Edinburgh University Press.

Blackstone, William. 1768a. *Commentaries on the laws of England. Book the second.* 3rd ed. Oxford: Clarendon.

Blackstone, William. 1768b. *Commentaries on the laws of England. Book the third.* 3rd ed. Oxford: Clarendon.

Blackstone, William. 1770. *Commentaries on the laws of England. Book the fourth.* 4th ed. Oxford: Clarendon.

Bradford, Samuel. 1720. *The honest and dishonest ways of getting wealth: A sermon preach'd in the parish-church of St. Mary le Bow, on Sunday, November 20. 1720.* London: John Wyat.

Butler, Joseph. 1736. *The analogy of religion, natural and revealed, to the constitution and course of nature.* London: J. and P. Knapton.

Campbell, R. 1747. *The London tradesman. Being a compendious view of all the trades, professions, arts, both liberal and mechanic, now practised in the cities of London and Westminster.* London.

Child, Josiah. 1698. *A new discourse of trade.* London.

Coke, Edward. 2003. *The selected writings and speeches of Sir Edward Coke.* Vol. 1. Edited by Steve Sheppard. Indianapolis: Liberty Fund.

Cowley, Robert LS. 2019/2020. *Industry and idleness* by William Hogarth (1697–1764) and the "doctrine of opposites." *The British Art Journal* 20:42–61.
Daunton, M. J. 1995. *Progress and poverty: An economic and social history of Britain 1700–1850.* Oxford: Oxford University Press.
Davenant, Charles. 1699. *An Essay upon the probable methods of making a people gainers in the balance of trade.* London: James Knapton.
Defoe, Daniel. 1725. Every-body's business, is no-body's business. In *Political and economic writings of Daniel Defoe*, vol. 8: *Social reform*, ed. W. R. Owens, 217–235. London: Pickering and Chatto, 2000.
Defoe, Daniel. 1728. A plan of the English commerce. In *Political and economic writings of Daniel Defoe*, vol. 7: *Trade*, ed. John McVeagh, 115–341. London: Pickering & Chatto, 2000.
Eden, William. 1771. *Principles of penal law.* London: B. White and T. Cadell.
Finn, Margot C. 2003. *The character of credit: Personal debt in English culture, 1740–1914.* Cambridge: Cambridge University Press.
Heyne, Paul. 2008. *"Are economists basically immoral?" and other essays on economics, ethics, and religion.* Indianapolis: Liberty Fund.
Hogarth, William. 1747. Industry and idleness. In *Engravings by Hogarth*, ed. Sean Shescreen, plates 60 to 71. New York: Dover, 1973.
Hoppit, Julian. 1987. *Risk and failure in English business 1700–1800.* Cambridge: Cambridge University Press.
Hoppit, Julian. 2000. *A land of liberty? England 1689–1727.* Oxford: Oxford University Press.
Howard, John. 1792. *The state of the prisons in England and Wales, with Preliminary observations, and an account of some foreign prisons and hospitals.* 4th ed. London: J. Johnson, C. Dilly, and T. Cadell.
Hume, David. 1987. *Essays, moral, political, and literary.* Edited by Eugene F. Miller. Indianapolis: Liberty Fund.
Innes, Joanna. 2009. *Inferior politics: Social problems and social policies in eighteenth-century Britain.* Oxford: Oxford University Press.
Johnson, Samuel. 1773. *A dictionary of the English language*, 4th ed. London: Consortium.
Johnson, Samuel. 1984. *Samuel Johnson.* Edited by Donald Greene. Oxford: Oxford University Press.
Jones, Erasmus. 1728. *A trip through London: Containing observations on men and things.* London.
Jones, Erasmus. [1736?] *Luxury, pride and vanity, the bane of the British nation.* London: J. Roberts.
Jonsson, Fredrik Albritton, and Carl Wennerlind. 2023. *Scarcity: A history from the origins of capitalism to the climate crisis.* Cambridge, MA: Harvard University Press.

Kames, Lord (Henry Home). 1774. *Sketches of the history of man*. Edinburgh: W. Creech.
Lemmings, David. 2011. *Law and government in England during the long eighteenth century: From consent to command*. Houndmills: Palgrave Macmillan.
Locke, John. 1988. *Two treatises of government*. Edited by Peter Laslett. Cambridge: Cambridge University Press.
Mandeville, Bernard. 1924. *The fable of the bees, or, Private vices, publick benefits*. 2 vols. Edited by F. B. Kaye. Oxford: Clarendon.
Marx, Karl. 1979. *Capital: A critique of political economy*. Vol. 1. Translated by Ben Fowkes. New York: Penguin.
Mun, Thomas. 1713. *England's treasure by foreign trade; or, The balance of our foreign trade is the rule of our treasure*. London.
Neocleous, Mark. 2003. The political economy of the dead: Marx's vampires. *History of Political Thought* 24:668–684.
North, Dudley. 1691. *Discourses upon trade; Principally directed to the cases of the interest, coinage, clipping, increase, of money*. London: Tho. Basset.
Paley, William. 2002. *The principles of moral and political philosophy*. Indianapolis: Liberty Fund.
Robertson, William. 1759. *History of Scotland, vol. 2*. Vol. 2 of *The works of William Robertson*. London: T. Cadell, 1840.
Robertson, William. 1777. *History of America, vol. 1*. Vol. 6 of *The works of William Robertson*. London: T. Cadell, 1840.
Ross, Ian Simpson. 1995. *The life of Adam Smith*. Oxford: Clarendon.
Schmidt, James. 2003. Inventing the Enlightenment: Anti-Jacobins, British Hegelians and the Oxford English dictionary. *Journal of the History of Ideas* 64:421–443.
Sherlock, Thomas. 1728. *The case of insolvent debtors, and the charity due to them, considered*. London: J. Pemberton.
Sherlock, Thomas. 1750. *A letter from the Lord Bishop of London, to the clergy and people of London and Westminster; on occasion of the late earthquakes*. London: John Whiston.
Shesgreen, Sean. 1976. Hogarth's Industry and idleness: A reading. *Eighteenth-Century Studies* 9:569–598.
Smith, Adam. 1976. In *An inquiry into the nature and causes of the wealth of nations*, ed. R. H. Campbell and A. S. Skinner. Oxford: Clarendon.
Steuart, James. 1767. *An inquiry into the principles of political economy*. Vol. 1. London: A. Millar and T. Cadell.
Thomas, R. P., and D. N. McCloskey. 1981. Overseas trade and empire 1700–1860. In *The economic history of Britain since 1700*, vol. 1: *1700–1860*, ed. Robert Floud and Donald McCloskey, 87–102. Cambridge: Cambridge University Press.
Trusler, John. [1781?] *Luxury no political evil. But demonstratively proved to be necessary to the preservation and prosperity of states*. London.

Tucker, Josiah. 1774. *Four tracts, together with two sermons, on political and commercial subjects*. Glocester.
Ure, Andrew. 1835. *The philosophy of manufactures: or, An exposition of the scientific, moral, and commercial economy of the factory system of Great Britain*. London: Charles Knight.
Waddell, Brodie. 2012. *God, duty, and community in English economic life, 1660–1720*. Woodbridge: The Boydell Press.
Waterman, A. M. C. 1991. *Revolution, economics and religion: Christian political economy, 1798–1833*. Cambridge: Cambridge University Press.
Wennerlind, Carl. 2011. *Casualties of credit: The English financial revolution, 1620–1720*. Cambridge, MA: Harvard University Press.
Wesley, John. 1778. *A serious address to the people of England, with regard to the state and the nation*. London.
Winch, Donald. 1978. *Adam Smith's politics: An essay in historiographic revision*. Cambridge: Cambridge University Press.
Winch, Donald. 1996. *Riches and poverty: An intellectual history of political economy in Britain 1750–1834*. Cambridge: Cambridge University Press.

CHAPTER 4

Consumption and Luxury

4.1 Consumption

If "industry" was a code word referring to all that was productive about economic activity, both individual and social, with "idleness" denoting a broad range of that which was not, another important word that made frequent appearances in different contexts of moral and economic discourse in the eighteenth century was "luxury." Unlike the terms investigated in the previous chapter, "industry" and "idleness," what precisely was to be denoted by the noun "luxury" or whether it was to be accepted as an inevitable or even salutary part of a commercial society was an issue which more often than not invited controversy rather than consensus. Its proneness to create contention, not surprisingly, has also captured the attention of scholars in our time, so that a venerable pile of literature on the debates about luxury has been accumulated (Sekora 1977, 23–129; McKendrick 1982, 14–20; Robertson 1983, 154–164; Raven 1992, 157–182; Berry 1994, 63–176; 2015, 158–172; Daunton 1995, 361–363; Winch 1996, 55–89; Berg and Eger 2003, 7–27). Our contribution can hope to do little more than add a few more details to this august edifice by opening the podium to authors who are not always remembered properly by intellectual historians.

"Luxury" was a topic that often divided rather than unified opinions among the published works, but one thing those who denounced or defended "luxury" could both accept was that it primarily concerned

H.-J. Yoon, *Moral Discourses of the Economy in Eighteenth-Century Britain*, https://doi.org/10.1007/978-981-95-0958-4_4

consumption, whereas "industry" referred primarily to production. Yet the sense and sensibility evoked by this very term "consumption" were in turn equally complex and ambivalent, particularly as it was understood during the first decades of the century. We first, therefore, have to delineate the contours of the meanings covered by "consumption" before moving on to look at those assigned to "luxury." In our current usage, "consumption" is firmly established as a foundational economic category, frequently coupled with "consumer." Both words carry mostly positive rather than negative connotations for us. An early precedent of this affirmative view of "consumption" can be found during the last decades of the seventeenth century, if not earlier. Nicholas Barbon arguably deserves to be credited as a leading author who set the pattern of using "consumption" in a purely economic context, freed from the noxious flavor attached to the word's physiological sense, which we shall shortly turn to. An author who made handsome money from London real-estate business, and described by one historian as an "archetype of the modern developer" (Inwood 1998, 256), Barbon confidently endorses the ability of the building industry to boost the economy. The term "consumption" plays a strategically indispensable role in this argument. Of the many reasons why "New Buildings are advantageous to the Country," the most important is the fact of their "taking off the Commodities of the Country" in the process. This colloquial expression, "taking off," is supplemented by a detailed elucidation:

> The Materials of these Houses, as Stones, Bricks, Lime, Iron, Lead, Timber, &c. are all the Commodities of the Country. And whatsoever the Inhabitants of these New Houses have occasion for, either for food, Apparel, or Furniture for their Houses, are at first the growth of the Country; And the bigger the Town grows, the greater is the occasion and consumption of these Commodities, and so the greater profit to the Country. (Barbon 1685, 23)

Construction of houses creates demand for building material, which is the first stage in the process of "taking off the Commodities of the Country." When the "New Houses" are finished and used as spaces of habitation, the business cycle moves forward to the second stage at which the "Inhabitants" purchase "food, Apparel, or Furniture." The "consumption" of these "Commodities" merits to be applauded, for it always incites the supply of the goods consumed, and thus occasions a "greater profit to the Country." The salutary effects of consumption, furthermore, transcended the jealous control of national borders. In *A Discourse of Trade* (1690), Barbon expressed his firm belief that unhampered international trade between England and its European neighbors will be beneficial for all. He flatly rejected the protectionist prejudice that English consumers of Continental goods will erode the productive potentials of native manufacture and agriculture:

> The common Argument for the Prohibiting Foreign Commodities, is, That the Bringing in, and Consuming such Foreign Wares, hinders the Making and Consuming the like sort of Goods of our own Native Make and Growth; therefore *Flanders*-Lace, *French* Hats, Gloves, Silks, *Westphalia*-Bacon, &*c.* are Prohibited, because it is supposed, they hinder the Consumption of *English*-Lace, Gloves, Hats, Silk, Bacon *&c.* But this is a mistaken Reason, and ariseth by not considering what it is that Occasions *Trade*. It is not Necessity that causeth the Consumption, Nature may be Satisfied with little; but it is the wants of the Mind, Fashion, and desire of Novelties, and Things scarce, that causeth *Trade*. (Barbon 1690, 72–73)

Apart from his openness toward England's foreign rivals, what makes this passage noteworthy is the author's elevation of "Consumption" to a realm of artificial needs created by society and the market, "the wants of the Mind, Fashion, and desire of Novelties, and Things scarce." Neither bound by "Necessity" nor dictated by "Nature," "the Bringing in" and "Consuming" of foreign goods ignite the "desire of Novelties" in the English consumers, which will have to be satisfied one way or another. The imported goods, besides, must be exchanged for native products, such as "Tobacco or Woollen-Cloth," and if these goods "Paid more Customs" and "Imployed more Hands in making," they can only add to the nation's wealth as a whole (Barbon 1690, 75–76). Consumption encourages and sustains "industry," to put the case in terms of the dichotomy discussed in the previous chapter, even in the domain of "idleness" patrolled by "Fashion." If so, to complain about the inordinate taste for luxury, particularly for foreign goods, is to complain about the very nature of a commercial society. Such was the argument implied in Barbon's apology for consumption.

In the list of advocates defending consumption, close to Barbon should be placed Bernard Mandeville, for whom all businesses were legitimate as long as they catered to what Barbon called the "wants of the Mind, Fashion, and desire of Novelties." Even the "worst of Women and most profligate of the Sex" have their share in keeping the economic engine rolling, for they "contribute to the Consumption of Superfluities, as well as the Necessaries of Life, and consequently were Beneficial to many peaceable Drudges, that work hard to maintain their Families, and have no worse design than an honest Livelihood" (Mandeville 1924, 1: 225). Consumption and production can never be separated, however dour one's moral outrage at the sleazy trade of the "most profligate" of women selling sexual service. The blessings scattered universally by this organic coupling of consumption with production, furthermore, make no discrimination between the "Consumption of Superfluities" and that of the "Necessaries of Life." To castigate certain types of goods and services as "Superfluities" and luxuries, therefore, is pointless and misleading. As we have seen in Chap. 2, Mandeville's arguments, so full of sound economic common sense when measured by our current standards, met with a fierce attack from various quarters in his time. Even so, Mandeville's assertions had a forceful appeal of being factual, if unpalatable. More "Customs" were indeed paid and more "Hands" were employed by ever-growing consumption of goods and services, both superfluous and necessary. The most articulate among the writers of the age could not but concede to the truth of Barbon's or Mandeville's thesis. The astute mind of David Hume, for instance, chose to cloak the benefits of consumption with the unimpeachable opposition between "industry" and "idleness," reconstructed by our sage as that between "labour" and "indolence":

> The encrease and consumption of all the commodities, which serve to the ornament and pleasure of life, are advantageous to society; because, at the same time that they multiply those innocent gratifications to individuals, they are a kind of *storehouse* of labour, which, in the exigencies of state, may be turned to the public service. In a nation, where there is no demand for such superfluities, men sink into indolence, lose all enjoyment of life, and are useless to the public, which cannot maintain or support its fleets and armies, from the industry of such slothful members. (Hume 1987, 272 ["Of Refinement in the Arts"])

Hume underscores the possibility of mobilizing the economic vitality stimulated by consumption for military purposes by the state, but more significant is the postulate upon which that state power stands, namely that consumption of "superfluities" offers an antidote to "indolence." Without a taste for the "ornament and pleasure of life," a society cannot hope to awaken its "slothful members." The adjective "innocent" inserted before "gratifications" seems to do little more than pay lip service to traditional moral prejudice toward "superfluities" or luxuries. If a nation is to be strong in war, it cannot afford to be too exacting about the morality of the people's "demand" for "superfluities." The important thing is to ensure a continuous transition from consumption to "industry" which will compel the "slothful" to grow diligent. By the same token, national debts, frequently lamented and denounced by moralists, can be beneficial. The system of national debts enables the "merchants" who invest in the state to possess a "species of money" which is "continually multiplying in their hands." This in turn empowers them to "trade upon less profit," as they can fall back on their dividends. The "small profit of the merchant," then, "renders the commodity cheaper" and, by doing so, "causes a greater consumption, quickens the labour of the common people, and helps to spread arts and industry throughout the whole society" (Hume 1987, 353 ["Of Public Credit"]). At the end of this virtuous chain of events stands, once again, "industry," which justifies all species of "consumption," whether "innocent" or not.

Writing after Hume, Adam Smith took a few steps further and conferred on consumption a natural parity with production. The "average produce of every sort of industry is always suited, more or less exactly, to the average consumption," asserts Smith in the first Book of *The Wealth of Nations* (Smith 1976a, 206 [I.xi.e.28]). In Book 4, Smith adopts this proposition as the ground for finding fault with the "mercantile system" (i.e., political and economic theories of protectionism):

> Consumption is the sole end and purpose of all production; and the interest of the producer ought to be attended to, only so far as it may be necessary for promoting that of the consumer. The maxim is so perfectly self-evident, that it would be absurd to attempt to prove it. But in the mercantile system, the interest of the consumer is almost constantly sacrificed to that of the producer; and it seems to consider production, and not consumption, as the ultimate end and object of all industry and commerce. (Smith 1976a, 660 [IV.viii.49])

Consumption is given a privileged role as the "sole end and purpose" of all production. In fact, Smith bestows on "consumption" the highest honor conceivable as the "ultimate end and object of all industry and commerce," and this without any further qualifying condition, such as the preference given to "innocent gratifications" by Hume. Moreover, the "consumer" emerges as a subject entitled to receive the respect due to this elevated post reserved for "consumption." The "consumer" in general is the endpoint of production, but some types of "consumer" can also be the initiator of production. Consumption, when matched with discretion, serves as a "*storehouse* of labour" that nourishes "industry" and banishes "idleness." "That portion of his revenue which a rich man annually spends," Smith believes, is "in most cases consumed by idle guests, and menial servants, who leave nothing behind them in return for their consumption." However, that "portion which he annually saves, as for the sake of the profit it is immediately employed as a capital, is consumed in the same manner, and nearly in the same time too, but by a different set of people." This "different set of people" are none other than the ranks and file manning the camp of "industry," the "labourers, manufacturers, and artificers," who, unlike those on the other side of the divide separating "industry" from "idleness," "re-produce with a profit the value of their annual consumption." When the "rich man," instead of dissipating the entirety of his revenue on the "idle guests" and the idle servants attending them, puts aside a "part of it" to invest it for profit, the "food, cloathing, and lodging, which may be purchased with it, are necessarily reserved" for those whom his investment will put to work. "The consumption is the same, but the consumers are different," concludes Smith (1976a, 338 [II. iii.18]). Consumption in itself is the "sole end and purpose of all production," but some consumption can be more beneficial than others, for it leads to a further and wider production, instead of destroying and wasting what is consumed. The contrastive juxtaposition of "industry" and "idleness" in this manner is revived in this emphatic vindication of consumption.

For Smith consumption is the destination of production, but as we have seen above, saving the "value" for future consumption "for the sake of profit" is more commendable than simple consumption. What my "idle guests" have eaten up and drunken off can never be recovered, whereas the part of my revenue, when it is re-invested, will be recovered with "profit," and this even after the laborers hired have consumed a good portion of it in the form of wages or of the raw material they are provided with during the working hours. Plausible as this analysis may sound, it is also true that such productive expenditure is not always what we mean by "consumption." Spending one's money on "idle guests" has the virtue of being far closer to the sense of "consumption" in the customary sense, even as it is branded by Smith with a stigma of destructiveness. This ambiguity can also be traced back to Mandeville, who is clearly Smith's major predecessor in this tradition of legitimizing consumption. As far as the "Consumption of things" is concerned, Mandeville writes, one will "find that the laziest and most unactive, the profligate and most mischievous are all forc'd to do something for the common good." They "continue to wear and otherwise destroy what the Industrious are daily employ'd about to make, fetch and procure" and thus "in spight of their Teeth" are all "oblig'd to help maintain the Poor and the publick Charges" (Mandeville 1924, 1: 86). This picture certainly supports Mandeville's main tenet of private vice ending up benefitting the public inadvertently, but the word "destroy" makes concession to the negative usage of the term as "Consumption of things." At least on one occasion, Mandeville the antimoralist succumbs to Mandeville the physician in admitting how the consumption of gin, however profitable it may be for those involved in its production and merchandise, can be quite detrimental to the consumer: "In hot and adust [i.e. dry] Tempers it makes Men Quarrelsome, renders 'em Brutes and Savages, sets 'em on to fight for nothing, and has often been the Cause of Murder. It has broke and destroy'd the strongest Constitutions, thrown 'em into Consumptions, and been the fatal and immediate occasion of Apoplexies, Phrensies and sudden Death" (Mandeville 1924, 1: 89). Mandeville the economic writer makes no distinctions between wholesome and unwholesome consumption, but Mandeville the medical doctor cannot ignore what objective science tells him about addiction to gin. To the physicians of the age, including Mandeville, "Consumptions" referred to a cluster of destructive diseases and their symptoms, frequently "fatal" to the point of inducing "Death," sudden or protracted.

A medical treatise widely read and consulted in Mandeville's time put the word "consumptions," in the plural form as in Mandeville's usage, on its title. Richard Morton's *Phthisiologia, or, A Treatise of Consumptions Wherein the Difference, Nature, Causes, Signs, and Cure of all Sorts of Consumptions Are Explained,* first published in 1694 in English (followed by a Latin edition), remained an enduring authority on the subject. Morton defines "Consumption" in general as "a wasting of the *Muscular* parts of the Body, arising from the Subtraction, or Colliquation of the Humours, and that either with, or without a Fever." It can be either "Original, or Symptomatical," and the representative type of consumption is that of lungs. A "Universal wasting of the Parts of the Body" can be caused by "some Distemper of the Lungs, as a stuffing, swellings, inflammation, and exulceration" (Morton 1694, 2–3). But wasting of lungs is by no means the only serious disease belonging to this family of "Consumptions." The first chapter of the book discusses a "Nervous Consumption," whose symptoms are a "decrease of the Patient's Strength, and a loss of Appetite, without any remarkable Fever, Cough, or shortness of Breath." A patient stricken with this type of "Consumption" affecting the "System of the Nerves" loses his or her taste for food. The patient has to forgo, as it were, "consumption" (in the economic sense) of delicacies offered by the market, and often the person has no one else to blame but himself or herself. This species of "Consumption" Morton suspects is often caused by "intemperate drinking of Spiritous Liquors and unwholsom Air," both of which London abounds with and due to which cause "the Tone of the Nerves, and the Temper of the Spirits are destroy'd" (Morton 1694, 5). It is a disease endemic to London, then, a town renowned for its ample supply of strong drinks and dirty air. Morton illustrates his theories with case studies which he calls "History." Supported by a series of numbered "History," Morton distributes various types of "Consumption" into different categories, many of which have direct or indirect connection to the consuming of goods and services in an immoderate or illicit fashion. The cause for the "Consumption from a Gonorrhoea and the Whites," for instance, can only be a sexual contact with a partner who has a venereal disease. For these individuals, typically males, afflicted by "Gonorrhoea," the delights of their erotic escapade often "terminate in a Consumption of the Lungs." Apparently less improper, "Consumption" attended by "Diabetes, or too great a Flux of Urine," results from unhealthy eating habits of leisurely consumers of both genders (Morton 1694, 19, 42). In all these cases, most of them earmarked for death, the disease makes an "insensible Progress" until it evinces itself in "direful Symptoms." When an autopsy was conducted on one of the author's female victims, a well-to-do gentlewoman, the "whole Substance" of the organs turned out to have been "by degrees corrupted and consumed" (Morton 1694, 218, 357, 360). When one conjures up such lurid and macabre picture painted by Doctor Morton of "Consumption" wreaking havoc on the human organism belonging to persons given to consuming delicacies, it will not be easy to use the same word to refer to that blithe economic action of those spending money to suit their fancy, who were extolled by Barbon, a contemporary of Morton, and defended by

Mandeville, whose bread-earning job was to treat rich clients suffering from "Nervous" diseases.

The correlation between economic consumption and "consumption" as a type of illness was clearly perceived and ascertained by a work that came out in 1733, *The English Malady: or, a Treatise of Nervous Diseases of All Kinds, as Spleen, Vapours Loweness of Spirits, Hypochondriacal, and Hysterical Distempers &c.* Reflecting the soaring status of Bath as a fashionable spot of conspicuous consumption and expensive medical treatment, the work was published both for "G. Strahan in Cornhill," London, and for "J. Leake at Bath" (Cheyne 1733, title page). The author was a well-known physician named George Cheyne, whose approach combined both deduction and induction. The "*Human Machin*," as designed by the "the Infinitely-wise Author of Nature," consists of "an infinite Number and Variety of different Channels and Pipes, filled with various and different Liquors and Fluids." This complex structure can be likened to a musical instrument played by the "Intelligent Principle, or *Soul*," which "resides somewhere in the Brain, where all the Nerves, or Instruments of Sensation terminate" (Cheyne 1733, 1, 62). The "*Intellectual* or *Spiritual* Operations" control and affect the physical functions of the "*Organs* of its Machin," just as a "skilful *Musician* playing on a well-tun'd Instrument" would do so. "So long as the Instrument is in due Order, so long is the Music perfect and compleat in its Kind," the author remarks. "As it weakens or breaks, the *Harmony* is spoil'd or stop'd," follows the corollary. When that happens, certain "Parts of this Instrument being more delicate than others," they are "sooner disorder'd or broken" (Cheyne 1733, 68–69). What then spoils the fine-tuned harmony of the instrument? It is none other than consumption of goods in the economic sense, an excessive and inordinate indulgence in expensive food. When this luxury of the palate is coupled with a habit of idleness, the consequences never fail to be devastating for the body. Contrary to what some "Free-drinking, or Free-thinking Physician" advocate, "Health, Cheerfulness, and long Life" should be preferred to a "short Life and a merry" (Cheyne 1733, viii–ix). From his professional experience, the author of this book came to be convinced that what was "intended by the Author of Nature for this *Climate* and *Country*" is "the *Diet* and *Manner of Living* of the middling Rank, who are but moderate and temperate in Foods of the common and natural Product of the Country." Their moderate meals reward them with a greater likelihood of "*prolonging Life*, and *preventing Distempers*" (Cheyne 1733, iv–v) than what one can expect from the "Tables of the rich and

Great (and indeed of all Ranks who can afford it)" which are "furnish'd with Provisions of Delicacy, Number, and Plenty, sufficient to provoke, and even gorge, the most large and voluptuous Appetite" (Cheyne 1733, 49–50). Cheyne does not hesitate a moment to identify the chief cause of the "English Malady." You fall sick largely owing to your insatiable desire for consumption:

> When I behold, with Pity, Compassion, and Sorrow, such *Scenes* of Misery and Woe, and see them happen only to the *Rich*, the *Lazy*, the *Luxurious*, and the *Unactive*, those who fare daintily and live voluptuously, those who are furnished with the rarest Delicacies, the richest Foods, and the most generous Wines, such as can provoke the Appetites, Senses and Passions in the most exquisite and voluptuous Manner: to those who leave no Desire or Degree of Appetite unsatisfied, and not to the *Poor*, the *Low*, the *meaner Sort*, those destitute of the Necessaries, Conveniencies, and Pleasures of Life, to the Frugal, Industrious, the Temperate, the Laborious, and the Active … *I must* … conclude, that it must be something received into the Body, that can produce such terrible Appearances in it, some flagrant and notable, Difference in the *Food*, that so sensibly distinguishes them from these latter. And that it is the miserable *Man* himself that creates his Miseries, and begets his Torture, or, at least, those from whom he has derived his bodily *Organs*. (Cheyne 1733, 28–29)

Woe to those who are rich and profligate. No matter how sound and healthy a child you may have been at youth, "rioting and wallowing in Luxury for some considerable Time" cannot fail to take toll on your "Fibres, Nerves, and Motive Organs." In due course, that luxurious lifestyle will "fill the Blood and Juices with an Excess of such oily, sulphureous, and inflammatory Particles, as are most readily turn'd into red Globules, which make the fibrous Part of the Blood" from which "inflammatory and acute Diseases are produc'd, with all the Varieties and Degress of their Symptoms" (Cheyne 1733, 32). All these symptoms drag their victim to the inevitable destination: consumption. The laws of "Animal *Œconomy*" are inexorable (Cheyne 1733, 51). It enacts that "all those whose Constitutions are spoiled, who have bad or corrupted Juices, violent and dangerous *Symptoms*, [and] great *Obstructions*" be subjected to the "great and eminent Degrees of these Disorders," in other words to be "threaten'd with *Hectic* or *Consumption*," which is nothing else than a "Destruction of some of the great *Viscera*." At this stage, "all the other Methods and Medicines that could be suggested" may be prescribed but all "without Success" (Cheyne 1733, 162–163). But this mortal specter of "Consumption" is shrouded by the glitter of consumption that blinds the consumers. In a chapter addressing the "Frequency of Nervous Disorders in later Years, beyond what they have been observed in former Times," Cheyne dilates on the political as well as the animal "*Œconomy.*" "Since your Wealth has increas'd, and our Navigation has been extended," he reproaches his fellow countrymen, "we have ransack'd all the Parts of the *Globe* to bring together its whole Stock of Materials for *Riot*, *Luxury*, and to provoke *Excess*." A globalized economy may be good for the traders involved, but it is ultimately lethal to those who consume what they sell. "Is it any Wonder then, that the Diseases which proceed from *Idleness* and *Fulness* of Bread, should increase in Proportion, and keep equal Pace with those Improvements of the Matter and Cause of Diseases?" asks our judicious doctor (Cheyne 1733, 52). The answer may be obvious, but the cure is by no means so. For the "Stock of Materials" for "Riot" and "Luxury" will never be exhausted, and the taste for the "richest Foods, and the most generous Wines" cannot be quelled in a free commercial society driven by consumption.

Even as "consumption," as we have seen, was gradually becoming a reputable term in the domain of "trade," the dreadful aura emanating from the physiological sense of the term persisted for quite some time in the century. If claiming, as does Margaret Schabas, that "until the late Enlightenment, the natural and the economic realms were one and the same" (Schabas 2005, 5) could be an exaggeration, there certainly was a fluid connection between the two at least in the case of "consumption." Johnson's *Dictionary* hesitates not to leave "consumption" fixed firmly with this negative connotation. The first sense of the noun is the "act of consuming; waste; destruction," even as the sample sentence taken from Locke—"In commodities, the value rises as its quantity is less and vent greater; which depends upon its being preferred in its *consumption*"—patently describes economic consumption. The second definition, "The State of wasting or perishing," is even more menacing, while the third and the last offers the most detailed definition among them. The word signifies a "waste of muscular flesh … frequently attended with a hectick fever, and is divided by physicians into several kinds, according to the variety of its causes" (Johnson 1773, s.v. "Consumption"). Ephraim Chambers' *Cyclopædia* (1741, fourth edition) assigns an article under the head word "consumption" understood as a medical category. The article defines "consumption" as "a disease arising from a defect of nourishment; or, a preternatural decay of the body, by a gradual waste of muscular flesh," the cause of which can be "*accidental, natural*, or *hereditary*." "Accidental consumptions may arise," we are further told, from physical disorders such as "ulcers, chalky stones or polypus's in the lungs." But "moral" disorders also play a significant role. The article lists "intemperance," "venereal disorders," "excess of venery," "grief," and "hard study" among the typical causes of "consumption" (Chambers 1741, s.v. "Consumption"). Other articles in *Cyclopædia* do accommodate the new sense of the word used as an economic category, such as the one on "Cavear." The English import "considerable quantities" of this "commodity" from Russia "not so much for home consumption, as to supply the French and Italians" (Chambers 1741, s.v. "Cavear"). Yet the predominant sense of the word in this ambitious publication whose title claims to be a "Universal Dictionary of Arts and Sciences" did not waver too far from the medical sense of the term signifying destructive diseases. William Robertson's *History of America* was published in 1777 just one year after Smith's *The Wealth of Nations*. Smith, as we have seen, honored "consumption" and "consumer" in many parts of his book. Robertson also speaks of "consumption," but does so, interestingly, in referring not to an expenditure of goods by individuals but to a destruction of a whole race of people. After Christopher Columbus was sent back to Spain, his successor Francisco de Bobadilla appeased the avarice and lust for power of the "dissolute and corrupted members" of the colonial society by giving them "such uncontrolled licence, as encouraged the wildest excesses." The Spaniards in the Americas being "too rapacious and impatient to try any method of acquiring wealth but that of searching for gold" drove the natives "in crowds to the mountains, and compelled to work in the mines by masters, who imposed their tasks without mercy or discretion." The result was catastrophic. "Labour so disproportioned to their strength and former habits of life," Robertson diagnoses, "wasted that feeble race of men with such rapid consumption, as must have soon terminated in the utter extinction of the ancient inhabitants of the country" (Robertson 1777a, 153–154). Even as the notorious "rage" and "cruelty of the Spaniards" did play their role in destroying the inhabitants of Mexico and Peru, the "inconsiderable policy with which they established their new settlements" proved to be far more lethal. Whereas the former were "temporary calamities, fatal to individuals," the latter was a "permanent evil, which, with gradual consumption, wasted the nation" (Robertson 1777b, 329–330). Robertson the historian is someone who never hastened to pass judgments or make philosophical generalizations, as have been noted by scholars (Smitten 1985, 75–76; Pocock 2005, 181–204). Yet his choice of the term "consumption" cannot be overlooked, even though consumption of goods and services in the refined society of enlightened Britain surely would ring a bell different in tone from the funeral knell of the Spaniards' genocide of Native Americans. As Robertson's expressions testify, "consumption" did not neatly shed its destructive connotations even in the 1770s, particularly in the various aspersions on "luxury" to be examined in the following section.

4.2 Luxury, the "Last of All Vices"

Luxury destroyed an individual's bodily health, Doctor Cheyne warned. It could also debilitate the body politic, above all, by eroding its military strength. *The Origin of the Distinction of Ranks* (1733) by John Millar presents this as a universal tendency. "The improvements of arts and manufactures," Millar writes in the present tense, "by introducing luxury, contributes yet more to enervate the minds of men, who, according as they enjoy more ease and pleasure at home, feel greater aversion to the hardships and dangers of a military life" (Millar 2006, 230). If any proof was needed of luxury inevitably pulling a nation toward a path of decay, one could readily point to the history of the Roman Empire. The representative historians of the age, even as they wrote in the latter part of the century when a purely moral discomfort with luxury was somewhat waning, still held on to this widespread view about what caused the demise of the Western Roman Empire. The second volume of Edward Gibbon's *The History of the Decline and Fall of the Roman Empire* (1781) enforced this judgment with a fair degree of regularity. Of the many unlikely and unseemly potentates of late Rome, Carinus, the elder son of Carus, fell prey to the "luxury of the capital" Rome, and his former "personal courage" evinced in the "Gallic war" quickly dissipated itself. He was "devoted to pleasure" but was "destitute of taste," being "soft, yet cruel" (Gibbon 1781, 83). Diocletian, when placed on the imperial throne, pampered his vanity and aspired to the "vain superiority of pomp and luxury" sustained by "increase of taxes" and attended by "oppression of the people" (Gibbon 1781, 140). Maxentius, who contended with Constantine for the ultimate power over the whole Empire, was ill-suited to be the latter's rival, for he "passed his indolent life" in Rome, whose "elegant luxury" he craved and sought to enjoy as long as he could. His soldiers, following their master's example, were "enervated by indulgence and luxury," above all, by "baths and theatres of Rome." Not surprisingly, when Constantine's "hardy legions of Gaul" approached Rome, Maxentius' army could put up only a feeble resistance at the fatal battle of Milvian Bridge (Gibbon 1781, 181, 183).[1] Unlike Gibbon, Robertson's primary focus was not on ancient Rome but on the Holy Roman Empire and its head Charles V, but the long pre-history of Charles V's sixteenth century appended to the first volume of *The History of the Reign of the Emperor Charles V* (1769a) under the heading of "A View of the Progress of Society in Europe" starts from the last stage of the Roman Empire. The changes that led the martial and virtuous Rome to fall into a trajectory of decline were triggered to a large extent by the "taste for the luxuries of the East," which "increased to such a pitch in the imperial court, that great sums were carried into India, from which, in the channel of commerce, money never returns." The lethal formula of luxury leading to a state's decay was also detected by Robertson as functioning in other empires in other times, such as that of the Moors in the Iberian Peninsula. The victorious Moors of Al-Andalus fell victim to their own success, as the "arts which they cultivated, together with the luxury to which these gave rise, relaxed, in some measure, the force of their military institutions, and abated the vigour of their warlike spirit" (Robertson 1769a, 7, 135). On the eve of the Protestant Reformation, the German princes of the Holy Roman Empire, ensnared by the ecclesiastical ambitions of the papacy, "drained their wealth to supply the luxury of a foreign court" in Rome. Luther's Reformation may have cut the noose that bound some German princes to the lavish Pope, but it almost simultaneously saw itself implicated in the German Peasants' War, whose cause, in Robertson's judgment, has a good deal to do with the inordinate "luxury" of the rulers. With the "progress of elegance and luxury, as well as the changes introduced into the art of war," came a sharp "increase in the expense of government," which the princes met by increasing the duties "upon beer, wine, and other necessaries of life." This naturally

[1] In Volume 1, published in 1776, Gibbon had admitted that "luxury," though "severely arraigned by the moralists of every age," plays a positive role "in the present imperfect condition of society," as it did in Rome during the wholesome era under the Antonines, and even alleged that luxury "seems to be the only means that can correct the unequal distribution of property" (Gibbon 1776, 54). This statement has received more attention than it deserves, for what "luxury" does to exacerbate the "decline and fall" of the Roman empire ought to be more significant, given the title of his work. For discussions of Gibbon's attitude toward luxury, see Sekora (1977, 103); Winch (1996, 65–66); Pocock (2003, 437–438).

"affected the common people in the most sensible manner" (Robertson 1769b, 46, 185). In the history of his own country Scotland, Robertson also detected the nefarious influence of "luxury" on her rulers, which would further exacerbate the distress of those placed below them. When their monarch James VI moved from Edinburgh to Westminster to be crowned as James I of England, the Scottish nobles had no choice but to travel to England to attend him at his English court. The cost of their journey south already put an extra strain on their meager finances, but when they made "attempts to imitate the manners and luxury of their more wealthy neighbours" south of the border, they had to multiply "exactions upon the people." As a result, Scotland's commoners and peasants, "subjected at once to the absolute will of a monarch, and to the oppressive jurisdiction of an aristocracy," had to suffer "all the miseries peculiar to both these forms of government" (Robertson 1759, 244–245).

The "manners and luxury" of the English courtiers, which the Scottish lords aspired to emulate with such dire consequences for the people of Scotland, were officially at least something the medieval statutes of the realm had intended to curtail, albeit without much success. William Blackstone traces the fate of the medieval "sumptuary laws against luxury" under the reign of James I, who himself was eager to relish all the gallant pleasures the English court had to offer. A number of penal laws restraining excess in apparel were duly repealed by 1 Jac. 1. c.25. But one law survived that reformation: an ancient statue, 10 Edw. III. st. 3., which commanded "that no man shall be served, at dinner or supper, with more than two courses; except upon some great holydays there specified, in which he may be served with three." It remained unrepealed most probably since few people cared to remember or honor it (Blackstone 1770, 171). Was the British nation, by becoming increasingly tolerant toward luxuries, courting the danger of falling into the Roman trap of decline and fall? The well-educated author of *The Spectator*, Joseph Addison, would have no qualms about acknowledging the general truth about luxury following military conquests and eroding the strength of the conquering forces. Upon the authority of the "most Elegant and correct of all the *Latin* Historians," he asserts that when a "Government flourishes in Conquests, and is secure from foreign Attacks, it naturally falls into all the Pleasures of Luxury." Since "these Pleasures are very expensive," those "addicted" to them are easily persuaded to raise "fresh Supplies of Mony, by all the Methods of Rapaciousness and Corruption." As a result, "Avarice and Luxury very often become one complicated Principle of Action, in those whose Hearts are wholly set upon Ease, Magnificence, and Pleasure" (Addison 1711, no. 55 [3 May]). Addison is less willing to admit that the same universal maxim can also be applied to his own country, for he celebrates in another essay the benefits of international "Traffick" or trade, which easily exceeds the narrow boundary of frugal necessities: "Our Tables are stored with Spices, and Oils, and Wines," marvels the author. "Our Rooms are filled with Pyramids of *China*, and adorned with the Workmanship of *Japan*: Our Morning's Draught comes to us from the remotest Corners of the Earth: We repair our Bodies by the Drugs of *America*, and repose ourselves under *Indian* Canopies." His "Friend Sir Andrew" calls the "Vineyards of *France* our Gardens; the Spice-Islands our Hot-beds; the *Persians* our Silk-Weavers, and the *Chinese* our Potters." "Mr. Spectator" finds no reason to contradict his friend "Sir Andrew," for "Nature indeed furnishes us with the bare Necessaries of Life," but one cannot do without "Traffick," since it "gives us greater Variety of what is Useful, and at the same time supplies us with every thing that is Convenient and Ornamental" (Addison 1711, no. 69 [19 May]).[2]

"Mr. Spectator," in admiring the benefits of "Traffick," cares not to be too exacting in separating the consumption of what is "Convenient" from what is "Ornamental," as both "Mr. Spectator" and his friend "Sir Andrew" disdain the realm of "bare Necessaries of Life" provided by mere "Nature." Other gentlemen besides "Mr. Spectator" also noted their society was evincing a greater openness toward secular and hedonistic attitudes, among whom one could easily find those who held a view distinctly opposed to Addison's cheerful acceptance of commercial cornucopia, particularly when we go back to the last decade of the previous century. *The Friendly Monitor, Laying Open the Crying Sins of Cursing, Swearing, Drinking, Gaming, Detraction, and Luxury or Immodesty* (1692) included "Luxury" among the foes it proposed to wage war against. "Luxury" aligns itself with the "Sin of Immodesty," which is the most "Dangerous and Universal" of "all Vices," for together they "block up all the Avenues and Passes, and so bring them to distress, without exposing the Besiegers to that hazard, which a nearer approach would necessarily oblige them to." As they assault "all the *Senses*," one should "secure those" senses so that "this Evil must be weaken'd by degrees, and will infallibly fall of it self" (Anon. 1692, 65–67). A more concerted engagement with the same

[2] This catalogue of domestic luxuries does not seem to display in our view a particular bias against women, which E. J. Clery associates "Mr. Spectator" with (Clery 2004, 23–24, 44–45).

enemy was offered by George Mackenzie's *The Moral History of Frugality, with Its Opposite Vices, Covetousness, Niggardliness, and Prodigality, Luxury* (1691). Like "Mr. Spectator," he adduces the historical example of the "Roman Luxury" that had "debauched" its empire (Mackenzie 1691, 6), but his analysis is more geared than Addison's toward surveying the "moral" dimension of Roman history underlying its political vicissitude:

> Luxury was the last of all Vices that prevailed over Mankind, for after Riches had been hoarded up, they rooted as it were unto Luxury, and after that Tyranny and Ambition had robbed many poor Innocents, Luxury more cruel than they, was made use of by Providence, to revenge their quarrel: and so triumphed over the Conquerors. Thus when Rome had by Wit, and Courage subdued the World, it was drowned in that inundation of Riches, which these brought upon it. (Mackenzie 1691, 26)

Luxury is the final victor, a double-edged weapon that destroys one who wields it. "Providence" works through "Vices" that enslave "Mankind," in such a way as to make the "last" of them seduce the Roman conquerors to be "drowned" in their "Riches" they idolize. In his own time and society, the subtle mischief of the wily "Luxury" works itself through other adjacent "Vices," such as "Avarice" turning humans away from the "Principles of Religion, Reason and Honour," so as to enrapture them by the "Charms ... and the Ease" which "Riches" promises. Together they "now unreasonably tyrannize over the World," tempting the moderns to be "wicked" in order to "satisfie their Imaginary fantastick Necessities," all the while persuading themselves and others that "we must prefer our selves to our friends, and that Necessity is exempted from Law" (Mackenzie 1691, 1–2).[3] Luxury is no mere excess in one's economic consumption. It becomes an amoral code of conduct which bids a "Man" to prefer "himself to all others, robbing and cheating them by all arts and devices, to get thereby superfluities, to feed himself and his Lusts" (Mackenzie 1691, 27). In refutation of Mackenzie's indictment of the moral corrosion luxury leaves behind, one may argue that "superfluities" and "Charms," when desired and procured at least without "robbing and cheating," help the nation's "Riches" to increase and that the "inundation

[3] Addison, while linking the same pair of vices noted by Mackenzie, puts, by contrast, "*Avarice*" and "*Luxury*" at opposite camps as "two very powerful Tyrants engaged in a perpetual War against each other" seeking to establish a "Universal Monarchy over the Hearts of Mankind" (Addison 1711, no. 55 [3 May]).

of Riches" which engulfed ancient Rome need not repeat itself in modern Britain. This apologetic stance was assaulted in the same decade by John Bellers, who pointed out how consumption of "superfluities," while it may benefit those who sell them, can never advance the welfare of the nation as a whole. "Traders may grow Rich, whilst a Nation grows Poor through Extravagancy," Bellers contends, "for when the Dealers may get 20 Thousand Pound by Claret, the Nation pays and spends 100 Thousand Pound for it, and no Body grows Rich by Drinking it, whatever the Seller doth." As far as he sees it, "nothing can be strictly said to inrich a Nation, but what increaseth its People, and with them, Supplies it with things [that] are lasting and necessary, more than they Spend." Your favorite bottle of Bordeaux never qualifies to join the group of "lasting and necessary" goods. Nor can it ever contribute to an increase in native population. On the contrary, as the English "Manufactures" and "Food" must be shipped to France to "supply the Pride and Luxury" of some Englishmen, it can only serve to "Depopulate our Country" (Bellers 1699, 10–12).

The combined moral and economic arraignment of luxury during the last decade of the previous century did not fall silent in the eighteenth century proper, even as Britain marched onward to encourage the nation's adoration of the "Charms" of "fantastick Necessities." John Dennis' rebuttal of his contemporary Mandeville, as we have seen in Chap. 2, predictably included a diagnosis of the deleterious effects of luxury. Luxury "weakens Mens Bodies, stupefies their Minds, consumes their Substance, and wastes their Time, and keeps even those in a State of Indolence and Inactivity, who are by Nature Diligent and Industrious." Notably the medical sense of consumption, that it "consumes their Substance," joins the symptoms of luxury's harms, entering the realm of economic behavior and forming alliance with the established diatribe against "Indolence" or idleness. When it permeates the entire society, luxury contaminates the national economy, since an "excessive National Luxury is sure to end at last in Slavery" ensuing from the "Diminution, if not the Ruin of Trade" (Dennis 1724, 74–75). Numbed by the pleasures of luxury, they will cease to be industrious, goes the argument. The logical leap from "excessive" consumption to "Slavery" sounds fortuitous indeed, but the rhetorical effect retains its potency thanks in part to the charge of "idleness" implied in it. A generation or so later, Thomas Cole, whom we also have met in Chap. 2, inveighed against what by then seemed an almost universal triumph of luxury over all its opponents. Cole, the author of *On Luxury, Infidelity, and Enthusiasm* (1761), was an "Assistant Preacher at St. Paul's

Covent-Garden," according to the title page. His church happening to be located in Covent Garden, the epicenter of a metropolis that was fast becoming one massive emporium of luxury goods (McKendrick 1982, 21; Daunton 1995, 138–139), Reverend Cole could not avoid observing how the "ruling manners of the age" were being entirely subjected to excessive pleasure:

> An ostentatious extravagance is continually displaying itself in every part of this voluptuous city, and amongst all ranks and conditions of men. An emulous endeavour to outvie each other in all the elegant accommodations of life, seems to be, not only the ruling principle of a few, but the main ambition of a vast majority; the characteristic, and almost universal passion of the age. There is scarce any one, but seems to be ashamed, as it were, of living within the compass of his own proper sphere, be it either great or small. (Cole 1761, 10–11)

As the injunction to pursue and emulate "ostentatious extravagance" is obeyed with such universal subservience, "pleasure," in Cole's diagnosis, has not only "become a business itself, but the parent also of an infinite variety of other occupations," so much so that the "commerce of vanity and intemperance" appears to have become the "principal traffick of the nation," and "vice and folly" to be the pillars of the kingdom's economy (Cole 1761, 14–15). Mandeville's paradox, arduously refuted by Dennis, in other words, has been materialized into vivid reality in Cole's London, with lurid impunity, to boot. Within the package of ills attending the "national love of pleasure" (Cole 1761, 45) lurks criminality. If you aim to satisfy your taste for "vanity and intemperance," you need to spend money. In their "emulous endeavour to outvie each other," the worshippers of "luxury" always find money to be in short supply. "As their love of pleasure will necessarily keep them poor," their relative "poverty" will "hardly suffer them to be honest" (Cole 1761, 47). Those at the lower echelons of the social ladder resort to petty crimes of larceny and robbery. Among those at the highest, the "deep-mortgaged, though richly pensioned, statesman," is "obliged, in order to relieve his still superior distresses, to betake himself to some grander expedient of iniquity," which can be "nothing less than the plunder of the publick" (Cole 1761, 48–49). From the top to the bottom, the nation resorts to illicit means to sustain its extravagant consumption. All the classes and members of British society, in Cole's view, have "already far advanced in the same destructive road of luxury" (Cole 1761, 51).

Whether due to luxury or avarice, or a fatal mixture of both, the corruption of high-ranking public officials was considered to be a major issue of public morality, as we shall see in our next chapter. In the meantime, the censure against the "vast majority" of the middling and lower sorts rushing forth to "outvie each other in all the elegant accommodations of life" deserves to be heeded a little more. In the allegorical denunciations of "Luxury" (often capitalized) as a most formidable vice, specific areas of this emulation for luxury would often be identified and itemized. Above all, women's apparels were frequently targeted as an indubitable sign of luxury. *Of Luxury, More Particularly with Respect to Apparel* (1736), whose author signed himself as a "Country Clergyman" on the title page, combines two "*Discourses*" or sermons based on the New Testament text, 1 Timothy 2:9. The Scripture commands women to "adorn themselves in modest apparel, with shamefacedness and sobriety; not with broidered hair, or gold, or pearls, or costly array" (Authorized [King James] Version). This counsel is blithely spurned by the British ladies of the time, dreading the strictures of "*Fashions*" rather than of the Bible. "But who, or what, I pray, are they, who *gives us* our *Fashions*?" asks our Country Clergyman. The culprits are none other than the French, a "*Nation* remarkable for *Vanity*; and a *Levity*, almost beneath the *Dignity* of *Human Nature*," and who "excel us in *Nothing*, save *Finenesse*, as they term it; which, *in plain English*, is neither *more*, nor *less*, than *Trick* and *Falsehood*" (Anon. 1736, 10). The author is prepared to leave alone "*Persons* of *Quality* and *great Fortune*, who were *born to Estates*" to spend their wealth on what pleases them, but "*Rich* and *costly Array*, especially if it be *above* the *Condition* of those who wear it," contaminates the morals of those who do, for it is "apt to *disorder the Head*, and to *fill the Mind* with *vain* and *idle Conceits*." Even more unseemly are those upstarts "who were formerly *cloathed* in *Rags*, or what was very *mean*, thro' some *lucky Accident*, as inheriting the *Industry*, or perhaps the *Iniquity*, of some remote Relation, do *arrive to great Wealth*." When they stroll the streets "cloathed in *gorgeous Apparel*, they *know* neither *themselves*, nor *any one else*," as they consider themselves "quite another *sort of Creatures*, from what they were before." Not only that, but after first making an "*Idol* of themselves," they fancy they are "*adored* by others; by every one, at least, that is not so *richly attired* as themselves" (Anon. 1736, 21–22). This view is shared by a later treatise written by Samuel Fawconer, *An Essay on Modern Luxury* (1765), for whom modern dress, "in all its variety of excess, and profusion of expence, is another striking instance of the luxury of the present times" (Fawconer 1765, 13). This is nothing less than a virtual slavery:

> How is the whole scope of our fancy continually on the stretch, in designing and contriving this drapery of the species! How do we travel from east to west, and ransack the several elements for materials to decorate these our corruptible bodies! To please a vitiated imagination of our own, or attract the eyes of the beholders, and provoke their envy, how content are we to forego our own ease!. ... This is the reigning taste: and what will not the slave to mode do, or suffer, in order to comply with it! (Fawconer 1765, 16)

Enthralled by this desperate need to "attract the eyes of the beholders, and provoke their envy," "we" British have no inclination to be alert to the nefarious effects of luxury, which "impairs the faculties of the soul, clouds the understanding, renders the will listless and inactive, stupefies the judgment, blunts the edge of our spirits" (Fawconer 1765, 33). At this pass, "the noblest virtues" lie "dormant and neglected, in the attentive pursuits of pleasure," and "we" can have "neither the power, nor inclination, to improve ourselves in those moral attainments, which are the only valuable ornament of the rational nature" (Fawconer 1765, 30).

Eating, drinking, and smoking was another area where luxury waged a successful campaign of conquest among the commoners. With the proliferation of retail shops, which numbered by 1759 a total of 141,700 in England and Wales, the middling sorts of the kingdom had a wide choice of goods offered by their local shops, many of which came from overseas, such as the different types of sugar, pepper, and cinnamon listed in the inventory of Henry Hancock, a Sheffield grocer (Brewer 1989, 184). The tastes of plebians were changing, very much to the dismay of those attached to traditional values. No plain fare will do to satisfy the expectations of the host or the guest, for "such is the expensive Humour of the Times," in Erasmus Jones' observation, that there is "not a Family, no hardly of the meanest Tradesmen, but treat their Friends with *Wine* and *Punch* and other *Exotic* Liquors." "Their *Tables*" are so far "advanc'd in their Proportion of Expence to other Things" that they have become "now the Emblems, not of Plenty, but Luxury, not of good Housekeeping, but Profusion, and that of the highest kind of Extravagancies." This pervasive gluttony even trickles down to the very beggars, at least those in London, who "eat more white Bread than the whole Kingdom of

Scotland" (Jones [1736?], 9–10). The social anatomy of our "Country Clergyman" concurs with this account, except that he puts more emphasis on the manner of cooking than on the foodstuff itself. To appease the "*Wantonness of Appetite*," the English "fetch Persons from every Quarter" of Europe to "*beat* and *slice*, to *mince* and *mangle*, to *confound* and *adulterate* with *unnatural Mixtures*, our *well-fed*, and *well-tasted*, Provisions, before we can eat them." The "*Foreign Cooks*" have been bred in their native soil to acquire the expertise in this type of cooking devised to "*disfigure* and *disguise* their Dishes," their countries being chronically in "want of that *Plenty*" which the English enjoy. "But is it not *ridiculous*," the author asks, "that our *Plenty* should ape their *Penury*; and that we should do, *out of Choice*, what they are obliged to, *out of Necessity*?" (Anon. 1736, 34–36). Fawconer also notes the fact that in the "convivial entertainments" of the common people they scruple not "to explore the treasures of sea and land, and traverse every quarter of the globe, in quest of new dainties to regale a luxurious palate" (Fawconer 1765, 12).[4] Cooked meal, however "unnatural," at least nourishes the body. Tobacco, on the other hand, has no such alimentary property. Yet, as Thomas Alcock rebukes, even those who are starving "lay out almost as much in Tobacco, as in Bread, and declare, they can as ill go without the first as the last" (Alcock 1752, 45). Alcock wrote in the 1750s, but already *Of Luxury, More Particularly with Respect to Apparel* lists consumption of tobacco as a formidable "Piece of *Luxury*" in the 1730s "which almost universally prevails among us." The "*meaner* Sort," in particular, are so much addicted to the "*taking of Snuff* in immoderate Quantities" as to render them "*incapable* of *Service*, and almost *useless* to *themselves* and *others*." Adorers of tobacco include the adorable ladies, as well, which confounds all common sense. Our author cannot possibly understand what is there "so *bewitching* in this *various-scented* Dust," that "for the sake of it, so many of the *fair Sex* … should be content to part, not only with their *Health*, but their *Beauty* too" (Anon. 1736, 37).

The concern of the writers quoted above about tobacco was by no means unfounded. The percentage tobacco occupied in the imports of grocery was only 8.9% in 1559. It rose to 16.9% in 1700, and then further on to 27.6% in 1750, to peak at 35.8% in 1772, after which it declined

[4] The other signs of luxury Fawconer observes include the "immoderate display of splendour and expence … in our domestic structures," the "splendour of our equipages," and the "largeness of our retinue" (Fawconer 1765, 20–21).

slightly to 28.9% in 1790 (Shammas 1993, 179). This vast amount of tobacco was avidly consumed by the British, regardless of the warnings given by Alcock and other pundits. Tobacco was one of the potent weapons used by the vice of "luxury" to dismantle both moral probity and physical health, but once again it proved the truth of Mandeville's proposition. The consumption of tobacco contributed to trade. Should it then be exonerated? Some may have thought so, but the luxury goods in question did not receive a unanimous ratification by those writing with a practical knowledge of international trade. *The British Merchant: A Collection of Papers Relating to the Trade and Commerce of Great Britain and Ireland*, written by the "*most eminent Merchants of the City of London*" (1743), begins its first volume with the "General MAXIMS in Trade, particularly applied to the COMMERCE between *Great Britain* and *France*." Of the nine types of trade that are advantageous to Britain, first comes the "Trade which exports Manufactures made of the sole Product or Growth of the Country," which is "undoubtedly good." The list of four species of trade "disadvantageous to a Nation," by contrast, is led by a trade which "brings in things of meer Luxury and Pleasure, which are entirely, or for the most part, consumed among us," such as the "Wine-Trade," especially when French "Wine is purchased with Money, and not in exchange for our Commodities" (King 1743, 1, 3). James Steuart, who otherwise had no wish to anathemize "luxury" itself, as we shall shortly see below, thought it needful to draw a borderline marking its acceptability. "Luxury, among those who live upon a revenue already got, and who, by their rank in the state, are not calculated for industry," Steuart states, "has the good effect of affording bread to those who supply them." However, the case is utterly different for those whose fate it is to "supply" industry rather than hire others to do so. Steuart warns that "there never can be any advantage in having luxury introduced among the lower classes, because it is then only a means of rendering their subsistence more chargeable, and consequently more precarious" (Steuart 1767, 349–350). The authors of *The British Merchant*, as well as the pioneering economist Steuart, would give their consent to Fawconer's verdict that "[l]uxury is prejudicial to trade, and undermines the very foundation, on which our political fabric" stands, and that "our land is drained and impoverished by the importation of foreign superfluities" (Fawconer 1765, 41). The adverse effect luxury will have on the "political fabric" was also underscored by Adam Ferguson in *An Essay on the History of Civil Society* (1767). Without directly pointing to Britain itself, Ferguson believed that all "nations under a high state of the commercial arts" are liable to be "exposed to corruption," for "by their admitting wealth, unsupported by personal elevation and virtue," they foster an unalloyed "respect towards mere wealth" as the "great foundation of distinction" (Ferguson 1995, 241). At all levels of reflections—physiological, ethical, sociological, and political—"luxury" as an aspect or area of consumption, particularly of the general populace, was a word that rang the bell of alarm among many authors including those who did not profess a commitment to traditional morality.

4.3 Refinement

Dubious and sinister as its moral implications were, "luxury" occupied an inalienable post in the buoyant market economy of eighteenth-century Britain, where "consumption," despite its macabre medical connotations, could not be confined to the strictly necessary and the indisputably wholesome items. Surely not in London. Already in the 1680s, in Barbon's proud assessment, London made pretensions to be deemed the "Metropolis of *Europe*," not inferior to other European capital cities when measured by the "number of good Houses," "many and large Piazzas," and the "richness of Inhabitants" (Barbon 1685, 2). Yet her "Grandeur" kindles "envy" on the part of those who are "affrighted" at its magnificence and are "angry with the Builders," like Barbon himself, "for making her so great." They refuse to appreciate the fact that the construction business contributes to the nation's wealth by "taking off the Commodities of the Country" and that the finished buildings "provide an habitation and livelihood for the Supernumerary and useless inhabitants of the Country" who are "unskilful and unfit for Country-life" (Barbon 1685, 22–24). These "useless" city-dwellers, nonetheless, help to keep the economy vibrant as they follow the "Fashion," the "great Promoter of *Trade*." "Fashion," instead of being castigated as abetting the vice of "luxury," is praised by Barbon as the "Spirit and Life of *Trade*" that "keeps the great Body of Trade in Motion." By its "Invention to Dress a Man," it enables one to continue to live in a "perpetual Spring," for "he never sees the Autumn of his Cloaths." Fashion is unjustly smeared with "an ill Name amongst many Grave and Sober People." When they denounce the "New Fashion" as "Vanity" and "commend the Decency of the Old one," they conveniently choose to forget that "every Old Fashion was once New, and then the same Argument might have been used against it" (Barbon 1690, 65–66). The antidote to misguided denigration of "luxury" can be found in

"Trade." In the alleged "Vanity" of building "good Houses" and catching up with the latest "Fashion" consists the very essence of "Trade," Barbon believes. Those who legitimized luxury in the subsequent decades adopted, whether wittingly or not, this discursive strategy of Barbon. In the 1710s, Thomas Mun, a London entrepreneur like Barbon, defended "Bounty and Pomp" by asking "how shall we then Vent our own Commodities" if "we should become so frugal, that we should use few or no Foreign Wares"? "What will become of our Ships, Mariners, Munitions, our poor Artificers, and many others?" Mun wished to know (Mun 1713, 59). *A General History of Trade, and Especially Consider'd as It Respects the British Commerce, as well as Home, as to All Parts of the World* published for the "Month of July" of 1713, paid tribute to the civilizing mission of "Trade." Consumers seek a "new method of Living," which should never be "reckon'd a Vice" if it supports "Trade," and it is "Trade" that "increases Wealth, raises Families, lifts the Poor up from the low and necessitous way of living, to subsisting comfortably and plentifully on their Labour." The "new way of Living," by means of "Trade," propels the people who had been "dwelling in Tents" to reside in "Houses of Cedar" decked with "costly Furniture" (Anon. 1713, 27). When the word "commerce" came to be used alongside "trade" in the latter part of the century, the same argument still exerted its force. The benefits of commerce or trade became something of a commonplace truism, as demonstrated by an article reviewing Malachy Postlethwayt's *Universal Dictionary of Trade and Commerce* published in *The Monthly Review* in 1755. The reviewer begins his account of the book by setting forth a general theory of "trade," in which "luxury" is justified as an inevitable element of "commerce":

> Commerce derived its origin from our wants, real or imaginary. Little satisfies nature, but the cravings of luxury and ambition are almost numberless; so that the rich employ the industrious, to supply the demands of splendor and magnificence. *Convenience* introduced *trade*; and its progress has been principally owing to the increase of mankind, who have found a proportional extension of commerce necessary for their mutual support. (Anon. 1755, 85)

The intimate relationship between "luxury" and "*trade*" is upheld also by Adam Anderson's *An Historical and Chronological Deduction of the Origin of Commerce, from the Earliest Account to the Present Time* (1764). While Anderson feels it incumbent on him as a historical writer to reiterate the established view that the "Sloth, Luxury, and Effeminacy of the Emperors and People" brought about the demise of the Roman Empire, he would add an important caveat. The fall of Rome was caused by the lack of vigorous commerce. Habitually dependent on plunder by military conquest, the mighty Empire felt no need for a "Revival of the never-failing Resources of Commerce, as well at home, as in her remoter Provinces." By contrast, the "great Increase of the Number and Splendor of *Equipages,*—of *Plate, Jewels, Pictures, Household Furniture,* &c." in London and elsewhere in Britain are all so many healthy signs of the nation's thriving "Commerce" rather than of luxury destroying its might (Anderson 1764, i, xi).

In vindicating "luxury" as a valuable component of "trade" or "commerce," Barbon, *The Monthly Review* reviewer, and Anderson all prefer to overwrite "luxury" with other positive words such as "Grandeur," "magnificence," "convenience," and "Splendor." With his characteristic ingenuity, Hume came up with a convenient new term. His choice was "refinement," which had the merit of embracing the favorable connotations these nouns carried while squarely denoting what "luxury" stood for. Hume's essay "Of Refinement in the Arts" initially stood under the title of "Of Luxury" in the editions of his *Essays* from 1752 to 1758, but was changed from 1760 onward into that title (Hume 1994, xxxix, 297 [editorial notes]). Hume being an author thoroughly celebrated and commented upon by others, here I merely will acknowledge his contributions by citing some of his key statements. First, regarding the broadly held view that luxury destroyed Rome, Hume corrects those who "mistook the cause of the disorders in the ROMAN state." The real cause of its decline was not "luxury and the arts" but its "ill modelled government, and the unlimited extent of conquests" (Hume 1987, 276 ["Of Refinement in the Arts"]). "Refinement on the pleasures and conveniencies of life has no natural tendency to beget venality and corruption," Hume assures the reader. Second, he keeps an equal distance from those who give ground to the "preposterous opinions" that extoll even "vicious luxury" and from those "of severe morals" who "blame even the most innocent luxury." He is not unwilling to grant that "wherever luxury ceases to be innocent, it also ceases to be beneficial," and that "when carried a degree too far, is a quality pernicious, though perhaps not the most pernicious, to political society" (Hume 1987, 269 ["Of Refinement in the Arts"]). The hedging phrase of "though … not the most pernicious" is a carefully planted rhetorical device, for he soon exonerates "luxury" of all moral mischiefs.

What really matters is whether "luxury nourishes commerce and industry." Whenever it does, everyone is better off. The "peasants, by a proper cultivation of the land, become rich and independent," while the "tradesmen and merchants acquire a share of the property, and draw authority and consideration to that middling rank of men, who are the best and firmest basis of public liberty." Far less ambiguous is the central thesis that the "ages of refinement are both the happiest and most virtuous." Besides, "luxury," even when "excessive," is to be preferred to "sloth and idleness," which are "more hurtful both to private persons and to the public," since when "sloth reigns, a mean uncultivated way of life prevails amongst individuals, without society, without enjoyment" (Hume 1987, 277, 280 ["Of Refinement in the Arts"]). For Hume, the "good life is the busy, occupied life," as Duncan Forbes put it (Forbes 1975, 87), whether for individuals or for nations. The ever-dependable dichotomy of "industry" and "idleness" thus comes to rescue "luxury" from moral turpitude. This alignment of "luxury" with "industry" is given full rein in Hume's essay, "Of Commerce." "If we consult history," Hume is confident, "we shall find, that, in most nations, foreign trade has preceded any refinement in home manufactures, and given birth to domestic luxury." When "men become acquainted with the *pleasures* of luxury and the *profits* of commerce," their "*delicacy* and *industry*, being once awakened, carry them on to farther improvements, in every branch of domestic as well as foreign trade" (Hume 1987, 263–264 ["Of Commerce"]). Hume deftly collocates "*delicacy*" with "*industry*" to further strengthen the moral force lent to "luxury" by the contrastive pairing of "industry" with "idleness." When one consults modern European history, which is the province of Hume's fellow Scottish thinker William Robertson, the conclusion is more or less the same. Robertson, whom we have seen above as underscoring the destructive potentials of "luxury," could also concede that it can have positive effects, at least when attended by "refinement." Describing the changes in medieval Europe after it began to recover from the devastations inflicted by barbarian invasions, he writes how as the "spirit of industry revived," "commerce" once again "became an object of attention, and began to flourish," ushering in other beneficial changes:

> Population increased. Independence was established; and wealth flowed into cities which had long been the seat of poverty and oppression. Wealth was accompanied by its usual attendants, ostentation and luxury; and though the former was formal and cumbersome, and the latter inelegant,

> they led gradually to greater refinement in manners, and in the habits of life. Together with this improvement in manners, a more regular species of government and police was introduced. (Robertson 1769a, 34)

The "usual attendants" of wealth include "ostentation and luxury," but they are subsumed under the auspicious trend of a "greater refinement in manners," which further leads to "improvements" in government. If such is the path toward progress launched by "ostentation and luxury" from "barbarism to refinement," there seems to be little reason to find fault with "luxury" (Robertson 1769a, 11). In Robertson's account of the auspicious role of "luxury," a minor but indispensable service is rendered by "improvement." The term, as David Hancock traces, was given a broader significance than the traditional sense it had of agricultural or moral amelioration in the previous centuries (Hankock 1995, 282), as it referred in Robertson's century both to growth in business and to "greater refinement" in social taste.

Steuart's views about luxury, unlike those of his fellow Scots, Hume and Robertson, are at once more comprehensive and more ambiguous. They surely deserve to be given a greater attention than has been usually granted by intellectual historians (see Sekora 1977, 125–127; Hont 1983, 296–297; Berry 1994, 138–139; de Vries 2003, 44). We have already seen how Steuart drew a clear line between the luxury of those who could afford it and that of those who could not. But he expressed his discomfort with the very word itself as being a notoriously slippery term. To some it signifies the "means of providing employment for such as must live by their industry, and of promoting an equable circulation of wealth and subsistence," while others regard it as the name of that which is "prejudicial to foreign trade" and corrupts the "morals" of people (Steuart 1767, x). For his part, Steuart cannot inculpate luxury as a moral vice, since when understood as "superfluous consumption," it can be "compatible" with both "virtue" and "vice" of individuals (Steuart 1767, 142). A "sober man," Steuart believes, "may have a most delicate taste, as well as a glutton." He therefore chooses to understand the term strictly in its "political sense," separated from "morals," as a "principle which produces employment, and gives bread to those who supply the demands of the rich" (Steuart 1767, 310, 32n). Here again, the crucial distinction to be made is that between the "superfluous consumption" of the "rich" and the unscrupulous spending of those who have to earn their bread through labor. He also would wish to differentiate "excess" from "luxury." A "moderate gratification" of human desire cannot be culpable, whereas if "immoderate gratification" is implied in the word "luxury," it is more proper to call it an "*excess*" and as such can hardly be justified (Steuart 1767, 177). When "luxury" is thus defined in its "political sense" as "*the providing of superfluity with a view to consumption*," it follows that "no man can become luxurious" without "giving bread to the industrious, without encouraging emulation, industry, and agriculture, and without producing the circulation of an adequate equivalent for every service." The last in the list of public benefits, for Steuart, is the "palladium of liberty, the fountain of gentle dependence, and the agreeable band of union among free societies" (Steuart 1767, 310). Luxury, then, plays a pivotal role in guaranteeing "gentle" interactions within a free commercial society and between free societies. However, it obliges the policy makers to keep luxury organically tied to "industry" rather than "idleness." The "introduction of luxury" may be a "rational and prudent step of administration" when its progress is "not accelerated from any other principle, but that of preserving the industrious, by giving them employment" (Steuart 1767, 263). Moreover, one should always keep an eye on the international trade opportunities, since the balance between "luxury and frugality," in tandem with that of "industry and idleness," fluctuates constantly in different nations. When the domestic market cannot absorb the output of the "industrious," the government ought to encourage their merchants to become "carriers" of goods for the neighboring countries so that the "national stock" can be increased (Steuart 1767, 342). If anything, far too fickle a fashion encircling items of luxury needs to be dampened. In general, those who are "systematically luxurious" from "confirmed habit" are far fewer than those who become so "from levity, vanity, and the imitation of others." While the "real allurements of ease and taste of luxury" rarely influence their decisions, the "fashion," which is to be understood to be synonymous with "imitation," guides most of them to incur "superfluous expence" to purchase articles of luxury. Such consumption can be controlled indirectly by the statesman when he sets an example of being free from the "caprice of fashion" by keeping his private and domestic expenditure within bounds (Steuart 1767, 280–281). In sum, luxury should be sagaciously channeled from inordinate "excess" and wasteful "imitation" into domestic "industry" and export. For Steuart, luxury is a political issue or, better still, a problem of public policy rather than that of individual morality.

Luxury No Political Evil. But Demonstratively Proved to be Necessary to the Preservation and Prosperity of States (1781) is a work anonymously published but written by John Trusler, a clergyman author remembered at least by one historian (Raven 1992, 168–172). Trusler combined and reasserted the arguments advanced by others before him, from Barbon to Steuart, in vindicating its advantages. To begin with, luxury stands on the side of "industry" rather than "idleness" in that eternal confrontation between the two. The "arts," whether "useful or frivolous," create in the consumers "a variety of indulgences" which transform themselves by degrees into a "kind of want." In this manner, a "spirit of industry" is "kept up" and manifests itself in an "abundance of every thing we wish." Indeed, without a "desire for Luxuries" implanted in human nature, our "intellectual faculties" would never be fully awakened, and we would "languish away our hours in stupidity, occupied only with the momentary want" (Trusler [1781?], 5, 7–8). The "arts, manufactures, trades, and all the luxuries of life" of a civilized society arise thanks to that desire. If that is so, there is no point in trying to separate luxuries from necessities. If all "superfluities" are "Luxuries," and "what is not immediately necessary" is "superfluous," there are few items that can escape that opprobrium. Besides, a "manufacture of the most trifling article" is "not without its advantage to the state," when one considers how it "tends to create that disbursement from which the state draws its resources, and employs a number of hands" (Trusler [1781?], 13–14, 16). Branding "articles which indulge a sensual gratification" as luxury is "begging the question," since all that civilized societies consume beyond those that are "immediately necessary to our existence" will be classified as luxury. Trusler would admit that there can be "certain species of Luxuries" injurious to the "morals of a community." The "Legislative power" of a nation should see to it that such items are properly regulated. But adducing extreme cases can be "no argument for condemning Luxuries in the gross." Indeed, it is by "Luxury alone" that "any state can exist." Luxury, for Trusler, is another name of civilization itself, of the "natural consequence of perfection in the arts, and the progress of the mind and taste" (Trusler [1781?], 22, 24). This is demonstrated by actual examples past and present, for "in countries where Luxury is predominant, we see a vast number of towns, an infinite population, good order existing, and nature embellished to the utmost," whereas, "in those new climates, where the industry of man, still enveloped, leaves him but little exertion for superfluities, the best soils are but boundless desarts" (Trusler [1781?], 86). Wise statesmen should and would encourage a "general spirit of Luxury," knowing how it boosts "labour" and remembering that labor is the "fund of riches and enjoyments" that fortifies the "power of the State" and ensures the "happiness of its subjects" (Trusler [1781?], 34).

4.4 Prudence

Steuart entrusts "luxury" to the care of statesmen whose duty it is to make it contribute to "industry." Trusler makes a similar case, but evinces an even greater confidence in the ability of the "spirit of industry" to mingle naturally with the "general spirit of Luxury." For Josiah Tucker, however, "industry" aroused by "luxury" itself needs to be subjected to a more sober scrutiny. He would not deny that luxury, in the "most favourable View of it," can for "a short Time" create a "greater Demand for the ornamental Parts of Furniture, Dress, and Equipage, than in Prudence there ought to have been." The important factor is temporality and sustainability. The economy can be enlivened by luxury but that vitality cannot last long, since "this brisk temporary Circulation of Industry in the Body politic is just the same as a feverish Circulation of the Blood in the natural Body; a Circulation, which may give a transient Flow of Spirits, and may raise a false Fire for a little while, but is sure of bringing on afterwards a general Weakness and Debility, and must prove fatal, if not corrected in Time" (Tucker 1774, "Sermon 2," 32). This caustic view of luxury rests upon Tucker's premise that "luxury" refers to instances where "the Expence exceeds the Ability." The luxurious men "figure away in the great World for a Time, and then either sink into Poverty and Obscurity, or else must take to bad Courses to support their Extravagances" (Tucker 1774, "Sermon 2," 25). Their level of lavish consumption may perhaps be preserved during their lifetime, but the "Luster of that must necessarily diminish" in the second generation, with even more depressing prospects for remote posterity:

> And then as to the third Generation, the Oil of their dim Lamp would be totally spent; and if we were still to go on by extending our Reasonings to the Contemplation of the State of the fourth, the fifth, and sixth Generation, the Prospect would grow worse and worse; and by a natural Transition from Waste to Poverty, the few wretched Descendents of the first Prodigals would

> be glad to inhabit some Corner of the mouldering Palaces of their Ancestors, fitted up as Huts or Hovels for their Reception. (Tucker 1774, "Sermon 2," 27)

History of the decline and fall of the Roman Empire due to "luxury" repeats itself, as it were, in these families. Instead of "luxury" pushing society toward civilized "refinement" as Hume assumed, it pulls the race of "Prodigals" back to sheer barbarism. And it is fitting that it should be so, for God ordained that the path of mankind's progress toward genuine prosperity to be that of "virtue" and not "luxury." God never could have willed that "in order to do the most Good to Mankind, by feeding and supporting the greatest Numbers of God's rational Creatures, we must be disobedient to the Laws of the Creator." Nor did He forbid our enjoyment of the goods of the world. The important thing is to be reasonable and prudent. One's expenditure should never exceed one's income. We should always save some money for unforeseen "Contingencies" and make "decent and adequate Provisions" for our "Family and Dependents." Above all, one should seek after "no Gratifications, which may injure either the Health of his Body, or the Faculties of his Mind." When he thus restrains his "Pleasures, Diversions, or Expences, by these Regulations, he is not a luxurious, but a temperate Man: He doth not abuse the good Things of Providence, but rightly uses them, according to the gracious Design of the Donor" (Tucker 1774, "Sermon 2," 32–34). In this way, "luxury" is taken back from economic policy where Steuart placed it to the domain of individual morals, except that it is an economic morality regulating one's consumption. The antidote to "luxury," according to Tucker, is "Prudence," rather than frugality or abstention.

As a topic straddling morals and economics, "luxury" received ample attention among those who wrote on social issues of the time, above all, the Anglican divines. Along with Trusler and Tucker who expressed their clear convictions about what constitutes "luxury" and what ought to be done about it, we should also remember what William Warburton from the first half of the century and William Paley from the latter half thought about the subject. Warburton, in the context of refuting Mandeville, cannot condone Mandeville's celebration of "luxury" if he means to use it as a tool for puncturing moral certainties. Mandeville's argument is skewed for he locates the objections to "luxury" only at the extreme corners of "Superstition" and "Fanaticism," "the Hypocrisy of *Monks*, and the Misanthropy of *Ascetics*." Similarly, Mandeville gives "luxury" a loose definition signifying whatever exceeds "bare Necessaries of Life." The inevitable corollary of these two positions would be that "luxury," condemned as "vice" by those critics summoned by Mandeville's first proposition, is in fact public "benefit," according to his second. By this sleight of hand, Mandeville can easily dismantle morality and discredit Christianity. Warburton cannot leave this distortion to march onward unimpeded. For "true Christianity, as delivered by its Author, and his Disciples," he emphasizes, is "quite another thing than what Bigots and Fanatics are wont to represent it," in that it "enjoins and forbids nothing, in moral Practice, but what natural Religion had before enjoined and forbid" (Warburton 1738, 82–83). Denying any enmity between the "revealed" and "natural" religions on this issue, Warburton assigns "luxury" to the latter department. "Luxury," as "natural Religion" sees it, is none other than the "using (and therefore abusing) *the Gifts of Providence, to the Injury of the User, either in his Person or Fortune; or to the Injury of any other, towards whom he stands in any Relation, which obliges him to Aid and Assistance*." What defines "luxury" is the consequences following the use and not so much the items used themselves. "When the Consumption is attended with such Injury," Warburton argues, it "becomes *Luxury*," and as such it also "becomes a Vice." If that is the case, "*this Vice*, like all others," can hardly be "advantageous to Society." Similarly, when consumption does not stumble into the trap of "Abusing the Gifts of Providence," that is, when it is "made without *Luxury*," "infinitely greater Numbers share in it" (Warburton 1738, 85–86). The direct continuity between the Bishop and the Dean of Gloucester, Warburton and Tucker, is obvious: "luxury" is an injurious use and, as such, patently an "abuse." When "injury" is fended off, the use of the "Gifts of Providence"—which can never be a "vice" deserving to be condemned by "*Monks*" and fanatics, or conversely sardonically celebrated by libertines—benefits the public. Not that different in stance from the divines of Gloucester was that of James Beattie, fighting the good fight in Aberdeen against contemporary detractors of Christianity. Rebuffing the charge that Christianity inculcates unpracticably lofty and strict moral standard, Beattie asserts that the Christian religion only rejects "injustice, contention, covetousness, pride" and other such destructive vices, and proscribes "all pleasures, passions, and purposes, that tend to debase the soul, or molest our neighbour." What it does encourage, such as the nature of charity described by St Paul in 1 Corinthians chapter 13, is fully compatible with modern commercial society. Christian charity, ever devoted to the welfare of others, can never "interrupt the business or innocent comforts of life." Only the "injurious man, and the sensual, the proud, the covetous, and the hard-hearted" will "object to the morality of the gospel, as the cheat and robber may to the laws of the land, as unreasonably severe." In fact, the "devout and generous affections, that continually prevail in the breast of a true Christian, are in themselves exquisitely delightful; and, instead of lessening other innocent pleasures, cannot fail to increase, ennoble, and refine them" (Beattie 1786, 106–108). A good Christian will consume his or her goods with an added relish furnished by God, as it were.

In contrast to Warburton or Tucker, and more realistic than Beattie regarding the moral force of religion on his contemporaries, Paley is alert to the possibility of "luxury" harming the happiness of the individual consumer. It is in our nature to seek pleasure and happiness, but pleasure is in general fleeting and fugitive. The pleasures of sense, particularly of the "grosser sort," can last "but a little while at a time," and when repeated, "lose their relish." When you seek to make up for this diminishing rate of pleasure by the "frequency" of repetition, you "suffer more than you gain, by the fatigue of the faculties, and the diminution of sensibility." Moreover, when that transitory pleasure is "purchased by the encumbrance of our fortune," it is "purchased too dear," and thus such pleasure can never compensate for the "perpetual irritation of embarrassed circumstances" (Paley 2002, 34). Happiness or pleasure, then, comes not so much from the objects consumed as from the "prudent constitution of the habits." Therefore, the "art in which the secret of human happiness in a great measure consists" has to do with regulating one's "habits in such a manner, that every change may be a change for the better." Articles of expensive luxury in themselves can guarantee no augmentation of pleasure, despite the costs that went into procuring them. "The luxurious receive no greater pleasure from their dainties, than the peasant does from his bread and cheese," remarks Paley. As a matter of fact, the peasant has a better chance of enjoying his pleasure, for "whenever he goes abroad," he "finds a feast," whereas the "epicure must be well entertained, to escape disgust" (Paley 2002, 38–39). The contrast between the "luxurious" epicure with his jaded palate and the peasant at his humble fare may sound trite. It reiterates to some extent Shaftesbury's somewhat circular reasoning that gratification of mere sensory appetite is "false and unnatural," whereas "satisfactions of the natural appetite, in a plain way, are infinitely beyond those indulgences of the most refined and elegant luxury." This is "often perceived by the luxurious themselves," who, whether accidentally or by necessity, come to "experience the sweet of a plain diet." Without specifying any further who these "luxurious" are, Shaftesbury tells us that they "have with freedom owned that it was then they received the highest satisfaction and delight which a table could possibly afford" (Shaftesbury 1999, 220). Paley, however, revives the contrast between the natural and unnatural pleasures to perform yet another variation on the grand theme of "industry" opposing "idleness." Here one may grant him some degree of originality. The idle "epicure," prone to be ridden with "disgust" and "distress," despite all his luxuries, can never know the hearty pleasure of the industrious laborer.

Paley knew very well that individual "prudence," when faced with "luxury," can exercise its force only up to a certain point. His society was becoming far more complex than one that can be characterized as one bifurcated into dronish "epicures" and industrious peasants. An increase in "industry" thanks to "luxury" could not be ignored, as it was evidenced by an increase in the volume of circulating money, a large part of which was spent by the wage-earners providing that "industry." What consequences would it have on the question of population, which increasingly came to be seen as vital to a nation's might? By promoting "industry," "luxury" enables the industrious masses to grow in number. But at the same time, "by introducing more superfluities into general reception," it makes the "usual accommodations of life more expensive, artificial, and elaborate." As a result, men will have scruples about marrying and keeping a family, for the standard of spending one's life "comfortably with the established mode of living" is ever elevated. They "will not marry, to *sink* their place or condition in society," or to "forego those indulgences" which "their own habits" have made indispensable. This tendency will be applicable to "every article of diet and dress, to houses, furniture, attendance," and it will affect "every class of the community." "Fashion" creates demand and arouses "industry" on the part of those who produce articles "fashion" calls for. Yet this interrelationship is by no means an unmixed blessing:

> [O]nce fashion hath annexed the use of these articles of dress to any certain class, the middling ranks, for example, of the community, each individual of that rank finds them to be *necessaries* of life; that is, finds himself obliged to comply with the example of his equals, and to maintain that appearance which the custom of society requires. This obligation creates such a demand upon his income, and adds so much to the cost and burden of a family, as to

> put it out of his power to marry, with the prospect of continuing his habits, or of maintaining his place and situation in the world.

Hence men opt rather to "waste their lives in a barren celibacy," damaging the "very source of population." All of this is "justly placed to the account of luxury" (Paley 2002, 314–315). Whether married or celibate, the "cost and burden" of having to "comply with the example of his equals" in consumption weighed heavily on all. It caused a steady increase in the price of butcher-meat, for instance, according to Adam Dickson. Attempting a more detailed diagnosis of the sociological parameters of "luxury," Dickson suspected that the increase in the price of provisions was owing to the universally acknowledged fact that the "inhabitants of this kingdom have of late years changed their way of living in a very remarkable manner, and greatly increased in luxury." More specifically, the consumption of butcher-meat in the course of two or three decades has "doubled, in others tripled." What caused it? The manner of dressing meat is to blame. On the "tables of our great people," of the "meat which some time ago appeared in its natural form, nothing is now presented but its essence in soups, sauces and gravies, while the meat itself is thrown into the kennel." What about the table of the less affluent? "If we take a view of the tables of the principal inhabitants in our cities and towns," he maintains, "we find a proportional waste of provision; and if we attend to the manner of living amongst the lower class, we find many families living now chiefly upon animal food, that formerly seldom tasted it except on holydays" (Dickson 1773, 22–23). At this stage of debate, "luxury" loses its specific significance as a moral concept referring to an individual's excess or prudent decision in purchase and consumption. Whatever may have been deemed luxury a few years before would soon become necessaries, which you can relinquish only at the unthinkable cost of losing caste.

Where moralizing fails to command authority, political economy takes over, undeterred by ethical dilemmas. Smith in *The Wealth of Nations* has a ready answer as to what to make of the rising cost of butcher-meat traced by Dickson. This is something to be expected in any "improved and cultivated country," when the "interest" on the supply side of "landlords and farmers" will not be impaired by it. Yet at the same time, "their interest as consumers" may be affected by "the rise in the price of provisions" (Smith 1976a, 251 [I.xi.m.12]). Such schizophrenic division of an individual subject into two opposed roles of producer and consumer can scarcely be avoided in a free-market economy. This self-division is not confined to the landlords living off their rent or the farmers who put their laborers to work. Even if you are nothing more than a wage-earner, you want to see your wages increase, naturally enough, but that increase "necessarily increases the price of many commodities, by increasing that part of it which resolves itself into wages, and so far tends to diminish their consumption both at home and abroad" (Smith 1976a, 104 [I.viii.57]). The list of what needs to be consumed and their prices tend to increase, as the dynamism of the market economy constantly erodes the distinction between necessaries and luxuries. With a full awareness of what has been said by many to castigate or to vindicate "luxury" throughout his lifetime, Smith wishes to suggest a more balanced view that may put an end to what to him is a bootless controversy:

> By necessaries I understand, not only the commodities which are indispensably necessary for the support of life, but whatever the custom of the country renders it indecent for creditable people, even of the lowest order, to be without. A linen shirt, for example, is, strictly speaking, not a necessary of life. The Greeks and Romans lived, I suppose, very comfortably, though they had no linen. But in the present times, through the greater part of Europe, a creditable day-labourer would be ashamed to appear in public without a linen shirt, the want of which would be supposed to denote that disgraceful degree of poverty, which, it is presumed, no body can well fall into without extreme bad conduct. … Under necessaries therefore, I comprehend, not only those things which nature, but those things which the established rules of decency have rendered necessary to the lowest rank of people. All other things I call luxuries; without meaning by this appellation, to throw the smallest degree of reproach upon the temperate use of them. (Smith 1976a, 869–870 [V.ii.k.3])

If "custom," rather than "nature," determines what are to be included in the "necessaries" of a given society, necessaries inhabit a realm of an artificial second nature, as it were, where it is extremely difficult to keep "necessaries" neatly and permanently segregated from "luxuries." Considering this difficulty, Smith wishes to cleanse "luxuries" of all vestiges of moral "reproach," except when they overstep the boundary of "temperate" use. This last brings Smith's stance close to that of Steuart, Warburton, and Tucker, who warned against "excess" of luxury, the "abuse" of things, and indulgences in "extravagances," respectively. Let the "necessaries" broaden their territory, and let "luxuries" be restrained by the rod of prudent moderation, and all things will be well. As Donald

Winch points out, Smith offers a way out of the debate about luxury's danger or benefit by moving toward a horizon of continual growth "generating irreversible social change and processes" that are "potentially limitless" (Winch 1996, 89). We may add that Smith also assumed that certain "rules of decency" would control that "change" by drawing a line between "necessaries" and "luxuries."

Yet our last word in this chapter may not be Smith of *The Wealth of Nations*, but the same author's *Theory of Moral Sentiments*. The sixth edition of this work published in the very year of his death (1790) came out fortified with a carefully and eloquently written Part VI, "Of the Character of Virtue," added to the earlier editions. The first "Section" of this "Part" presents "prudence" as a most viable "virtue" in an age of fluctuating values, both economic and moral. People strive to secure the "advantages of external fortune," not merely to "supply the necessities and conveniences of the body" but to obtain the "respect of our equals," the desire for which incites our "anxiety to obtain" these advantages (Smith 1976b, 212–213 [VI.1.3]). In other words, luxuries requisite for the "respect" of society, rather than natural and physical necessity, propel our pursuit of material prosperity. Who then is the virtuous man of prudence? He is one "who lives within his income" and is "naturally contented with his situation, which, by continual, though small accumulations, is growing better and better every day." Having shunned extravagance, he can afford "gradually to relax" both the "rigour of his parsimony" and the "severity of his application." The reward he reaps is a "double satisfaction" of seeing a "gradual increase of ease and enjoyment" heightened by his memory of "having felt before the hardship which attended the want of them" (Smith 1976b, 215 [VI.1.12]). Admittedly, this does not go far enough to claim the admiration of the general public. "Prudence," when applied to the "care of the health, of the fortune, and of the rank and reputation of the individual," may be "respectable" but not the "most endearing" or the "most ennobling of the virtues." As such, it "commands a certain cold esteem" and cannot quite hope to be "entitled to any very ardent love or admiration" (Smith 1976b, 216 [VI.1.14]). This degree of moderate "esteem," even so, would be sufficient for the vast majority of middle-class tradesmen and professionals, who have known the "rigour" of "parsimony" and who can feel a modicum of pride at least in the "steadiness" of their "industry and frugality" (Smith 1976b, 215 [VI.1.11]), which have enabled them to enjoy their temperate "luxuries." They surely will avoid the pitfall of going after the mirage of happiness extravagant consumption promises. From the first edition onward, Smith had inserted in Part IV of the same book the hypothetical but typical case of a "poor man's son" stricken with undue "ambition" and condemned to a life-long admiration of the "rich." As far as his "industry" is concerned, he has nothing to be ashamed of, for he has striven hard "night and day" to climb out of his poverty and to excel in competition with his peers. His arduous quest after "wealth and greatness" is attended by an improvement of his circumstances, but he never acquires satisfaction from it. Throughout the "whole of his life," he pursues the "idea of a certain artificial and elegant repose which he may never arrive at," but for which he "sacrifices a real tranquillity that is at all times in his power" (Smith 1976b, 181 [IV.1.8]). The man of prudence will never fall into this trap. Joyce Appleby considers "comfort" to be a new key word proffered by the Scottish Enlightenment, one that suits the "middle-class character of the Scottish ideal" (Appleby 1993, 169). It seems to me that a far more important term, for Smith at least, is "prudence," being more sonorous and richer in its moral connotations than "comfort." Smith's conception of "prudence," as Leonidas Montes sees it, is an antidote to self-interest as it guides one to forbear from pursuing blindly "one's own wishes, wants, or desires regardless of others" (Montes 2016, 144). A better way of putting it, perhaps, would be to state that the prudent man in Part VI of *The Theory of Moral Sentiments* pursues a higher sort of self-interest, one that keeps in view his own emotional happiness.

Prudence can also be a solid criterion of judging and censuring the imprudent schemes of those who happen to be in influential positions in the public realm. In the name of that "esteem" cautiously acquired by respectable commoners, and the peace which "prudence" brings by quenching the turbulence of misplaced ambition, Smith and his friend Edmund Burke raised their voices to reprimand those who offended public morality by embarking on overly avaricious or daring "projects" that often brought about harrowing consequences to other members of society. This new platform of moral discourse we shall examine in the next chapter.

References

Addison, Joseph. 1711. *The spectator: A new edition*. Vol. 1. Ed. Henry Morley. London, 1891. https://www.gutenberg.org/cache/epub/12030/. Accessed 21 December 2023.

Alcock, Thomas. 1752. *Observations on the defects of the poor laws, and on the causes and consequences of the great increases and burden of the poor, with a proposal for redressing these grievances*. London: R. Baldwin.

Anderson, Adam. 1764. *An historical and chronological deduction of the origin of commerce, from the earliest account to the present time, containing, an history of the great commercial interests of the British Empire*. London: Consortium.

Anon. 1692. *The friendly monitor, laying open the crying sins of cursing, swearing, drinking, gaming, detraction, and luxury or immodesty*. London: Sam. Crouch.

Anon. 1713. *A general history of trade, and especially consider'd as it respects the British commerce, as well as home, as to all parts of the world*. London: J. Baker.

Anon. 1736. *Of luxury, more particularly with respect to apparel, being the substance of two discourses, on 1Tim.ii.9*. London: T. Green.

Anon. 1755. The universal dictionary of trade and commerce … by Malachy Postlethwayt. *The Monthly Review* February: 85–94.

Appleby, Joyce. 1993. Consumption in early modern social thought. In *Consumption and the world of goods*, ed. John Brewer and Roy Porter, 162–173. London: Routledge.

Barbon, Nicholas. 1685. *An apology for the builder: or A discourse shewing the cause and effects of the increase of building*. London.

Barbon, Nicholas. 1690. *A discourse of trade*. London.

Beattie, James. 1786. *Evidences of the Christian religion; Briefly and plainly stated*. Vol. 2. London: A. Strahan and T. Cadell.

Bellers, John. 1699. *Essays about the poor, manufactures, trade, plantations, and immorality, and of the excellency and divinity of inward light*. London.

Berg, Maxine, and Elizabeth Eger. 2003. The rise and fall of the luxury debates. In *Luxury in the eighteenth century: Debates, desires and delectable goods*, ed. Maxine Berg and Elizabeth Eger, 7–27. New York: Palgrave Macmillan.

Berry, Christopher. 1994. *The idea of luxury: A conceptual and historical investigation*. Cambridge: Cambridge University Press.

Berry, Christopher. 2015. *The idea of commercial society in the Scottish Enlightenment*. Edinburgh: Edinburgh University Press.

Blackstone, William. 1770. *Commentaries on the laws of England. Book the fourth*. 4th ed. Oxford: Clarendon.

Brewer, John. 1989. *The sinews of power: War, money and the English state, 1688–1783*. New York: Knopf.

Chambers, Ephraim. 1741. *Cyclopædia: or, An universal dictionary of arts and sciences*. London: Consortium.

Cheyne, George. 1733. *The English malady: or, A treatise of nervous diseases of all kinds*. London: G. Strahan.
Clery, E. J. 2004. *The feminization debate in eighteenth-century England: Literature, commerce and luxury*. Houndmills, Basingstoke: Palgrave Macmillan.
Cole, Thomas. 1761. *On luxury, infidelity, and enthusiasm*. London: J. Dodsley.
Daunton, M. J. 1995. *Progress and poverty: An economic and social history of Britain 1700–1850*. Oxford: Oxford University Press.
De Vries, Jan. 2003. Luxury in the Dutch Golden Age in theory and practice. In *Luxury in the eighteenth century: Debates, desires and delectable goods*, ed. Maxine Berg and Elizabeth Eger, 41–56. New York: Palgrave Macmillan.
Dennis, John. 1724. *Vice and luxury publick mischiefs: or, Remarks on a book intituled, The fable of the bees; or, Private vices public benefits*. London: W. Mears.
Dickson, Adam. 1773. *An essay on the causes of the present high prices of provisions, as connected with luxury, currency, taxes, and national debt*. London: E. and C. Dilly.
Fawconer, Samuel. 1765. *An essay on modern luxury: or, An attempt to delineate its nature, causes, and effects*. London: James Fletcher.
Ferguson, Adam. 1995. *An essay on the history of civil society*. Edited by Fania Oz-Salzberger. Cambridge: Cambridge University Press.
Forbes, Duncan. 1975. *Hume's philosophical politics*. Cambridge: Cambridge University Press.
Gibbon, Edward. 1776. *The history of the decline and fall of the Roman Empire, Volume the first*. London: W. Strahan and T. Cadell.
Gibbon, Edward. 1781. *The history of the decline and fall of the Roman Empire, Volume the second*. London: W. Strahan and T. Cadell.
Hankock, David. 1995. *Citizens of the world: London merchants and the integration of the British Atlantic community, 1735–1785*. Cambridge: Cambridge University Press.
Hont, Istvan. 1983. The "rich country–poor country" debate in Scottish classical political economy. In *Wealth and virtue: The shaping of political economy in the Scottish Enlightenment*, ed. Istvan Hont and Michael Ignatieff, 271–316. Cambridge: Cambridge University Press.
Hume, David. 1987. *Essays, moral, political, and literary*. Edited by Eugene F. Miller. Indianapolis: Liberty Fund.
Hume, David. 1994. *Political essays*. Edited by Knud Haakonssen. Cambridge: Cambridge University Press.
Inwood, Stephen. 1998. *A history of London*. London: Macmillan.
Johnson, Samuel. 1773. *A dictionary of the English language*, 4th ed. London: Consortium.
Jones, Erasmus. [1736?] *Luxury, pride and vanity, the bane of the British nation*. London: J. Roberts.

King, Charles ed. 1743. *The British merchant: A collection of papers relating to the trade and commerce of Great Britain and Ireland*. Vol. 1. London: C. Marsh and T. Davies.

Mackenzie, George. 1691. *The moral history of frugality, with its opposite vices, covetousness, niggardliness, and prodigality, luxury*. London: J. Hindmarsh.

Mandeville, Bernard. 1924. *The fable of the bees, or, Private vices, publick benefits*. Edited by F. B. Kaye. Oxford: Clarendon.

McKendrick, Neil. 1982. Commercialization and the economy. In *The birth of a consumer society: The commercialization of eighteenth-century England*, ed. Neil McKendrick, John Brewer, and J. H. Plumb, 9–194. Bloomington: Indiana University Press.

Millar, John. 2006. *The origin of the distinction of ranks*. Edited by Aaron Garrett. Indianapolis: Liberty Fund.

Montes, Leonidas. 2016. Adam Smith: Self-interest and the virtues. In *Adam Smith: His life, thought, and legacy*, ed. Ryan Patrick Hanley, 138–156. Princeton: Princeton University Press.

Morton, Richard. 1694. *Phthisiologia, or, A treatise of consumptions*. London: S. Smith and B. Walford.

Mun, Thomas. 1713. *England's treasure by foreign trade; or, The balance of our foreign trade is the rule of our treasure*. London.

Paley, William. 2002. *The principles of moral and political philosophy*. Indianapolis: Liberty Fund.

Pocock, J. G. A. 2003. *The first decline and fall*. Vol. 3 of *Barbarism and religion*. Cambridge: Cambridge University Press.

Pocock, J. G. A. 2005. *Barbarians, savages and empires*. Vol. 4 of *Barbarism and religion*. Cambridge: Cambridge University Press.

Raven, James. 1992. *Judging new wealth: Popular publishing and responses to commerce in England, 1750–1800*. Oxford: Clarendon.

Robertson, William. 1759. *History of Scotland, vol. 2*. Vol. 2 of *The works of William Robertson*. London: T. Cadell, 1840.

Robertson, William. 1769a. *The history of the reign of the Emperor Charles V, vol. 1, with A view of the progress of society in Europe*. Vol. 3 of *The works of William Robertson*. London: T. Cadell, 1840.

Robertson, William. 1769b. *The history of the reign of the Emperor Charles V, vol. 2*. Vol. 4 of *The works of William Robertson*. London: T. Cadell, 1840.

Robertson, William. 1777a. *History of America, vol. 1*. Vol. 6 of *The works of William Robertson*. London: T. Cadell, 1840.

Robertson, William. 1777b. *History of America, vol. 2*. Vol. 7 of *The works of William Robertson*. London: T. Cadell, 1840.

Robertson, John. 1983. The Scottish Enlightenment at the limits of the civic tradition. In *Wealth and virtue: The shaping of political economy in the Scottish Enlightenment*, ed. Istvan Hont and Michael Ignatieff, 137–178. Cambridge: Cambridge University Press.
Schabas, Margaret. 2005. *The natural origins of economics*. Chicago: The University of Chicago Press.
Sekora, John. 1977. *Luxury: The concept in western thought, Eden to Smollett*. Baltimore: The Johns Hopkins University Press.
Shaftesbury (Anthony Ashley Cooper), the Third Earl of. 1999. *Characteristics of men, manners, opinions, times*. Edited by Lawrence E. Klein. Cambridge: Cambridge University Press.
Shammas, Carole. 1993. Changes in English and Anglo-American consumption from 1550 to 1800. In *Consumption and the world of goods*, ed. John Brewer and Roy Porter, 177–205. London: Routledge.
Smith, Adam. 1976a. *An inquiry into the nature and causes of the wealth of nations*. Edited by R. H. Campbell and A. S. Skinner. Oxford: Clarendon.
Smith, Adam. 1976b. *The theory of moral sentiments*. Edited by D. D. Raphael and A. L. Macfie. Oxford: Clarendon.
Smitten, Jeffrey. 1985. Impartiality in Robertson's *History of America*. *Eighteenth-Century Studies* 19:56–77. https://doi.org/10.2307/2739130.
Steuart, James. 1767. *An inquiry into the principles of political economy*. Vol. 1. London: A. Millar and T. Cadell.
Trusler, John. [1781?] *Luxury no political evil, but demonstratively proved to be necessary to the preservation and prosperity of states*. London.
Tucker, Josiah. 1774. *Four tracts, together with two sermons, on political and commercial subjects*. Glocester.
Warburton, William. 1738. *The divine legation of Moses demonstrated, on the principles of a religious Deist*. Vol. 1. London: Fletcher Gyles.
Winch, Donald. 1996. *Riches and poverty: An intellectual history of political economy in Britain 1750–1834*. Cambridge: Cambridge University Press.

CHAPTER 5

"Projects," Monopolies, and "Nabobing"

5.1 "Projects" and "Projectors"

"Project" in our time is a word that has no pejorative implications, and "projector" refers not to persons but instruments, often combined with other nouns such as "beam projectors." The status of these terms was quite different in the seventeenth and the eighteenth centuries. A sample usage of "project" as an important category selected by the *Oxford English Dictionary* comes from Thomas Scott's *The High-waies of God and the King. Wherein All Men Ought to Walke in Holinesse Here, to Happinesse Hereafter: Deliuered in Two Sermons Preached at Thetford in Norfolke, anno 1620* (*OED* 2023, s.v. "Project"). As identified by the title, it is a sermon by an Anglican clergyman, who was a fairly prolific author with a large number of titles attributed to him by the *English Short Title Catalogue*. In the perceptive eyes of Reverend Scott, things are falling apart in his society. Not just "this or that finger or toe," but the "whole body" of the nation is "corrupted." First of all, "*Religion*" is put under siege by "adversaries on all sides" made up of "schimes, sects, heresies, and private spirits." In that parlous state, religion leaves the "defect of charity" to remain uncorrected, as the false doctrine spreads that inculcates "solitary faith" to the detriment of good "works." With true Christianity thus assaulted, the kingdom's policy is manipulated by worshippers of mammon:

H.-J. Yoon, *Moral Discourses of the Economy in Eighteenth-Century Britain*, https://doi.org/10.1007/978-981-95-0958-4_5

> [W]as there ever generally such an itch of private wealth which ever fore-runnes and effects the ruines of the Common-wealth? Looke upon all our *Projects*, of draining surrounded grounds, or whatsoever other profitable pretence they carry, see if they ayme not at the draining of the publique purse, at the milking of the state by private *Monopolies*, as if *England* were a hard step dame, and no indulgent Mother to her prodigall and ungratefull children. (Scott 1624, 80)

The "*Projects*" in question pretend to contribute to the public welfare, but are mere schemes brewed by "private *Monopolies*" to drain the "publique purse." The two key words of this chapter both appear in this context as the names of the parasitical "milking of the state" by groups of schemers bonded by their shared greed. Whereas "industry," "idleness," "luxury," "prudence," and other virtues or vices covered in the previous chapters primarily reside in the individual's heart, soul, or purse, "*Projects*" and "*Monopolies*" always involve public policy decisions of some kind that implicate but transcend the individual's moral disposition. The moral discourse of the economy targeting these issues necessarily spills onto politics, yet it is still a moral politics in that those taking part in this species of discourse wield the language and tropes of morals to attack or defend certain social and political agents or their roles, as exemplified by this published sermon peppered with bitter political phlegm.

Scott's voice may have gone unheeded in his time, but before a generation passed, there erupted a dramatic political upheaval in 1642, which led to the English Civil War along with a pamphlet war. Although political controversy generally inspired those who published their opinions, economic questions could easily be summoned for their chosen purposes. The number of pamphlets published with "projectors" and "projecting" in the titles, which often promised to denounce them, soared in the 1640s, as Koji Yamamoto shows (Yamamoto 2018, 33). Those without mentioning these terms in the title could equally be vocal in assaulting nefarious "projects." Among them, the stance adopted by Gerrard Winstanley is particularly impressive, for he chose as his antagonists all owners of large private estates. Winstanley penned and published *A Declaration from the Poor Oppressed People of England, Directed to All that Call Themselves, or Are Called Lords of Manors, Through This Nation; That Have Begun to Cut, or that Through Fear and Covetousness, Do Intend to Cut Down the Woods and Trees that Grow upon the Commons and Waste Land* in 1649, which true to its intent declared in the title, engages to battle the "Lords of Manors," accusing them and their "Ancestors" of nothing less than "murther and theft." They deserve this severe indictment because they are all worshippers of "that disturbing devil, called *Particular Propriety.*" God so willed that the "Earth, with all her Fruits of Corns, Cattle, and such like," be possessed and kept as "common Store-house of Livelihood to all Mankinde, friend, and foe, without exception." These satanic conspirators dismantled that godly order by introducing the use of money and made money the false deity to overthrow the authority of the true God. Winstanley desires to put an end to this despotism of money once and for all. He is resolved never to allow the use of money in his reformed world:

> [K]now this, That we must neither buy nor sell; Money must not any longer (after our work of the Earths community is advanced) be the great god, that hedges in some, and hedges out others; for Money is but part of the Earth: And surely, the Righteous Creator, who is King, did never ordain, That unless some of Mankinde, do bring that Mineral (Silver and Gold) in their hands, to others of their own kinde, that they should neither be fed, nor be clothed; no surely, For this was the project of Tyrant-flesh (which Landlords are branches of) to set his Image upon Money. (Winstanley 2009, 32–33)

This "project" of "Tyrant-flesh," indicted by Winstanley as a seditious conspiracy to usurp the throne of the "Righteous Creator," marched on triumphant during the political turmoil, as not many were willing to follow his command to abandon money. When the Interregnum ended with the Restoration, Winstanley himself changed course to lead, first, a life of a small-scale landowner, and then, that of a London trader, using money stamped with the mark of the Devil, according to his erstwhile radicalism, to buy and sell vigorously in both capacities (Alsop 1979, 73–81). Winstanley's revolutionary scheme may have been a futile dream, but his use of the term "project," itself carrying on the senses assigned to it by his predecessors such as Scott, retained its solid post in the English vocabulary used by the moral and economic discourses of the long eighteenth century.

We may begin with Josiah Child's *A New Discourse of Trade* published in the last decade of the seventeenth century, where he presented a hypothetical argument "City Usurers" would use to declaim against Parliament's imposing a cap on interest rates. Being experts in "draining" the "publique purse" and "milking" the "state," as Scott had put it earlier in the century, they will loudly complain that this is a "Plot carried on only by

Noblemen and *Gentlemen*, whose Estates are all in Land, for their own advantage, and that it will spoil all the Trade of the *Kingdom*, being a Project at one instant to take off just one third of all Mens Estates that are Personal, and add the same Proportion to all such whose Estates are real" (Child 1698, 78). That this is by no means a class-aligned "Project" of the landed interest against the monied interest, but one that boosts the "industry" of the nation is what Child seeks to persuade the reader, as we have seen in Chap. 3. Apart from the merits of the argument recommending legislation restricting high interest rate, Child's treatise illustrates what "project" still signified at the time. A "project" was a stratagem for making money by mobilizing state power on behalf of certain interested parties. One notable evolution of the term in the next century was the increasingly frequent usage of "projector(s)" as a noun referring to those who planned and conducted "projects" as understood in this conspiratorial sense. A "projector" bore thus the stigma of moral disapproval, as did "miser" or the "prodigal," but unlike these other labels, it also pointed to particular positions or roles of certain agents in the nation's economy. For instance, David Hume predicted in his essay "Of Public Credit" that when the nation resorted to a maximum increase of indirect taxes, matched with the drastic measure of mortgaging public funds to "perpetuity," the "invention and wit of all our projectors" will most likely be summoned to find some "new imposition" to service the national debt. The outcome is not hard to conjecture, for the "seeds of ruin" to the nation's "commerce and industry" will be "scattered with such profusion as not to escape the eye of the most careless observer." When the nation "becomes heartily sick" of public debts, after being "cruelly oppressed" by them, once again, it will open up an opportunity for "some daring projector" to come up with "visionary schemes for their discharge" (Hume 1987, 357, 361 ["Of Public Credit"]).[1] Adam Dicksons' *Essay on the Causes of the Present High Prices of Provisions*, quoted in the company of Smith in the previous chapter, reiterated Child's contention that the rate of interest must be controlled. As he did so, he offered a moral anatomy of the "projectors":

> When access to money is under no restrictions, encouragement is given to projectors, as well as to real improvers; and every person knows, and I may

[1] Hume's prediction did prove to be true, as new excise were voted by Parliament again and again to service the soaring national debt particularly during the wars with France. See Holmes and Szechi (1993, 369); Brewer (1989, 114–119).

> add, many have felt, that some of the gentlemen of that turn of mind, soon dissipate their own money with as much of other peoples as they can lay their hands upon, while others of them have nothing in view from the beginning, but to impose upon the public, and to live away at the expence of the industrious and unsuspecting part of mankind. (Dickson 1773, 79)

Added to the binaries of "industry v. idleness" and "necessaries v. luxuries," we see in this quotation yet another contrast, that of "projectors" and "improvers." The former, in turn, are divided into those who fully adopt the easy recipe of "idleness" and "dissipate" their own and other's money and those who are capable of some degree of "industry" which they activate as they diligently strive to "impose upon the public." Even for the latter sort, of course, that is where their "industry" stops, for as soon as they have secured the fund, they "live away" at the expense of the "industrious."

In the free market of published opinions centered in London, there was no likelihood that all authors would hold the same jaundiced view of "project" and "projectors." The word indeed found its defenders in various quarters. *The Case of Bankrupts and Insolvents Consider'd*, in keeping with its sympathetic stance on those unfortunate insolvents (in contrast to the malicious defaulters), advanced a plea for the value of "projects" and those courageous enough to undertake them. An unavoidable fact in "all Trading Nations" is that "Numbers of People are undone by *new Projects*, and by what is commonly called, *Pushing a Trade*" (Anon. 1734, 51). Should they be condemned, then, for their rashness? The author did not think so:

> As to *new Projects*, tho' they generally prove *unlucky* to the first Projector, yet they often prove *beneficial* to the Country, because others perceive the Rocks upon which the first Projector split, and from thence learn to steer safe, and to carry on the Project successfully, to the great Benefit of their Country, as well as themselves. ... [A]s no Man is infallible, the best concerted, and the best conducted Scheme in this way may prove abortive; and by its proving so, the Undertaker may become Insolvent. We know how often, how easily Men are deceived by Hopes; especially those Men who are of sanguine Constitutions, and therefore generally the most active, and the most useful Subjects. (Anon. 1734, 51–52)

This being the case in a "Trading Country," those who become insolvent by "pursuing Projects" should be "gently dealt with," even when they have failed while "venturing another Man's Money upon a *reasonable* Project, or Scheme of Trade." Besides, our moral sentiments entreat clemency, since the disappointed "Projects" is what is "incident to Human Nature." No one is "infallible" and the "best conducted Scheme" may go awry. Furthermore, it would be politically wise to connive at the unfortunate insolvents, for the early failures may "redound very much to the Improvement of the Trade of any Country where it is practiced." For these reasons, an insolvency due to "*Misfortune* or *Disappointment*" merits to be "*pitied*" rather than "*punished*" (Anon. 1734, 52–53). Adam Anderson, the author of *An Historical and Chronological Deduction of the Origin of Commerce, from the Earliest Account to the Present Time*, a work remarkable for its solid historical research and one that reflects a distinctively Scottish experience of historical change during his lifetime (Tonks 2020, 74–78), affirmed the worth of "projects." Anderson's vindication steers clear of moralizing and, instead, adduces the authority of known precedents. His chronology of commerce will not exclude "many unsuccessful and abortive Proposals, Embrios, and Projects," for even the "bare Catalogue of those airy Schemes" may prove "more instructive to some, than may, at first Glance, be apprehended," when one bears in mind how "some of them formerly deemed impracticable and visionary" have, on "subsequent and repeated Experiments," turned out to be "both practicable and beneficial to the Public, as well as to Individuals, as others of them may possibly prove hereafter!" (Anderson 1764, ix). The exclamation mark closing his statement attests to his emotional attachment to "Proposals, Embrios, and Projects" past, present, and future. The "airy Schemes" have and will baffle the critics, but they should not be ridiculed since they may eventually prove to be "practical" rather than "impracticable," to be "beneficial" and not merely "visionary."

Daniel Defoe was an author whose complex and elusive portfolio sports his experience as a secret agent and his business failures, and who was ever sedulous to impersonate various personas in diverse genres of writing he ventured into (Backscheider 1989; Owens 2000). A "projector" of sorts himself, Defoe could not keep his hands off from offering his proposals for improving his society under the title, *Essays upon Several Projects* (1702), even though it was published anonymously like most of his works. For Defoe, "Project" is a term that needs to be used neutrally, at least in a commercial nation like England, since any "new Voyage" of any "Merchant" is to be considered a "Project," dependent on contingencies fraught with "strange and Universal Intelligence," of which some are "so exquisite, so swift, and so exact, that a Merchant sitting at home in his Counting-house, at once converses with all Parts of the known World" (Defoe 1702, 8). Rather than castigating all new schemes as iniquitous "projects," one has to distinguish those that are "of publick Advantage" tending to the "Improvement of Trade, and Employment of the Poor" from those that are not or, in other words, between the "Honest and the Dishonest" projects (Defoe 1702, 10–11). Trained in his youth at a Dissenter's academy and knowing his Bible like the back of his hand, Defoe summons the Old Testament to fortify his case, pointing out that the "Building of the Ark by *Noah*, so far as you will allow it a human Work," was a grand "Project," even though "no question seem'd so ridiculous to the Graver Heads of that Wise, tho' Wicked Age, that poor *Noah* was sufficiently banter'd for it" (Defoe 1702, 20). What then would be a comparable plan in his own "Wise, tho' Wicked Age"? Establishing funds for poor discharged sailors is one, and suppressing beggars by setting up well-managed workhouses is another. As the subtitle of his treatise claims, Defoe would always be alert to spot the most "Effectual Ways for advancing the Interest of the Nation." All the same, he would by no means tolerate a "meer Projector," whom he severely rebukes as a "Contemptible thing":

> [He is] driven by his own desperate Fortune to such a Streight that he must be deliver'd by a Miracle, or Starve, and when he has beet his Brains for some such Miracle in vain, he finds no remedy but to paint up some Bauble or other … and then cry it up for a New Invention, gets a Patent for it, divides it into Shares, and they must be Sold; ways and means are not wanting to Swell the new Whim to a vast Magnitude; Thousand, and Hundreds of thousands are the least of his discourse, and sometimes Millions; till the Ambition of some honest Coxcomb is wheedl'd to part with his money for it, and then … the Adventurer is left to carry on the Project, and the Projector laughs at him. (Defoe 1702, 33–34)

This depiction of those poisonous creatures who use their cunning to deceive and defraud the credulous with their glib "discourse" is redolent with the stylistic vividness of the author's fictions such as *Moll Flanders* or *Roxana* whose heroines wield their charms to entice "some honest Coxcomb" to "part with his money." In Defoe's classification of human types, both in his fiction and in non-fiction, there are those who have "more Money than Brains," who fall prey to those who have more "Brains" than "Money." But this should not obfuscate the fact that some are worthy of being deemed to be the rightful descendants of Noah the projector. The "Honest Projector" is "he, who having by fair and plain principles of Sense, Honesty, and Ingenuity, brought any Contrivance to a suitable Perfection, makes out what he pretends to, picks no body's pocket, puts his Project into Execution, and contents himself with the real Produce, as the profit of his Invention" (Defoe 1702, 35). Interestingly, in his "Project" of penning fictional pseudo-biographies, which helped him gain a lasting reputation posthumously though with little profit to himself in his own lifetime, the only character that comes close to this description would be Robinson Crusoe in his desert island, surely resourceful in using his "Ingenuity" and in bringing his "Contrivance to a suitable Perfection." Crusoe certainly picked "no body's pocket" as he put his "Project into Execution," simply because he had no occasion to do so. He always remained contented with the "real Produce" of his "Project," largely because he had no other choice. The first-person protagonists residing in England or Europe of his time, so far removed from the fantastic setting of Crusoe, had a good chance of joining the group of the "Dishonest," rather than the "Honest," projectors.

To Defoe, the prototype of an "Honest Projector" was the biblical figure of Noah dedicated to building his Ark, braving all the ridicule and slander of his contemporaries. To William Robertson the historian of Spanish America, Columbus in modern history exemplified in his character the "ardent enthusiasm of a projector," which however was offset by a salutary "modesty and diffidence of true genius." Endowed with such potent mixture of requisite dispositions, he did not "rest with such absolute assurance either upon his own arguments, or upon the authority of the ancients, as not to consult such of his contemporaries as were capable of comprehending the nature of the evidence which he produced in support of his opinion" about the possibility of sailing through the Atlantic to India. At first Columbus proposed his scheme to his native country the Republic of Genoa. In spite of its proud history of having been once a mighty maritime power, Genoa rejected his proposal, unable to trust an expatriate who had spent so many years in foreign lands. Moreover, the mandarins of the city state were not well informed about the new "distant voyages" beyond the Mediterranean the Portuguese were undertaking. To the leaders of Genoa what Columbus proposed seemed a vain "dream of a chimerical projector," and thus they "lost for ever the opportunity of restoring their commonwealth to its ancient splendour" (Robertson 1777a, 64–65). When Columbus finally embarked on his historic journey with the support of the Spanish monarchs, he had to face the intransigence and timidity of the crew. But once again, the strength of his character came to his assistance. "Happily for himself, and for the country by which he was employed," our historian observes, in the character of Columbus was "joined to the ardent temper and inventive genius of a projector, virtues of another species, which are rarely united with them." Namely, Columbus "possessed a thorough knowledge of mankind, an insinuating address, a patient perseverance in executing any plan, the perfect government of his own passions, and the talent of acquiring an ascendant over those of other men" (Robertson 1777a, 80–81). Such was the rare moral asset Columbus was endowed with. He had all the characteristic features typical of a "projector," but they were enriched by "virtues of another species." Robertson made a similar diagnosis of another memorable figure in the history of early colonization of the Americas by the Spaniards, Bartolomé de las Casas, who conducted an indomitable campaign to battle the dehumanizing brutality inflicted on the natives by the avaricious Spanish colonizers. Las Casas left no effort untouched including that of working through the Flemish courtiers of Charles V. Whereas "projectors are usually too sanguine to conduct their schemes with much dexterity," Las Casas, in addition, "possessed a bustling indefatigable activity, which sometimes accomplishes its purposes with greater success than the most exquisite discernment and address" (Robertson 1777a, 214). If Columbus was a "projector" with an infinite resource of "patient perseverance," Las Casas was a "projector" exceptionally capable of executing his plan energetically. By contrast, the first English colonizers of America, such as Walter Raleigh, "had the spirit" but also all the "defects of a projector," and this notwithstanding all his "extraordinary talents, enlightened by knowledge no less uncommon." "Allured by new objects, and always giving the preference to such as were most splendid and arduous," Raleigh, in Robertson's assessment, was prone to be engaged in "undertakings so vast and so various as to be far beyond his power of accomplishing." The "multiplicity of projects" that stirred in his mind, included "taking possession of inexhaustible wealth, flowing from the richest mines in the New World" (Robertson 1777b, 29). Raleigh was infected by that moral disease endemic to the "Dishonest" projectors, as Defoe defined them, that of craving for a "Miracle" of instant and massive profit.

Robertson, like Defoe, recognized the value of the positive energy emanating from "projects" and "projectors," even though it requires to be moderated by virtues of honesty, generosity, and dedication. Adam

Smith would recognize no such redeeming qualities in those he calls "projectors" and their "projects," which may come as something of a surprise given his belief that the "system of natural liberty" in a free-market economy "establishes itself of its own accord" when private individuals are "left free to pursue" each "his own interest his own way" (Smith 1976, 687 [IV.ix.51]). In discussing how merchants serviced their debts by discounting and redrawing bills of exchange initially issued by commercial banks in Scotland, Smith points out how through that method, many "vast and extensive projects" were sustained "without any other fund to support them besides what was raised at this enormous expence" of 8% interest (Smith 1976, 310 [II.ii.69]). These bills of exchange, circulating as currency in lieu of hard cash, were often the "whole fund destined for carrying on some vast and extensive project of agriculture, commerce, or manufactures," frequently exceeding the sum the "projector" could produce from the money he actually had in possession. The individual "projector" and his "projects" could be kept afloat by this means but it put at risk the health of the nation's economy. The potential danger lurked in the fact that the "greater part of this paper" was "over and above the value of the gold and silver which would have circulated in the country, had there been no paper money." It was a fictive capital that could not be "exchanged for gold and silver" upon demand, a "capital which those projectors had very artfully contrived to draw from those banks, not only without their knowledge or deliberate consent, but for some time, perhaps, without their having the most distant suspicion that they had really advanced it" (Smith 1976, 311 [II.ii.71]). Specters of bankruptcy and insolvency haunt the issuer, endorser, and acceptor of a bill of exchange, for instance, drawn in Edinburgh on a London merchant, as it is redrawn repeatedly with interests and commissions deducted from it. As the bills circulate at increasingly discounted rates, the original sum advanced was steadily diminished, and the payments became increasingly "fictitious" rather than genuine (Smith 1976, 311 [II.ii.70]). What makes Smith call those entrepreneurs who juggle with the bills of exchange "projectors" is not so much their ingenuity itself as their unnatural and groundless desire to conjure up airy money from the papers besmirched with their signatures. Any default by one of the signatories often did trigger a chain of losses and even insolvency. The economy based on credit which evolved in Smith's society had "vices as well as virtues," as M. J. Daunton states (Daunton 1995, 248–249).

Even as he warned about the "vast and extensive projects" undertaken by "projectors," Smith would by no means condemn categorically the use of paper money itself. He was more than willing to concede that "judicious operations of banking can increase the industry of the country." The hidden premise, once again, is that any increase of "industry" is a supreme good in itself since it banishes "idleness," or the "unproductive" state of the national stock, to use Smith's preferred term. Even so, the "commerce and industry of the country" will be much less secure when they are "suspended upon the Daedalian wings of paper money, as when they travel about upon the solid ground of gold and silver" (Smith 1976, 321 [II.ii.86]). If any further persuasion was needed, one did not have to go too far back in time in search of historical corroboration. Smith summons his fellow countryman John Law, the mastermind behind the Mississippi Bubble. Before Law launched his daring scheme to create quick wealth in France, Smith reminds the reader that Law had first "proposed his project" in a "discourse concerning money and trade, which he published in Scotland." Despite Law's dubious career, the work itself contained some "splendid, but visionary ideas," which retained some luster. To Smith's dismay, Law's propositions "still continue to make an impression upon many people, and have, perhaps, in part, contributed to that excess of banking, which has of late been complained of both in Scotland and in other places" (Smith 1976, 317–318 [II.ii.78]). The title of Law's 1720 treatise *Money and Trade Consider'd; with a Proposal for Supplying the Nation with Money* is at once ominous and alluring. Having grasped the secret of a nation's prosperity, Law feels sorry for the abject state of his fatherland. Even though Scotland is "more capable of an extended Trade than any other Country of *Europe*, yet it is reduc'd to a very low State." Her "Trade is ruin'd," the "National Stock is wasted," and the "People forsake the Country" (Law 1720, 100–101). The remedy can be none other than furnishing Scotland with "Paper Money" secured by "Land" and given equal "Value" to "Silver Money." This will cure the nation of its compound diseases. As the new paper currency circulates, the "People will be employ'd, the Country improv'd, Manufacture advanc'd, Trade domestick and foreign will be carried on, and Wealth and Power attained; and not being liable to be exported, the People will not be set Idle, &c. and Wealth and Power will be less precarious" (Law 1720, 92–93). Fortunately for Scotland, Law found no opportunity in his homeland to put into practice his seductive theory.

Law lists the woes of a nation caused by a dearth of money and the myriad blessings an abundance of money will bring to it. Paper or silver, the material form of money matters not for him, because in his cerebral scheme, the value of one is equal to the other. In the same year Law "proposed" his "project" in his English pamphlet, his brazen self-confidence was sorely shattered by the financial crash which erupted in Law's adopted country of France in 1720 (Brewer 1989, 125–126; Neal 1990, 70–76; Hamilton 1991, 42–79; Dale 2004, 56–72). His catastrophic failure, as Smith perceived, did not dispel the allure of Law's encomium on paper currency, which could always find ready adherents in the bustling economy of mid-eighteenth-century Britain. Yet Smith considered excessive adoration of silver and gold to be equally dangerous. "Of all those expensive and uncertain projects" which "bring bankruptcy upon the greater part of the people who engage in them," Smith writes, "there is none perhaps more perfectly ruinous than the search after new silver and gold mines." It is the "most disadvantageous lottery in the world," since, "though the prizes are few and the blanks many," the "common price of a ticket" is nothing less than the "whole fortune of a very rich man." All in all, this is a perfect example of a nugatory "project":

> Projects of mining, instead of replacing the capital employed in them, together with the ordinary profits of stock, commonly absorb both capital and profit. They are the projects, therefore, to which of all others a prudent law-giver, who desired to increase the capital of his nation, would least chuse to give any extraordinary encouragement, or to turn towards them a greater share of that capital than what would go to them of its own accord. Such in reality is the absurd confidence which almost all men have in their own good fortune, that wherever there is the least probability of success, too great a share of it is apt to go to them of its own accord. (Smith 1976, 562 [IV. vii.a.18])

Unlike the "projects" of financiers jeopardizing other peoples' private savings or public funds, those searching for silver and gold mines mostly hazard their own money. They may, therefore, appear to harm the public less, but this species of "projects" incurs the waste of the nation's "capital" as a whole. In Smith's view such loss of valuable investment is a political issue that needs to be addressed by wise statesmen. The gold and silver mining "projects" are also yoked to moral defects in human nature, since these "projects" arise from the fertile soil of human delusion, the "absurd confidence which almost all men have in their own good fortune." Those investing their money in these "projects" have learned nothing from the folly of Spaniards in America who lusted after silver and gold with such calamitous consequences for the natives and for Spain's economy. "Though the judgment of sober reason and experience concerning such projects has always been extremely unfavourable," Smith observes, "that of human avidity has commonly been quite otherwise." The "same passion" of "human avidity" which had "suggested to so many people the absurd idea of the philosopher's stone" imparts in others the "equally absurd one of immense rich mines of gold and silver." Forgetting the obvious fact that the value of those metals is founded on their "scarcity," and on the "labour and expence" of finding the scarce metals, the fortune hunters in the Americas "flattered themselves that veins of those metals might in many places be found as large and as abundant as those which are commonly found of lead, or copper, or tin, or iron" (Smith 1976, 563 [IV.vii.a.19]). Mighty indeed is the force of "avidity" which seduces humans into believing the improbable.

Smith's deployment of moral argument in his anatomy of the social and political dangers of "projects" becomes even more salient when he discusses the regulation of interest rates. An inordinately high interest rate would only benefit "prodigals and projectors." "Sober people" would "give for the use of money no more than a part of what they are likely to make by the use of it" and thus are "most likely to make a profitable and advantageous use" of the "capital of the country." When the interest rates rise too high, these reasonable borrowers will be pushed out of the money market by these "prodigals and projectors." The legal rate of interest, therefore, ought to be fixed "but a very little above the lowest market rate," if the "sober" tradesmen are to be supported by timely loan (Smith 1976, 357 [II.iv.15]). The "projectors" who borrow others' money even at unnaturally high rates include the "stock jobbers," who were often denounced by different authors throughout the century. *An Account of the Trade to the East Indies, Together with the State of the Present Company, and the Best Method for Establishing and Managing that Trade, to the Honour and Advantage, of the Nation*, by "Mr. George White of London, Merchant," first published in 1692 and reissued in 1772, inveighed against "a new society of *artificers*," plaguing the market of East India shares. They "blow the price of stock up and down, as best suits their design of enriching themselves by the ruin of others." This "*leger-demain* is manag'd by a strange sort of *insects* call'd *Stock-jobbers*, who devour men on our

Exchange, as the *locusts* of old did the herbage of Egypt" (White [1694] 1772, 20). Thomas Mortimer's *Every Man His Own Broker: or, A Guide to Exchange-Alley* (1769) described these "*insects*" in a more measured language. The "stock-jobbers" are the "stock-brokers and their employers," who "with very little, and often with no property at all in the funds," trade or "job" shares on credit, and "transact more business in the several government securities in one hour, without having a shilling of property in any one of them, than the real proprietor of thousands transacts in several years" (Mortimer 1769, 34–35). They cunningly tickle that potent passion of "avidity" in those who trade with their money, as they deftly "throw out all possible baits to engage people to be continually changing from one fund to another," all the while garnering "fresh commission-money" from the transactions (Mortimer 1769, 22n). They play with people's hopes and fears by fabricating a "great variety of articles in the newspapers" and spreading "rumors and reports in coffee-houses" (Mortimer 1769, 32–33). This business of stock-jobbing for this and other reasons is condemned by Mortimer as an "iniquitous art" (Mortimer 1769, 24). The "iniquitous art" of stock-jobbing thrives at the interstices of the credit economy. The "*insects*" or "*locusts*" prey on the greed of the monied classes. Being petty agents, they are called "jobbers" instead of "projectors," the latter being something of a distinction reserved for those who undertake "vast and extensive projects," in Smith's expression. Yet they clearly belong to the tribe of "prodigals and projectors" whom "sober people" ought to shun.

Stock-jobbers could thrive in this early stage of globalization when international news from distant parts of the world traveled slow and were largely immune to objective verification. News of war and troubles overseas, often exaggerated if not outright fabricated, could not fail to create loud resonance in the "fiscal-military state" (Brewer 1989, 24; Graham and Walsh 2016, 1–21) which Britain had become, as the vast number of civilians with spare money who invested in the government securities were excited or alarmed by the news. The public sentiment more often than not favored belligerence rather than pacifism, particularly when rumors were spread about Britain's international trade being menaced by foreign powers. Hume had reasoned in the 1750s in his essay "Of the Jealousy of Trade" that "foreign commerce" can only be beneficial to "domestic industry," since the "emulation among rival nations" invigorates "industry" in both nations. No "single man" in a society can be "industrious" when "all his fellow-citizens are idle," for only when they are all "industrious," will they "consume the produce of my industry, and afford me the produce of theirs in return." The relationship between neighboring nations is essentially the same. It is far better for your "industry" to have an industrious rival as your neighbor than an "idle" one (Hume 1987, 329–330 ["Of the Jealousy of Trade"]). Josiah Tucker, in the 1770s, raised his voice to exorcise the "Witchcraft of the Jealousy of Trade," which, far from having been dispelled by Hume's enlightened disquisition, raged, if anything, with greater fierceness, as it often was presented as legitimate *casus belli*. Tucker could not concur with those who considered "going to War for the Sake of getting Trade" to be a reasonable policy. "Grant that you subdue your Rival by force of Arms: Will that Circumstance render your Goods cheaper at Market than they were before?" he asks. As the answer can only be in the negative, and as foreign nations "will never enquire, whether you were victorious or not; but only, whether you will sell cheaper, or at least as cheap as others," the inescapable conclusion must be that "Trade will always follow Cheapness, and not Conquest" (Tucker 1774, 74–75). Despite this patent truth, the "Thirst of inordinate Riches" in certain "private Subjects" goads them to "wish so vehemently for War" (Tucker 1774, 57). These war-mongers Tucker classifies into different categories. He begins with that "Monster of modern Times, who is perpetually declaiming against a Peace, *viz.* the Broker, and the Gambler of Change-alley," to whom peace among nations is an anathema. Tucker depicts their typical stratagem with a barrage of satirical details:

> Letters from the *Hague*, wrote in a Garret at Home for Half a Guinea;—the first News of a Battle fought (it matters not how improbable) with a List of the Slain and Prisoners, their Cannon, Colours, *&c.* Great Firings heard at Sea between Squadrons not yet out of Port;—a Town taken before the Enemy was near it;—an intercepted Letter that never was wrote;—or, in short any Thing else that will elate or depress the Minds of the undiscerning Multitude, serves the Purpose of the Bear or the Bull to sink or raise the Price of Stocks, according as he wishes either to buy or sell. And by these vile Means the Wretch, who perhaps the other Day came up to *London* in the Waggon to be an Under-Clerk or a Message Boy in a Warehouse, acquires such a Fortune as sets him on a Par with the greatest Nobles of the Land. (Tucker 1774, 80–81)

Not too much removed from this army of fabricators seeking to amass a sudden "Fortune" by juggling the "Bear" and the "Bull," in Tucker's judgment, are the news-writers scribbling in their garrets. They form a "Species which abound in this Country more than in any other; for as Men are in this Kingdom allowed greater Liberty to say, or write what they please; so likewise is the Abuse of that Blessing carried to a higher Pitch." Left alone to write what they will, they "*trade in Blood*," as it were, for "War is their Harvest; and a Gazette Extraordinary produces a Corp of an hundred Fold." "Friends of Peace" they never can be, and they see to it that all government "Ministers" be "Ministers of War." By penning and printing periodical articles, they aspire to "govern the Minds of the good People of England," and conspire "to turn their Affections whithersoever they please." They can render "any Scheme unpopular which they dislike" and make their "Approbation, or Disapprobation" be "regarded by Thousands, and almost by Millions, as the Standard of Right and Wrong, of Truth or Falshood." Britain, Tucker deplores, is "as much News mad, and News-ridden now, as ever it was Popery-made, and Priest-ridden, in the Days of our Forefathers." But both the stock-jobber and the news-writer are dwarfed in their villainy when put next to those profiting directly from the projects of war, the "Jobbers and Contractors of all Kinds and of all Degrees for our Fleets and Armies;—the Clerks and Pay-Masters in the several Departments belonging to War;—and every other Agent, who has the fingering of the public Money." These Tucker likens to a "distinct Brood of Vultures, who prey upon their own Species, and fatten upon Human Gore" (Tucker 1774, 81–82). These bloodthirsty "Jobbers and Contractors" share with the projectors a keen relish for "public Money," but they are protected, unlike the stock-jobber and the news-monger, by an aura of respectability and legitimacy transmitted to them by the state apparatus. J. G. A. Pocock suggested that there existed an odd combination of a strong belief in "economic freedom" with an advocacy of "submission to civil authority" in Tucker's thoughts (Pocock 1985, 161). This spirited denunciation of those living off the state coffers ought to qualify Pocock's assessment, for this "Brood of Vultures" pervert both the civil government and the free market. In this respect, they are similar to the monopolists, whom we will encounter in the next section.

5.2 Monopolies

Criticism of monopoly could be founded either on some moral principles or on theories of governance. The former would accuse it of going against the natural order of things, while the latter would delve into its harmful consequences for the general public. In the eyes of the laws of the realm, a monopoly, as William Blackstone defines it, was a "licence or privilege allowed by the king for the sole buying and selling, making, working, or using, of any thing whatsoever; whereby the subject in general is restrained from that liberty of manufacturing or trading which he had before." Being a political favor granted by the supreme executive authority, however unfair it may be, monopoly in itself could not be challenged by the king's subjects "in general." Riding the tide of ascending monarchical power under the Tudors, monopolies were "carried to an enormous height" under Eliabeth I. But as the market economy in Britain began to grow in complexity, the abuse of monopolies began to be "remedied" by James I's parliament, which declared by statute (21 Jac. I. c. 3) that all monopolies are "contrary to the Lawes of this Realme, and so are and shalbe utterlie void," except for those protected by royal patents, which, in turn, were stipulated to expire after fourteen years. "Forestalling the market," or signing a compact to artificially boost the price of any merchandize or victual, had already been made an offense under Edward VI, as was "regrating," which is the "buying of corn, or other dead victual, in any market, and selling it again in the same market, or within four miles of the place" to raise the price. "Engrossing," or "getting into one's possession, or buying up, of corn or other dead victuals, with intent to sell them again" was likewise deemed an injury to the public, as it put it in the "power of one or two rich men to raise the price of provisions at their own discretion" (Blackstone 1770, 158–159). These legal restrictions on monopolies and other conspiratorial interventions in the market mechanism were intended to eradicate, in the language of the preamble to the 1623 *Statute of Monopolies* (21 Jac. I. c. 3), the "greate Greevance and Inconvenience" of the king's "Subjects." The same statute, however, exempts the "Graunts Chartres or Lettres Patents" given to the "City of London" and to "any Companies or Societies of Merchants within this Realme, erected for the mayntenance enlargement or ordering of any Trade or Merchandize," so that "their Liberties Priviledges Powers and Immunities, shalbe and continue of such force and effect as they were before the making of this Act" (*Statute of Monopolies 1623* n.d.).

By the eighteenth century, the unequal advantages enjoyed by "Companies, or Societies of Merchants" protected by "Graunts Chartres or Lettres Patents" began to grate against the spirit of the age, which upheld free trade as sacrosanct. That free trade was divinely ordained was almost a standard trope circulating widely among writers both forgotten and celebrated by posterity. *A General History of Trade*, cited in the previous chapter, evoked the authority of the "Wise Disposer" of the world, who has "separated all those valuable things, by vast Oceans, unknown Gulphs, and almost impassable Seas, that he might joyn them all again, and make them common to one another, by the Industry of Men, and thereby propagate Navigation, Plantation, Correspondence, and Commerce to the Universal benefit of every part of the World" (Anon. 1713b, 25–26). Lord Kames was likewise convinced that the "commercial balance held by the hand of Providence, is never permitted to preponderate much to one side; and every nation partakes, or may partake, of all the comforts of life" (Kames 1774, 82). Free international trade, therefore, has the sanction of Divine Providence for these authors, one anonymous and the other famous. Kame's friend Hume endorsed both the substance and the spirit of this anonymous author of *A General History of Trade* when he accused all "those numberless bars, obstructions, and imposts, which all nations of EUROPE, and none more than ENGLAND, have put upon trade" of depriving "neighbouring nations of that free communication and exchange which the Author of the world has intended, by giving them soils, climates, and geniuses, so different from each other" (Hume 1987, 324 ["Of the Balance of Trade"]). Edmund Burke, though not always sedulous to mend the fate of the land he hailed from, yet forcefully argued that all restrictions on Ireland's international trade imposed by the British clearly flouted divine natural law. To shackle free trade by such despotic legislation was to "counteract bounty of Providence" and to stifle the free "use of the natural faculties which God has given" to the Irish (Burke 1991c, 509). Above all, although there were other champions of free trade before Smith (Hoppit 2017, 164–165), a plea for freedom from artificial legal restrictions was most eloquently made by the author of *The Wealth of Nations*. Smith declared that to restrain common people "from making all that they can of every part of their own produce, or from employing their stock and industry in the way that they judge most advantageous to themselves, is a manifest violation of the most sacred rights of mankind" (Smith 1976, 582 [IV.vii.b.44]). Anticipating objections to this maxim as an idealistic moral argument based on an abstract principle of the "rights of mankind," Smith also presented with taut succinctness a practical political argument addressing the question of expediency. "The price of monopoly," Smith reminds his readers, is "upon every occasion the highest which can be got," whereas the "natural price, or the price of free competition" is the "lowest which can be taken" (Smith 1976, 78

[I.vii.27]). Heedless of the rhyme and reason of the admonition given by Smith and others, monopoly corporations of Britain jealously guarded their "Liberties Priviledges Powers and Immunities."

The stronghold of the chartered companies was the City of London, whose "Liberties" were inseparable from those of the "Companies, or Societies of Merchants" located there. Smith, needless to say, was no Londoner, and he betrays in his masterpiece *The Wealth of Nations* a pervasive reluctance to acknowledge the leading role London played in creating and increasing the "wealth" of the British "nation." London makes only a marginal or subsidiary appearance in the detailed discussions and accounts of the long book, where no single chapter or even a section is assigned to account for the contribution London made to the nation's economic might. Smith must have intentionally adopted such a guarded and reserved attitude toward the English metropolis, not because of his personal aversion to the city or because of his relatively insufficient knowledge of a town where he resided extensively and collected the sources for his book (Ross 1995, 223–267). Though a prudish middle-aged Scotsman, Smith could not have been entirely immune to the charms of London that enthralled his younger compatriot James Boswell, who sang the praises of London in his journal, as in the following entry for 5 December 1762:

> London is undoubtedly a Place where Men & Manners may be seen to the greatest advantage. The liberty & the whim that reigns there occasions a variety of perfect & curious characters. Then the immense crowd & hurry and bustle of business & diversion, the great number of public places of entertainment, the noble churches and the superb buildings of different kinds agitate[,] amuse & elevate the mind. Beside[,] the satisfaction of pursuing whatever plan is most agreeable, without being known or look'd at, is very great. (Boswell 2010, 28–29)

The "liberty & the whim" Boswell celebrates of the town, which for Boswell were more attuned to "diversion" and "entertainment" than to serious "business," cannot be all that inimical to that "freedom of trade" and "natural liberty" in whose name Smith castigates the "exclusive privileges of corporations" (Smith 1976, 470 [IV.ii.42]). It seems more plausible that Smith's reticence regarding London's centrality has to do with his effort to construct a model of economic progress founded on the universal premise of "industry" (or "labour") which ought to be free from the historical and geographical conditions favoring a particular locale such as London. To preserve this stance, Smith has to grapple with vast variations in the price of "industry," as they inevitably tend to diminish the force of his generalizations. The chapters, "Of the Wages of Labour" and "Of Wages and Profit in the Different Employments of Labour and Stock," are among the longest in the book, as the two add up to some 185 paragraphs in total. In this long excursus, the exceptionally high London wages could not possibly go unmentioned. The impact of a rich and populous city like London inhabited by voracious consumers on adjacent agrarian lands similarly could not be ignored in the chapter, "Of the Rent of Land," which thorny subject makes for a mini-treatise of its own comprising three sub-chapters whose third "Part" alone sprawls into one long "Digression" running into some nine sections. London in these accounts stands out as an exception to the general pattern. The metropolis behaves almost like a foreign country when it comes to prices. In London, no "bank notes are issued under ten pounds value," since "ten pounds" in London, "amidst the profuse expence" of the city, equal "five pounds" in "most parts of the kingdom" (Smith 1976, 323 [II.ii.91]).

Smith the advocate of the "sacred rights of mankind" to engage in free trade, at least, indirectly admitted London's exceptional status in the nation's economy. What is left as an open question in the chapters where Smith traces the exorbitant cost of living in London is whether it is due to the legalized forestalling and engrossing by chartered monopolies, or to "regrating" and other illicit deeds by different traders, or merely due to the "freedom of trade" the city sustains and is sustained by. A typical view of London's thriving economy would focus more on the dynamic flow of the city's commerce rather than those visible or invisible hands guiding or blocking its flow. Nicholas Barbon, who had boasted already in 1685 that London had become the "Metropolis of *Europe*" (as he was seen in the previous chapter) (Barbon 1685, 36), is proud to see it reign over the nation as her "Metropolis," which he compares to the "heart of a Nation, through which the Trade and Commodities of it circulate, like the blood through the heart, which by its motion giveth life and growth to the rest of the Body." Woe, then, to those that dare to defame or disable this vital "heart" of the nation's economic "Body," for when the heart "declines, or be obstructed in its growth, the whole body falls into consumption" (Barbon 1685, 30). *The Exact Dealer's Daily Companion: Instructing Him Thoroughly in All Things Absolutely Necessary to Be Known by All Those Who Would Thrive in the World; and in the Whole Art and Mystery of Trade and Traffick* (1721) by "N. H. Merchant, in the City of London," as the title introduced the author, pays court to the importance of "industry" in its first chapter. "The happiness and welfare of all People arises," asserts the author, "by having or acquiring, thro' some Industry or other, such conveniency of Lively-hood, as may not only keep them from Want and Poverty, but render them pleasant and sociable to one another." What has been acquired "thro' some Industry" then enters the domain of "Trade." "*Great Britain*," being "properly a Nation of Trade" well "situated for Commerce," and the "Inhabitants" being "Ingenious, and fit for it, if encouraged," the only thing the British need to do is to "keep at unity with ourselves, and enjoy a free Trade; keeping only some Forts and Islands in profitable Places, whereby we become Masters of Trade" (Anon. 1721, 1–3). To all British subjects "free trade" founded on "industry" is to be allowed, but at the same time, some collective ownership of foreign stations in "profitable Places" of the world are also recommended. Although a broadly catholic "we" is used in the last clause, "we become Masters of Trade," whether any individual or only the certified "Companies, or Societies of Merchants" are entitled to be the "Masters of Trade" making use of these trading posts is not clear. What to our "N. H. Merchant, in the City of London" is indubitably obvious is the preeminence of London, rooted in the geographical "Advantages." London is blessed by the "goodly River of *Thames*," which, "opening Eastward towards *Germany* and *France*, is much more Advantagious for Traffick, than any other River in *England*." In fact, no "River in the World can shew a braver Sight of Ships than are commonly to be seen (like a floating Forest) from *Black-Wall* to *London-bridge*; which in continual Voyages, Import all sorts of Goods, either for Need or Ornament, and Export our Superfluities, to the extraordinary Advantage of all Sorts of People, high or low." Added to this is the immense "Advantage that *London* hath" of getting "plentifully supplied with all necessary Provision from the Country, at easie and indifferent Rates, and the Manufactures of the respective Counties, which the City disperses to Markets beyond Seas." The entire "Country," on the other hand, is amply furnished by London with "all Sorts of necessary Merchandizes, wanting there." London, in sum, is one "large Magazine of Men, Money, Ships, Horses, Ammunition; of all Sorts of Commodities necessary or expedient for the use or pleasure of Mankind" (Anon. 1721, 23–24).[2] A reasonable conjecture would be that some Londoners or some

[2] Historians corroborate this author's proud estimation of London's enormous preponderous in the nation's economy. In 1750, some 11% of England's population lived in London,

"Companies, or Societies," of them would profit more than others from the "Advantage" of this "large Magazine" ideally situated to be the first among all the "profitable Places" in the world.

A Companion to the Plan of London (1765?) follows the discursive strategy adopted by *The Exact Dealer's Daily Companion* published more than four decades earlier, of celebrating London's water traffic managed by its "commodious Port" to which "many thousand Ships of Burthen annually resort from all Parts of the Globe, and those of moderate Bulk can come up as far as London-Bridge, tho' the very largest are obliged to lie lower down the River" (Anon. [1765?], 2). That "large Magazine" of goods and services has its headquarters in the Royal Exchange, where "Factors and Agents" from "so many different Nations" gather to "transact their respective Business." The "prodigious *Trade*" conducted by merchants domestic and foreign supports the "Grandeur and Opulence of the City," and for our author nothing pleases him more than to behold the "numerous Concourse of Merchants and Traders, who frequent this great Mart of Commerce during Change Hours" and to muse on the "Benefits arising to this Kingdom from such an extensive Correspondence" (Anon. [1765?], 9). Relishing this particular kind of pleasure was an activity or hobby that had some illustrious precedents. Joseph Addison writing as "Mr. Spectator" eulogized in 1711 the "great Mart" of international "Commerce" which London's Royal Exchange housed. It gave him a "secret Satisfaction" to see "so rich an Assembly of Countrymen and Foreigners consulting together upon the private Business of Mankind, and making this Metropolis a kind of *Emporium* for the whole Earth." To this "great Council" have dispatched "all considerable Nations" their "Representatives," who conduct in this "Trading World" what ambassadors do in the "Politick World." Here they convene to "negotiate Affairs, conclude Treaties, and maintain a good Correspondence between those wealthy Societies of Men that are divided from one another by Seas and Oceans, or live on the different Extremities of a Continent." Not content to be merely an outside observer, Mr. Spectator walks into this "Emporium" in search of a more intimate sensation of the "Trading World" assembled there:

when Paris took up only about 2.5% of France's population (Daunton 1995, 138). About 80% of overseas trade passed through London in the early part of the century, before Bristol and Liverpool began to emerge as significant but still weaker rivals of London in the later decades (Thomas and McCloskey 1981, 92). London also had higher rates of bankruptcy than the provinces, about 33–43% above the national average (Hoppit 1987, 73). See also Hankock (1995, 86–87).

> I have often been pleased to hear Disputes adjusted between an Inhabitant of *Japan* and an Alderman of *London*, or to see a Subject of the *Great Mogul* entering into a League with one of the *Czar of Muscovy*. I am infinitely delighted in mixing with these several Ministers of Commerce, as they are distinguished by their different Walks and different Languages: Sometimes I am justled among a Body of *Armenians*; Sometimes I am lost in a Crowd of *Jews*; and sometimes make one in a Groupe of *Dutchmen*. I am a *Dane*, *Swede*, or *Frenchman* at different times; or rather fancy my self like the old Philosopher, who upon being asked what Countryman he was, replied, That he was a Citizen of the World. (Addison 1711, no. 69 [May 19])

These foreigners whom Addison was delighted to survey in the Royal Exchange, picturesque as their presence may be, surely were not the main players of the market. They were, in the legal parlance of the City of London, as explained by *City-Liberties: or, The Rights and Privileges of Freemen*, which claimed to offer in the remainder of the subtitle a "*Concise Abridgment of all the Law, Charters, By-Laws, and Customs of London, down to this time*" (1732), were "*Merchant Strangers*" permitted to "sojourn with the Citizens" as lodgers in the City. They could "not sell any Goods by Retail" and could only "sell Goods in Gross," according to the medieval statute passed under Edward III. In order to enjoy the full "City-Liberties" one had to obtain the status of "Freeman of London." One could do so through one of the three paths: first, by serving as an apprentice in the City of London; second, by being born as a son to a London freeman; and, third, by "Fine and Ransom" or "Order of the Court of Aldermen." Hogarth's industrious apprentice (discussed in Chap. 3) trod the first track to become a most prominent "Merchant." Those who earned the title of "Merchant" of London had the right to "carry on Merchandize" in the City and "within ten Miles thereof." Before one could reach that stage, one first had to prove his having obtained the qualification of "Freeman" by producing a "Testimonial" issued by the "Chamberlain" (Anon. 1732, 86, 109).

Among the "Merchants" in the City of London the most respectable, if not the most affluent, according to the *City-Liberties* quoted above, would be those with membership in the "Companies of Merchants" empowered by the Crown or by parliamentary legislation to undertake "joint Trades to Foreign Parts" on a considerable scale (Anon. 1732, 110). That indeed was the case. More than half of those elected as aldermen of London between 1695 and 1714 had connections to overseas trade (Hoppit 2000, 322). The Bank of England, established in 1694, also belonged to the category of the "Companies" of London, as it consisted of "Merchants and others wholly employ'd in the turning of Money" (Anon. 1732, 114). Even if one lacked the requisite qualifications of "Merchant" and "Freeman," one could still seek one's fortune in the City as a "broker" licensed by the Lord Mayor and the Court of Aldermen of London. A "broker" could assist the "making and concluding" of "Bargains between Merchant and Merchant or others" such as the "*Merchant Strangers*" sojourning in London. Brokers of London had to take an oath and give a bond of £500 for the "faithful Execution of their Offices," which bond they could forfeit when found guilty of misconduct or mischief. The total number of licensed brokers could not exceed 100 at any given time, and their "Names and Places of Habitation" had to be "publickly affixed on the *Royal Exchange*": Any one acting as a broker without the aforesaid license, and without being included in the official list, were liable to be fined and to forfeit the fee they may have earned. This regulation, apparently, did not prevent the "stockjobbers," the poorer cousins of "projectors" we have already met above, from proliferating in the City. To extirpate this breed of unlicensed brokers and the "*Bubbles* and Cheats" they foment, a statute was enacted in 1720 declaring that "all Stockjobbing, Subscriptions, &*c.* not authorized by Act of Parliament, or by Charter" to be "void" and such "Undertakings" to be deemed "publick Nuisances." The brokers of this description caught "buying and selling any Shares of Stock" were liable to pay a penalty of £500 (Anon. 1732, 29, 145). The City of London, upon the whole, behind the façade of a glamorous "Emporium," maintained a complex, or even rigid, self-governance. It enjoyed a considerable autonomy vis-à-vis the national government, and maintained an extensive jurisdiction over those who did business within it. Tucker's third "Tract" written in the form of a letter sent by a "Merchant in *London* to his Nephew in *America*" has the "uncle" rebuke the insolence of the "nephew" who claim exemption from taxation on the grounds that Americans are not represented in the British parliament. That this exemption is untenable is proven, as far as the "*Merchant* in London" sees it, by the example of the City of London. Despite being a "Body Politic as respectable" and not inferior to the "greatest" among the North American Colonies with "Regard to *Property*," and despite having "long enjoyed, before the Colonies were ever thought of, the threefold Power of Jurisdiction, Legislation, and Taxation in certain Cases," no one ever supposes in

London, that the "City of *London* either was, or could be exempted by these Charters from Parliamentary Jurisdiction, or Parliamentary Taxes." Whether or not the comparison can be justified in this context, the point Tucker makes about the City of London's virtual sovereignty is what we can readily accept (Tucker 1774, 98–99).

In the "Body Politic" constituting the City of London, the most powerful organs of its potency by mid-century were not the ancient guilds with quaint names such as the companies of the "Haberdashers" or the "Mercers," but the incorporated societies of merchants specializing in particular regions or items of foreign trade. They upheld the absolute preeminence of London as a trading port of the nation, evidenced by London's massive contribution to the Crown's customs receipt, which took up some 80.3% of the national total in 1710, and remained only partially modified in the later decades (67.0% in 1750, and 68.2% in 1780) (Hoppit 2017, 285). Anderson, writing in the 1760s, names four corporations established by charter to manage the kingdom's international trade: the "Hamburgh" Company formerly known as "*Merchant's-Adventurers*," the "*Russia* Company," the "*Levant* or *Turkey* Company," and the "*African* Company." Even more powerful were the four "exclusive Joint-Stock Companies," led by the East India Company, and followed in terms of seniority by the "*Hudson's-Bay* Company," the "*South-Sea* Company," and the Bank of England, which last Anderson, like the author of *City-Liberties*, counts among London's joint-stock companies. Both the chartered and the joint-stock companies were all of them "exclusive" companies, for "no other Company" or "any private Partnership" could encroach on the particular area of business assigned to them by parliamentary legislation (Anderson 1764, xxv). These "exclusive" monopolies, naturally, could easily be arraigned for causing "great grievance and inconvenience" to the king's "subjects" (in the expression of the seventeenth-century *Statute of Monopolies*) who desire but are denied access to their trades. The British East India Company, which will receive further attention in our next section, was frequently pilloried by those criticizing the ills attending the "exclusive" monopoly granted to the corporation. White's *An Account of the Trade to the East Indies*, cited earlier in this chapter, deplored the "evil practice" of the managers of the Company of "multiplying their votes according to their stocks, rating every vote at 500 *l.*" This is "utterly destructive of our *darling property*, and directly contrary to those measures which the justice and wisdom of the nation has taken in choice of our representatives, who are the preservers of it." Furthermore, it was pernicious because it has been shown that "he who has the biggest purse, is not always the most honest, nor able to manage so weighty an affair." In fact, "such *notorious frauds* have been acted in underselling the company's goods by *private contracts and unheard of deductions afterwards*" (White [1694] 1772, 16–17). Without naming names, White alleges that a "certain man" in London, "who is at present no more than one of the committee," made away with "several of their books and papers" from the company's offices at the Leadenhall street to "his own house about six miles from London," which "if true" should be a "Felony that ought not to have the Benefit of Clergy" (White [1694] 1772, 36). Criminality lurks at the very top and at the heart of the "committee" of this "exclusive" company of London merchants, who, being "not always the most honest" among the city's dwellers, seek to fatten their already bulky "purse" by fair means or foul.

White wrote with his practical knowledge of London companies in the 1690s, and surely some of the abuses which he berated and which indeed did exist were rectified since then, as the East India Company itself was reformed a number of times by Parliament (Stern 2023, 45–48). Yet complaints about the monopoly companies did not subside, often pointing to the deleterious sway they held over the nation's economy. *An Essay on the Increase and Decline of Trade, in London and the Out-Ports* (1749) flaunts a lengthy subtitle characteristic of the period enumerating the themes treated. The first in the list is the claim that "Monopolies have been the Ruin of several Branches of the London Commerce," and the second is that "Luxury and high Living have, in all Ages, been the Bane of Trade, and have had remarkable Effects upon the British Commerce," with many more theses coming after these two, such as that "all the Merchants in the Out-Ports are not clandestine Dealers, and licensed Smugglers, as hath in too general Terms been asserted." The first thesis, linked directly to the topic in the title, "the Increase and Decline of Trade," is given full elaboration in the main body. It stands upon a historical awareness of how things have changed since the "Infancy of Trade" when "*Monopolies*" and the "numerous Charters granted on such Accounts" by the Crown all "in *Favour of London*" and her merchants could be said to have been "expedient." Times have changed, however, and the "great Powers and exclusive Privileges granted to several of them, have since been found a sore Nuisance to Trade; and not only a *heavy Grievance* to the rest of the *Nation*, but a *great Detriment* to the Trade of *London* itself" (Anon. 1749, 8). The author would not underrate the manifold advantages of London as a center of international commerce. The capital is most "commodiously situated for the foreign Trade to *Holland, Germany*, and the *Baltick*," and "exceedingly well stocked with Shipping and skilful Navigators." The metropolis also accommodates a "prodigious home Consumption, and the best and largest Market for all Commodities, which the Merchant can there at any Time turn into ready Money." As this is the city where the "monied Men chiefly reside," any "*London* Merchant of Credit" can easily be "supplied with Cash at a short Warning, and for any Term, which is not the Case in the Out-Ports." In London, moreover, "Bills are negotiated, and Insurances made with more Ease to the Merchant, and at a less Expence than in any other Port of *Britain*." Do we need then, on top of all these benefits, to bestow on this "great and opulent City" all those "Grants and Charters" reserving "several of the richest Branches of Commerce" for London's monopoly companies, and excluding other ports of Britain (Anon. 1749, 5–6)? The answer should be in the negative, for the following reasons:

> For Experience hath taught us, that when Trade is under the Direction of large Companies, it is seldom managed with the same good Œconomy, and with the same Care and Eagerness, as when in the Hands of private Adventurers. Hence those large Companies are very liable to be abused, imposed upon, and cheated by *those they employ*, and (which is a Misfortune peculiar to them) even by the *Employers*; so that in no other way of trading Neglects, Mismanagement, Jobbs, Frauds, and treacherous Dealings are so frequent. No wonder therefore, that many Branches of Trade, when carried on in this Manner, tho' they have been lucrative to some Particulars, have not been profitable to the Company in general. No wonder that Bankruptcies have often been the Consequence of such Management.

Indeed, had it not been for these "Monopolies" which have "at length turned greatly to the Disadvantage of *London*, and have been one great Cause of the Decline of its Trade," those "Branches of Commerce thus lost, would probably still have flourished there, had they in due Time been left open to the private Adventurer, in them to have exerted his Skill and Industry" (Anon. 1749, 9–10). The linchpin of his argument, once again, is "Industry," which is best exercised by "private Adventurers." At the other end of the spectrum are those "Particulars" belonging to these "large Companies" who seek their own private profit often to the detriment of the "Company in general." The 1773 Regulating Act (13 Geo. 3, c.63) sought to reform the East India Company's governance by raising the voting qualification of the members of the Court of Proprietors, from £500 to £1000 of stock, and by requiring each stock to be held for a minimum of 12 months (Holmes and Szechi 1993, 376). The legislation intended to strengthen the control of the monopoly corporation by large-scale investors. It did little to promote "industry" or to prevent and punish petty infringements of its legal rights. As Burke pointed out in his speech at the House of Commons in 1774, monopoly conferred on the East India Company, like the "immense duties" placed on French brandy, after all, had its inevitable loopholes. The law may use draconian language promising severe punishment, but there is "not a creek from Pentland Frith to the Isle of Wight, in which they do not smuggle immense quantities of teas, East India goods, and brandies" (Burke 1981a, 429). Burke may have exaggerated a little, as the extent and volume of smuggling, by definition, could never be accurately ascertained, but it could not be denied that high duties meant to preserve monopolies did convert themselves into incentives for smuggling (Hoppit 2017, 297–298).

Among the monopoly corporations, the Royal African Company had the honor of being the first to sustain a full-scale attack by the supporters of free trade. Established to oversee slave trade on the West African coast, the Company bore the brunt of a sally of accusations about its inaptitude in the first quarter of the century, decades before a moral criticism of slave trade itself emerged, which will be discussed at length in the next chapter. *A True State of the Present Difference Between the Royal African Company, and the Separate Traders* (1710) denounced the "Company's Mismanagements, and unfair Practices at home, the Irregularities, Abuses to the *British* Nation, committed to their Governours and other Agents abroad, their great Civilities to, and frequent Correspondence with our Enemies Ships, and the French Settlement in Africa, the indefensible Weakness of their little more than Titular Fortifications on that Coast," all of which, if true, would amount to serious misdeeds indeed or even to treasonous crimes. Tucked away in the exotic tropical posts, the "vast Sums" of money collected by the Company's agents from the "Merchants trading upon their own private Stocks, for the Protection of their Forts" is always put to "ill Use and Misapplication" (Anon. 1710, 33). The Company, after suffering severe financial difficulties, lost its exclusive monopoly in 1712, but still retained its presence on the African coast (see Neal 1990, 50–51, 54; Thomas 1997, 199–206; Morgan 2007, 56–61; Wennerlind 2011, 219–220; Pettigrew 2013, ch. 2). At this new stage, the Company did not lack its defenders in the London print market. *The Case of the Royal African Company of England* (1730) found fault with the private free traders who wished to "partake of the Benefits and Advantages" of the African trade, but was reluctant to contribute to "such Charges, as are absolutely necessary for the *Preservation* of the *Whole*." To protect even these selfish free riders, it was vital to maintain a "certain Number of *Forts* and *Castles*, in proportion to the *Power* of such other *Rival Nations*, as are strongly settled in the same Parts." Only the African Company could carry out this arduous and costly task (Anon. 1730, 90). Toward the mid-century, a compromise of sorts was advocated by pundits debating the issue. Charles Hayes, a Deputy Governor of the African Company, published anonymously *The Importance of Effectually Supporting the Royal African Company of England Impartially Consider'd; Shewing, That a Free and Open Trade to Africa, and the Support and Preservation of the British Colonies and Plantations in America, Depend upon Maintaining the Forts and Settlements, Rights and Privileges Belonging to that Corporation, Against the Encroachments of the French, and All Other Foreign Rivals in that Trade* (1744). What the verbose title announced as its main position is spelled out in the main text as a proposal to terminate the "unnatural Divisions" between the "Private Traders" and the African Company by clearly separating their roles. The "Company, by the Situation of their *Forts*, and by the Means of navigable Rivers, will naturally have it more in their Power to open and extend the Trade to the remotest *Inland Parts* of *Africa*," whereas "*Private Traders* are better able to supply our Plantations with *Negroes*," for they can "fit out their Ships cheaper than the Company" from the "*Out-Ports*; and as they carry on a constant Intercourse of General Trade with the *British* Plantations" (Hayes 1744, 143–144). Malachy Postlethwayt took part in this debate by writing two pamphlets, *The African Trade, the Great Pillar and Support of the British Plantation Trade in America* (1745) and *The National and Private Advantages of the African Trade Considered* (1746). Postlethwayt urged the reader to be impartial and judicious toward the much-maligned Company. One should take into consideration the "extraordinary Charge" the Company took upon itself of maintaining the forts at "so immense a Cost" and acknowledge that the 25-year monopoly granted by the Royal Charter to the Company barely sufficed to enable the Company to recover its massive investments (Postlethwayt 1746, 285–286, 293–294). The Company, in his view, should play the role of the police, providing protections from foreign rivals, leaving the actual trading to private merchants. When their respective powers are thus defined, "every Trader in the Kingdom will have it in his Power to engage in it, such Part of his Fortune as he shall chuse to employ therein, either as a *Member* of the *African Corporation*, or as a *Separate Trader*" (Postlethwayt 1745, 192). These different opinions about the monopoly rights and the role of the African Company, even among those sympathetic to it, seemed to agree on one view at least. The "*Private*" or "*Separate Trader*," they all accepted, was more resilient than the monopoly corporation in getting the business done and in making money from it, reflecting no doubt the surging entrepreneurial ethos of what Immanuel Wallerstein classifies as the first phase of West Africa's incorporation into the "European world-economy" as supplier of enslaved labor force (Wallerstein 2011, 147).

Quite apart from the question whether the obloquy upon the monopoly joint-stock trading companies was justified, London in a figurative sense "monopolized" the nation's international trade, such as the "African Trade," that is, the slave trade which the much-resented African Company sought but ultimately failed to control. In the early eighteenth century before the emergence of Liverpool, London faced the challenge offered by Bristol, but still the capital city's share of the "African Trade" remained substantial. *An Account of the Ships Employed in the African Trade, from the Ports of London and Bristol, Belonging to the Separate Traders to Africa* (1713) lists a total of 37 ships sailing from London, not counting two ships "Lost" in the "Hurricane." This sizable number of ships together carried in total some £137,000 worth of cargo. The monetary value of this cargo, of course, mostly reflects the worth of the enslaved humans the ships carried. The same *Account* records a total of 11,380 of all the "Negroes loaded in each Ship." The ships from the Port of Bristol numbered 24, with the total value of cargo reaching £98,820 and the total number of "Negroes" counted at 7540 (Anon. 1713a, 1–2). Bristol was certainly emerging as London's rival at least in this business sector, but it did not threaten the leading position of England's capital city. *A Register of the Trade of the Port of London Specifying the Articles Imported and Exported, Arranged Under the Respective Countries*, compiled by Charles Whitworth, for January–March 1776, calculated the export and imports through London to be "three-fourths" of the "whole Trade of the Kingdom" (Whitworth 1777, vi). Not to be compared in quantity and quality with the bulky transactions looked after by the grandees of London mercantile class, the business of providing foodstuff for the city's denizens also constituted an important sector of London's economy. Here again it was not difficult to meet with pamphlets crying out against "monopoly." One good example is *The London Fishery Laid Open: or the Arts of the Fishermen and Fishmongers Set in a True Light* (1759), written in the form of a letter sent to an unnamed recipient. The author reminds him (and the reader) how "this great town" was supplied with fish "in so sparing a manner, and at so dear a rate," all because of "monopolies," which are always "injurious in all trades, but in none worse, than in those on which this supply depends." The fish market of London suffers from the mischief of "forestalling," moreover, which "generally attends that of monopoly." The fishmongers of Billingsgate, before Parliament passed a bill forbidding their forestalling, had conspired to "employ one of two persons, as their buyers, to take up all the best and choicest fish that came to market, and then divided it, by such lots or parcels, as was agreed among themselves." By doing so, they wielded despotic power over both the supplier and the consumer. Billingsgate's wholesalers could buy "at what rates they pleased" and could charge "extravagant prices upon it, of which every one complained, and every one still complains" (Anon. 1759, 1, 4, 27).

The literally "fishy" bonding of Billingsgate monopolists who were keen to enhance their gains may explain to some extent the "profuse expence" of London Smith speaks of. Although London fish market fails to appear in *The Wealth of Nations*, Smith does deal with the "popular fear of engrossing and forestalling" in the realm of corn trade, which he suggests can be "compared to the popular terrors and suspicions of witchcraft." "The law which put an end to all prosecutions against witchcraft," Smith reflects, "seems effectually to have put an end to those fears and suspicions, by taking away the great cause which encouraged and supported them." Can the same remedy be applied to this modern brand of witch-hunting? Perhaps not, but the spirit of that precedent of restraining the punitive power of the law bears on this issue. The "law which should restore entire freedom to the inland trade of corn," he assumes, "would probably prove as effectual to put an end to the popular fears of engrossing and forestalling" (Smith 1976, 534 [IV.v.b.26]). The adverbial qualifier "probably" admits how uncertain the actual outcome would be. Whether in concert with others or just by himself, a corn merchant may "sometimes raise the price of his corn somewhat higher than the scarcity of the season requires" simply from an "excess of avarice." Even so, "all the inconveniencies which the people can suffer from this conduct" have to be put up with, if famine is to be avoided. Besides, the avaricious corn merchant himself is "likely to suffer the most by this excess of avarice," in part by being exposed to the "indignation which it generally excites against him," but more substantially by the "quantity of corn which it necessarily leaves upon his hands in the end of the season, and which, if the next season happens to prove favourable, he must always sell for a much lower price than he might otherwise have had" (Smith 1976, 525 [IV.v.b.3]).

But can any mechanism or power counteract the "excess of avarice" not of this or that corn dealer but of the magnates of the state and their friends the mighty merchants? Smith was less confident about this question. Not much can be done to stop them when they undertake their "invidious and malignant project" of profiting from their monopoly on colonial trade (Smith 1976, 595 [IV.vii.c.18]), or of maintaining a "great empire" solely for the purpose "of raising up a people of customers," which is "a project altogether unfit for a nation of shopkeepers; but extremely fit for a nation whose government is influenced by shopkeepers" (Smith 1976, 613 [IV.vii.c.63]). Particularly dangerous and devastating will be the outcome when these sorts of people pursue their avarice-inspired "project" far away from Britain, in the sultry regions of East Indies, to which we now turn.

5.3 "Nabobing"

Smith the philosopher of the "nature and causes" of the "wealth of nations" often builds his arguments upon universal premises. The "mean rapacity, the monopolizing spirit of merchants and manufacturers, who neither are, nor ought to be the rulers of mankind" present a new source of woe to the modern commercial nations, not less harmful than the "capricious ambition of kings and ministers" in the earlier eras (Smith 1976, 493 [IV.iii.c.9]). They pervert by their "interested sophistry" the natural common sense that in any country it "always is and must be the interest of the great body of the people to buy whatever they want of those who sell it cheapest" (Smith 1976, 494 [IV.iii.c.10]). Moreover, they use their "sophistry" and influence to usurp the power of "kings and ministers." The "protection of trade" against foreign rivals and enemies properly belongs to the "duty of the sovereign." But in the "greater part of the commercial states of Europe," such as Britain, "particular companies of merchants have had the address to persuade the legislature" to divide that sovereign power with them. The companies thus formed and empowered may have been "useful for the first introduction of some branches of commerce" by diffusing the risk the government might face, but they soon outlived their usefulness, proving "either burdensome or useless" (Smith

1976, 733 [V.i.e.4-5]). This is best illustrated by the Royal African Company, the debates about which we have revisited above. Buffeted by criticism, the Company was finally reformed in 1750 by new regulations purporting to "restrain effectually the oppressive and monopolizing spirit which is natural to the directors of a regulated company" (Smith 1976, 737–738 [V.i.e.12]). The new African Company was entrusted with the mission of maintaining forts on the African coast to protect private traders but was forbidden from engaging in direct trade itself. However, the "spirit of monopoly" died hard, as the Company sought to find loopholes in the law to interfere with private traders, as was accused by the Company's critics but hushed by the committee in the House of Commons investigating it. That was only to be expected, Smith observes, since the committee consisted of nine members, "all merchants, and the governors and factors, in their different forts and settlements" and thus "all dependent upon them" (Smith 1976, 739 [V.i.e.13]).

The East India Company, which had even mightier friends in Parliament, and had ready supporters in the publishing market, was quickly becoming a veritable sovereign power with a huge military capacity in the Indian subcontinent. In 1696, *An Essay on the East-India-Trade*, written by Charles Davenant, eulogized the "*East-India* Trade" as a blessing to the nation, claiming that it added "to the gross Stock of *England* at least 600,000 *l. per Annum* in time of Peace" by "carrying to other Places the Commodities brought from *India*" (Davenant 1696, 17, 22). Davenant's impressive figure was conjectural rather than actual. What seemed more convincing to others was that the trade with East India drained England of hard cash. Other earlier defenders, therefore, such as Child writing in the 1690s, had to justify the unfavorable balance of trade by emphasizing how what the Company imported in exchange for large "quantities of Gold and Silver" had vital strategic values, above all, saltpeter which was indispensable for gunpowder, as well as "*Pepper, Indico, Callicoes*, and several useful *Drugs*" (Child 1698, 159, 161). White in 1694 conceded that it would be better, no doubt, if British woolen manufacture could be exchanged with these valuable East-Indian commodities, but he would request the detractors of the Company to take in view the whole picture. The special circumstances of the East India Trade should be taken into account, and one should remember the "irrefragable maxim, that *trade is no more to be forced than faith*: and, as we *believe* according to the dictates of our *consciences*; so we *buy* and *sell* both as to quantities and sortments, as our *interests* direct" (White [1694] 1772, 10). And surely, it was

Britain's interest to secure sufficient quantities of saltpeter even when the balance of trade was unfavorable. Anderson repeated the same argument in 1764. Due to that "single, though indeed great, Article of *Saltpetre*," not just Britain but all Europe are involved in a "pernicious Trade," pernicious in that it forces Europe to part with "*all* or *most* of the Silver which *America* brings to it." But since "*Saltpetre* is so absolutely necessary for our national and private Magazines for Gun-powder, for which we must otherwise be at the Mercy of dangerous Rivals," the British "must ever be of Opinion, that our *East-India* Trade, under its present Circumstances, is really a beneficial one for *Great Britain*" despite the "pernicious" trade deficit (Anderson 1764, xxiii). For Smith, and later for Burke, the key point of contention was no longer the large sums of money spent to import East-Indian saltpeter, but the promiscuous expenditure of gunpowder made from saltpeter in the Company's interminable military adventures in India. Through a combination of luck and daring, the Company had become the ruler of Bengal, but in Smith's diagnosis, instead of taking upon their new role with sincere dedication, they still considered themselves "a company of merchants" and the "character of the sovereign as but an appendix to that of the merchant, as something which ought to be made subservient to it, or by means of which they may be enabled to buy cheaper in India, and thereby to sell with a better profit in Europe." Dictated by their "mercantile habits," which "perhaps insensibly" entice them to "prefer upon all ordinary occasions the little and transitory profit of the monopolist to the great and permanent revenue of the sovereign," they strive to "keep out as much as possible all competitors from the market of the countries which are subject to their government." Those doomed to live under them suffer the most, as "some part of the surplus produce of those countries" ruled by the Company is reduced to "what is barely sufficient for supplying their own demand, or to what they can expect to sell in Europe with such a profit as they may think reasonable" (Smith 1976, 637–638 [IV.vii.c.103]). Smith cannot but pass a sour judgment on the record of their conduct in the territories they control:

> No two characters seem more inconsistent than those of trader and sovereign. If the trading spirit of the English East company renders them very bad sovereigns; the spirit of sovereignty seems to have rendered them equally bad traders. While they were traders only, they managed their trade successfully, and were able to pay from their profits a moderate dividend to the proprietors of their stock. Since they became sovereigns, with a revenue

> which, it is said, was originally more than three millions sterling, they have been obliged to beg the extraordinary assistance of government in order to avoid immediate bankruptcy. (Smith 1976, 819 [V.ii.a.7])

The petty "trading spirit" of these inept "sovereigns" seduces them to spurn their duty to serve the interests of the shareholders back in Britain. Nothing would better suit the tempers of the Company's "servants and dependents" than the "pleasure of wasting" or "embezzling whatever surplus might remain, after paying the proposed dividend of eight per cent" to the investors. All the while, they never ceased their effort to extend "either their dominion, or their depredations, over a vast accession of some of the richest and most fertile countries in India," only to leave them utterly "wasted and destroyed" (Smith 1976, 753 [V.i.e.27–28]). Unflustered by the ruin they left behind, they returned back home with deep pockets. Tucker gave voice to the widespread aversion in the home country to "that ill-gotten and ill-spent Wealth, which was obtained by robbing, plundering, and starving the poor defenceless natives of the East-Indies." To refer to this new and unprecedented "Species of Villainy," Tucker remarked, the English language was forced to invent a new word: "*Nabobing*" (Tucker 1774, 205–207n).

"Sir Matthew Mite," the "Nabob" in Samuel Foote's popular play *The Nabob: A Comedy*, and whom we met in Chap. 1 as we embarked on our investigative journey, combines all the themes dealt with in this chapter thus far. He is a "projector" seeking to purchase status by marrying the daughter of a landed gentleman. "How is the stock?" (Foote 1778, 40) is the stock phrase he habitually uses to question his two stock-jobbers hired to aid him in his regular "project" of making money at the stock market. He first amassed his fortune in Bengal where he worked for Britain's monopoly corporation governing that land. Nabobs like Mite made themselves rich in India by "cunningly" encroaching "little by little" on the native's estates until the foreign intruders have grown strong enough to turn the natives "out of their lands" and to "take possession of their money and jewels," as Mite's servant Touchit boasted (Foote 1778, 39). Foote's play represented the general sentiments of the public regarding the "Nabobs." People frowned at these upstarts with dubious moral credentials and their unseemly conducts back home (Raven 1992, 147–148, 232–235). But many also felt that what the British rulers and merchants did to the people in Bengal did not concern them. Burke, however, begged to differ. In the same line of accusation pioneered by Smith, Burke made his speeches of impeachment of Warren Hastings charging him with "high crimes and misdemeanor" as the governor of the British India Company's "Presidency" in Bengal. Burke's earlier stance toward the Company in the late 1760s was one that opposed any government interference in the Company's affairs and one that was less hostile than Smith's toward the privileges conferred on the monopoly corporation (Collins 2019, 373–388; Sato 2022, 87). But Burke increasingly came to harbor strong distrust of the Company's integrity and efficiency from the 1770s onward. By the mid-1780s, he had become firmly convinced of the need to chastise those responsible for the Company's mismanagement in Bengal (Locke 2006, 31–34, 62–66; Bourke 2015, 347–350, 629–639). Burke's speeches denouncing Hastings deserves to be included in our inquiry into the moral discourse dealing with matters economic, for even though the impeachment became a protracted drama involving high politics, Burke targeted primarily the unholy mixture in Hastings of the "trading spirit" with sovereign power. It may appear incongruous to mention Tucker in the same paragraph discussing Burke, who publicly ridiculed the divine in his speeches in 1774 defending the American colonies. Tucker, siding with the "vermin of court reporters," attacked any opposition to the Stamp Act as an encouragement of sedition in America. Burke alleged that Tucker, "already a dean," published such pro-government views with an eye to getting himself a "bishoprick" (Burke 1981a, 446).[3] But as far as the British East India Company was concerned, and in the different ambience of the 1780s, Burke and Tucker, despite their well-known mutual animosity (Shelton 1981, 194–199), stood on the same side. Braving the staunch opposition of fellow MPs with strong East Indian connections (Philips 1961, 23–24, 41–53), Burke in the late 1780s made it his chosen mission to dissect and denounce Hastings' grand "Nabobing." Hastings, who was nominated by the Crown on the basis of the 1773 Regulating Act as the governor-general of Bengal at the handsome salary of £25,000 annum (Holmes and Szechi 1993, 376), still felt entitled to reward himself with extra income, both licit and illicit. To Burke, he exemplified moral depravity grafted on injudicious political economy. To some commentators in our time, Burke's assault on the individual morality or the lack thereof of

[3] Tucker seemed to have had no such expectations and had never neglected his spiritual duties as dean of a cathedral that weathered the storm of various controversies arising from both within and without the Church (Sykes 1934, 169, 184; Shelton 1981, 165; Barry 1993, 191–208).

Hastings appears fundamentally misfocused, since what really mattered was a structural "disjunction" brought about by "imperial wealth" (Ahmed 2011, 136, 145). But that personalizing of the "disjunction" owed largely to Hastings's own flatulent exaggeration of his role in the official and personal letters sent back home even before his appointment (Marshall 2020, 187). Hastings successfully elevated his name to become the preeminent symbol of British Bengal. His name stood for Bengal and all its problems. By punishing him, therefore, Burke believed that public morality could be restored for the nation and its burgeoning empire in the East Indies. However, the odds were piled against Burke from the outset. To begin with, impeaching a commoner upon charges of misdeeds in a remote colonial territory was quite unprecedented. Impeachment rightfully belonged to the constitutional powers of Parliament, since the legislature also acted as the "supreme court" of the realm, as Blackstone glossed it, convened for the "trial of great and enormous offenders, whether lords or commoners." In practice, however, those usually impeached were peers of the realm, who could be tried for any crime or misdemeanors. A commoner like Hastings, unlike the lords, could be impeached only for "high misdemeanors," since their crimes were more appropriately tried at the high courts of law (Blackstone 1770, 256–257). Indeed, most of the impeachment cases Blackstone discusses are of peers rather than commoners (Blackstone 1770, 258–262). Whereas an impeachment of a high-ranking nobleman in the House of Lords was a legal process that followed the constitutional principle of the right to be tried by one's peers, that of a commoner was essentially a political trial initiated by the House of Commons, and as such it inherently challenged the authority of the "artificial reason" of the common law, which stood apart from that of "natural reason," according to the classic distinction made by Edward Coke (2003, 481). All the more so, when evidence incriminating Hastings was exceptionally "complex and murky," as Frederick G. Whelan put it (Whelan 1996, 670), and when witnesses had to be brought offshore from the exotic colony of Bengal, the trial was bound to go off course from the strict legal procedure of English law. Though trained in law at one of the Inns of Courts, Burke had decades ago in *A Vindication of Natural Society* (1756) inveighed against the "strange and unaccountable Fancies and Contrivances of artificial Reason." The "Lawyer" attached to his "Artificial Law" upholds "his Forms, and his positive Institutions," with a "Veneration altogether as religious" as that of the "Professors of Artificial Theology" regarding their doctrines, so that the "worst Cause cannot be so prejudicial to the Litigant, as his Advocate's or Attorney's Ignorance or Neglect of these Forms" (Burke 1997, 178, 173). When the "right honourable" Mr. Burke representing the Commons presented his case against Hastings to the House of Lords and the huge audience that packed Westminster Hall, he cared not to respect the formalism of "Artificial Law." He appealed, instead, with his superb oratory, to natural law founded on universal morality, which clashed with the formalities of the English law constantly (see Marshall 1965, 64–87; Whelan 1996, 81–82, 277–278; Locke 2006, 119, 162, 177; Bourke 2015, 666–670).

Burke had defined in 1770 the ideal role of a politician as that of a "philosopher in action." In contrast to the "speculative philosopher" who theorizes about the "proper ends of Government," the "philosopher in action" seeks to "find out proper means towards those ends, and to employ them with effect" (Burke 1981b, 317–318). His speeches of impeachment in the Hastings trials of 1788 were to him the "proper means" of realizing the "proper ends of Government" in the British East Indies and, by doing so, of keeping British government on the right path toward its own "proper ends." The "ends" which the British India Company pursued, as Burke saw it, were most improper and sordid. Even before Hastings took charge of the Company's management of its territory in Bengal, the Company had already displayed a mean "trading spirit," as Smith called it, by seeking to cash in on a series of political upheavals, since by the "vast sums of money acquired by individuals" in the process of regime changes, "it was discovered that a revolution in Bengal was a mine much more easily worked and infinitely more productive than the mines of Potosi and Mexico." Particularly after the first of the Nabobs Lord Clive returned to Britain to "enjoy his fame and fortune," he was succeeded by "another set of people, who thought a revolution upon that revolution might be made as lucrative to [them] as this was to the first projectors." The business items these "projectors" dealt in were blood and gunpowder. Not long after their lackey "Meere Jaffiear" was placed on throne, they "projected another revolution" in order to collect bribes from those contending to gain power. This was a "revolution which was to unsettle all the former revolutions, to make way for new wars and disturbances, and for that train of peculation which ever since has vexed and oppressed that Country" (Burke 1991a, 317).[4] The same pattern of first securing to the

[4]On the military turbulences in Bengal ignited by the British East India Company, see Travers (2007, chapters 1 to 3); Dalrymple (2019, chapters 5 to 7).

Company an "enormous bribe" and then "under the Shadow of that, to take all the little emoluments they could to themselves" repeated itself again and again. Hastings in due course became the supreme leader of these "projectors" who enriched themselves through their deadly "projects" (Burke 1991a, 331). He first supported the coup of "Cossim Ally Cawn," a treacherous and merciless tyrant, after taking bribes from him. Later, this figure was replaced by the legitimate ruler, but not until he was forced to pay Hastings an "amazing sum" of money. The restored ruler was a puppet of Hastings. His role was to collect and hand over taxes to the Company (Burke 1991a, 336–337). A few years later, the Company, through Hastings' maneuver, acquired "Dewanee, or Stewardship," which gave them direct control of tax revenue. The tax collected was never used for the benefit of those taxed. It was merely a "play thing of avarice" (Burke 1991a, 342, 337). In Burke's diagnosis, "pecuniary corruption and avarice" formed the "root" of all the charges of misdemeanor made against Hastings (Burke 1991b, 374). The defendant built a "corrupt system," at once "frightful and odious," of "receiving bribes from poor, miserable, indigent people" by abusing his authority as a "Chief Governor of a great empire." "The Government of India undoubtedly originated first in ideas of safety and necessity," Burke grants. He also acknowledges that the inevitable "next step" could not but be a "step of ambition," as "generally happens in conquest." But at that stage, things began to go awry, for it was "followed by gains of money." Money soon became the sole consideration, with "no mixture at all" of "ambition," so that under Hastings' governorship, it became "altogether a business of money" (Burke 1991b, 377). Thoroughly addicted to the "vice of base avarice" (Burke 1991b, 377), Hastings used his power to maximize his personal profit. He imposed an impossibly high rate of tax on land and then took bribes in exchange for tax exemption. He thus oppressed and corrupted the natives "first by making extravagant demands, and afterwards by making corrupt relaxations of them" (Burke 1991b, 383). To pay bribes to Hastings, the people had to borrow money at usurious interest rates, often reaching hundreds of percent, the "hard hand of usury being the only resource against the cruel scourge of oppression." When they failed to pay either their tax or bribe money, they were "stripped" of everything they had. As a last resort, they had to sell their family, children and wives, for "they thought that it was a tolerable escape from famine into servitude" (Burke 1991b, 417–418). Hastings was no better than a "fraudulent Bullock Contractor" carrying on "fraudulent Bullock transactions." Yet he was "exalted to great unmerited power," and as a result, "defrauded and taught others to defraud" as he "desolated Countries" (Burke 2000, 277).

In his own defense Hastings argued that Burke's accusation of moral laxity is literally misplaced, since "actions in Asia do not bear the same moral qualities as the same actions would bear in Europe." Hastings claimed that he had merely followed the "law, custom and usage" of India, doing nothing more than what other native rulers there had done before him. This Burke calls a perverse "Geographical morality," utterly unacceptable, for to make such statement is to aver that the "duties of men in public and in private situations are not to be governed by their relations to the Great Governor of the Universe, or by their relations to men, but by climates, degrees of longitude and latitude, parallels not of life but of latitudes." Such moral relativism amounts to contending that "when you have crossed the equinoctial line," you go through some sort of satanic "baptism" by which the Europeans "unbaptize themselves of all that they learned in Europe, and commence a new order and system of things." Burke will have none of that, for "the laws of morality" are unaffected by geography. "There is no action which would pass for an action of extortion, of peculation, of bribery and of oppression in England, that is not an act of extortion, of peculation, of bribery and of oppression in Europe, Asia, Africa, and all the world over," Burke proclaimed (Burke 1991a, 346–347). Not content to rely merely on "Geographical morality," Hastings also sought protection, provided by his well-paid lawyers, in the "artificial reason" of English law, which ultimately helped him to be acquitted. Even when faced with the inevitable defeat, Burke never budged, firmly upholding his belief in the greater "laws of morality." For Burke, there is "but one Law in the world, namely, that Law which governs all Law: the Law of our Creator, the law of humanity, Justice, Equity, the Law of Nature and of Nations" (Burke 2000, 280).[5] That Burke's was not a lone prophetic voice in the wilderness will be seen in our next

[5]The legal and political issues involved were no doubt complicated. Marshall considers Hastings, like Robert Clive before him, to have been swayed more by "ambition" than by avarice (Marshall 2003, XV: 11–15). The clash between Burke and Hastings, according to Travers, was one that hinged upon their respective views of the Mughal constitution, as well as of the "laws of morality" (Travers 2007, 207–223). Marshall deemed the impeachment which relied largely on "Burke's tirades" a well-deserved failure of Burke and a fitting victory of "legal orthodoxy" (Marshall 1965, 84, 87). Recent views of Burke's reliance on moral or natural law tend to be more sympathetic toward Burke (Smith 2008, 86–89; Goodman 2020, 466–472).

chapter devoted to the Abolitionists who waged war in the name of the "Law of our Creator, the law of humanity, Justice, Equity" against the "Geographical morality" and the "artificial reason" protecting Britain's transatlantic slave trade and slave plantations in the British West Indies.

References

Addison, Joseph. 1711. *The spectator: A new edition*. Vol. 1. Edited by Henry Morley. London, 1891. https://www.gutenberg.org/cache/epub/12030/. Accessed 21 December 2023.

Ahmed, Siraj. 2011. *Stillbirth of capital: Enlightenment writing and colonial India*. Palo Alto: Stanford University Press.

Alsop, James. 1979. Gerrard Winstanley's later life. *Past and Present* 82:73–81.

Anderson, Adam. 1764 *An historical and chronological deduction of the origin of commerce, from the earliest account to the present time, containing, an history of the great commercial interests of the British Empire*. London: Consortium.

Anon. 1710. A true state of the present difference between the Royal African Company, and the separate traders. In *The British transatlantic slave trade*, vol. 2: *The Royal African Company*, ed. Kenneth Morgan, 17–57. London: Pickering and Chatto, 2003.

Anon. 1730. The case of the Royal African Company of England. In *The British transatlantic slave trade*, vol. 2: *The Royal African Company*, ed. Kenneth Morgan, 61–94. London: Pickering and Chatto, 2003.

Anon. 1713a. *An account of the ships employed in the African trade, from the ports of London and Bristol, belonging to the separate traders to Africa*. [London?]

Anon. 1713b. *A general history of trade, and especially consider'd as it respects the British commerce, as well as home, as to all parts of the world*. London: J. Baker.

Anon. 1721. *The exact dealer's daily companion: Instructing him thoroughly in all things absolutely necessary to be known by all those who would thrive in the world; and in the whole art and mystery of trade and traffick*. London.

Anon. 1732. *City-liberties: or, The rights and privileges of freemen, being a concise abridgment of all the law, charters, by-laws, and customs of London, down to this time*. London: W. Mears.

Anon. 1734. *The case of bankrupts and insolvents consider'd*. London.

Anon. 1749. *An essay on the increase and decline of trade, in London and the out-ports*. London: R. Dodsley.

Anon. 1759. *The London fishery laid open: or The arts of the fishermen and fishmongers set in a true light*. London.

Anon. 1765. *A companion to the plan of London, describing the government, churches … City-companies … general and penny-post offices, and other interesting particulars relative to the cities of London and Westminster, and borough of Southwark*. London: T. Kitchin and H. Parker.

Backscheider, Paula R. 1989. *Daniel Defoe: A life*. Baltimore: The Johns Hopkins University Press.

Barbon, Nicholas. 1685. *An apology for the builder: or A discourse shewing the cause and effects of the increase of building*. London.

Barry, Jonathan. 1993. Cultural patronage and the Anglican crisis: Bristol c. 1689–1775. In *The Church of England c.1689–c.1833: From toleration to tractarianism*, ed. John Walsh, Colin Haydon, and Stephen Taylor, 191–208. Cambridge: Cambridge University Press.

Blackstone, William. 1770. *Commentaries on the laws of England. Book the fourth*. 4th ed. Oxford: Clarendon.

Boswell, James. 2010. *London journal 1762–1763*. Edited by Gordon Turnbull. London: Penguin.

Bourke, Richard. 2015. *Empire and revolution: The political life of Edmund Burke*. Princeton: Princeton University Press.

Brewer, John. 1989. *The sinews of power: War, money and the English state, 1688–1783*. New York: Knopf.

Burke, Edmund. 1981a. Speech on American taxation. In *The writing and speeches of Edmund Burke*, vol. 2: *Party, Parliament, and the American crisis 1766–1774*, ed. Paul Langford, 406–463. Oxford: Clarendon.

Burke, Edmund. 1981b. Thoughts on the present discontents. In *The writing and speeches of Edmund Burke*, vol. 2: *Party, Parliament, and the American crisis 1766–1774*, ed. Paul Langford, 241–323. Oxford: Clarendon.

Burke, Edmund. 1991a. Opening of impeachment, 16 Feb 1788. In *The writings and speeches of Edmund Burke*, vol. 6: *India: The launching of the Hastings impeachment 1786–1788*, ed. P. J. Marshall, 313–373. Oxford: Clarendon.

Burke, Edmund. 1991b. Opening of impeachment, 18 Feb 1788. In *The writings and speeches of Edmund Burke*, vol. 6: *India: The launching of the Hastings impeachment 1786–1788*, ed. P. J. Marshall, 373–427. Oxford: Clarendon.

Burke, Edmund. 1991c. Two letters on the trade in Ireland. In *The writing and speeches of Edmund Burke*, vol. 9.2: *Ireland*, ed. R. B. McDowell, 506–517. Oxford: Clarendon.

Burke, Edmund. 1997. A vindication of natural society. In *The writing and speeches of Edmund Burke*, vol. 1: *The early writings*, ed. T. O. McLoughlin and James T. Boulton, 129–184. Oxford: Clarendon.

Burke, Edmund. 2000. Speech in reply, 28 May 1794. In *The writing and speeches of Edmund Burke*, vol. 7: *India: The Hastings trial 1789–1794*, ed. P. J. Marshall, 231–281, Oxford: Clarendon.

Child, Josiah. 1698. *A new discourse of trade*. London.

Coke, Edward. 2003. *The selected writings and speeches of Sir Edward Coke*. Vol. 1. Edited by Steve Sheppard. Indianapolis: Liberty Fund.

Collins, Gregory M. 2019. The limit of mercantile administration: Adam Smith and Edmund Burke on Britain's East India Company. *Journal of the History of Economic Thought* 41:369–392. https://doi.org/10.1017/S1053837218000354.

Dale, Richard. 2004. *The first crash: Lessons from the South Sea Bubble*. Princeton: Princeton University Press.

Dalrymple, William. 2019. *The anarchy: The relentless rise of the East India Company*. New York: Bloomsbury.

Daunton, M. J. 1995. *Progress and poverty: An economic and social history of Britain 1700–1850*. Oxford: Oxford University Press.

Davenant, Charles. 1696. *An essay on the East-India-trade*. London.

Defoe, Daniel. 1702. *Essays upon several projects: or, Effectual ways for advancing the interest of the nation*. London.

Dickson, Adam. 1773. *An essay on the causes of the present high prices of provisions, as connected with luxury, currency, taxes, and national debt*. London: E. and C. Dilly.

Foote, Samuel. 1778. *The nabob; A comedy, in three acts, as it is performed at the Theatre-Royal in the Haymarket*. London: T. Cadell.

Goodman, Rob. 2020. The low principles of jurisprudence: Legal indeterminacy in Edmund Burke's impeachment of Warren Hastings. *The Review of Politics* 82:459–483. https://doi.org/10.1017/S0034670520000364.

Graham, Aaron, and Patrick Walsh. 2016. Introduction to *The British fiscal-military states, 1660–c.1783*. Edited by Aaron Graham and Patrick Walsh. New York: Routledge.

Hamilton, Earl J. 1991. Prices and wages at Paris under John Law's system. In *John Law (1671–1729) and Bernard Mandeville (1660–1733)*, ed. Mark Blaug, 42–79. Aldershot: Edward Elgar.

Hankock, David. 1995. *Citizens of the world: London merchants and the integration of the British Atlantic community, 1735–1785*. Cambridge: Cambridge University Press.

Hayes, Charles. 1744. The importance of effectually supporting the Royal African Company of England impartially consider'd. In *The British transatlantic slave trade*, vol. 2: *The Royal African Company*, ed. Kenneth Morgan, 97–145. London: Pickering and Chatto, 2003.

Holmes, Geoffrey, and Daniel Szechi. 1993. *The age of oligarchy: Pre-industrial Britain 1722–1783*. London: Routledge.

Hoppit, Julian. 1987. *Risk and failure in English business 1700–1800*. Cambridge: Cambridge University Press.

Hoppit, Julian. 2000. *A land of liberty? England 1689–1727*. Oxford: Oxford University Press.

Hoppit, Julian. 2017. *Britain's political economies: Parliament and economic life, 1660–1800*. Cambridge: Cambridge University Press.

Hume, David. 1987. *Essays, moral, political, and literary*. Edited by Eugene F. Miller. Indianapolis: Liberty Fund.

Kames, Lord (Henry Home). 1774. *Sketches of the history of man*. Edinburgh: W. Creech.

Law, John. 1720. *Money and trade consider'ed: with a proposal for supplying the nation with money*. London: W. Lewis.

Locke, F. P. 2006. *Edmund Burke*. Vol. 2: *1784–1797*. Oxford: Clarendon.

Marshall, P. J. 1965. *The impeachment of Warrant Hastings*. Oxford: Oxford University Press.

Marshall, P. J. 2003. *"A free though conquering people": Eighteenth-century Britain and its empire*. Farnham: Ashgate.

Marshall, P. J. 2020. The East India Company's "ancient form of government" and the exigencies of empire: Bengal 1765 to 1773. In *Envisioning empire: The new British world from 1763 to 1773*, ed. Robert A. Olwell and James M. Vaughn, 173–195. London: Bloomsbury Academic.

Morgan, Kenneth. 2007. *Slavery and the British Empire: From Africa to America*. Oxford: Oxford University Press.

Mortimer, Thomas. 1769. *Every man his own broker: or, A guide to Exchange-Alley*. London: S. Hooper.

Neal, Larry. 1990. *The rise of financial capitalism: International capital markets in the Age of Reason*. Cambridge: Cambridge University Press.

OED/Oxford English dictionary. 2023. https://www-oed-com-ssl.access.yonsei.ac.kr. Accessed 14 November 2023.

Owens, W. R. 2000. Introduction to *Political and Economic Writings of Daniel Defoe*, vol. 8, *Social Reform*. Edited by W. R. Owens. London: Pickering & Chatto.

Pettigrew, William A. 2013. *Freedom's debt: The Royal African Company and the politics of the Atlantic slave trade, 1672–1752*. Chapel Hill: University of North Carolina Press.

Philips, C. H. 1961. *The East India Company 1784–1834*. Manchester: Manchester University Press.

Pocock, J. G. A. 1985. *Virtue, commerce, and history: Essays on political thought and history, chiefly in the eighteenth century*. Cambridge: Cambridge University Press.

Postlethwayt, Malachy. 1745. The African trade, the great pillar and support of the British plantation trade in America. In *The British transatlantic slave trade*, vol. 2: *The Royal African Company*, ed. Kenneth Morgan, 149–194. London: Pickering and Chatto, 2003.

Postlethwayt, Malachy. 1746. The national and private advantages of the African trade considered. In *The British transatlantic slave trade*, vol. 2: *The Royal African Company*, ed. Kenneth Morgan, 197–328. London: Pickering and Chatto, 2003.

Raven, James. 1992. *Judging new wealth: Popular publishing and responses to commerce in England, 1750–1800*. Oxford: Clarendon.

Robertson, William. 1777a. *History of America, vol. 1*. Vol. 6 of *The works of William Robertson*. London: T. Cadell, 1840.

Robertson, William. 1777b. *History of America, vol. 3*. Vol. 8 of *The works of William Robertson*. London: T. Cadell, 1840.

Ross, Ian Simpson. 1995. *The life of Adam Smith*. Oxford: Clarendon.

Sato, Sora. 2022. Rethinking Burke and Smith: Political economy and foundations of industry. *The European Journal of the History of Economic Thought* 29:82–103. https://doi.org/10.1080/09672567.2021.1914699.

Scott, Thomas. 1624. *The high-waies of God and the King. wherein all men ought to walke in holinesse here, to happinesse hereafter: Deliuered in two sermons preached at Thetford in Norfolke, anno 1620*. London.

Shelton, George. 1981. *Dean Tucker and eighteenth-century economic and political thought*. London: Macmillan.

Smith, Adam. 1976. *An inquiry into the nature and causes of the wealth of nations*. Edited by R. H. Campbell and A. S. Skinner. Oxford: Clarendon.

Smith, Brian. 2008. Edmund Burke, the Warren Hastings trial, and the moral dimension of corruption. *Polity* 40:70–94. https://doi.org/10.1057/palgrave.polity.2300051.

Statute of Monopolies 1623. n.d. Legislation.gov.uk. https://www.legislation.gov.uk/aep/Jal/21/3/section/IX. Accessed 3 January 2022.

Stern, Philip J. 2023. *Empire, incorporated: The corporations that built British colonialism*. Cambridge, MA: Harvard University Press.

Sykes, Norman. 1934. *Church and state in England in the xviiith century*. Repr., Hamden: Archon Books, 1962.

Thomas, Hugh. 1997. *The slave trade: The story of the Atlantic slave trade: 1440–1870*. New York: Simon & Schuster.

Thomas, R. P., and D. N. McCloskey. 1981. Overseas trade and empire 1700–1860. In *The economic history of Britain since 1700*, vol. 1: *1700–1860*, ed. Robert Floud and Donald McCloskey, 87–102. Cambridge: Cambridge University Press.

Tonks, Paul. 2020. British union and empire in the origin of commerce: Adam Anderson as eighteenth-century historian and Scottish political economist. *History* 105:60–81.

Travers, Robert. 2007. *Ideology and empire in eighteenth-century India*. Cambridge: Cambridge University Press.

Tucker, Josiah. 1774. *Four tracts, together with two sermons, on political and commercial subjects*. Glocester.

Wallerstein, Immanuel. 2011. *The modern world-system III: The second era of global expansion of the capitalist world-economy 1730–1840s*. Berkeley: University of California Press.

Wennerlind, Carl. 2011. *Casualties of credit: The English financial revolution, 1620–1720*. Cambridge, MA: Harvard University Press.

Whelan, Frederick G. 1996. *Edmund Burke and India: Political morality and empire*. Pittsburgh: University of Pittsburgh Press.

White, George. [1694] 1772. *An account of the trade to the East Indies, together with the state of the present company, and the best method for establishing and managing that trade, to the honour and advantage, of the nation*. London: Brotherton and Sewell.

Whitworth, Charles. 1777. *A register of the trade of the Port of London specifying the articles imported and exported, arranged under the respective countries ... number 1. for January, February, and March, 1776*. London.

Winstanley, Gerrard. 2009. *The complete works of Gerrard Winstanley*. Vol. 2. Edited by Thomas N. Corns, Ann Hughes, and David Loewenstein. Oxford: Oxford University Press.

Yamamoto, Koji. 2018. *Taming capitalism before its triumph: Public service, distrust, and "projecting" in early modern England*. Oxford: Oxford University Press.

CHAPTER 6

Slaves and Trade

6.1 The "African Trade" and Sugar

Edmund Burke's indictment of Warren Hastings' misdemeanor and crimes, even though he acted as the representative of the lower house of Parliament, was made in many names. He closed his opening speech of impeachment on 19 February 1788 using anaphora, beginning each statement with "I impeach him in the name of" and varying the object of the preposition "of." Twice in the name of the "Commons of Great Britain" Hastings is impeached for having "betrayed" his "trust" and having "dishonoured" the "national character" of the nation. He is also impeached in the name of the "people of India," whose "laws, rights and liberties he has subverted, whose properties he has destroyed, whose Country he has laid waste and desolate." Not content to stop there, Burke looks up to heaven to impeach the governor of British Bengal in the "name and by virtue of those eternal laws of justice which he has violated." He then looks down into "human nature itself," in whose name also he impeaches Hastings, for the impeached has "cruelly outraged, injured and oppressed" human nature in "both sexes, in every age, rank, situation and condition of life" (Burke 1991, 459). That a parliamentarian could wax eloquent upon such universal terms upon such an unusual trial, flaunting the legal niceties concerning how the "people of India," the "eternal laws of justice," and "human nature itself" could possibly qualify as plaintiffs, attests to the prevalence of moral concerns in a society supposedly devoted to profit.

H.-J. Yoon, *Moral Discourses of the Economy in Eighteenth-Century Britain*, https://doi.org/10.1007/978-981-95-0958-4_6

Spurning mere calculation of expediency or juggling of technicalities, Burke raises the stakes to such a high level that the moral status not just of the British East India Company but of Great Britain itself as a trading empire is made the central issue. While Burke warmed toward the afflicted "people of India" and burned with righteous rage over the injustice they suffered, there were others who felt a comparable pang of pity and outrage deep in their heart over what went on in the British slave plantations in the West Indies and on the West African coast.[1] Just one year before Burke made his passionate impeachment speech at the Westminster Hall, Thomas Cooper joined the critics of the transatlantic slave trade in his pamphlet published in Manchester, *Letters on the Slave Trade* (1787). He made a simple but lucid point about how consumption of sugar comes at the price of consuming human lives:

> The Abbé Raynal computes, that at the time of his writing, nine millions of slaves had been consumed by the Europeans. Add one million at least since, for it is about 10 years ago. Recollecting then, that for one slave procured, ten at least are slaughtered; that a fifth die in the passage, and a third in the seasoning; and the unexaggerated computation will turn out, that the infernal voracity of European avarice has been glutted with the MURDER of ONE HUNDRED and EIGHT MILLIONS of our FELLOW-CREATURES! Good God, cries the astonished Reader, for what purpose?—*That the Gentlefolk of Europe, (my friend) may drink Sugar to their Tea*! (Cooper 1787, 45)

Cooper taps on the well-established admonishment against excessive consumption we have discussed in Chap. 4. Moreover, his approach reminds one of William Robertson's remarks about the "consumption" of native American lives by the Spaniards, except for the disturbing fact that whereas the notoriously brutal incidents in Spain's first American possessions took place some centuries before in the past, this destruction of human life was an ongoing atrocity at the very present, with Britain having the shameful honor of being the main agent of abetting and appeasing the "infernal voracity of European avarice." Rectifying this callous devastation of Africans, however, was by no means easy, as Cooper himself implicitly admitted. His readers sipped their tea brought from the East Indies

[1] Burke as a parliamentarian was aware of the plight of the African slaves and lent his support to reform the existing practices, if not consistently supportive of an outright abolition of slave trade and slavery (Marshall 2019, 205–210).

sweetening it with the sugar imported from the West Indies plantations, where, the typical apology would allege, no one but the black Africans could bear the harsh climate and carry out the excruciating task of growing sugar canes. William Fox, a Quaker lawyer and Abolitionist remembered at least by one historian (Davis [1975] 1999, 381–385), asserted in 1791 that it was the "British luxury" that the "African Slave Trade depends on for support." The "consumption of sugar" in Britain has become "so immense" that it "nearly equals the consumption of all Europe." This was hardly something to be proud of, for in Fox's eyes, "every pound of sugar used" by the British, being the "produce of slaves imported from Africa," incurs "consuming two ounces of human flesh, besides an alarming number of seamen destroyed by the slave-trade, and the inconceivable anguish and misery that must result from parents being torn from their families, and children from their parents, villages burnt, and continual suspicion, terror and dismay, spread thro' an extensive country." The familiar and by the 1790s somewhat outmoded denunciation of "luxury" is revived, as Fox, though a lawyer, proposes a moral solution to the problem, namely a voluntary abstention by individuals from using this bloodstained commodity. Since "to form new plantations for the supply of this our increasing luxury" the "wretched Africans are torn from their native land," if less sugar is consumed in Britain, more lives will be saved in Africa and in the West Indies (Fox 1791, 326–327). The question, of course, was how many of his readers would pay heed to his advice and put it to daily practice.

Sugar was steeped in blood, according to Cooper, Fox, and other Abolitionists. Yet it was seductively sweet, particularly to those who loved that even sweeter taste of profit garnered from businesses connected one way or another to sugar. From the early decades of the century, the "African trade" and the "West Indies trade," marching together shoulder to shoulder, were believed, whether plausibly or not, to be a lucrative affair. This belief explains, among other things, the debate about the injustice—surely not of trafficking in humans itself—but of the monopoly held by the Royal African Company, which we touched upon in the previous chapter. Any sympathy solicited by the authors broaching the subject was rarely extended to the Africans themselves and their native communities (Wennerlind 2011, 224). In the 1690s, Josiah Child drew the reader's attention to the impact of "*Barbadoes*, and the other *West-Indies Plantations*" on England's population rather than on the inhabitants of Africa forcefully brought to these islands. Will the migration of the English to these colonies result in depopulation? Child did not believe so. Instead of a decrease, such "evacuation" contributes to "an encrease of People," for "one Englishman, with the ten Blacks that work with him, accounting what they eat, use and wear, would make employment for four Men in England" (Child 1698, 215–216). His calculation breaks down into different branches of Britain's economy such as those responsible for "Provisions, Cloaths, and Houshold-goods, Sea-men, and all others employed about Materials for Building, Fitting and Victualling of Ships." A reasonable inference would be that "*Every* English-man *in* Barbadoes *or* Jamaica *creates employment for four men at home*" (Child 1698, 190–191). In addition to these trades supporting shipping, the "*Sugar-Bakers* in *London*" also benefit from the sugar plantations in the West Indies. Child plays the advocate of these businessmen running sugar refineries, warning the government not to endanger their "Callings" by letting them suffer from high interest rates (Child 1698, 23). Nor should the plantations themselves be subjected to excessive taxation, as the "*Parliaments*, if they please, by taking off all Charges from Sugar," can make sugar "more intirely an *English Commodity*, than white Herrings are a *Dutch Commodity*," and "draw more profit to this Kingdom thereby, than the Dutch do by that" (Child 1698, 204). An admission that slave trade, though undoubtedly indispensable, was not entirely immune to scruples could sometimes be found. The author of *A General History of Trade* (1713) remarked that "our Merchants Plant and Reside" in the "torrid *Zone* of *Africa*" notwithstanding the "violence of the Heat," to secure some "Capital Articles of Commerce," namely, "*Gold, Ivory, Civet*, and *Slaves*." "The Trade of *Africa* is singular," he observes, in that "those four Kinds of Goods we fetch there, are not to be had in any other part of the World." The first three can pass without any further apology, but the last does detain him for a short while:

> Some Attempts have been made for the Planting this part of the World with Cotton, Ginger, Sugar, Indico, &c. but the mistaken Policy of Trade among those who fancy they understand it, has put a check to that encrease of Commerce which is yet reserv'd for wiser Posterity, till when, we continue foolishly to carry the Negroes to the Plants, when we might bring the Plants to the Negroes, and make the Coast of *Africa* as good to us, as Ten of the Islands, either of *Barbadoes* or *Jamaica*. (Anon. 1713, 10)

The costly process of shipping the "Negroes" to the "Plants" in Barbados or Jamaica is what he disapproves, not the purchase and exploitation of slave labor itself. Questions about the justice of enslaving humans were rarely raised. Only how an "increase of Commerce" can be pursued less "foolishly" was all that mattered.

The prevalent stance on African and the West Indies trades of the mid-eighteenth century, when Child's ardent wish to see sugar become "more intirely an *English Commodity*, than white Herrings are a *Dutch Commodity*," came close to being realized, and when slaves came to push out other rivals in the African Trade's four "Capital Articles of Commerce," is well represented by *Candid and Impartial Considerations on the Nature of the Sugar Trade* (1763). The author, John Campbell, makes it clear who it is that enables sugar cultivation in the West Indies to remain a "very lucrative commerce." Those living in the "*sugar colonies*" are neatly divided into "*Whites* and *Blacks*, or in other words *British* subjects and *African* slaves." The "skill and industry of the former" are not unimportant, but it is above all thanks to the "painful and indefatigable labour of the latter" that "not sugar only, but various other commodities also to an immense value, are raised in those countries, and exported to different parts of the world." The "cheapness of the labour of these poor people" enables the British "sugar trade" to be "confined to *America*," which in turn is the "principal cause of its affording such a variety of advantages, and more especially of its contributing so highly to the support of navigation, and in consequence of that to the maintenance of naval power" (Campbell 1763, 19–21). Would the corollary, then, be that the "painful and indefatigable labour" of the African slaves should be maintained at the cheapest level? Evading this question, Campbell dilates on the manifold advantages of slave trade and its intimate relationship with sugar plantations. "These so necessary *Negro* slaves," to begin with, are "purchased in *Africa* by the *English* merchants" with a "great variety" of British goods and manufactures, woolens, fire arms, powders, spirits, cutlery, and some "*East India* goods." The precious human cargos exchanged with these goods ensure handsome profit to those who ship them across the Atlantic and to those who use them in the West Indies. If the British islands happen to be burdened with a "surplus of slaves," the ships unload their slaves at the ports belonging to other "foreign nations" where they are sold at a "very high price." When the slaves are put to work in the plantations, they are made to use tools manufactured in Britain. The slaves also have to be clothed, fed, and kept under roof. The vast army of slaves consume "vast quantities of check linen, striped hollands, fustian, blankets for their bedding, long ells and bays for warm cloathing, coarse hats, woollen caps, cotton and silk handkerchiefs, knives, razors, buckles, buttons, tobacco pipes, fishing tackle, small glasses, thread, needles, pins, and innumerable other articles," the beauty of it all being that these are "all of *British* growth and manufacture" (Campbell 1763, 21–24). What about the British consumers back home? More and more people in Britain are becoming keenly attached to sugar. This should not alarm anyone, for "if we consume it, this is owing to the increase of our industry, that is of our affluence." The dichotomy of "industry v. idleness" (discussed in Chap. 3) comes briefly to rescue the consumers of sugar from the opprobrium of "luxury" (examined in Chap. 4). That repugnant term "luxury" has no business meddling itself with this wholesome circulation of wealth and "industry," for it stands as an "indubitable proof of the increase of our riches" and "consequently of our commerce" (Campbell 1763, 31, 33). The author of *Candid and Impartial Considerations on the Nature of the Sugar Trade* finishes his work by evoking "DIVINE PROVIDENCE," with whose "blessing," the "envied happiness" of the British "nation" he hopes will ever be preserved. This is the only reference in the entire book to God or Christianity. Campbell's religion enters the scene at the last moment in a severely diluted and diminished form to bless Britain's sugar trade, so crucial to the happiness of the "nation." The brutality instigated by this wonderful commerce among the African nations supplying the slaves is a subject he cares not even to mention briefly (Campbell 1763, 228).

Candid and Impartial Considerations on the Nature of the Sugar Trade, if not genuinely candid or impartial, cannot be classified as an outright apology of slave trade and sugar plantations, primarily because he felt no need to refute any charges of injustice or inhumanity. There simply was not enough of such pressure in the published public opinion of the times in the 1760s. By contrast, there was no shortage of printed voices in the first half of the century testifying to the necessity and the expediency of slave trade and slave labor, which anyone discussing the subject could readily consult. Already in the latter part of the seventeenth century, William Petty estimated in his *Political Arithmetick* the "value of the *Slaves*, brought out of *Africa*, to serve in our *American* Plantations" to be "Twenty thousand pounds" (Petty 1690, 240). Petty's figure was more rhetorical than factual, for it was meant to convince the reader of the importance of the slaves for England's "*American* Plantations," even when the economic significance of these colonies was relatively paltry. Whether Petty's calculation was accurate or not, the total "value of the Slaves" in the eighteenth century increased substantially when compared with Petty's days. That the "*Negro* slaves" were "so necessary" to the plantations, as *Candid and Impartial Considerations on the Nature of the Sugar Trade* so candidly confessed, was in fact a widely accepted truism. *A True State of the Present Difference Between the Royal African Company, and the Separate Traders* (1710) castigated the African Company for its ineptitude from a heartfelt appreciation of the value of the slaves they were entrusted to supply "her Majesty's *American* Colonies" with. The "Prosperity of our West-India Plantations depend, beyond Exception, upon the *African* Trade," the author puts it emphatically, "since they have no other way to occupy their Grounds, raise their Products, or manufacture their Commodities, but by hard Labour, and that not to be endur'd in such a sultry Climate by any but Negroes, who are by Nature season'd to the excessive Heat of those *American* Countries." The value of these "Negroes" consists in the fact that they are not "Horses or Oxen," for "their Grounds must be broken up and manag'd with the Hoe and other Instruments that can be no ways useful without humane Judgment and manual Dexterity." Their capacity to make "humane Judgment" as rational agents combined with their "manual Dexterity," however, is acknowledged only to subordinate them ruthlessly to the economic necessity of producing marketable commodities such as "Sugar, Cotton, Indico, Ginger, [and] Tobacco," which cannot be "brought to a Perfection, but by the constant Slavery and Attendance of such Men and Women who are qualify'd by Nature for the hardest Service in the hottest Countries." If no less an authority than "Nature" willed that the Africans be suitable for "constant Slavery," and if one was properly "acquainted with the true Nature of foreign Commerce," there can be no reason to demure or hesitate in advocating "a constant Supply of Negroes" to the colonies through whatever means conceivable (Anon. 1710, 48). Biological "Nature," fortified by economic "Nature," precludes all dissent and skepticism. Can white Europeans carry out the job? This is ruled out by both species of "Nature." "Has not long Experience," Malachy Postlethwayt asked in 1745, "shewn that *White* Men are not constitutionally qualified to sustain the Toil of Planting in the Climates of our *Islands Colonies* like the Blacks?" Besides, the "Nature" of "Commerce" would not permit any divergence from an utter dependence on the "Blacks." "*White Men* cannot be obtained near so cheap, or the Labour of a sufficient Number be had for the Expence of their Maintenance only, as we have of the *Africans*," is the candid, though hardly an impartial, statement made by the same author. Along with their physical assets the Africans are endowed with, the unquestionable cheapness of their labor when compared with free white labor is something that could never be ignored (Postlethwayt 1745, 164). Profoundly interested in Britain's access to African slave labor (Brown 2006, 263–265), Postlethwayt was firmly convinced that the "Nature of foreign Commerce" dictates that the British be on a constant alert to fend off competition from "those Europeans … who have an establish'd Interest and Power among the Natives," such as the French, and who seek to procure good slaves to be sold at good prices (Postlethwayt 1746, 240–241). Charles Hayes, the author of *The Importance of Effectually Supporting the Royal African Company of England* (1744), shared Postlethwayt's concern. "Should our most formidable Rivals monopolize the whole *African Trade* to Themselves," Hayes could not but ask, "will they not naturally furnish their *own Colonies* with the *best* of *Negroes*, and suffer *Englishmen* to purchase their *Refuse* only; and that too at an exorbitant Rate?" (Hayes 1744, 101). Britain had to beat its rival France in this as in other contests.

The benefits of slaves consuming British manufacture were also frequently magnified, for instance, by Postlethwayt. "Are we not indebted to those valuable People, the *Africans*, for our *Sugars*, *Tobaccoes*, *Rice Rum*, and all other *Plantation Produce*?" he questions, confident that it will be greeted with a universal consent. From this premise follows the conclusion that the "greater the Number of *Negroes* imported into our *Colonies*, from *Africa*," the "Exportation of *British* Manufactures among the *Africans*" will be "in Proportion." The African and the West Indian trades are inextricably intertwined so that the "more either flourishes or declines, the other must be necessarily affected," and simultaneously, the "general Trade and Navigation of their *Mother Country*, will be proportionably benefited or injured" (Postlethwayt 1745, 156). The indubitable importance of "those valuable People, the *Africans*" in the sugar islands could be conceded without much reservations but without tincturing it with even a modicum of sympathy for their plight. *The Civil and Natural History of Jamaica* (1756) written by Patrick Browne, an erudite physician with vast scientific ambitions, demonstrates this attitude. In this work greeted by a warm reception by *The Critical Review* (Anon. 1756), the "Civil" history of Jamaica takes up only a tiny portion in comparison with the elaborate "Natural History" of the island which the author pretends to have an intimate personal knowledge of. Before classifying and elucidating the minerals, vegetables, and animal creatures of the island, Browne speaks of its human inhabitants, of which inevitably the "Negroes" are the most numerous category "computed to be more than 120000 in number." Our learned doctor readily acknowledges that it is by the "labours and industry almost alone" of these "Negroes" that the "colony flourishes, and its productions are cultivated and manufactured." He forgets not to note that these "Negroes" are, "for the most part, the property of the Whites; and bought and sold like every other commodity in the country, being always reckoned a part of their estates either real or personal." His language turns opaque when he has to describe the condition of their existence: "When we consider the inconveniences under which these creatures labour, the toils they are obliged to undergo, the vicissitudes of heat and cold, to which they are exposed, and the grossness of their food in general; we ought not to be surprized if they had been still more slothful and sickly than they are commonly observed to be; or if the diseases to which they are obnoxious, had differed more apparently from our own" (Browne 1756, 24–25). Euphemisms such as "inconveniences" and the "toils they are obliged to undergo" mix uneasily with more explicit expressions such as "grossness." The emphasis falls not on the hardship they are "exposed" to, but on the natural consequences of these factors that tend to make these "creatures" generally "slothful and sickly." No one should be surprised if their diseases are different "from our own" as their lives are so starkly different from the "Whites" whose property they remain. Having made this brief nod in the direction of the enslaved human "creatures" to whose "labours and industry" Jamaica depends so much, Browne hastens to move on to his chosen task of describing the island's curious elements, plants, and animals.

Postlethwayt and others maintained that sugar was beneficial for both the colonies and the "Mother Country" and ascertained that the production of sugar could not but depend on African labor. Greater the quantity of African labor supplied, therefore, greater the benefit for all parties concerned. What these writers were less vocal about was the process of collecting the African slaves to be sold to the Europeans. The "MURDER of ONE HUNDRED and EIGHT MILLIONS of our FELLOW-CREATURES!" which appalled Cooper in the late 1780s did not as yet come to the surface as a point of contention, but when it did, as we shall see below, through the concerted assault waged by the opponents of the slave trade, the London print market also welcomed those authors who chose to rebuff the allegation that the British were encouraging rampant homicide in Africa. These authors would first of all point to the fact that Africans, and never the British, were directly involved in capturing the slaves. If blood had to be shed in order to subdue the resistance of the victims, it was the African slave hunters who deserved to be blamed rather than the British merchants, since the latter merely bought those who were sold by the former. A most potent testimony of the British slave traders' reasonable conduct on the West African coast was provided by John Matthews' *A Voyage to the River Sierra-Leone, on the Coast of Africa; Containing an Account of the Trade and Productions of the Country, and of the Civil and Religious Customs and Manners of the People* (1788). The title page introduced the named author as a "Lieutenant in the Royal Navy" who resided in "that country in the years 1785, 1786, and 1787." Not being a merchant himself but a trustworthy officer of His Majesty's Navy, the author gives the reader an apparently impartial account of the matter. Africans, according to him, are habitually at war among themselves, and that owing to their innate moral constitution. "The vindictive and violent spirit of revenge which every African possesses when he imagines he is injured or insulted," Matthews can vouchsafe, is the "cause of frequent wars among the natives." Their perennial wars are really "petty wars, or quarrels," which only "involve the particular town, or towns, which are engaged." Their warfare is "always of the predatory kind" and to "surprise and burn a village, and make a few prisoners, is the utmost extent of their ambition" (Matthews 1788, 128). Did Europeans ever instigate these petty predatory feuds? Matthews assures the reader that "never was [it] the case in any instance which fell under my observations," and "from every account" he could collect, it "never had been the case." When he first arrived at his post, which was the "Isles of Loss," he found an "almost general war" raging throughout the whole region, due to quarrels between chiefs (Matthews 1788, 130–131). In fact, Europeans cannot induce a native warrior to attack other tribes, because it is simply impossible to "make war upon any other tribe without the consent and approbation of the principal people of his nation" (Matthews 1788, 206). On the contrary, native slave dealers took advantage of the war between European powers, particularly between the Dutch and the Portuguese, which rivalry did serve to change the "nature" of the trade, in that the "natives soon availed themselves of the eagerness and avidity, with which each adventurer strove to outvie the other, and their demands increased accordingly." As the thirst for slave labor grew intense, the price of slaves rose, so that slaves "which were formerly purchased with a few cheap and simple articles" could no longer be purchased at the old rate. European buyers were then forced to hand the African supplier a "more extensive and valuable assortment of cloths, fire arms powder, shot, great variety of bead, and silver ware" (Matthews 1788, 182). War being perpetual, "great numbers" of slaves are "prisoners taken in war" clustered in "fifty or a hundred together, by the black slave merchants." Every prisoner of war in this part of Africa is executed instantly or, if spared, is sold as a slave (Matthews 1788, 187). Our author does not deny that Europeans, by the "eagerness with which they push this trade" and by "their competition with each other," did at times "excite the avarice of the individuals to procure slaves, by means as repugnant to their own laws as any act of dishonesty is to ours." But upon the whole, "slavery can never be abolished in a country like Africa, consisting of a prodigious number of small independent states, perpetually at variance, and under no restraining form of government, where the people are of a vindictive and revengeful spirit, and where the laws make every man a slave who is convicted of the most trifling offence" (Matthews 1788, 189–190). Matthews may have answered one of the charges of homicide leveled at British slave traders. But the "MURDER of ONE HUNDRED and EIGHT MILLIONS of our FELLOW-CREATURES" calculated by Cooper included not only the ratio "for one slave procured, ten at least are slaughtered," but also the fact that "a fifth die in the passage, and a third in the seasoning." Even when a part of the blame was passed on to Africans who captured slaves, the flanks of Britain's slave trade and her slave plantations were still left vulnerable to moral assaults by Abolitionists, which, as we shall see below, had their own venerable heritage dating back to the very first phase of the alliance of African and West Indian trades.

6.2 Abolitionists: Forerunners

As is broadly recognized by historians, evangelical Christianity played a prominent role in the Abolitionist movement in the late eighteenth and the early nineteenth centuries. The account given by David Brion Davis rings a representative note. "New World slavery provided Protestant Christianity with an epic stage for vindicating itself as the most liberal and progressive force in human history," Davis states. After "a century of embattled and often reactionary defense," British Christianity "had at last proved that it could be far more 'progressive' than the revolutions spawned by the infidel Enlightenment, even when measured by the Enlightenment's standards of secular freedom and happiness" (Davis [1975] 1999, 129, 223). What one should also acknowledge is that Christian ethics and the theology which supported it also pioneered a moral crusade against the staunch citadel of slave trade and slave plantations from a fairly early stage of the affair. The Anglican clergyman Morgan Godwyn, based on his own experience as a minister stationed in Virginia, published in 1680, *The Negro's and Indians Advocate, Suing for Their Admission into the Church: or, a Persuasive to the Instructing and Baptizing of the Negros' and Indians in Our Plantations.* No publisher apparently offered to undertake the publication business so that the title page informs us that the pamphlet is "printed for the Author." The reason is not difficult to conjecture, since from the very first page of the "Preface" the author cares not to mince his words as he denounces the British planters who possess slaves. They are virtual infidels who "do know no other *God* but *Money*, nor *Religion* but *Profit*." Their religion of "*Money*" and "*Profit*" bids them to oppose the "Christianizing of our *Negro's* and other Heathen in those *Plantations*, and for settling (or rather reviving) of *Religion* amongst our own People there" (Godwyn 1680, preface). Godwyn is rebuked in our time for having recommended "not liberation of enslaved bodies, but the redemption of souls enslaved to sin" (Brown 2006, 57), but the two were by no means neatly separated. Baptism of the "Negros' and Indians" carried civil as well as religious ramifications, for it meant recognizing that they were humans with souls created by God and as such were entitled to moral, if not full-fledged legal, rights. Knowing what was implied, the planters did their best to thwart the admission of their slaves into the Church of England. In the profane colonies prevailed a "spirit of *Gentilism*" which condoned "*Licentiousness*." Rampant pursuit of pleasure and profit is almost "*kept as a Law*: To gain-say which is lookt upon as no less *impious*, than elsewhere it is (and formerly it universally was) *reputed Meritorious*." In this sorry state, they treated their slaves in a most deplorable manner, justifying themselves by contending that "the *Negro's*, though in their Figure they carry some resemblances of Manhood, yet are indeed no Men," which argument they used to cut off the "*Negroe's all pretence to Religion*." This is a vital premise for them, as the "*Owners*" of the African slaves are "hereby set at Liberty, and freed from those importunate Scruples, which Conscience and better Advice might at any time happen to inject into their unsteadie Minds" (Godwyn 1680, 2–3). The satanic war the religion of "*Profit*" waged against the religion of Christ was further indicted by

Godwyn in his 1685 pamphlet *Trade Preferr'd Before Religion, and Christ Made to Give Place to Mammon*. The substance of the work was a "Sermon Relating to the Plantations" first preached at Westminster Abbey and later in other churches of London, and this time, printed not for the "Author" but for two London publishers. Christ's principal foes in the modern world, in Godwyn's view, are the "*MAMMONISTS*" who hold that "whatever conduceth to the getting of Mony, and carrying on of *Trade*, must certainly be lawful." Conversion of the slaves in the plantations disturbs their "getting of Mony," since the baptized slaves, they claim, are bound to be "more tumultuous and rebellious," as well as crafty in their dealings with their masters. This "cursed aversion in our Planters" to their slaves' baptism comes from "no other cause, than from their brutish and *Atheistical* temper" (Godwyn 1685, 1, 5-6). The worshippers of Mammon, of which there are no shortage both in the colonies and in the home country, practice the "Religion" of "*Trade* and *Commerce*" and regard "even Heaven and Salvation to be of less moment than *the getting of Money*." Fervently reverencing the "*filthy Lucre*," they spurn "*Charity*, which is the true *mark* of a Child of God, and the *badge* of a Christian." This amounts to an "absolute *deposing* and rejecting of *Christ*, *for the Exaltation of Mammon*" (Godwyn 1685, 23). The campaign to banish Christian charity is nowhere more poignantly achieved than in the way the English treat their African slaves, denying them humanity and the possibility of spiritual salvation. That the English nation, "once so *famous* for *Zeal* and Piety," should "*prostrate* her self to that *foul Idol Mammon*, and *worship Trade*," is a shame indeed. That "being so much indebted to those *poor Barbarians*, for the Riches, Trade and Commerce, both *by*, and *from them* acquired," the English "should be so far destitute of common Justice" as to refuse to "*make known the Gospel unto them*," is nothing less than to conspire with "*Satan*" to set up a "*confederacy with Hell it self*" (Godwyn 1685, 26–27).

Godwyn's ardent plea on behalf of those "poor Barbarians," thanks to whom "Riches, Trade and Commerce" were accumulated made only a feeble impact, if at all, on the deafening silence enforced even on the Church of Christ, if not by an organized worship of "*Mammon*," clearly by a widespread veneration of "Trade." Godwyn feared that God would punish the English for their "*prophane* Silence, and *unchristian* connivance" at those "*Spiritual Murthers* and Soul-depredations," and cause them "not to prosper" in their worldly affairs (Godwyn 1685, 20). The mysterious workings of Providence did not bear out his predictions made in the 1680s. Instead, in the next century, the British progressively increased both the production and consumption of sugar, which could not but go hand in hand with a steady increase in the purchase, transfer, and exploitation of slaves brought from Africa. The multiple advantages of "African" or slave trade combined with that of the "American" or "West Indies" trade were elevated by the mid-eighteenth century to become orthodox articles of faith certified by the almighty religion of "Trade," as the views sampled in the previous section illustrate. Many printed works of various descriptions extolled the combined blessings of the "African'" and "American" trades, which appeared to be founded on solid grounds. In the sixteenth and seventeenth centuries, the Portuguese planters in Brazil, with equipment imported from Italy and financed by the Fuggers of Augsburg, supplied Europe with sugar. Sugar canes were carried mostly by Dutch ships, making Amsterdam the greatest sugar wholesale market in the West (Thomas 1997, 135). The English, however, quickly caught up with the Dutch, with whom they contended for naval supremacy in the latter half of the seventeenth century. They soon began to seize islands in the Caribbean. In Barbados, the leading English colony in the seventeenth century, at first tobacco was the cash crop cultivated not by imported slaves but by white farmers, which numbered around 11,000 in 1645. The island's economy, however, was drastically altered by 1667, when some 745 sugar plantations thrived on the island employing more than 80,000 slaves, making the island nearly 20 times richer compared with 1645 (Thomas 1997, 187–188). The pattern set by Barbados of specializing the island's economy exclusively in sugar produced by enslaved African labor was repeated and magnified by Jamaica, which overtook Barbados as the foremost sugar island of British West Indies by the 1730s, with an explosive increase of scale from 124 sugar plantations in 1705 to 1601 in 1786. Jamaica's slave population, needless to say, increased in tandem from 9500 in 1675 to 45,000 in 1703 and further onto 226,000 by 1788. Between 1763 and 1778, some 84% of the slaves in Jamaica worked at sugar plantations (Curtin 1969, 51; Hankock 1995, 146–147; Thomas 1997, 275). Such steep surge in the West Indies in the volume of sugar production and in the number of the enslaved producers could not have been possible without a similar growth in demand for the product in the home country. British consumption of sugar in 1669 was 2.13 pounds per capita (annual average). It rose in the 1700s to 5.81 pounds and further to 14.9 in the 1730s, after which there would be a less dramatic but nonetheless steady increase to 16.94 in the 1750s, 20.2 in the 1760s, and 23.2 in the 1770s. The figure, after a brief decline to 21.14 in the 1780s, peaked at 24.16 pounds in the 1790s. The price of sugar in the domestic market dropped as the supply increased. It was sold on average at one shilling per pound in the sixteenth century, making it surely a forbidding luxury item back then. As the seventeenth century progressed, the price was halved and then dropped to the level of one-third of that half between 1700 and 1750 (Shammas 1993, 182). Per capita consumption of sugar in 1776 was 25 pounds, which doubled the figure for 1748 (Morgan 2000, 67). The insatiable demand for sugar, which was being made increasingly affordable, could only be met by an equally insatiable demand in the West Indian plantations for African labor, of which, between 1701 and 1810, Jamaica absorbed some 37.9%, along with Barbados' 14.4% and 17.3% going to Leeward Islands, of the grand total of 1,749,200 (Curtin 1969, 140). No doubt some serious money was made from this trade by merchants engaged in slavery and sugar, although the profitability has been contested by historians, and even though the nation as a whole may not have benefitted all that much due to the expense of keeping and maintaining a vast merchant fleet (Anstey 1975, 47–48; Thomas and McCloskey 1981, 99–100; Davis 1984, 73; Morgan 2000, 38, 44; Morgan 2007, 35–36, 81).

Against this backdrop, few were willing to wage a pitched battle with the combined forces of slave and sugar traders. One could rummage the archives for some pioneering voices, and come up, for instance, with *Two Dialogues on the Man-Trade* (1760), written by a pseudonymous author "J. Philmore," who also features as the main character taking part in the dialogue. "Philmore" urges his friend "Mr. Allcraft," a merchant engaged in the slave trade, to admit the following indubitable truths, first, that to the "African blacks are, as properly and truly, men, as the European whites," and second, that to trade in the "blacks" is to "trade in men," an inexcusably "wicked trade" indeed (Philmore 1760, 6–7, 13). His propositions rest on more or less the same footing as that of Godwyn's argument. Black Africans are God's creatures like the Europeans, endowed with the "same rational powers," and are "under the same moral law, the eternal law of reason, which God hath written upon the table of man's heart." To "sell and buy human creatures" as if they were "brute creatures," therefore, is "great impiety." To persist in the evil practice and to sacrifice "thousands of the human race" to the "voracious God mammon!" is sacrilege (Philmore 1760, 9, 18–19, 46). But the outcry of "Philmore," although he succeeds in the text to convert his slave-trading friend—toward the end his friend vows to leave the trade and to "lay aside some part" of his income to "redeem some of the blacks, and set them at liberty" (Philmore 1760, 62)—seems to have been largely ignored by the readers of the period.[2]

Even the pulpit, nominally beholden to the laws of God, did not quite preserve the torch lit by Godwyn to battle that "*foul Idol Mammon*" worshipped in slave plantations. In some respects, one may concur with Eric Williams when he makes his sweeping accusation of all denominations of British Christianity for conniving at the slave trade and slavery, which, according to Williams' dogmatic Marxism, is hardly surprising, since the "attitude of the churchman was the attitude of the layman," and since the "eighteenth century, like any other century, could not rise above its economic limitations" (Williams [1944] 1966, 43). Of course, such generalizations are always liable to stumble on exceptions, and in this instance, one offered by a prominent leader of the Church: *Sermon Preached Before the Incorporated Society, for the Propagation of the Gospel in Foreign Parts ... on February 21, 1766*, by William Warburton, formerly Dean but now Bishop of Gloucester. According to the review of the printed sermon in *The Monthly Review*, after surveying the state of the New World, Warburton finished his homily by making a common cause with the "*savages in bonds*"—those "vast multitudes yearly stolen from the opposite continent" by the "free savages," namely the British slavers and plantation owners who sacrifice these slaves to "their great idol, the GOD OF GAIN." The reviewer remarks that what the good bishop says regarding this last topic of his sermon "will give pleasure to every humane and discerning reader" (Anon. 1766, 286). Even so, Bishop Warburton's sermon, although significant enough to merit mention by historians (Davis [1975] 1999, 272; Brown 2006, 401), was perhaps far too short and far too isolated to batter the citadel of that great "idol" of "GAIN." Nor did all "humane and discerning" minds of the period share Warburton's concern and outrage. Occupying the other end point of the religious spectrum, David Hume showed no signs of his philosophical tranquility being disturbed by the human sacrifices made at the altar of Mammon far off in the West Indies. Hume's most detailed dissertation on the topic did not confront the contemporary slavery to which the sugar he consumed with his tea owed its

[2] Similarly, Aphra Behn's *Oroonoko: or, the Royal Slave*, which depicted the tragic fate of an enslaved African prince and evinced the author's sympathy at least for him and his bride, if not for all African slaves (Brown 1993, 62–63), had only a limited literary impact, if at all, even though the novel is immensely popular among English literature syllabi of our time.

provenance, but instead, enlarged on the documented slavery of classical antiquity. "Of the Populousness of Ancient Nations" is the title of the essay where he examines what role slavery may have played in the increase or decrease of population. Resplendent in his impressive erudition, Hume opts for a rather anticlimactic inference that "slavery is in general disadvantageous both to the happiness and populousness of mankind, and that its place is much better supplied by the practice of hired servants" (Hume 1987, 396 ["Of the Populousness of Ancient Nations"]). But slaves nonetheless were used extensively "in the AMERICAN colonies," whether wisely or not. Regarding this modern slavery, Hume merely recognizes that "domestic slavery" has a corrupting influence on the owners' "humanity," as the masters will be inured to habitual tyranny over fellow humans "from their infancy." He also observes how the privileges enjoyed by domestic slaves in antiquity are withheld by "our planters" in the colonies, who, to their credit, "would not be fond of rearing many of that kind" (Hume 1987, 383, 389 ["Of the Populousness of Ancient Nations"]). A note attached to this observation mentions how it is "computed in the WEST INDIES, that a stock of slaves grow[s] worse five *per cent.* every year, unless new slaves be bought to recruit them." This calculation leads him to muse, not so much on the callousness of the masters as on the trouble of keeping the slaves alive and fit:

> They [the masters] are not able to keep up their number, even in those warm countries, where cloaths and provisions are so easily got. How much more must this happen in EUROPEAN countries, and in or near great cities? I shall add, that, from the experience of our planters, slavery is as little advantageous to the master as to the slave, wherever hired servants can be procured. A man is obliged to cloath and feed his slave; and he does no more for his servant: The price of the first purchase is, therefore, so much loss to him: not to mention, that the fear of punishment will never draw so much labour from a slave, as the dread of being turned off and not getting another service, will from a freeman. (Hume 1987, 389–390n ["Of the Populousness of Ancient Nations"])

Hume wonders how worse the case would be in Europe, where the climate is harsher. His question serves to diffuse any alarm the "five per cent" of annual wastage of human lives and human vitality in British-owned plantations may have raised. Hume returns to the "warm countries" of the West Indies, yet his sympathy glides away from the "slave" to "our planters," forced to depend on the expensive and easily depleted "stock" of slaves. These Africans, besides, do not seem to be the most promising sort of people when it comes to exhibiting commendable qualities as humans. In another footnote in a different essay, he opined how he is "apt to suspect the negroes to be naturally inferior to the whites," for there "scarcely ever was a civilized nation of that complexion, nor even any individual eminent either in action or speculation." By contrast, even the "most rude and barbarous of the whites" have "something eminent about them," which can only be explained by the decision of "nature" to have things that way and was pleased to make an "original distinction between these breeds of men." "Not to mention our colonies," which of course Hume never visited in his entire life, "there are NEGROE slaves dispersed all over EUROPE, of whom none ever discovered any symptoms of ingenuity" (Hume 1987, 208n ["Of National Characters"]).[3] The general symptom of a clear defect in "ingenuity" betrayed by the "NEGROE slaves" can easily be compounded into something worse. In one explicit reference to the slave trade in Africa, this is what Hume states without much demurral: "You may obtain any thing of the NEGROES by offering them strong drink; and may easily prevail with them to sell, not only their children, but their wives and mistresses, for a cask of brandy" (Hume 1987, 214 ["Of National Characters"]). Slaves are purchased in Africa not through predatory wars among African tribes but through the inordinate affection the "NEGROES" have for strong European liquors. The censure and derision are passed on, in this sentence, to the drunken "NEGROES" away from the white traders bartering brandy for slaves.

"Dr. Adam Smith" is listed by Thomas Clarkson in *The History of the Rise, Progress, and Accomplishment of the Abolition of the African Slave-Trade by the British Parliament* (1808) among the "forerunners" of the noble crusade of Abolitionists. Belonging to the category of those "men of great talents and learning" who "promoted the cause of the injured

[3] Hume has been charged of racism in our time for these remarks, and Edinburgh University felt obliged to rename David Hume Tower, to appease current political sensibilities (Anon. 2004). An extensive study and ultimate defense of Hume's views about the African race has been presented by Asher (2022a, 2022b). Whether Hume really held racist views may remain an eternally inconclusive question, but less arcane is the fact that his remarks were considered to be unacceptable and incited criticism by some of his own contemporaries, most severely by James Beattie, who laid bare the logical weaknesses (hasty generalization based on faulty sampling and dubious premises) of Hume's statements about the Africans (Beattie 1771, 507–512).

Africans" in their writings, Clarkson quotes first from *The Theory of Moral Sentiments*, where the author, "so early as the year 1759," presented the Africans in an "honourable, and their tyrants in a degrading light." The passage quoted by Clarkson is as follows:

> There is not a negro from the coast of Africa who does not … possess a degree of magnanimity which the soul of his sordid master is too often scarce capable of conceiving. Fortune never exerted more cruelly her empire over mankind, than when she subjected those nations of heroes to the refuse of the jails of Europe, to wretches who possess the virtues neither of the countries which they come from, nor of those which they go to. (Clarkson 1808, 1: 85)

The quoted portrayal by Smith of the "negro from the coast of Africa" patently presents a clear contrast to what Hume had to say about the dull-witted or brandy-loving "NEGROES." The context, however, somewhat qualifies this complaint about the fickle disposition of "Fortune" who plays such a cruel prank on these "nations of heroes." The title of the chapter where this passage appears is "Of the Influence of Custom and Fashion upon Moral Sentiments." Custom and fashion exercise their power not randomly but along the fault line separating civilization from barbarism. Smith illustrates by the description above the "Spartan discipline" of savages, who can endure the most severe pain or torture with fortitude and indifference. This shows us how in "civilized nations," those softer "virtues which are founded upon humanity" are "cultivated," whereas among the "rude and barbarous nations," thanks to their rough circumstances of life, the "virtues of self-denial are more cultivated than those of humanity." It is a curious combination of the trope of noble savage with an accusation of the cruelty meted out by the "sordid masters" in slave plantations (Smith 1976b, 205–206 [V.2.8–9]). The "Spartan" virtue of the "negro" is admired but at the same time the commercial network which binds both him and his "sordid master," such as the "Custom and Fashion" of consuming sugar, is allowed to stay put undisturbed.

Clarkson also applauds Smith of *The Wealth of Nations* for having shown in a "forcible manner," by appealing to the "interests" of those concerned, the "dearness of African labour, or the impolicy of employing slaves" (Clarkson 1808, 1: 86). The passage Clarkson alludes to, although he provides no precise reference, most likely is Smith's generalization about slave labor appearing in the second chapter of the third Book, "Of the

Different Progress of Opulence in Different Nations." Here Smith deals with the "Discouragement of Agriculture in the Antient State of Europe after the Fall of the Roman Empire":

> The experience of all ages and nations, I believe, demonstrates that the work done by slaves, though it appears to cost only their maintenance, is in the end the dearest of any. A person who can acquire no property, can have no other interest but to eat as much, and to labour as little as possible. Whatever work he does beyond what is sufficient to purchase his own maintenance, can be squeezed out of him by violence only, and not by any interest of his own. (Smith 1976a, 387–388 [III.ii.9])

The reasoning is sound, no doubt, but whether it could persuade the slave-owning masters of sugar plantations to heed his counsel is a moot point, since the context, once again, is slightly off-focus. Smith does not intend here to confine his discussion to the case of employing "African labour" but to broaden his purview to the "experience of all ages and nations" from ancient Rome onward. The actual experience of the "sordid masters" putting Africans to work in the West Indies features in the fourth Book of *The Wealth of Nations*, where Smith tends to leave the very foundation of slavery alone, even as he grapples with the issue of managing slaves. "In all European colonies," Smith admits, the "culture of the sugar-cane is carried on by negro slaves." He also reiterates the justification proposed by those who support this practice, that the physical "constitution" of white Europeans cannot "support the labour of digging the ground under the burning sun of the West Indies." Smith then builds an argument based on analogy. Just "as the profit and success of the cultivation which is carried on by means of cattle, depend very much upon the good management of those cattle," so the "profit and success of that which is carried on by slaves, must depend equally upon the good management of those slaves" (Smith 1976a, 586–587 [IV.vii.b.54]). If any factual evidence is required to uphold this plain truth, Smith adduces the cases of the French sugar colonies, where the slaves are given a better treatment than in the British plantations and where, as a consequence, they yield greater profit than their British counterpart. Smith is confident that the "prosperity of the sugar colonies of France has been entirely owing to the good conduct of the colonists, which must therefore have had some superiority over that of the English; and this superiority has been remarked in nothing so much as in the good management of their slaves" (Smith 1976a, 588 [IV.vii.b.56]). To have gone thus far to plead for the welfare of enslaved African laborers in the West Indies was quite an achievement indeed. Yet Smith takes care not to overstep the boundary of an economic counsel against excessive cruelty toward slaves. Humane treatment of their slaves is to be preferred to inhumane tyranny, for it rewards the owners with greater "profit and success."

Two years before Smith published *The Wealth of Nations*, with some remarks directly or implicitly critical of slavery included in it, another well-known author, venerated by his followers but often maligned by others, declared an all-out war on slave trade and slavery. *Thoughts Upon Slavery* (1774) hoisted a deceptively terse title, matched with the name of the author printed in the title page, "John Wesley, A.M.," but the title was flanked by an explosive epigraph taken from Genesis, chapter 4, verse 10: "And the Lord said—What hast thou done? The voice of thy brother's blood crieth unto me from the ground" (Wesley 1774, title page).[4] His readers, most of them familiar with their King James Bible, could not have failed to notice that this is God reproaching Cain for his crime of murdering Abel. Slavery is fratricide, abhorrent in the eyes of God, because the black African slave is the white British reader's "brother." Unless this shocking proposition held its ground, the entire argument demolishing justifications of slavery was bound to falter. The founder of Methodism builds his case methodically indeed, citing authorities based on first-hand accounts. He first repels the racist prejudice that alleges that Africans are inferior by nature, as Hume casually suggested. The inhabitants in the so-called Slave Coasts are equal in their human faculty to anyone in Europe. They are "industrious and laborious," their trades are diversified, and their observances of the "Mahometan" religion strict and pious. Far from being given to an excessive "Spartan discipline," which Smith believed to be the hallmark feature of a barbarian custom, they are "sensible, courteous," and even "gentleman-like" (Wesley 1774, 11, 13). Why then are they engaged in a constant warfare with one another? Wesley would not deny the war-ridden condition of the region, but as they were originally "sincere and inoffensive" people and generally "fair, just, and honest in all their dealings," it is obvious that the "fair-faced natives of *Europe*" have

[4] The Scripture text is slightly longer than Wesley's quotation: "And the LORD said unto Cain, Where *is* Abel they brother? and he said, I know not: *Am* I my brother's keeper? And he said, What hast thou done? the voice of thy brother's blood crieth unto me from the ground" (Genesis 4:9–10; Authorized [King James] Version).

"taught them to be otherwise." Seeing how risky it was to capture the natives by direct invasion, Europeans "found a more compendious way of procuring *African* Slaves, by prevailing upon them to make war upon each other, and to sell their Prisoners." "Till then," Wesley emphasizes, "they seldom had any wars: but were in general quiet and peaceable." The "white men" changed it all. They "first taught them drunkenness and avarice, and then hired them to sell one another" (Wesley 1774, 15–16, 18). The British merchants who purchase these victims of predatory internecine war put pressure on the native kings under their influence and goad them to fight one another by supplying them with British weapons, raising the casualty rate to an astounding level (Wesley 1774, 20–22). Furthermore, the painful passage from the African slave stations to the British plantations across the Atlantic further incurs destruction of lives, all due to the intolerable state in which the slaves are carried on British ships. Finally, when they are unloaded, sold, and put to work, further atrocities await them, not any less murderous than whatever they may have suffered when they were captured by fellow Africans in their homeland (Wesley 1774, 23–26). The conclusion to be drawn from all these proven facts is that all those involved directly or indirectly in the business and all those benefitting from it immediately or mediately are accomplices to the heinous crime of human trafficking. The laws made by men may turn a blind eye to the criminal deed or even encourage it. But Wesley, as God's minister, has God's laws before him. Since the "Just GOD" will "reward every man according to his works," Wesley beseeches those engaged in the slave trade to desist and repent: "Before you drop into eternity! Think now, *He shall have Judgment without mercy, that shewed no mercy*" (Wesley 1774, 46). The italicized quotation comes from the New Testament book the Epistle of James (chapter 2, verse 13), but the whole affair is placed in an Old Testament ambience of God directly punishing the evil-doers, such as the sinful inhabitants of Sodom and Gomorrah:

> When you squeezed the agonizing creatures down in the ship, or when you threw their poor mangled remains into the sea, had you no relenting? Did not one tear drop from your eye, one sigh escape from your breast? Do you feel no relenting *now*? If you do not, you must go on, till the measure of your iniquities is full. Then will the great GOD deal with *You*, as you have dealt with *them*, and require all their blood at your hands. And at that day it shall be more tolerable for Sodom and Gomorrah than for *you*! (Wesley 1774, 46–47)

The last sentence quotes and applies the words of Lord Jesus Christ, who warns (in Matthew 10:14-15) that those who do not receive His disciples and refuse to hear their words should expect in the "day of judgment" a fate far worse than that which was meted out to Sodom and Gomorrah. The author then fleshes out the full implication of the epigraph. "Therefore the blood of all these wretches, who die before their time, whether in their country, or elsewhere lies upon *your* head," Wesley warns. "*The blood of thy brother* (for, whether thou wilt believe it or no, such he is in the sight of Him that made him)," he stresses the propriety of using the term, "*crieth against thee from the earth*, from the ship, and from the waters" (Wesley 1774, 50). In the name of the Father, the Son, and the Holy Spirit (who inspires Wesley to denounce the "iniquities" of slave trade), Wesley condemned Britain's slave trade and admonished his fellow countrymen engaged in it to immediately terminate their sinful actions.

Upon its publication Wesley's treatise met with a favorable notice in *The Monthly Review*, which assigned some four pages of its September 1774 number to review the work. After providing extracts and summary of the work, the article closed with the assurance that the pamphlet "contains many facts on good authority, or as good as could be found," and that the writer "has made many pertinent observations, into which we cannot enter, but which do honour to his humanity" (Anon. 1774a, 236–237). Wesley's treatise incited one anonymous author to write and publish an instant refutation, *A Supplement to Mr. Wesley's Pamphlet, Intitled, Thoughts upon Slavery*, which was also reviewed in the same number, though far less favorably. This author, according to the review, refuted Wesley's account primarily by attempting to discredit the author's credentials. Wesley being an infamous "enthusiast in his religious principles," what he asserts is bound likewise to be tainted by extremism. This defect, however, the reviewer cannot accept as a compelling reason to dismiss Wesley's rebuke of the "tyrannic dominion we assume" over the "negroes," however "stupid" they may be (Anon. 1774b, 237). Readers of the periodical also entered the controversy, one of whom, claiming to be "a constant Reader" as well as an "Admirer" of the magazine, sent a letter to the editor attempting to debunk Wesley's characterization of the plantation owners, which to him seemed totally biased and false (Anon. 1774c, 324–325). The censured author did not remain aloof and placid. Wesley sent his own letter to the same periodical two months later rebuffing "what your Correspondent affirms" about the humanity of American slave owners, by citing two sample advertisements sent to him by his acquaintances in Philadelphia. The advertisements promised decent reward for anyone presenting the advertised runaway slave's "head severed from his body" (Anon. 1774d, 487–488). Wesley had many other battles to wage against his many adversaries over multiple issues besides the brutal enslavement and exploitation of African slaves, but that he always was deeply concerned about their plight is evidenced by *A Serious Address to the People of England* (1778), cited in Chap. 3, whose last word targets the "Trade of our *West-Indian* Islands," that "horrid Trade" of "buying the Bodies and Souls of Men." He wishes that it will cease altogether, even if "all our Sugar-Islands (so the inhabitants escaped) were swallowed up in the depth of the sea," for he is certain England's economy will flourish "tho' we no more suck the blood and devour the flesh of the less barbarous *Africans.*" The blood of the murdered brother Abel is once again evoked in the closing exclamation: "O Earth, hide not thou their blood, and no more cover the slain!" (Wesley 1778, 28). Far less well-known in Britain in the 1770s than Wesley was the American Quaker Anthony Benezet, whose pivotal work *Some Historical Account of Guinea; with an Enquiry into the Rise and Progress of the Slave-Trade, Its Nature, and Lamentable Effects* (1772) received only a brief notice in *The Monthly Review*. The review magazine merely mentioned that the work was "[w]holly collected, and not injudiciously, from a considerable variety of authors; and intended to shew both the iniquity of the slave-trade, and of our enslaving the negroes, &c. in our colonies," and that it was "first printed at Philadelphia, in 1771" (Anon. 1772, 73). Similar in many respects to Wesley's pamphlet but preceding it by three years, historians suggest that Wesley could have been directly influenced and inspired by Benezet (Anstey 1975, 232–233; Davis [1975] 1999, 215–220; Drescher 1987, 117). The similarity between the two pioneers of Abolitionism, whether reflecting Wesley's respect for Benezet or not, can be traced in their common intention to cover all the facets of the issue from the sourcing of slaves in Africa to their use by plantation owners.

Benezet's historical overview of slave trade reaches back in time to the Portuguese in the sixteenth century, who were "stimulated" by an "unwarrantable lust of gain" to engage in the "horrid traffic" on the West African coast (Benezet 1772, 58–59). It was a blatant betrayal of the "gentle spirit" of Christianity, and those engaged in the trade flouted Christ's teachings about brotherly love. As the Middle Ages progressed, Christian doctrine inculcating the "original equality of mankind, as well as the impartial eye with which the Almighty regards men of every condition" had gradually pulled the European nations away from the institution of slavery. Revival of slavery by the Portuguese in the sixteenth century and by the British in his own century who followed their suit clearly perverted Christianity in "those parts of America which are in the practice of it" and pulled the world back to the "ignorance and barbarity of the darkest ages." The nominal Christians who out of greed foment "cruel wars among the blacks" stifle the possibility of the "barbarous people" becoming "civilized" by acquainting them with the true "nature of the Christian religion" (Benezet 1772, 65–66, 68). As those who undertake this business were least likely to care very much about religion, at least when trade is at stake, Benezet appeals to their vaunted "liberty" founded on English law. "It is matter of astonishment, how a people, who, as a nation, so much value themselves for their uncommon sense of the benefit of liberty," Benezet asserts, "can live in the practice of such extreme oppression and inhumanity, without seeing the inconsistency of such conduct, and feeling great remorse." Their enlightened rationality is equally hypocritical, since one hears "these men calmly making calculations about the strength and lives of their fellow men" as if they were domesticated animals. The planters in Jamaica would consider it a "gaining purchase" if "six in ten of the new imported Negroes survive the seasoning," that is, the first phase of their enforced labor in the plantations. In most of the "other plantations," the cost of purchasing slaves is reckoned to have been sufficiently reimbursed if they "live eight or nine years." The "iniquity" of the slave drivers apparently has not been directly punished by God, whose existence or authority they care not to acknowledge anyway. Yet "divine displeasure" is evidenced by their utter fall from grace, "that hardness of heart, that forgetfulness of God, and insensibility to every religious impression, as well as that general depravation of manners, which so much prevails in these colonies, in proportion as they have more or less enriched themselves at the expence of the blood and bondage of the Negroes" (Benezet 1772, 92–93). Grow rich if you will, but do so at the price of losing your humanity, if not your soul. The fundamental question for Benezet is the injustice of unpaid wages, which he indicts by quoting both the New and the Old Testaments (Luke 10:7 and Jeremiah 22:13). "Is it not a Christian doctrine, *that the labourer is worthy of his hire*?" the author inquires. "And hath not the Lord, by the mouth of his prophet, pronounced," Benezet reminds the reader, "'*Wo unto that man who buildeth his house by unrighteousness, and his chambers by wrong; who uses his neighbour's service without wages, and giveth him nought for his work?*" The "poor Negro slaves," by the supposedly Christian Whites, are "constrained, like the beast, by beating, to work hard without hire or recompence, and receive nothing from the hand of their unmerciful masters, but such a wretched provision as will scarce support them under their fatigues" (Benezet 1772, 93–94). Benezet challenges the "opulent planter, or merchant" to "prove that his Negro slave is not his brother, or that he is not his neighbour, in the scripture sense of these appellations." If "he is not able so to do," Benezet asks, "how will he justify the buying and selling of his brethren, as if they were of no more consideration than his cattle?" How will the planter or merchant ever justify the "wearing them out with continual labour, before they have lived out half their days?" or the "severe whipping and torturing them, even to death, if they resist his insupportable tyranny?" (Benezet 1772, 94–95). It is ultimately the duty of British Parliament to rectify this injustice. In fact, Benezet cannot but inquire how the political authorities of the realm could possibly wink at it: "[When] the principles of which the British constitution is founded, are so favourable to the common rights of mankind, how it has happened that the laws which countenance this iniquitous traffic, have obtained the sanction of the legislature? and that the executive part of the government should so long shut their ears to continual reports of the barbarities perpetrated against this unhappy people, and leave the trading subjects at liberty to trample on the most precious rights of others, even without a rebuke?" (Benezet 1772, 126). A ready answer to these questions would be that leaving the "trading subjects at liberty" to pursue their interests is what Britain's government ought to do, for, after all, slaves are legal properties of the "opulent planter, or merchant," and property is enshrined in the "British constitution." At this point, we have to see to what extent slave ownership enjoyed the firm protection of the common law.

6.3 "Somerset, the Negro"

In addition to asserting that the African slaves are the "brethren" of the White planters and merchants, Benezet also claimed that the slave has "a *superior* property or right to the fruit of his own labour; and more especially to his own person," which was "given him by God, and which none but the Giver can justly claim" (Benezet 1772, 95). Man-made laws may protect the property rights of the planters and slave merchants over their slaves, but the law of God granted a "*superior*" right to the slaves over their own lives. The conflict or strife between these two laws was what Granville Sharp, another pioneer Abolitionist, made it his special task to amplify. In the "Preface" to Sharp's first pamphlet on slavery, *An Essay on Slavery, Proving from Scripture Its Inconsistency with Humanity and Religion* (1773), the author contended that "Slavery" has been deemed to be "not consistent with the English constitution, nor admissible in Great-Britain," according to the "late solemn determination in the court of King's Bench at Westminster, in the case of—Somerset, the Negro." It is thus utterly unconscionable that slavery "should be revived and continued in the colonies, peopled by descendants of Britain, and blessed with sentiments as truly noble and free as any of their fellow subjects in the mother country" (Sharp 1773, vi).[5] The main body of this work, however, focuses largely on the Biblical texts adduced to condemn slavery and to refute Thomas Thompson's treatise that sought to justify slavery on the basis of Scripture. Thompson draws support from the Old Testament book Leviticus, where enslavement as such is never condemned, and from 1 Corinthians in the New Testament, where St Paul advises the "servants" (i.e., slaves) to "abide in the same calling" assigned to them by God (Thompson 1772, 12–13, 16). Sharp regards this interpretation as utterly spurious. "The glorious system of the gospel," Sharp emphasizes, "destroys all *narrow, national partiality*; and makes *us citizens of the world*, by obliging us to profess *universal benevolence*: but more especially are we bound, as Christians, to commiserate and assist to the utmost of our power all person in *distress*, or *captivity*." If so, "we must not, for the sake of *Old-England*, and its *African trade*, or for the supposed advantage, or imaginary necessities of our American colonies, lay aside our *christian charity*" toward the sorely distressed African slaves in the colonies (Sharp 1773, 22–23). Sharp began his pamphlet war against slave trade by battling a

[5] For a detailed account of Sharp's life and thoughts, see Davis ([1975] 1999, 375–376, 389–397); Brown (2006, 93–97, 171–175). Readers of Sharp's works may readily agree with Davis when he observes that Sharp "was something of an anomaly in eighteenth-century England," in that "he still embodied the polarized traits of a Puritan reformer" and "saw himself as the vindicator of a primal and eternal law which had been obscured by centuries of encrustation" (Davis [1975] 1999, 389). Going in the opposite direction, Baucom compares Sharp to Immanuel Kant, largely on the strength of Sharp's involvement in the campaign to punish those responsible for the random drowning of slaves on board the Liverpool slave-trading ship *Zong*, in a language Sharp (or even Kant) would have found somewhat incomprehensible. Baucom finds Sharp's "serial" or "obsessive reiteration" of the "'singular' facts" to construct an "appearance of the spectral truth event" to be "entirely like Kant's" (Baucom 2005, 128).

rather tenuous theological justification of slavery attempted by Thompson. His arsenal was enriched by a more diversified enlisting of Bible books in his second work, *The Law of Liberty, or, Royal Law, by Which All Mankind Will Certainly be Judged! Earnestly Recommended to the Serious Consideration of All Slaveholders and Slavedealers* (1776). The epigraph was taken from James 2:12: "So speak ye, and so do, as they that shall be judged by the law of liberty." From this verse he picked the phrase the "law of liberty" and placed it at the head of the title. This "Law" exhorts all Christians to practice Christian charity to the full, for they in turn will be judged by that law. Armed with this divine ordinance, Sharp engages his enemy, the "continued multiplication of Statutes" designed to fortify slavery. This artifice of human laws "affords matter only for *Equivocation, Doubt*, and *Evasion*, whereby SOUND LAW is vitiated and corrupted." As a result, "*bad Precedents*" hold sway over the law courts "instead of LAW." Sharp's "LAW" in all caps refers to the "general Laws of Morality," which always recognize the supremacy of the "*natural Rights of Mankind*," particularly when applied to the question of the "*Legality or Illegality of Slavery among Christians.*" Since even the "Tyrants, Slaveholders, Extortioners, and other Oppressors, would most certainly dislike to be treated as they treat others," this "Law of Liberty" necessarily excludes "*the least Toleration of Slavery*, or of any other *Oppression*, which an *innocent Man* would be unwilling to experience in his own person from another" (Sharp 1776b, 21–23). The golden rule of Christ, of doing to others as you would have them do unto you, makes slavery "absolutely inconsistent" with Christianity, "because we cannot say of any *Slaveholder*, that he *doth not* to another, what he would not have done to himself." The slaveholder is "continually exacting *involuntary Labour* from others *without Wages*, which he would think monstrously unjust, were he himself the Sufferer" (Sharp 1776b, 33). But the laws of the realm can conveniently forget Christ's laws. African slave trade, even though it incurs the "most contemptuous Violations of *Brotherly Love* and *Charity* that men can be guilty of," is "openly encouraged and promoted" by the British legislature, while the "most detestable and oppressive *Slavery*, that ever disgraced even the unenlightened Heathens, is notoriously *tolerated* in the British Colonies by the *public Acts* of their respective Assemblies." Sharp, therefore, accuses the "WHOLE BRITISH EMPIRE" as an accomplice to the crime of "*Slave-dealing* and *Slave-holding*" and not just the "few hardened *Individuals*" employed to carry out "those baneful Practices" (Sharp 1776b, 48–49).

In the same year of 1776 was also published Sharp's third assault on slavery, *The Just Limitation to Slavery in the Laws of God, Compared with the Unbounded Claims of the African Traders and British American Slaveholders*, which came with a "copious Appendix," as promised by the subtitle, offering, among other things, a detailed account of the trial of "Somerset, the Negro" and other cases related to runaway slaves. The main text fired a heavy barrage of Scripture texts to dismantle the pretended legitimacy of slavery in the eyes of God. Reiterating many points made in his two previous works, the author this time stepped into the terrain of English law proper, even as he kept his feet firmly planted on the moral codes of Christ. Can the law justify an "absolute property" over African slaves extended "for life"? When their case is compared with that of British convicts transported to perform forced labor without recompense, the obvious question is whether they had ever "offended any member of our community either at home or abroad to justify such a severe punishment under *British Government*." Alternatively, justifying it as some "legal contract for service" is equally groundless, since the slaves are "absolutely incapacitated by *unlawful duress*, to *enter into any contract* as long as they are retained by force of fear in the British dominions" (Sharp 1776a, 52-53n). No crime justifies their forfeiture of freedom. Neither has any voluntary contract ratified their lifelong subjection to the master. Therefore, the African slaves cannot be an absolute property of any master, from which follows the inference that an "ACTION of TROVER *cannot lye for a slave*" or, in other words, "that no man can lawfully be prosecuted for protecting a negroe, or any other slave whatever, that has '*escaped from his master*' because that would be punishing a man for doing *his indispensable duty* according *to the laws of God*" (Sharp 1776a, 55). The "copious Appendix" of this book was meant to silence any doubts raised by this forthright claim made about the illegality of seeking to recover a runaway slave as a lost property. Before we discuss the celebrated case of "Somerset, the Negro," we would have to see how far Sharp diverges from the general position of the English law about slavery, as explained by William Blackstone.

Slavery is touched upon by Blackstone in the first Book, "Of the Rights of Person," of the first volume of *Commentaries on the Laws of England* (1st edition, 1753). Blackstone evinces a great deal of satisfaction and pride that "political or civil liberty" flourishes in Britain, where it "falls little short of perfection, and can only be lost or destroyed by the folly or demerit of its owner." This "spirit of liberty is so deeply implanted in our constitution, and rooted even in our very soil, that a slave or a negro, the moment he lands in England, falls under the protection of the laws, and so far becomes a freeman, though the master's right to his service may probably still continue" (Blackstone 1768a, 126–127). Free but bound to render service? This jarring discord between right and obligation is not fully silenced by the modifier "probably." Blackstone attempts to elucidate it as follows:

> [A] slave or negro, the instant he lands in England, becomes a freeman; that is, the law will protect him in the enjoyment of his person, and his property. Yet, with regard to any right which the master may have acquired to the perpetual service of John or Thomas, this will remain exactly in the same as before: for this is no more than the same state of subject for life, which every apprentice submits to for the space of seven years, or sometimes for a longer term. (Blackstone 1768a, 424)

How then did the master acquire the right to the "perpetual service" of his slave, which not even the constitutional "spirit of liberty" of Britain can interfere with? Surely, the slave's direful condition cannot be likened to that of a free apprentice, however long his apprenticeship may last? Instead of answering these questions, Blackstone moves on to the issue of baptism of slaves which mattered so much to Godwyn, as we have seen above. The "infamous and unchristian practice of withholding baptism from negro servants, lest they should thereby gain their liberty," is both "without foundation" and "without excuse," since England's law, even as it ensures "liberty" or "protection, to a jew, a turk, or a heathen, as well as to those who profess the true religion of Christ," will "not dissolve a civil obligation between master and servant, on account of the alteration of faith in either of the parties." To put it simply, being baptized or not has nothing do with the legal status of the "negro servants" (Blackstone 1768a, 425). Of course, our enlightened jurist wishes not to condone slavery itself, namely "pure and proper slavery" understood as an "absolute and unlimited power" of the master over the "life and fortune of the slave." England's law never grants this absolute right, which is "repugnant to reason, and the principles of natural law." Captivity in war, "assigned by Justinian," hardly justifies slavery, for presenting enslavement as an alternative to killing a prisoner is to admit that the prisoner posed no threat that can only be prevented by his instant death. Neither can one sell oneself, also according to Roman law, since "what equivalent can be given for life, and liberty," Blackstone asks, "both of which (in absolute slavery) are held to be in the master's disposal?" (Blackstone 1768a, 423–424). On this issue at least, Sharp's contention that slaves cannot be an absolute property seems to harmonize with Blackstone's stance. But for Blackstone, even as "absolute" or "pure" slavery is banished beyond the pale of the laws of England, virtual *de facto* slavery is allowed to pass itself off as a lawful civil contract. How and upon what terms the slave entered into that fictional compact and how it has any better legitimacy than one provided by *Codex Justinianus*, once again, Blackstone declines to delve into. Yet the case seems far from abstruse when considered a question of natural common sense. If, as Sharp, Benezet, and Wesley accused, the British purchasers of slaves, whether on the African coast or at the ports of West Indies, are accomplices in brutal slaughter and man-hunt, their criminal possession and detention of human captives is patently illegal, or at least immoral.

What if a slave, although legally free in England but still legally compelled to obey his or her master, refuses to do so, and even runs away, as did "Somerset, the Negro"? Obviously, this case happened after Blackstone published the fourth and last volume of his magnum opus. But already some clues can be found in the book as to the position England's law would take about it. In the second volume of his *Commentaries* devoted to the "Right of Things," after discussing extensively that cherished object of England's law, "things real," i.e., landed estate, Blackstone catches breath to deal with "things personal," which embrace "all sorts of things moveable, which may attend a man's person wherever he goes," unlike the immovable land or a building. Of the "things personal," the more narrowly defined category is "chattels personal," which are things that "may be annexed to or attendant on the person of the owner, and carried about him from one part of the world to another," such as "animals, household-stuff, money, jewels, corn, garments, and every thing else that can properly be put in motion, and transferred from place to place" (Blackstone 1768b, 385, 387). At this stage, human slaves are not included in the list, although the expression "attendant on the person of the owner, and carried about him from one part of the world to another" could be interpreted as being applicable to a slave such as Somerset brought by his master from Jamaica to England. The rights over chattels are either "absolute" or "qualified." The former pertains to "possession absolute" of "inanimate things" or "vegetable productions," while to the latter belongs possession of animals tamed and domesticated "*per industriam hominis*," namely, by a "man's *reclaiming* and making them tame by art, industry, and education; or by confining them within his own immediate power, that they cannot escape and use their natural liberty" (Blackstone 1768b, 389, 391). Inevitably, one cannot but wonder whether an analogy with animals cannot be established regarding the slaves confined forcefully so that they "cannot escape" nor "use their natural liberty." Blackstone concedes that the right over slaves is a species of a "qualified property" in chattels, but it is ratified by the "original and natural right of occupancy." What is meant by this legal phrase is best clarified in his own words:

> [A]s in the *goods* of an enemy, so also in his *person*, a man may acquire a sort of qualified property, by taking him a prisoner in war; at least till his ransom be paid. And this doctrine seems to have been extended to negro-servants, who are purchased, when captives, of the nations with whom they are at war, and continue therefore in some degree the property of their masters who buy them: though, accurately speaking, that property consists rather in the perpetual *service*, than in the *body* or *person* of the captive. (Blackstone 1768b, 402)

Slaves were prisoners of war and therefore the property first of those who captured them and then of those who purchased them from the captors. This logic reverts to the Roman law which Blackstone chose to criticize in the first volume. To be fair, he hedges his statement with "seems to have been" and "in some degree," and he underscores again what to him is an important distinction between the "*person*" of the "negro-servants" and the "*service*" exacted from them. But the martial authority of the "original and natural right" of "occupancy," which means taking possession by physical force, cleanses the slave-catchers and slave-buyers of all moral opprobrium. This supposed "right of occupancy" stands as another fence—if not a wall—that separates Blackstone from the Abolitionists.

The case of Somerset concerned the right of his master Charles Stewart (or Steuart) to recapture Somerset and to incarcerate him on Captain Knowles' ship anchored on Thames for the purpose first of transporting him from England and then of selling him in Jamaica. As we have seen, Sharp argued that no *trover* applies to a runaway slave in England. An action of trover, according to Blackstone, is an action of "trespass" seeking to recover damages against such person "as had *found* another's goods, and refused to deliver them on demand, but converted them to his own use." Although it is called an action of "*trover*," i.e., of finding, the fact of finding is "totally immaterial," since the plaintiff needs only to assert that he lost certain goods and that the defendant has them. The plaintiff then has to prove that the said goods are *his* property and that the defendant had them in his possession. The injury lies in the "conversion" or use of the plaintiff's property by the defendant, so that only when a "conversion" is also proved can the plaintiff recover damages equal to the value of the thing converted. Now to recover the thing itself, the plaintiff needs to initiate an action of *detinue* or *replevin* (Blackstone 1768c, 151–152). Sharp apparently did not intend to enter into these intricate formalities of the law, but merely to emphasize the fact that a slave is not a "chattel personal" to be recovered by an action of "trover." Those who championed Somerset's cause, using their legal expertise, challenged the right of Stewart to recover his alleged property Somerset by requesting the court to issue a "writ" of *habeas corpus*, which, as Blackstone describes it, is the "most celebrated" among the "writs" (or court order) terminating an unlawful imprisonment or detention of a person whether in a prison or in a private house. Among different writs of *habeas corpus*, what was applied to Somerset's case was "*habeas corpus ad subjiciendum*," directed to the "person detaining another, and commanding him to produce the body of the prisoner with the day and cause of his caption and detention," and then to submit to "whatsoever the judge or court awarding such writ shall consider in that behalf" (Blackstone 1768c, 127–128, 131). It was a most powerful prerogative writ issued by the high court of King's Bench, where, in the case of Somerset, sat Lord Mansfield (William Murray) to adjudicate this delicate plea. His decision, which was to grant a writ of *habeas corpus* releasing Somerset from his master, may appear to posterity to be a "Delphic verdict laced with ambiguities" (Brown 2006, 97), but it was celebrated at the time as a significant victory by those who found slavery repugnant. John Millar hailed the landmark court decision of 1772 in the revised 1773 edition of *The Origin of the Distinction of Ranks* as an "authentic testimony of the liberal sentiments entertained in the latter part of the eighteenth century" (Millar 2006, 279-280). Sharp was confident that the ruling set a new precedent which "obliged by the common law (which always favours LIBERTY) to discharge" a slave from the "*unnatural* and *unprecedented* claims of his master" that a slave such as Somerset was his lawful property to be disposed of as he saw fit (Sharp 1776a, 74). Not surprisingly, the decision ignited outrage on the part of the slave-traders and slave-owners. Samuel Estwick, born to a Barbados planter, wrote and published in the same year of the trial, under the generic name of "West Indian," *Considerations on the Negroe Cause Commonly So Called, Addressed to the Right Honourable Lord Mansfield, Lord Chief Justice of the Court of King's Bench, &c.* (1772). The "West Indian" would drop the "odious word" slavery and take the debate to the "land of *Property*," where he is first greeted by the acts of Parliament empowering the Royal African Company. These statutes, as far as he can read them, clearly bestowed the "mark and stamp of property upon Negroes" (Estwick 1772, 10–11). When no one dared to deny that "Mr. Stewart was the bona fide purchaser of Somerset, in the legal course of trade" (Estwick 1772, 20), depriving him of his property right by the subterfuge of *habeas corpus* was a scandal in this "kingdom of commerce," for it was nothing less than "robbing" the law-abiding "merchants" of their property (Estwick 1772, 18).

The reports of the trial, notwithstanding the enthusiasm of one party or the anger of the other, convey the impression that Lord Mansfield himself sought to keep a measured and cautious stance regarding the famous "LIBERTY," which the common law, as Sharp believed, "always favours." The trial which took place on 14 May 1772 (Easter Term) occasioned a lengthy and heated debate between the counsels of respective parties. Lord Mansfield, however, deferred his decision, merely stating what difficulties were involved in the dispute. He began by identifying the key point of the litigation. The question was whether the "owner had a right to detain the slave, for the sending of him over to be sold in Jamaica." If he had, then, the writ of *habeas corpus* cannot compel the owner. "Contract for sale of a slave is good here" in England, and such sale is a "matter to which the law properly and readily attaches" protection, but in this case the "person of the slave himself is immediately the object of enquiry." This made a "very material difference." Now, "Mr. Stewart," the master, "advances no claim on contract," but "rests his whole demand on a right to the negro as slave," that is, as his rightful property, according to the laws of Virginia or Jamaica. The question, then, is whether "any dominion, authority or coercion can be exercised in this country, on a slave according to the American laws" (*Somerset v. Stewart* 1772, 509). Decision was made on 22 June (Trinity Term) rejecting Stewart's claim that he can exercise lawful right over his property Somerset. Lord Mansfield, true to the spirit of the common law, first acknowledged the influence the relevant precedents may have on his decision. Lord Mansfield first granted "all due attention to the opinion of Sir Philip Yorke, and Lord Chief Justice Talbot," two Crown law officers who answered in 1729 an inquiry made by slave-trading merchants about the "legal consequences of slaves coming over to this kingdom or being baptized." Their opinion was that a slave coming to England, or being baptized, had no material consequences on his status as a slave.[6] "Lord Chancellor Hardwicke, sitting as Chancellor on the 19th of October 1749," had also ruled that "trover would lie" on a slave in England. Mansfield, therefore, would demur from touching upon the legality of slavery itself, but focus only on the "question before us," which is whether the "return to a habeas corpus" (i.e., a request not to submit to the writ) has a sufficient cause. If it has, the "negro must be remanded," and if not, "he must be discharged." The "return," as Mansfield summarizes it, states that the "slave departed and refused to serve; whereupon he was kept, to be sold abroad." Mansfield then chose to move beyond the narrow boundary set by precedents:

> So high an act of dominion must be recognized by the law of the country where it is used. The power of a master over his slave has been extremely different, in different countries. The state of slavery is of such a nature, that it is incapable of being introduced on any reasons, moral or political; but only positive law, which preserves its force long after the reasons, occasion, and time itself from whence it was created, is erased from memory: it's so odious, that nothing can be suffered to support it, but positive law. Whatever inconveniences, therefore, may follow from a decision, I cannot say this case is allowed or approved by the law of England; and therefore the black must be discharged. (*Somerset v. Stewart* 1772, 510)

Contrary to what Sharp suggested, Lord Mansfield did not exactly judge slavery itself to be "*unnatural* and *unprecedented*." The precedents were there withdrawing the much-vaunted English liberty from African slaves, whether baptized or not. What Mansfield said about the "nature" of slavery was that it found no support in morals or politics. Being unnatural perhaps and even "odious," slavery can only be sustained by "positive law," such as those enacted by the slave-owning colonies in North America and the West Indies. By the same token, however, unless a clear positive

[6] Estwick, not surprisingly, quotes their words in full: "We are of opinion, that a slave by coming from the West-Indies, either with or without his master, to Great-Britain or Ireland, doth not become free, and that his master's *property* or *right* in him is not thereby determined or varied; and baptism doth not bestow freedom on him, nor make any alteration in his temporal condition in these kingdoms: We are also of opinion, that the master may *legally* compel him to return to the plantations. / P. York. / C. Talbot. / Jan. 24, 1729" (Estwick 1772, 33).

law of England can be said to have "allowed and approved" slavery, the "power of the master" over the alleged slave cannot be honored to such a high degree as to overrule the supreme writ of *habeas corpus.* This was a carefully drafted speech, steering clear of the more contentious issues about the slaves' rights, and keeping in view one of the most important tasks of England's law, the prevention of unlawful detention of persons. By extending *habeas corpus* to the "black," this decision acknowledged that he was not quite a chattel personal to be treated like brutes.

6.4 Abolitionists of the 1780s

Lord Mansfield had said to the contending lawyers, on 22 May 1772, that the question of slavery and the commercial interests attached to it would ultimately have to be left to Parliament to decide, for it will be the "best and perhaps the only method of settling the point for the future" (*Somerset v. Stewart* 1772, 509). In the 1780s, this advice was put into action. The opponents of slavery sought to enact a law prohibiting slave trade and, after that measure was taken, to abolish slavery itself. Those with vested interests in the slave trade and slave plantations did all their best to thwart that effort. One way or another, slavery was increasingly becoming an unavoidable topic, owing no doubt to the disturbances and controversy caused by the American Revolution in the 1780s. To summarize a sophisticated account given by Christoper Leslie Brown, first, slave ownership was associated with the rebel colonies to debunk their claim that Britain's arbitrary rule was turning them into slaves, but when the American revolutionaries banned slave imports, Britain's slave trade became the target (Brown 2006, 110–126, 151–152). The hypocrisy of the slave-owning American rebels appalled many, including Wesley. "Slavery is a state, wherein neither a man's goods, nor liberty, nor life, are at his own disposal," Wesley made it clear. That indeed is the "state of a thousand, of ten thousand negroes in the American Colonies." "And are their masters in the same state with them?" the champion of enslaved "negroes" inquired (Wesley 1776, 25). On the other hand, censuring the Americans for being self-righteous slave owners had an unexpected effect of highlighting Britain's dominant role in the transatlantic slave trade. Great Britain's massive share in that "iniquitous commerce" of slave trade, according to *Thoughts and Sentiments on the Evil of Slavery* (1787), a work written by a former slave Quobna Ottobah Cugoano, obliged the nation to "set an example" by changing course, "lest they have to repent for their wickedness when it becomes too late" (Cugoano 1999, 84). That "example," for Cugoano, had to meet the highest moral standards. He demanded a "universal emancipation of slaves" in the name of "Christian religion" by a "proclamation" issued by Parliament "setting forth the Antichristian unlawfulness of the slavery and commerce of the human species," which was then to be "sent to all courts and nations in Europe" (Cugoano 1999, 98). While Cugoano's proposal no doubt went far beyond the domain of practical policy, slavery and slave trade were becoming topics to ponder even by those removed from the theaters of fierce pamphlet war. Paley set aside a chapter on slavery in *The Principles of Moral and Political Philosophy* (1785) in the portion of his work dealing with those "Relative Duties which are Indiscriminate." What justifies the obligation of a slave to work for the master? In general, there are three grounds on which it stands, "crimes," "captivity," and "debt." None of these bestows a permanent and absolute power on the master. When crime is punished by enslavement, the "continuance of the slavery, as of any other punishment, ought to be proportioned to the crime." In the second and third cases, it "ought to cease, as soon as the demand of the injured nation, or private creditor, is satisfied." The "slave-trade upon the coast of Africa," however, seems immune to such restraint based on common reason. "When slaves in that country are brought to market," the "origin or justice of the vendor's title" is never checked. But the "defect of right in the first purchase" pales in criminality when placed next to the method of securing the slaves to be sold, since the "natives are excited to war and mutual depredation, for the sake of supplying their contracts, or furnishing the market with slaves." The "slaves," after being "torn away from parents, wives, children, from their friends and companions, their fields and flocks, their home and country," are shipped to European colonies in America, "with no other accommodation on shipboard than what is provided for brutes." When the "miserable exiles" are "delivered" from this "second stage of cruelty," they are "placed, and that for life, in subjection to a dominion and system of laws, the most merciless and tyrannical that ever were tolerated upon the face of the earth." An "inordinate authority" is granted by the "plantation-laws" to the slave-holder, and the "*English* slave-holder," among the Europeans in that part of the world, enjoys the deplorable distinction of being most excessive in his cruelty. Paley then confronts the customary defense of slavery made by appealing to "necessity," under which term "every enormity is attempted to be justified." Paley retorts by asking, "And, after all, what is necessity?" His answers give no quarter to his opponents:

> It has never been proved that the land could not be cultivated there, as it is here, by hired servants. It is said that it could not be cultivated with quite the same conveniency and cheapness, as by the labour of slaves: by which means, a pound of sugar, which the planter now sells for sixpence, could not be afforded under sixpence-halfpenny—and this is the *necessity*.

Human lives are expended to bring down the price of sugar from sixpence-halfpenny a pound to sixpence. This economic calculation makes no moral sense. Neither can it be endorsed by political calculus, for writing just after the end of the war with the Thirteen Colonies of North America, the "fall of this abominable tyranny" may and should be hastened by a chastened Parliament, even though Paley has misgivings about Britain's legislature, "which had so long lent its assistance to the support of an institution replete with human misery" (Paley 2002, 129–130).

Paley had led a quiet life as a Cambridge don at Christ's (the college of John Milton, among others) before he became Archdeacon of Carlisle, when he published his work based largely on his lectures at Cambridge. James Ramsay, hailing from Aberdeen, Scotland, had led a far more dramatic life. His first profession was that of a naval surgeon, in which capacity he could see under what appalling conditions slave ships carried their human cargo. Believing it to be his mission to minister to the enslaved and the brutalized, he left the navy, joined the Church, and returned to the West Indies as an Anglican priest (Davis [1975] 1999, 377–378; Brycchan 2005, 109–124; Brown 2006, 234–237, 244–253). More than any other Abolitionists, Ramsay had an immediate and vivid experience of what he wrote about, and when he published *An Essay on the Treatment and Conversion of African Slaves in the British Sugar Colonies* in 1784, it did not fail to catch the attention of the reading public. *The Monthly Review* placed the review of the book as the leading article of its June 1784 number, furnishing the reader with long extracts to allow the author to speak for himself. Even when the reviewer could not fully accept the author's rather partisan praise of the natural "capacity of the negroes" (in the fourth chapter of his book, "The Natural Capacities of African Slaves Vindicated"), he found no difficulty sharing the author's strictures on slave-owners. It is a mockery of common sense to argue that "because one race of men have blacker skins and larger heads than their neighbours, they are to be treated with ferocious inhumanity, with a barbarity more savage than that with which the beasts of the field are treated by the most unfeeling and thoughtless." All in all, the reviewer could vouchsafe that this "Author's book" is "written with great benevolence of intention, and a competent knowledge of his subject" (Anon. 1784, 415, 418). In the preface to this reviewed work, Ramsay assures his readers that what he writes is founded on his "twenty years" of "experience in the West Indies," of which "above fourteen years" have "particular application to the subject." The author Rev. Ramsay, like Rev. Wesley before him, stands *coram Deo*, before God's presence, as he endeavors to draw "humane, benevolent attention to wretches, whom the crimes and avarice of selfish men have placed in our power" (Ramsay 1784, vii, xiii). It is the will of the "Author of nature," the "heavenly fountain of benevolence," to allow all humans the "free use of their powers and acquisitions, or of life, liberty, and property." In the "artificial, or unnatural relation of master and slave," however, "power constitutes right," and "according to the degree of his capacity of coercion, every man becomes his own legislator, and erects his interest, or his caprice, into a law for regulating his conduct to his neighbour" (Ramsay 1784, 2–3). The origin of this perversion can only be "traced to the infernal enemy of all goodness" (Ramsay 1784, 3), namely, Satan. Yet the hypocritical Christians of Europe, where slavery was abolished thanks to the teachings of Christianity, have brazenly established slavery in the new world with "all the venturous energy of a commercial spirit" and "through an infernal love of gold" (Ramsay 1784, 33–34). The British, remarkable for an "insolence arising from the keen sense of our own freedom" (Ramsay 1784, 103), have been particularly unabashed in sacrificing everything to their "love of gold" (Ramsay 1784, 34), for (as Smith also noted) slaves in the French colonies are treated much more humanely than in the English plantations, thanks to the "fasts and festivals of the Romish church" and to the "attention and benevolence in the French government" (Ramsay 1784, 52–53). "Our countrymen," unlike the French, are "left, each to be guided by his own changeable temper, and to be influenced by a semblance of self-interest; nor have they any tie on them, in their behavior to the wretches under them, but this interest." "Slaves are esteemed" by the laws of these colonies, only as the "entire property of their masters, and as having, distinct from him, no right or interest of their own." Britain's constitution, on its part, overlooks the tyranny of these free-born British planters, for it has "such an excessive bias to personal liberty" that it "cannot, or will not, meddle with private behaviour" of these colonists (Ramsay 1784, 64).

Exacerbating the vice of their avarice and tyrannical tempers, in Ramsay's diagnosis, is the "luxury" the planters indulge in. Before "luxury had rapaciously converted every little nook of land into sugar," Ramsay testifies, the "slaves had a field or two of the fallow crane-land yearly divided among them, for a crop of yams, pease, and potatoe" (Ramsay 1784, 78–79). "When luxury came in, like a torrent, among the planters," it "seized with violence on the slaves' little spots, and demanded the whole of their time, not leaving even to sleep its due." The "cravings of luxury and extravagance" have even curtailed the "slave's partial respite from toil on the sabbath" (Ramsay 1784, 94, 106). The specter of luxury's devastation, which apparently was dispelled by the latter part of the century in the home country, as we have seen in Chap. 4, still haunted the souls and houses of the British planters in the West Indies. Luxury in collusion with avarice erodes not only the moral and spiritual welfare of those directly involved in the sugar business, but the nation's economy as well. Money is made from sugar by various parties, the owners of the West Indian plantations, the sugar bakers in Britain, those collecting freight charges, insurance fees, and so forth, but the "whole is put in motion" by, and "draws its worth" from, the labor of slaves (Ramsay 1784, 111–112). If it cannot be denied that the slaves "alone stamp a value on West-Indian property" by their labor,

> it will clearly follow, that to improve and advance their condition in social, to encourage and instruct them in moral life, would be as politically profitable, as it is religious and humane. Were their condition advanced, they would become more worthy, more valuable subjects. They would produce much more by their labour, and agreeably to that great purpose of modern police, financiering, by the consumption of more manufactures, they would increase the public revenue. (Ramsay 1784, 113–114)

To banish the curse of luxury, the dichotomy of "industry v. idleness" is once again activated. Sugar-related wealth comes from the "industry" of slaves. When they are better treated, the greater the products of their "industry" will be. Moreover, they will emerge as a new source of consumption for the "industry" in the home country. This reasoning has only one possible flaw. What if the Africans are innately inferior to other races? If they are constituted by nature to be slothful and incapable of self-help, the trustworthy mechanism of "industry" guiding the industrious to march along the path of improvement would not function properly. Ramsay spends an entire chapter to tear apart this racist reasoning, combatting, among others, his own fellow Scottish writers of great eminence,

Hume and Lord Kames. If the Blacks appear to be created inferior by nature, as Hume suggested, we should recall also that Britons were utter barbarians in the eyes of the Roman conquerors. History demonstrates that "arts, sciences, and the polished life accompanying them, are slowly progressive through nations and climates, rather than that the natives of any particular country are born incapable of them" (Ramsay 1784, 199). Lord Kames speculated that the natives of America could have been created separately as a different species altogether. The dangerous implications of this view Ramsay cannot leave unchecked. Against such "conjectures of philosophy, and the paradoxes of infidelity," the "system taught by revelation" gives "man one simple origin," whose "author" is the "God of universal nature," and "by bestowing on him a common nature, a foundation was laid for the ultimate re-union of mankind, as well now in improved social life as in futurity" (Ramsay 1784, 205, 207).[7] Above all, any racial inferiority can hardly be used to justify slavery. "Suppose different races, and that they vary in point of excellence," Ramsay remarks, "yet, in what chapter of nature's law is it declared, that one quarter of the globe shall breed slaves for the rest?" (Ramsay 1784, 233). Having battered the scientific racism of the age, Ramsay closes his work by proposing some practicable plans for improving the physical, moral, and spiritual conditions of the slaves, such as allowing them full rest from toil in the weekend and permitting them to earn their freedom by doing extra work as paid laborers. "These regulations would lay a foundation for that far distant view which we take of this subject," namely, the "time when liberty shall claim every exiled African for her own child" (Ramsay 1784, 285–286).

The critics of slave trade and slavery we have heard speak thus far all have one thing in common: their adoption of Christian moral precepts in the form of an alliance of natural with revealed religion. The partial differences in their approaches reflect the compartments of the topic receiving special emphasis. Benezet sought to historicize African slave trade, Wesley to inculpate all parties concerned, Sharp grappled with the legal balustrades guarding slavery, and Ramsay alerted the reader to the conditions

[7] To be fair to Lord Kames, he proposed this as a hypothesis, rather than as a proven fact. If one supposes that the "human race to have been planted in America by the hand of God later than the days of Moses, Adam and Eve might have been the first parents of mankind, i.e. of all who at that time existed, without being the first parents of the Americans" (Kames 2007, 559–560).

of the slaves in the plantations based on his first-hand experience. Ramsay also struck a new note in appealing to the economic advantage, reminiscent of Smith in *The Wealth of Nations*, of treating the slaves more humanely. Clarkson, dedicated to moving Parliament to abolish slave trade, was perhaps far more important as an activist than as a writer. As is amply testified by his own account *The History of the Rise, Progress, and Accomplishment of the Abolition of the African Slave-Trade by the British Parliament*, he indefatigably worked in close alliance with William Wilberforce (who, like himself, studied at St. John's College, Cambridge) to mete out justice to the oppressed slaves in the British territories abroad (Clarkson 1808, vol. 2, chap. 3 to 8).[8] Clarkson's works, even so, merit to be noticed for their efficient synthesis of denunciations of injustice made by others before him, such as that of instigating predatory wars, concocting specious racial theories, flaunting hypocritically the master's right as freedom, spurning Christian teaching, and indulgence in rampant violence on board the slave ships and in the plantations. But more interesting than all these charges is Clarkson's relatively new strategy of putting extra stress on the economic expediency of abolishing slave trade and slavery. His first publication on the topic was *An Essay on the Slavery and Commerce of the Human Species, Particularly the African, Translated from a Latin Dissertation, Which Was Honoured with the First Prize in the University of Cambridge, for the Year 1785, with Additions* (1786). As specified in the title, it was originally a university essay written in Latin and comprises a great deal of book learning related to the topic from antiquity to the modern age. But already here, in the preface to the English translation coming "with additions," he argued that greater profit is the reward for liberating slaves. Referring to certain published cases, he maintains that plantation slaves, even "when unconditionally freed" willingly "returned without any solicitation to their former masters, to serve them, at stated wages, as free men." Their work, moreover, was "found to be better done than before," and a "greater quantity was done in the same time." The planters who emancipated their slaves, thus, "contrary to their expectations," reaped a "considerable advantage from their benevolence" (Clarkson 1786, ix). The greatest stumbling block to accepting the plain economic maxim that

[8] The importance of Clarkson is acknowledged even by Williams. Clarkson, that "indefatigable worker" dedicated to his chosen cause, "personifies all the best in the humanitarianism of the age," and was "one of those friends of whom the Negro race has had unfortunately only too few" (Williams [1944] 1966, 179).

free motivated labor is attended by greater productivity is racism. To all the Scriptures the clerical authors quote—and "Thomas Clarkson, M.A." or "Rev. Thomas Clarkson" was the author's name on the title pages of his works—the apologists of slavery will turn a deaf year. Business is business, and besides, did not the rational philosophers freed from "superstition," such as Hume, assure us that the Blacks were decidedly inferior by nature? Clarkson has his answer for those who believe in nature without caring to concede that there is an "Author" of nature. Even when one rejects natural or revealed religion, it can never be proven that "one species" of humans is "inferiour to another," nor that the alleged inferiority solely "depends upon their *colour*, or their *features*, or their *form*." A more reasonable inference would be that nature "tempered the bodies of the different species of men in a different degree, to enable them to endure the respective climates of their habitation," by giving them a "variety of colour and appearance" (Clarkson 1786, 183–184). For those who feel less confident about the absolute non-existence of God the creator, he can reiterate the admonitions of Benezet, Wesley, and Sharp rebuking their impiety. It is sacrilege to suppose that "God has made an order of beings, with such mental qualities and powers, for the sole purpose of being used as *beasts*, or *instruments* of labour." The conduct of the British is all the more "impious" since they have sought to reduce the African slaves under them to an "equality with the brute creation" (Clarkson 1786, 215-216). Wielding the double-edged sword of natural and revealed morality, Clarkson marched onward in his subsequent pamphlets to repudiate the pretentions of expediency and necessity the defenders of slavery habitually resorted to. This typical argument of the apologists of slavery needs to be sampled first before we move on to Clarkson's counter-arguments.

The British cannot be blamed, to begin with, for the brutal warfare raging among the Africans. Matthews' *A Voyage to the River Sierra-Leone, on the Coast of Africa* (1785) placed the blame on the Africans themselves, as we have seen. This would be a point relished by others, such as the author of *Commercial Reasons for the Non-Abolition, in the West-India Islands* (1789), written, as the title page advertised, by a "Planter, and Merchant of many Years Residence in the West-Indies." Enslavement, in fact, was an act of mercy, for the "swarthy Potentates being continually at War with each other" are prone to condemn the "Captives of their Arms to a Death too shocking to bear a Recital." Hence, it is a far better lot to be the "Slaves of Christians, than the Victims of Heathen Ferocity" (Anon. 1789, 13). Besides, the Africans "take vast Quantities of trivial Articles, such as

Toys, Tools, and Hardware, in the manufacturing of which Thousands of industrious Men in London, Birmingham, Sheffield," are employed. Abolish the slave trade, and you smother "laborious Industry" whose place "Want and Indolence" will promptly usurp (Anon. 1789, 10–11). The unimpeachable need for "Industry" to curb "Indolence" also explains why new slaves have to be imported to the West Indies, for the "Native Creoles possess so indolent a Disposition, they are incapable of the most trivial Employments" (Anon. 1789, 14). Moreover, all allegations of cruelty of the masters toward the slaves are utter nonsense, these defenders insisted. Out of self-interest, if not humanity, any master would take good care of "his valuable Property" (Anon. 1789, 23–24). Another apologist, Gilbert Francklyn, would remind the reader that the master typically spends forty to forty-five pounds in purchasing a slave and that a slave purchased at that high rate, when "seasoned," will be worth "near double the money." How, then, could he be so foolish as to have "so little regard to his interest, as to starve, abuse, ill treat, and mutilate these people, and thus ruin himself and his family" (Francklyn 1788, 57)? Besides, the Africans in the West Indies are not the only slaves the British put to work. The white British soldier and the "pressed sailor" are virtual slaves, subjected to cruel punishments, and even instant death, when they refuse to obey the command of their officers. The laborer in England, moreover, can be said to be a "*slave* of *necessity*," who "serves a harder task master than the African finds in the West Indies" (Francklyn 1788, 47). Last but not least, if you enjoy sugar, then forbear from accusing the owners of sugar plantations of tyranny. Can the accusers "drink no rum, no sugar in their tea, consume no chocolate or coffee, eat no sweetmeats, tarts, or pudding, no currant jelly sauce to their venison, unless they are convinced such sugar" is "prepared without any assistance from slaves"? That surely would be impossible (Francklyn 1788, 106). Francklyn's pamphlet, armed with solid commercial reasoning, succeeded at least in encouraging the enemies of the Abolition to persist in their opposition (Morgan 2007, 162).

Mere moral argument was insufficient, then, if the likes of Francklyn were to be vanquished. Clarkson dedicated *An Essay on the Impolicy of the African Slave Trade* (1788) to "William Wilberforce, Esq.," MP of York and a "zealous advocate in behalf of the oppressed Africans." Clarkson's contribution as a pamphlet-writer (apart from his vigorous activism) to Wilberforce's "exertions in the cause of humanity and freedom" (Clarkson 1788, i–ii) in this collective endeavor was to emphasize the economic potentials of free Africans, both in their country and in the British plantations. Africans have a sufficient capacity for "industry" and of imbibing a genuine "*commercial spirit*" as was demonstrated by those who traded with them in articles other than captured humans, particularly those native dealers in "wood trade." Contrary to what Europeans believed, Africans proved they were by no means "an indolent people." The natives "went more than two hundred miles into the inland country" for the woods, which they brought to sell to the European merchants (Clarkson 1788, 4). Compared with this innocuous trade, trafficking in enslaved humans, far from being indispensable to Britain's trade with Africa, blights the potentials for durable growth. Africa "abounds with hidden treasures" not tapped yet, such as gums, peppers, cotton, mahogany woods, rice, spices, and indigo. Once you abolish slave trade, then new trades in these articles will flourish to "great advantage and extent" (Clarkson 1788, 7–8, 10). There are geopolitical gains to be reaped as well. The age-old monopoly of the Dutch over spices could be circumvented and the "unprincipled conduct of many of the Americans," now independent from Britain, can be chastised (Clarkson 1788, 14–15, 17). Slave trade in Africa, however, "hinders the country from being farther explored, and those inexhaustible treasures from coming forth, which are now buried and concealed" (Clarkson 1788, 14). The last point was corroborated by Olaudah Equiano, a former slave with a colorful life-story to share. Toward the end of his memoir, *The Interesting Narrative of the Life of Olaudah Equiano, or Gustavus Vassa, the African* (1789), Equiano certifies that the "bowels and surface of Africa, abound in valuable and useful returns." When the slave trade is abolished, the "hidden treasures of centuries will be brought to light and into circulation" and "an endless field of commerce" will be opened to the "British manufactures and merchant adventurer" (Equiano 1789, 357).

Why then does the slave trade continue to exercise its false magic over the British? The ready answer is "sugar." Clarkson admits the importance of sugar consumption, but uses that to debunk the claims of his opponents. Sugar is of supreme value, for it is "*sugar* that produces the revenue, and not the slave." Let us then have sugar, but let us not deny that the "cane can be cultivated by *free men*, and farther, that it can be cultivated, under certain regulations, without the importation of another African from the coast." But what about the adverse impact on Britain's shipping business? "Do they mean again, that slaves employ ships to transport them? that these ships employ seamen, and that these seamen are the pillars of the state?" Clarkson cannot but ask. To be exact, these are "but *appendages* of the trade," and shipping various products of Africa instead of enslaved Africans would be "equally beneficial" to those making money from transatlantic navigation (Clarkson 1788, 6). Besides, the slave trade has become far risky and disadvantageous for the individuals engaged in it. First, the competition is becoming more virulent each year among the buyers; second, the high mortality rate of the slaves on board makes the trade "peculiarly hazardous"; third, the market in the West Indies has already been "glutted" with supply; and fourth, the bills of exchange sustaining the transactions are drawn at exceedingly long dates. All of these factors make slave trade a "most *hazardous*" investment and "have occasioned it to be justly distinguished by the appellation of a *lottery*" (Clarkson 1788, 23–24). Furthermore, the cost of human loss is stupendous not just among the slaves themselves but among the British sailors manning the ships, against whom their superiors habitually commit unimaginable atrocities. First lured into signing unfavorable contracts, the sailors have no means to protest against the "deliberate barbarity exercised" on them, and the harsh working conditions on board the ships destroy their health incurably, making them "rather *shadows* in their appearance than *men*" when they are discharged from their bondage (Clarkson 1788, 34–35, 44, 56–57). Slave trade, on all counts, is to be condemned as "*impolitick as it is inhuman and unjust.*" All the "arguments" which the "*moralist* is able to collect from the light of reason," or the "*man of humanity* from his feelings," or the "statesman is able to collect others from the source of *policy*," all equally call "aloud for its ABOLITION" (Clarkson 1788, 133–134).

Does it have to be an outright abolition rather than regulation? Clarkson was adamant about this question. In *An Essay on the Comparative Efficiency of Regulation or Abolition, as Applied to the Slave Trade. Shewing That the Latter Only Can Remove the Evils to Be Found in That Commerce* (1789), published one year after, while recapitulating many of the points he made in his 1788 pamphlet, Clarkson gave a clear reason as to why regulation was unacceptable. Regulation presupposes a "continuance upon stated terms," and "*so long as the trade continues*, so long will there be temptations, and so long will the needy and avaricious embrace them, to obtain the persons of men" (Clarkson 1789, 13). The bogey of economic inexpediency is chased off by a candid admission of the innate depravity of human moral constitution. This is a remarkable moment in the history of the moral intervention in economic affairs. It would be fitting to close this chapter with Clarkson's own words concerning this issue:

> Unless the British legislature can alter the passions and habits of men, and make human nature what it certainly is not; unless they have a perfect and acknowledged dominion over the Africans, can exercise such dominion, and can alter the African codes of law at their own will: and unless additionally they can do things equally impossible with those now stated, so long will the very best regulations that human wisdom can devise, be totally inadequate to remove the evil, sustained by the Africans in their own country, in consequence of the prosecution of the slave trade. But what evil is this existing in Africa, that cannot be remedied by any act of foreign states? It is an evil, of all others the most flagitious, and of greater magnitude than those, which afterward occur, either in the prosecution of the trade, or in the colonial slavery. It is an evil, the parent and foundation of all other evils, by means of which every tie of love, consanguinity, and friendship, is torn asunder, by means of which the pestilential dungeon presents itself afterwards on the passage, and the scourge and manacle in the land of slavery. (Clarkson 1789, 16–17)

The "passions and habits of men" being what they are, only an utter extirpation of this "flagitious" "evil" can be the remedy. In a sense this echoes Bernard Mandeville's belief that human nature can never be changed, which we discussed in the third section of Chap. 2, but, unlike Mandeville, Clarkson will not leave private vices alone to yield public benefits, since the chain of "evils" unleashed by slavery overweighs all economic gains.

Potent as Clarkson's argument was, it still could not eradicate this "evil, the parent and foundation of all other evils," which held its grounds for almost two more decades until 1807. At the close of the century, the efforts of Clarkson and others on behalf of the African slaves had gained no victory. Geopolitics was added to the factors that detained the progress of the Abolitionist cause, as the French Revolutionary Wars and the fear of Jacobinism made the abolition of slave trade less urgent an issue for a government at war with France (Morgan 2007, 165–166). Wilberforce's 1792 bill was defeated by his opponents who appealed, as exemplified by *An Appeal to the Candour and Justice of the People of England in Behalf of the West India Merchants and Planters Founded on Plain Facts and Incontrovertible Arguments* (1792), to the sacred rights of property, the liberty of the planters, and the nation's naval interest (Anon. 1792). Against the primarily moral argument of the Abolitionists, they wielded an economic argument neatly severed from morality. Clarkson and other warriors against slave trade upheld the supremacy of morals over matters economic. In the next century and beyond, morality and economics will go increasingly separate ways, with the latter spurning the former as at best a shabby old schoolmate.[9]

References

Anon. 1710. *A true state of the present difference between the Royal African Company, and the separate traders.* In *The British transatlantic slave trade*, vol. 2: *The Royal African Company*, ed. Kenneth Morgan, 17–57. London: Pickering and Chatto, 2003.

Anon. 1766. A sermon preached before the incorporated Society, for the Propagation of the Gospel in foreign Parts … by the Right Reverend Father in God, William Lord Bishop of Gloucester. *The Monthly Review* October: 279–286.

Anon. 1789. *Commercial reasons for the non-abolition, in the West-India islands.* In *The British transatlantic slave trade,* vol. 4: *The Abolitionist struggle: Promoters of the slave trade*, ed. David Ryden, 3–28. London: Pickering and Chatto, 2003.

Anon. 1792. *An appeal to the candour and justice of the people of England in behalf of the West India merchants and planters founded on plain facts and incontrovertible arguments.* In *The British transatlantic slave trade,* vol. 4: *The Abolitionist struggle: Promoters of the slave trade*, ed. David Ryden, 135–168. London: Pickering and Chatto, 2003.

Anon. 2004. Edinburgh University renames David Hume Tower over "racist" views. *BBC*, 13 September 2020. https://www.bbc.com/news. Accessed 15 November 2024.

Anon. 1713. *A general history of trade, and especially consider'd as it respects the British commerce, as well as home, as to all parts of the world.* London: J. Baker.

Anon. 1756. The civil and natural history of Jamaica … by Patrick Browne. *The Critical Review* June: 390–409.

Anon. 1772. Some historical account of Guinea; with an enquiry into the rise and progress of the slave-trade … by Anthony Benezet. *The Monthly Review* July: 73.

[9] Of course, this cannot be the end of the story, even though this chapter stops here. The Abolition Bill was at long last passed in 1807. For a detailed account of the political background and procedure, see Clarkson (1808, vol. 2, chaps 9 to 10); Davis ([1975] 1999, 420–452); Morgan (2007, 169–171). Furthermore, a "moral" or even a "Christian" economic thinking emerged in the early nineteenth century, nourished at least in part by the "moderate evangelicals" who saw the economic realm as an "arena of great spiritual trial and suspense," as Boyd Hilton puts it (Hilton 1988, 13). By contrast, A. M. Waterman's "Christian political economy" traces the lineage of the economic thoughts, removed to a certain extent from the "evangelicals," of Thomas Malthus, John Bird Sumner, Edward Copleston, and Thomas Chalmers, stemming from the contributions made by Paley, as well as Smith (Waterman 1991, 11–12, 74–79, 150).

Anon. 1774a. Thoughts upon slavery, by John Wesley. *The Monthly Review* September: 234–237.
Anon. 1774b. A supplement to Mr. Wesley's pamphlet, intitled, Thoughts upon slavery. *The Monthly Review* September: 237.
Anon. 1774c. Correspondence. *The Monthly Review* October: 324–325.
Anon. 1774d. Correspondence. *The Monthly Review* December: 487–488.
Anon. 1784. An essay on the treatment and conversion of African slaves … by the Rev. James Ramsay. *The Monthly Review* June: 409–418.
Anstey, Roger. 1975. *The Atlantic slave trade and British Abolition 1760–1810.* Atlantic Highlands: Humanities Press.
Asher, Kendra. 2022a. Was David Hume a racist? Interpreting Hume's infamous footnote (Part I). *Economic Affairs* 42:225–239. https://doi.org/10.1111/ecaf.12519.
Asher, Kendra. 2022b. Was David Hume a racist? Interpreting Hume's infamous footnote (Part II). *Economic Affairs* 42:477–499. https://doi.org/10.1111/ecaf.12540.
Baucom, Ian. 2005. *Specters of the Atlantic: Finance capital, slavery, and the philosophy of history.* Durham: Duke University Press.
Beattie, James. 1771. *An essay on the nature and immutability of truth, in opposition to sophistry and scepticism.* 2nd ed. Edinburgh: A. Kincaid and J. Bell.
Benezet, Anthony. 1772. *Some historical account of Guinea, its situation, produce, and the general disposition of its inhabitants, with an inquiry into the rise and progress of the slave trade, its nature, and lamentable effects.* London.
Blackstone, William. 1768a. *Commentaries on the laws of England. Book the first.* 3rd ed. Oxford: Clarendon.
Blackstone, William. 1768b. *Commentaries on the laws of England. Book the second.* 3rd ed. Oxford: Clarendon.
Blackstone, William. 1768c. *Commentaries on the laws of England. Book the third.* 3rd ed. Oxford: Clarendon.
Brown, Laura. 1993. *Ends of empire: Women and ideology in early eighteenth-century English literature.* Ithaca: Cornell University Press.
Brown, Christopher Leslie. 2006. *Moral capital: Foundations of British Abolitionism.* Chapel Hill: University of North Carolina Press.
Browne, Patrick. 1756. *The civil and natural history of Jamaica.* London.
Brycchan, Carey. 2005. *British Abolitionism and the rhetoric of sensibility: Writing, sentiment, and slavery, 1760–1807.* Basingstoke: Palgrave Macmillan.
Burke, Edmund. 1991. Opening of impeachment, 19 Feb 1788. In *The writings and speeches of Edmund Burke*, vol. 6: *India: The launching of the Hastings impeachment 1786–1788*, ed. P. J. Marshall, 427–460. Oxford: Clarendon.
Campbell, John. 1763. *Candid and impartial considerations on the nature of the sugar trade; the comparative importance of the British and French islands in the*

West-Indies; with the value and consequence of St. Lucia and Granada, truly stated. London: R. Baldwin.
Child, Josiah. 1698. *A new discourse of trade*. London.
Clarkson, Thomas. 1786. *An essay on the slavery and commerce of the human species, particularly the African, translated from a Latin dissertation, which was honoured with the first prize in the University of Cambridge, for the year 1785, with additions*. London.
Clarkson, Thomas. 1788. *An essay on the impolicy of the African slave trade*. London.
Clarkson, Thomas. 1789. *An essay on the comparative efficiency of regulation or abolition, as applied to the slave trade. Shewing that the latter only can remove the evils to be found in that commerce*. London.
Clarkson, Thomas. 1808. *The history of the rise, progress, and accomplishment of the abolition of the African slave-trade by the British Parliament*. 2 vols. London: Longman, Hurst, Rees, and Orme.
Cooper, Thomas. 1787. *Letters on the slave trade: First published in Wheeler's Manchester chronicles; and since re-printed with additions and alterations*. In *The British transatlantic slave trade*, vol. 3: *The Abolitionist struggle: Opponents of the slave trade*, ed. John Oldfield, 21–56. London: Pickering and Chatto, 2003.
Cugoano, Quobna Ottobah. 1999. *Thoughts and sentiments on the evil of slavery and other writings*. Edited by Vincent Carretta. New York: Penguin.
Curtin, Philip D. 1969. *The Atlantic slave trade: A census*. Madison: The University of Wisconsin Press.
Davis, David Brion. 1984. *Slavery and human progress*. New York: Oxford University Press.
Davis, David Brion. [1975] 1999. *The problem of slavery in the age of revolution 1770–1823*. New York: Oxford University Press.
Drescher, Seymour. 1987. *Capitalism and antislavery: British mobilization in comparative perspective*. New York: Oxford University Press.
Equiano, Olaudah. 1789. *The interesting narrative of the life of Olaudah Equiano, or Gustavus Vassa, the African*. London.
Estwick, Samuel. 1772. *Considerations on the Negroe cause commonly so called, addressed to the Right Honourable Lord Mansfield, Lord Chief Justice of the Court of King's Bench*. London: J. Dodsley.
Fox, William. 1791. An address to the people of Great Britain, on the utility of refraining from the use of West India sugar and rum. In *The British transatlantic slave trade*, vol. 3: *The Abolitionist struggle: Opponents of the slave trade*, ed. John Oldfield, 323–334. London: Pickering and Chatto, 2003.
Francklyn, Gilbert. 1788. Observations occasioned by the attempts made in England to effect the abolition of the slave trade. In *The British transatlantic slave trade*, vol. 4: *The Abolitionist struggle: Promoters of the slave trade*, ed. David Ryden, 29–106. London: Pickering and Chatto, 2003.

Godwyn, Morgan. 1680. *The Negro's and Indians advocate, suing for their admission into the Church: or, A persuasive to the instructing and baptizing of the Negros' and Indians in our plantations*. London.

Godwyn, Morgan. 1685. *Trade preferr'd before religion, and Christ made to give place to Mammon*. London: B. Took and Isaac Cleave.

Hankock, David. 1995. *Citizens of the world: London merchants and the integration of the British Atlantic community, 1735–1785*. Cambridge: Cambridge University Press.

Hayes, Charles. 1744. The importance of effectually supporting the Royal African Company of England impartially consider'd. In *The British transatlantic slave trade*, vol. 2: *The Royal African Company*, ed. Kenneth Morgan, 97–145. London: Pickering and Chatto, 2003.

Hilton, Boyd. 1988. *The age of atonement: The influence of evangelicalism on social and economic thought, 1785–1865*. Oxford: Clarendon.

Hume, David. 1987. *Essays, moral, political, and literary*. Edited by Eugene F. Miller. Indianapolis: Liberty Fund.

Kames, Lord (Henry Home). 2007. *Sketches of the history of man, book 2: progress of men in society*. Edited by James A. Harris. Indianapolis: Liberty Fund.

Marshall, P. J. 2019. *Edmund Burke and the British Empire in the West Indies: Wealth, power, and slavery*. Oxford: Oxford University Press.

Matthews, John. 1788. A voyage to the river Sierra-Leone, on the coast of Africa; Containing an account of the trade and productions of the country, and of the civil and religious customs and manners of the people. In *The British transatlantic slave trade*, vol. 1: *The operation of the slave trade in Africa*, ed. Robin Law, 35–225. London: Pickering and Chatto, 2003.

Millar, John. 2006. *The origin of the distinction of ranks*. Edited by Aaron Garrett. Indianapolis: Liberty Fund.

Morgan, Kenneth. 2000. *Slavery, Atlantic trade and the British economy, 1660–1800*. Cambridge: Cambridge University Press.

Morgan, Kenneth. 2007. *Slavery and the British Empire: From Africa to America*. Oxford: Oxford University Press.

Paley, William. 2002. *The principles of moral and political philosophy*. Indianapolis: Liberty Fund.

Petty, William. 1690. *Political Arithmetick*. London: R. Clavel and H. Mortlock.

Philmore, J. [pseud.]. 1760. *Two dialogues on the man-trade*. London: Consortium.

Postlethwayt, Malachy. 1745. The African trade, the great pillar and support of the British plantation trade in America. In *The British transatlantic slave trade*, vol. 2: *The Royal African Company*, ed. Kenneth Morgan, 149–194. London: Pickering and Chatto, 2003.

Postlethwayt, Malachy. 1746. The national and private advantages of the African trade considered. In *The British transatlantic slave trade*, vol. 2: *The Royal African Company*, ed. Kenneth Morgan, 197–328. London: Pickering and Chatto, 2003.

Ramsay, James. 1784. *An essay on the treatment and conversion of African slaves in the British sugar colonies.* London: Consortium.

Shammas, Carole. 1993. Changes in English and Anglo-American consumption from 1550 to 1800. In *Consumption and the world of goods*, ed. John Brewer and Roy Porter, 177–205. London: Routledge.

Sharp, Granville. 1773. *An essay on slavery, proving from Scripture its inconsistency with humanity and religion.* Burlington.

Sharp, Granville. 1776a. *The just limitation to slavery in the laws of God, compared with the unbounded claims of the African traders and British American slave-holders ... with a copious appendix.* London: B. White and E. and C. Dilly.

Sharp, Granville. 1776b. *The law of liberty, or, Royal law, by which all mankind will certainly be judged! earnestly recommended to the serious consideration of all slaveholders and slavedealers.* London: B. White and E. and C. Dilly.

Smith, Adam. 1976a. *An inquiry into the nature and causes of the wealth of nations.* Edited by R. H. Campbell and A. S. Skinner. Oxford: Clarendon.

Smith, Adam. 1976b. *The theory of moral sentiments.* Edited by D. D. Raphael and A. L. Macfie. Oxford: Clarendon.

Somerset v. Stewart. 1772. In *English Reports full reprint*, vol. 98: *King's Bench.* HeinOnline 499–510. https://heinonline-org-ssl.access.yonsei.ac.kr. Accessed 8 May 2023.

Thomas, Hugh. 1997. *The slave trade: The story of the Atlantic slave trade: 1440–1870.* New York: Simon & Schuster.

Thomas, R. P., and D. N. McCloskey. 1981. Overseas trade and empire 1700–1860. In *The economic history of Britain since 1700,* vol. 1: *1700–1860*, ed. Robert Floud and Donald McCloskey, 87–102. Cambridge: Cambridge University Press.

Thompson, Thomas. 1772. *The African trade for Negro slaves, shewn to be consistent with principles of humanity, and with the laws of revealed religion.* London.

Waterman, A. M. C. 1991. *Revolution, economics and religion: Christian political economy, 1798–1833.* Cambridge: Cambridge University Press.

Wennerlind, Carl. 2011. *Casualties of credit: The English financial revolution, 1620–1720.* Cambridge, MA: Harvard University Press.

Wesley, John. 1774. *Thoughts upon slavery.* London.

Wesley, John. 1776. *Some observations on liberty: Occasioned by a late tract.* London.

Wesley, John. 1778. *A serious address to the people of England, with regard to the state and the nation.* London.

Williams, Eric. [1944] 1966. *Capitalism and slavery.* New York: Capricorn Books.

CHAPTER 7

Epilogue; or, Burke and Bentham

We presume not to finish our inquiry with a grandiose "Conclusion," but instead merely to delineate, under a more modest heading of "Epilogue," the transition in the 1790s from a moral to a political discourse of the economy, if one may be allowed to simplify what no doubt is a complicated transformation in the discursive grammar of certain published works that came to acquire lasting fame in the next century and beyond. The distinction, of course, is by no means clearcut, for there can hardly be anything more political than the heated controversy about the slave trade that erupted in the last years of the 1780s, which also was a period when Edmund Burke raised his voice to castigate the misdeeds of Hastings in the supreme political arena of Westminster Hall. These public debates on what certainly were highly divisive political issues took on the form of a moral discourse peppered with expressions and quotations bequeathed by Britain's Protestant Christianity and fortified by enlightened natural religion. This alliance of common moral sense and shared religious sentiments reached its culminating and terminal point in Burke's denunciation of "Jacobinism" both in France and in Britain. Even as Burke spent the last years of his life to pour out prophetic animadversions on the emerging new world, others were poised to challenge traditional certainties with a new rationalist morality, best represented in Britain by Jeremy Bentham, who spoke of "nature" but stringently severed its ties to the "author of Nature" and of His natural law. Burke and Bentham, we suggest, can be

H.-J. Yoon, *Moral Discourses of the Economy in Eighteenth-Century Britain*, https://doi.org/10.1007/978-981-95-0958-4_7

made to stand for two contrastive forces pulling moral discourses into opposite directions during the last phase of the eighteenth century.

The changes in the moral and political climate in the late 1780s can be demonstrated, among other instances, by the editorial evolution of *The Monthly Review*, which, as we have seen in Chap. 6, had been punctual in noticing and responding to the Abolitionists' works upon their appearance. This periodical divided each monthly number into two segments, the first main part for extensive review articles followed by the second—labeled the "Monthly Catalogue" for that month—set aside for shorter articles covering works that failed to receive the honor of receiving a full-length review. The "Monthly Catalogue" articles were generally divided into genres such as "Miscellanies," "History," and "Sermons," but on special occasions, a particular topic would be used as a rubric under which mutually related pamphlets and books were gathered. In January 1788, the magazine placed the category "Negroe Slavery" as such thematic heading, which was changed in February to "Slave Trade." In the same January number, the "Impeachment of Mr. Hastings" appeared as a header bringing together three short reviews of works dealing with the issue (*The Monthly Review* 1788a). The "Impeachment of Mr. Hastings" disappeared in March (to be revived briefly in July), but "Slave Trade" (alternating with "Negroes Slavery") as a classificatory category enjoyed a long shelf-life all the way until November 1789 (*The Monthly Review* 1788a, 1788b, 1789a, 1789b). One month before in October, a new challenger to "Slave Trade" made its debut, and soon muffled the Abolitionists' exclamations. The "Grand Revolution in France" became a new classificatory theme of the "Monthly Catalogue" (*The Monthly Review* 1789b). The magazine itself was also faced with a revolutionary challenge presented by the rapidly increasingly volume of new publications. The "productions of the press, in this country alone, began to overflow the narrow limits of the plan" the magazine had maintained thus far. The circumstances left no other option to the editors but that of "enlarging the assigned boundary" and "proportionally increasing the price of the work" by starting a new series in January 1790 with more words printed on more pages (Anon. 1789, ii).

In the enlarged *Monthly Review*, "Slave Trade" failed to retain its position as a term conferring a group identity to newly published works, simply because the print market shifted its attention away from it to other saleable political topics. Instead, in the new series launched that year, the "Grand Revolution in France" and its most eloquent critic in Britain,

Edmund Burke, occupied the center stage. Burke's *Reflections on the Revolution in France* was reviewed in November 1790 as soon as it came out. The reviewer found in this new publication "some truth" but also detected "much falsehood." The "former," namely the modicum of "truth," is "neither in such abundance, nor of such importance, as to throw us into raptures," but at the same time the "latter," the "falsehood" is not "so pernicious, nor so wilful, as to fill us with horror and indignation" (Anon. 1790c, 314). Whatever the reviewer's true feelings may have been, the importance of the author's name and the topical impact of the work could hardly be denied. A sequel to the review was included in the magazine's December 1790 number. Even as the work was summarized and extracted extensively in the articles, the author was not given an unreserved praise. Burke was "very deficient" in "judgment." Although an undoubtedly "eloquent writer," he was rarely a "sound reasoner" (Anon. 1790d, 465). Burke's reasoning revealed a weakness, above all, in his discussion of political rights, which cannot possibly be separated from "natural rights," in whose name the French Revolution was being pushed forward. *The Monthly Review* critic had to disagree with Burke when he ignored the plain truth that the "natural rights" of all men must be the foundation of "social, municipal rights" (Anon. 1790c, 321). *The Critical Review*, *The Monthly Review*'s old rival, also followed suit in ending the old editorial practice to begin a new series with densely printed pages sold at a higher price. *The Critical Review* covered Burke's work in the same month of its publication in the last volume of its old series. The article there showed more support for the author, even as it took note of the book's shortcomings. "If we except the effects of long received opinions, perhaps of prejudices, declamation occasionally too florid, and resentment a little too acrimonious, the Reflections on the Revolution in France is one of the most able, the most eloquent, and most interesting works that has appeared on this or any other political subject for a long series of years," the reviewer remarked (Anon. 1790b, 518). *The Analytical Review*, founded in August 1789 and sporting a distinctively radical color on religious and political matters, naturally offered to debunk Burke's criticism of the French Revolution. His "leading principles" that flatly contradict the "abstract principles of truth and reason" were to the reviewer a "monstrous and extraordinary doctrine—a doctrine which places an effectual bar to all progressive improvement" and "immerges the human mind in all the darkness of the darkest ages" (Anon. 1790a, 303). Despite "Mr. Burke's abilities," the reviewer found him a "dupe of his imagination or his passions," as he "despises arrangement or logical precision" and ends up losing "himself in a wilderness of words and figures" (Anon. 1790a, 307).

The mixed response to Burke's first publication on the revolutionary upheaval in France did not detain him at all. Nor was Burke daunted and silenced by the somber course of the last years of his life, which was marked by tragic disappointments on personal as well as on public front. His son Richard, upon whom he had placed so much hope, died in 1795 of diseases. Burke died two years later in 1797. The fortune of Burke's grand antagonist Warren Hastings, by contrast, was waxing. In 1795, Hastings was not only acquitted of all charges that Burke, representing the Commons, impeached him with, but was amply compensated by the East India Company (Locke 2006, 497). In the meantime, the civilized world as Burke knew it seemed to be on the verge of being dismantled as all its values were desecrated by the French Revolution, whose excesses, to his great dismay, certain political leaders in Britain, such as Charles James Fox (his ally in the crusade against Hastings), chose to justify as excusable in view of the benefits it will sooner or later bring to the French people and to mankind (Locke 2006, 257–259; Bourke 2015, 691, 764–766). The review magazines' discomfort—measured in the case of *The Monthly Review* and truculent in that of *The Analytical Review*—at Burke's criticism of the French revolutionaries, so complete in its rejection of their genuine intention and of their capacity for achieving what they professed to be their objective, reflected the generally positive view in Britain of the Revolution across the channel in its early stage. Burke's position, which we neither need nor can enlarge upon here, was not fundamentally different from one that sustained his campaign to indict and punish the moral corruption of Hastings who profited from revolutions and disruptions of established order. In Burke's terminology, "Indianism" and "Jacobinism" formed two sides of the same coin (Bourke 2015, 846). Indeed, Burke's accusation of the Jacobin's "authorizing treasons, robberies, rapes, assassinations, slaughters, and burnings throughout their harassed land" could be applied almost verbatim to Hastings (Burke 1998, 90). One apparent difference between the two would be the bogey of "natural rights," which Burke's critic at *The Monthly Review* conjured. But that conception of abstract "natural rights" stood upon a false postulate that politics and morals could be neatly segregated. An unswerving acceptance of this segregation was what bolstered Hastings' "geographical morality" (see Chap. 5, Sect. 5.3).

For Burke, any viable politics calls for a "deep knowledge of human nature and human necessities." The order of precedence between "nature" and "necessities" is not merely rhetorical but logical. Human "nature" has to precede human "necessities," or in other words, morals have to take precedence over economics. The "science of constructing a commonwealth, or renovating it, or reforming it" can never be "taught *à priori*" aloof from practical experiences, as "abstract principles of truth and reason" underscored by Burke's critic writing for *The Analytical Review*. The "real effects" made by politics can only come from "moral causes" which are "not always immediate." One could dilate on the "rights of man" theoretically, but when these "metaphysical rights" pass through the "dense medium" of complex political reality, they are compelled by the "laws of nature" to be "refracted from their straight line." The moral "nature of man" is "intricate," while the "objects of society," both political and economic, are marked by the "greatest possible complexity." If that is so, it is "absurd" to speak of the "metaphysical" or "primitive rights" as if they remain unaffected by all the "refractions and reflections" (Burke 1998, 111–112). If someone persists in insisting on their absolute authority, "in proportion as they are metaphysically true, they are morally and politically false." Furthermore, the metaphysical tidiness will be achieved at the cost of brutally suppressing dissent. "On the scheme of this barbarous philosophy," Burke warns, "laws are to be supported only by their own terrors, and by the concern which each individual may find in them from his own private speculations, or can spare to them from his own private interests." "In the groves of *their* academy, at the end of every vista, you see nothing but the gallows," Burke predicted (Burke 1998, 113). When this incisive and prophetic diagnosis of Burke is impartially assessed, one would hesitate to accept the verdict of *The Monthly Review* article, which decided than Burke was not a "sound reasoner" but merely an "eloquent writer."

Burke was not simply pointing to the dangerous disregard of the complex moral nature of humans which attended the "metaphysical" schemes of the French revolutionaries. In following that well-established tradition of denouncing political manipulation of the economy (which we have covered in Chap. 5), he accused them of setting afloat sundry "projects" to maximize their personal gain, as well as to aggrandize their power. The Third Estate, which quickly monopolized all political sovereignty, was largely composed of petty provincial lawyers, the "inferior, unlearned, mechanical, merely instrumental members of the profession" whose expertise consists in fomenting the "petty war of village vexation." When suddenly "snatched from the humblest rank of subordination" to "unprepared greatness," they, "at any expence to the state, of which they understood nothing," were bent on pursing "their private interests, which they understood but too well" (Burke 1998, 93–94). This a perfect description of the "projectors," as the writers such as Smith would understand the term. Inured to their old habit of "obscure contention, and laborious, low, unprofitable chicane" as mongers of petty lawsuits, these projector-revolutionaries are eager to "*join* (if their capacity did not permit them to *lead*) in any project which could procure to them a litigious constitution; which could lay open to them those innumerable lucrative jobs which follow in the train of all great convulsions and revolutions in the state, and particularly in all great and violent permutations of property" (Burke 1998, 94). As eager as Hastings to profiteer from the "great convulsions and revolutions," the second-rate lawyers in the Third Estate formed a lethal partnership with the descendants of John Law, the full-fledged projectors in the world of high finance. After first confiscating the properties of the Catholic Church and then using it to issue paper currencies (*assignats*), and through a dizzy "process of continual transmutation of paper into land, and land into paper," the revolutionaries gave full rein to the "spirit of money-jobbing and speculation" (Burke 1998, 238). At the price of making "industry" decline "without vigour," and with "commerce expiring," an "ignoble oligarchy" was established composed of "attornies, agents, money-jobbers, speculators, and adventurers" (Burke 1998, 242). The "age of chivalry is gone." Therefore, should the modernizers believing in progress congratulate themselves? Surely not, for the "age of sophisters, oeconomists, and calculators, has succeeded" it (Burke 1998, 127). Why should this be a problem for a nation's economy? Burke answers this implied question by proffering a starkly moral definition of the economy itself. "Even commerce, and trade, and manufacture, the gods of our oeconomical politicians," Burke asserts, "are themselves perhaps but creatures; are themselves but effects, which, as first causes, we choose to worship." The deceptive hedging of "perhaps" is discarded in the very next sentence: "They certainly grew under the same shade in which learning flourished." That is, they grew under the moral patronage and guidance of the Church in the "age of chivalry" when "learning" (in religion, morals, and manners) "flourished." When the moral ballast is thrown overboard, the economy will "decay" along with their "natural protecting principles" (Burke 1998, 130). Burke makes a rather unseasonable—and to many, an erroneous—prognosis:

> Where trade and manufactures are wanting to a people, and the spirit of nobility and religion remains, sentiment supplies, and not always ill supplies their place; but if commerce and the arts should be lost in an experiment to try how well a state may stand without these old fundamental principles, what sort of a thing must be a nation of gross, stupid, ferocious, and at the same time, poor and sordid barbarians, destitute of religion, honour, or manly pride, possessing nothing at present, and hoping for nothing hereafter? (Burke 1998, 130–131)

Posterity, blithely despising the "spirit of nobility and religion," would reply that "commerce and the arts," far from decaying due to the lack of that superstitious "spirit," flourished famously in the centuries following his death to such a degree as to enable those who possessed "nothing" to gain something in that process of economic advance.

One should not, however, relegate Burke to the limbo of dead sages yet, for Burke's *Reflections on the Revolution in France* was not the end but the beginning of his war on rationalist barbarians. Burke never tired of delivering at the top of his lungs his diatribes against the French "Jacobins." In 1796, one year before he died, he published an extremely irate and bitter pamphlet, *A Letter to a Noble Lord*, where he severely rebuked the Duke of Bedford, the "Noble Lord" in the title, not just for opposing the pension the government voted to reward Burke for his lifelong service to the country as parliamentarian but for his irresponsible sympathy for the Jacobins. The "Jacobins," renowned for their skill at confiscating vast properties owned by any "Noble Lord," should they ever invade Britain upon the Duke's invitation, will instantly take possession of his vast property. No formalities will be observed, since "insurrection" to them is the "most sacred of revolutionary virtues" and ingratitude is "their four cardinal virtues compacted and amalgamated into one." The Duke's enthusiasm for the "philosophick revolution" will be scoffed at and his ancient "deeds will be drawn out with the rest of the lumber of his evidence room and burned to the tune of *ça ira* in the courts of Bedford (then Equality) House" (Burke 1991a, 173–174). Who are these "philosophers" whom the "Noble Lord" feels so much attracted to? They are men of letters endowed with knowledge and talents, which are the "first gifts of Providence to the World," but who have abused them in such a manner as to throw off the "fear of God, which was in all ages too often the case, and the fear of man, which is now the case." In place of a frail, supple, and warm human heart, they carry something that approximates the "cold malignity of a wicked spirit" of the "incorporeal, pure, unmixed, dephlegmated, defecated evil." They will never heed the loud complaint of a dispossessed aristocrat such as the Duke of Bedford, for they "never see any way to their projected good but by the road of some evil." In fact, they sustain their spirit with the "contemplation of human suffering thro' the wild waste of centuries added to centuries, of misery and desolation." Having trampled upon human heart and all the moral sentiments it abounds with, these "philosophers, consider men in their experiments, no more than they do mice in an air pump, or in a recipient of mephitick gas" (Burke 1991a, 176–177). What then should be done about these inhuman and inhumane "philosophers"? Relentless war is the answer. Burke's *First Letter on a Regicide Peace*, also published in the same year of 1796, rebuffs those arguments advocating peace with France for the sake of preserving Britain's economic interests. The premises are important, once again. What is a nation? It is a "moral essence, not a geographical arrangement, or a denomination of the nomenclator," answers Burke (Burke 1991b, 253). But surely Britain has huge economic "interests" to protect? Indeed, Britain has a "vast interest to preserve, and we possess great means of preserving it," but "wealth" should not be the master, but instead, the "obedient and laborious slave of virtue and of publick honour." Burke in his last published work echoes the voice of Morgan Godwyn (heard in Chap. 6) who admonished his countrymen to beware of falling into mammon worship:

> But if this order is changed, and honor is to be sacrificed to the conservation of riches, riches which have neither eyes nor hands, nor any thing truly vital in them, cannot long survive the being of their vivifying powers, their legitimate masters, and their potent protectors. If we command our wealth, we shall be rich and free: If our wealth commands us, we are poor indeed. (Burke 1991b, 194)

This sonorous manifesto of the validity and importance of a moral control over the economy had to wait until the very end of the illustrious public career of this eloquent author on whom the "first gifts of Providence" had been lavished.

A writer equally talented in argument, if not in oratory, had offered to cleanse the realm of economy of all moral dross in 1787 when Burke was preparing his moral crusade to punish Hastings. His target was not Burke but his friend Adam Smith. The famous author, "Dr. Smith," in the assessment of this young writer, Jeremy Bentham, was to be faulted for being insufficiently liberated from the hoary prejudices about "projectors" and "usury." Bentham's *Defence of Usury* comprises of two parts, the first "Shewing the Impolicy of the Present Legal Restraints on the Terms of Pecuniary Bargains; in Letters to a friend," as the subtitle stated, and the second, "A Letter to Adam Smith, Esq. LL.D. on the discouragements opposed by the above restraints to the progress of Inventive Industry." What holds together the two parts is the author's desire to dethrone the "tyranny of sounds" resonating from certain accepted terms used to discuss economic issues such as "usury" or "projects" (Bentham 1787, 136). Not all of them are rejected, for that most important word "industry" (which we have discussed in Chap. 3), retains its authority in the title of his "Letter to Adam Smith." "Custom" is the main culprit, being the "sole basis" upon which the "moralist" or the "legislator" erects his "precepts" or "injunctions." Yet custom lacks any essential meaning apart from the "convenience which gave it birth" (Bentham 1787, 8, 12). Usury was condemned for fomenting prodigal expenditure, but legislation can do little to "prevent" prodigals from "doing themselves a mischief," for they will get credit at any rate of profit (Bentham 1787, 17, 28). Here Bentham follows Bernard Mandeville in taking as his grand premise the depraved human nature, which by being incorrigible enables economic profits. Like Mandeville, Bentham finds faults with organized religion for brewing irrational prejudice against self-gratification. Moreover, Christian regimes are accused of mixing the ascetic prejudice with anti-Semitism, cynically letting the "Jews get the money any how they could" so that they could "squeeze it out of them as it was wanted" (Bentham 1787, 98–99). Bentham, however, turns his back on those who applaud "luxury" (covered in Chap. 4), such as Mandeville, when he pleads the case of the money-lender. Bentham activates the dichotomy of "industry" and "idleness" when he contrasts the "man of dissipation" to the "man of thrift." In the case of the former type, the "luster, which the display of borrowed wealth has diffused over his character, awes men, during the season of his prosperity, into a submission to his insolence." When the glamour of indolent affluence vanishes, the "recollection of the height, from which he has fallen, throws the veil of compassion over his injustice." The latter, however, can hope for no such favorable reception. "His lasting opulence procures him a share, at least, of the same envy, that attends the prodigal's transient display." But when he remains content to derive from it a "pleasure of possession, and the idea of enjoying, at some distant period, which may never arrive," others frown upon him as a "kind of insolvent, who refuses to honour the bills, which their rapacity would draw upon him." To the latter breed belong the much-maligned "usurers" (Bentham 1787, 105–106). Equally maligned unjustly are the "projectors," whom even the author of *The Wealth of Nations* upbraids (see Chap. 5), and under which "invidious name" Smith refers in fact to "all such persons as, in the pursuit of wealth, strike out into any new channel, and more especially into any channel of invention" (Bentham 1787, 132). Many decades before Bentham, Daniel Defoe had offered a qualified defense of virtuous projectors, as we have seen. What is new about Bentham's argument is his displeasure at the very term itself and the "tyranny of sounds" emanating from it. We owe to these "adventurous spirits" all "that can be called *improvement*; whether it consist in the production of any new article adapted to man's use, or in the meliorating the quality, or diminishing the expense, of any of those which are already known to us" (Bentham 1787, 138). He asks the venerable "Adam Smith, Esq. LL.D." whether "whatever is now the *routine* of trade was not, at its commencement, *project*?" (Bentham 1787, 144–145). He then asks the general reader, "If so original and independent a spirit has not been always able to save itself from being drawn aside by the fascination of sounds, into the paths of vulgar prejudice, how strict a watch ought not men of common mould to set over their judgments, to save themselves from being led astray by similar delusions?" (Bentham 1787, 182). Beware of the snare of moral prejudices, Bentham warns, set by the familiar terms of moral-economic discourse such as "usury" or "project." Of the words responsible for the "tyranny of sounds" perhaps only "industry" may be salvaged, since "indolence," the arch antagonist of "industry," should always be subdued.

Bentham's belief in the virtues of "industry" was further manifested in a work published in the same year as *Defence of Usury* and one which has gained an inordinate fame in our time thanks to Michel Foucault's fascination with it (Foucault 1979, 201–209). The long title of the work merits a full quotation: "Panopticon; or, the Inspection-House: Containing the Idea of a New Principle of Construction Applicable to Any Sort of Establishment, in Which Persons of Any Description Are to Be Kept Under Inspection; and in Particular to Penitentiary-Houses, Prisons,

Houses of Industry, Work-Houses, Poor-Houses, Lazarettos, Manufactories, Hospitals, Mad-Houses, and Schools." In the title of this curious work that captivated Foucault and a legion of his disciples, one spots that familiar word "industry" so dear to so many eighteenth-century writers. That for Bentham, as well as for virtually all the authors we have met thus far, "industry" was an important category straddling morals and economics is testified by the very first sentence of his "Preface," printed in emphatic italics: "*Morals reformed—health preserved—industry invigorated—instruction diffused—public burthens lightened—Economy seated, as it were, upon a rock—the gordian knot of the Poor-Laws not cut, but untied—all by a simple idea in Architecture!*" "Morals reformed" and "industry invigorated" not by carefully working with that most "intricate" object, the "nature of man," as Burke advised, but by a "simple idea in Architecture." This is "metaphysical" and "barbarous philosophy," as Burke would have put it, parading as a panacea for all sorts of moral, political, and economic ills (Bentham 1843, title page, 39). The simple idea is that of observing without being observed isolated inmates in a circular prison kept in cells with barred but open doors. The myriad benefits of the scheme include that of "employing the idle" as well as "punishing the incorrigible" or "guarding the insane" (Bentham 1843, 40). The beauty of the scheme consists in the fact that it motivates private contractors to take up the management and profit from an establishment built according to this design. They will take off the burden from the local or central government. Indeed, Bentham has a good deal to say about the "*pecuniary economy*" of his proposal (Bentham 1843, 47). A contractor will be allowed to put his prisoners into whatever trade they think will be most profitable. As the financial success of this venture will depend very much on the "industry" of the workers, the contractor should know how best to distribute works according to the four kinds of "hands," the "*good* hands, the *capable* hands, the *promising* hands, and the *drones.*" Since the "drones" have also to work, the likelihood of anyone indulging in idleness is utterly ruled out. The "prisoner-workman" can be remunerated for his pains, for "the more the prisoner-workman got, the more the master could get out of him" (Bentham 1843, 49–50). Paying the inmates is optional, but their labor should be mandatory. No one will be allowed to be slothful. In fact, they would be inevitably motivated to do some work rather than remain idle "from morning to night" and "without a soul to speak to." All in all, the contractor would have a "much better security than he can have for the industry and diligence of any ordinary journeyman at large" (Bentham 1843, 54). The thorny issue of disciplining the idle poor to become industrious bees is thus resolved, once again, all by "*a simple idea in Architecture.*"

Bentham's confidence in his "simple idea" hinges upon his simplistic view of human nature, one that stands at the other extreme from that of Burke. *An Introduction to the Principles of Morals and Legislation*, which Bentham first printed in 1780 but reissued with a long list of errata and additions in 1789, is a work enshrined as a classic foundation of modern utilitarianism. All its merits and shortcomings originate from the definition of human nature or human condition given by the very first statement of the "Introduction": "Nature has placed mankind under the governance of two sovereign masters, *pleasure* and *pain*." This dual governance is marked by an exceptionally rigid despotism. "It is for them alone to point out what we ought to do, as well as to determine what we shall do," Bentham adds immediately. These two "masters," almost like gods, "govern us in all we do, in all we say, in all we think." The "tyranny of sounds" upheld by the jargons of traditional morality may have been deposed, but on its throne is placed a new tyranny of "*pleasure*" and "*pain*," which dual monarchs tolerate one philosophy only, the "*principle of utility*" that wisely "recognizes this subjection" (Bentham 1789, i). This degree of complete certitude about human nature would have baffled even Mandeville, who always had a penchant for satirical humor, and who envisioned a more diffuse governance of human action by various passions. Whereas *Defence of Usury* and *Panopticon* paid respect at least to contrastive pairing of "industry" with "idleness," which occupied the core of the eighteenth-century discussions of matters economic, in *Introduction to the Principles of Morals and Legislation*, Bentham, who was as yet relatively obscure compared with Burke in the 1780s, spelled the end of the moral discourse of the economy by constructing an economic morality founded on a rudimentary arithmetic of adding and subtracting pleasure and pain. When morality is trimmed to such a radical minimum, nothing much can be drawn from it when one attempts to speak of the economy using moral terms.

Modern microeconomics, evolved from Benthamite theories of marginal utility, would recognize its ancestor in Bentham most likely with pleasure rather than pain. The shade of Burke, if we can summon him back to this mortal world, would have been appalled. When alive, Burke never met Bentham, nor seemed to have read his works, but if he did, he would have identified him as a confederate of the same cold philosophers who instructed the Jacobins and who "consider men, in their experiments, no more than they do mice in an air pump, or in a recipient of mephitick gas."

References

Anon. 1789. To the literary world. *The. Monthly Review* 81: i–iii.

Anon. 1790a. Reflections on the revolution in France … by the Right Honourable Edmund Burke. *The Analytical Review* November: 295–307.

Anon. 1790b. Reflections on the revolution in France … by the Right Honourable Edmund Burke. *The Critical Review* November: 517–530.

Anon. 1790c. Reflections on the revolution in France … by the Right Honourable Edmund Burke. *The Monthly Review; or, Literary Journal, Enlarged* November: 313–326.

Anon. 1790d. Mr. Burke's Reflections on the revolution in France. *The Monthly Review; or, Literary Journal, Enlarged* December: 438–465.

Bentham, Jeremy. 1787. *Defence of usury; Shewing the impolicy of the present legal restraints on the terms of pecuniary bargains; in a series of letters to a friend. To which is added, a letter to Adam Smith, esq. LL.D. on the discouragements opposed by the above restraints to the progress of inventive industry.* London: T. Payne and Son.

Bentham, Jeremy. 1789. *An introduction to the principles of morals and legislation.* London: T. Payne and Son.

Bentham, Jeremy. 1843. *Panopticon; or, The inspection-house.* In *The works of Jeremy Bentham*, ed. John Bowring, vol. 4, 37–172. London: Simpkin, Marshall, & Co.

Bourke, Richard. 2015. *Empire and revolution: The political life of Edmund Burke.* Princeton: Princeton University Press.

Burke, Edmund. 1991a. A letter to a noble lord. In *Writing and speeches of Edmund Burke*, vol. 9.1: *The Revolutionary War 1794–1796*, ed. R. B. McDowell, 145–187. Oxford: Clarendon.

Burke, Edmund. 1991b. First letter on a regicide peace. In *Writing and speeches of Edmund Burke*, vol. 9.1: *The Revolutionary War 1794–1796*, ed. R. B. McDowell, 187–264. Oxford: Clarendon.

Burke, Edmund. 1998. Reflections on the revolution in France. In *The writing and speeches of Edmund Burke*, vol. 8: *The French Revolution 1790–1794*, ed. L. G. Mitchell and William B. Todd, 53–293. Oxford: Clarendon.

Foucault, Michel. 1979. *Discipline and punish: The birth of prison.* Translated by Alan Sheridan. New York: Vintage.

Locke, F. P. 2006. *Edmund Burke.* Vol. 2: *1784–1797.* Oxford: Clarendon.

The Monthly Review. 1788a. Vol. 78: January to June.

The Monthly Review. 1788b. Vol. 79: July to December.

The Monthly Review. 1789a. Vol. 80: January to June.

The Monthly Review. 1789b. Vol. 81: July to December.

Index[1]

[1] Note: Page numbers followed by 'n' refer to notes.

H.-J. Yoon, *Moral Discourses of the Economy in Eighteenth-Century Britain*, https://doi.org/10.1007/978-981-95-0958-4

Kolibri 360 GmbH
Ferdinand-Jühlke-Straße 7
99095 Erfurt, Deutschland
produktsicherheit@kolibri360.de